MONTEZUMA
Amish Mennonite
COOKBOOK II

Montezuma Amish Mennonite COOKBOOK II

Published by
Melvin & Ruth Yoder

For additional copies, use the form provided
in the back of the book. Or, write or telephone:

Melvin & Ruth Yoder
Amish Mennonite Cookbook
Rt. #2, Box 182
Montezuma, GA 31063
Phone (912) 472-8921
http://www.amishcooking.com

International Standard Book Number 0-9630704-1-X

First Printing   June 1998   5,000 copies

DEDICATION

I would like to dedicate this book to all good cooks.
Life seems to be centered around the kitchen and
with this in mind we have compiled our second
cookbook. We hope that you will enjoy this as
much as you did the first one.

Ruth Yoder

Printed in the USA by
WIMMER
The Wimmer Companies
Memphis

TABLE OF CONTENTS

ABOUT THE AUTHOR . . . RUTH KAUFFMAN YODER

Originally from Virginia Beach, Virginia, Levi and Mary Kauffman moved their family to Georgia when Ruth was nine years old. Also making the journey to their new home was her twin brother, Richard, and four brothers and six sisters.

Another tradition shared by these fine folks is the preparation of good and wholesome "home-cooked" food. Now more commonly known as Pennsylvania Dutch cooking, Ruth cultivated her cooking skills while growing up in her mother's kitchen. She also credits an older sister, Rhoda, as one of her early culinary influences.

Ruth says she has always had an adventurous spirit when it comes to trying new recipes. Her husband and eight children are the blessed recipients of these adventures and she assures that they have been good sports; even when it comes to the one percent "misfires" she has encountered along the way! She theorizes that every cook shoots his or her own foot once in a while . . .

The Yoders still make their home in Montezuma, Georgia, where Ruth leads a very busy life as a wife and mother, homemaker and caterer. She is grateful for the help and support she receives in the business from her husband, Melvin, and her daughter, Drusilla. She reports that even 5-year-old Gail Nicole pitches in from time to time.

"We have enjoyed the tremendous blessings of God, church, and family. Without a personal relationship with Jesus Christ and his intervention in our lives, we would never have made it through some of our crises—both personal and professional.

We sincerely hope that this cookbook will play a special role in bringing even more enjoyment to one of God's 'needful blessings' here on earth—FOOD!"

Ruth Yoder

APPRECIATION

To my husband and family for their wonderful support while I was working on this book. Also, to the many friends and relatives who shared their treasured recipes with me. I could not have published this book without your help.

Sincerely,
Ruth Yoder

Appetizers
&
Beverages

PECAN STUFFED MUSHROOMS
Sonia Hoffman

1 pound (about 24) large
  mushrooms
2 tablespoons butter or margarine
¼ cup chopped green pepper
2 tablespoons chopped onion

1 cup chopped pecan meats
½ cup shredded Swiss cheese
1 egg, slightly beaten
¼ teaspoon salt
Dash ground red pepper

Remove stems from mushrooms; chop stems. Arrange mushroom caps on greased baking sheet. In skillet, over medium heat, melt margarine. Add chopped mushroom stems, green pepper, and onion; cook until tender. Stir in pecans, cheese, egg, salt, and pepper. Spoon about 1 tablespoon pecan mixture into each mushroom cap. Bake at 400° for 15 minutes. Serve hot.

ORANGE BALLS
Ruth Yoder

12 ounces vanilla wafers, crushed
1 box powdered sugar
1 cup crushed pecans

1 (6 ounce) can frozen orange
  juice concentrate

Form into balls and roll in coconut. Very good!

Seven days without prayer makes one weak.

SAVORY BBQ PARTY MIX
Cynthia Helmuth

8 cups Crispix cereal
1 cup mini pretzel twists
1 cup honey roasted peanuts
2 teaspoons sugar or 1 packet
  sweetener
2 teaspoons paprika
½ teaspoon garlic salt
½ teaspoon onion salt

¼ teaspoon dry mustard powder
⅛ teaspoon cayenne pepper
3 tablespoons vegetable oil
1½ teaspoons Worcestershire
  sauce
½ teaspoon liquid smoke (hickory
  or mesquite BBQ flavoring)

In a 2-gallon zipper-type storage bag, combine cereal, pretzels, and peanuts. In a separate bowl, mix together sugar or sweetener and spices. Set aside. Combine oil, Worcestershire sauce, and liquid smoke. Mix well. Pour oil mixture over cereal mixture. Close bag and gently toss cereal mixture until well-coated. Add spice mixture and close bag. Gently toss until well coated. Store in airtight container.

OYSTER CRACKER SNACKERS

Tina Nussbaum

½ cup Crisco oil
½ teaspoon garlic powder
1 package dry ranch dressing mix

2 (12 ounce) packages oyster
crackers

Mix all ingredients and place on flat cookie sheet. Bake at 375° until crackers are crunchy.

Optional: You may just mix and place in a sealed container. Delicious!

PIZZA CUPS

Elsie Brenneman

1 pound hot or mild pork sausage
1 (14 ounce) jar pizza sauce
2 tablespoons ketchup
¼ teaspoon garlic powder

2 (10 ounce) cans refrigerated
biscuits
Shredded mozzarella cheese
Grated Parmesan cheese

In skillet, cook sausage over medium heat; drain. Stir in pizza sauce, ketchup, and garlic powder; set aside. Press biscuits into 20 well-greased muffin cups. Spoon 1 or 2 tablespoons of the meat sauce into each biscuit. Top with mozzarella cheese, and sprinkle with Parmesan cheese. Bake at 350° for 10-15 minutes or until golden brown. (Refrigerate or freeze any extra meat sauce). Yield: 20 pizzas.

CARAMEL POPCORN

Ruth Yoder

2 cups brown sugar
1 teaspoon salt
2 sticks margarine
½ cup light corn syrup

1 teaspoon baking soda
1 teaspoon butter or vanilla
Nutmeats
6 quarts popped corn

Boil sugar, margarine, salt, and light corn syrup. Add baking soda, butter or vanilla, and nutmeats. Add to sugar mixture. Pour mixture over popped corn and spread on cookie sheet. Bake at 200° for 1 hour, stirring every 15 minutes.

CARAMEL CORN

Viola Miller

1 cup butter
2 cups brown sugar
½ cup white Karo syrup or
    molasses
1 teaspoon salt

1 teaspoon vanilla
½ teaspoon baking soda
7 quarts popped corn
1 cup peanuts

Boil together first 4 ingredients for 5 minutes, then add the vanilla and baking soda. Pour over the popped corn and peanuts. Spread in loaf pans and bake 1 hour at 250°.

BROILED POTATO SKINS
Regina Overholt

4 large baking potatoes
2 tablespoons butter or margarine,
  softened
½ teaspoon salt

1 cup finely shredded Monterey
  Jack cheese with jalapeño
  peppers
4 slices bacon, crisply fried and
  crumbled

Prick potatoes with fork to allow steam to escape. Bake potatoes at 425°
until tender, about 1 hour. Cool slightly. Cut each potato lengthwise into
halves; scoop out insides, leaving a ⅜-inch shell. Spread insides with
butter or margarine and sprinkle with salt. Cut each into 6 pieces; sprinkle
with cheese and bacon. Broil potato pieces about 5 inches from heat until
cheese is melted, about 2 minutes. Makes 48 appetizers.

GARLIC PRETZELS
Janet Showalter Miller

¾ cup Orville Redenbacher
  popcorn oil
1 teaspoon dill weed
½ teaspoon garlic powder

1 envelope Hidden Valley Ranch
  dry dressing mix
10 to 14 ounces broken pretzels or
  "mini-bite" size pretzels

Combine popcorn oil, dill weed, garlic powder, and dry dressing mix in
blender and pour over pretzels that have been spread in 9x13-inch (or
larger) pan. Bake at 225° for 10 minutes. Stir and bake 10 more minutes.
Remove from oven and stir occasionally while cooling until dressing clings
to pretzels. Store in airtight container. Makes 6-12 servings.

SOFT PRETZELS
Wanda Steiner

2 tablespoons yeast
1½ cups warm water
½ teaspoon salt
1 tablespoon brown sugar
4½ cups flour

2 tablespoons baking soda
1 cup cold water
Coarse salt
Melted butter

Dissolve yeast in warm water. Add salt, sugar, and flour. Mix well and let
rise 15 minutes. Divide dough in balls; roll each ball into a rope. Twist into
pretzel shape. Dissolve baking soda in cold water; dip each pretzel into the
soda water. Place on well-greased baking sheet. Sprinkle with coarse salt.
Bake at 350° for about 15 minutes or until golden brown. Dip in melted
butter. Serve warm with mustard or cheese sauce. Makes 12-18 pretzels.

SOFT PRETZELS

Linda Zook, Deborah Kauffman

1 tablespoon yeast
1¼ cups water
¼ cup brown sugar

2 cups bread flour
2 cups all-purpose flour

Dissolve yeast in water. Add remaining ingredients. Let rise for 20 minutes. Shape into pretzels. Dip into 2 cups water mixed with 2 tablespoons baking soda. Place on greased baking sheet and sprinkle with salt. Bake at 400° for 10-12 minutes. Makes 12-16 pretzels.

PUPPY CHOW

Donna Stephens, Silla K. Yoder,
Mrs. Roger Helmuth, Sr.

1 (12 ounce) bag chocolate chips
1 cup chunky peanut butter
1 stick butter

1 large box Rice Chex cereal
2 cups (or more) powdered sugar

Melt first 3 ingredients together. Add box of Rice Chex and coat with chocolate mixture. Let cool a little and put into a large brown grocery bag. Add powdered sugar and shake well. Dump out onto paper towels to finish cooling. *(This really does look like dog food!)*

CURRIED SHRIMP APPETIZER

Sonia Hoffman

2-3 pounds shrimp
2 tablespoons butter
2 tablespoons flour
2 cloves garlic, minced
⅔ cup minced onion

⅔ cup minced apple
2 cups chopped tomatoes
4 tablespoons curry powder
3 cups mayonnaise
2 tablespoons lemon juice

Clean and peel shrimp. Put shrimp in boiling water for 2-3 minutes, just until pink. Do not overcook. Drain and chill. Melt butter in saucepan. Add flour and mix thoroughly, then add garlic, onion, apple, tomatoes, and curry powder. Stir over medium heat constantly for about 3 minutes. Remove from heat and let cool. When thoroughly cool, add mayonnaise, shrimp, and lemon juice. Refrigerate for several hours or overnight. Arrange on a plate or in a shallow bowl and serve with toothpicks.

SAUSAGE PARTY BALLS

Edna Schrock, Mrs. Robert Paul Yoder

2 pounds hot* sausage
2 pounds grated sharp cheese

4 cups Bisquick baking mix
1 teaspoon red pepper

Mix all ingredients and roll into 1-inch balls. Bake at 325° for 8-10 minutes. Serve with honey mustard and crackers. Makes 6 dozen 1-inch balls.

*Real hot. If you prefer milder flavor, use mild sausage instead.

*If you are centered in yourself, you are a problem.
If you are centered in God, you are a person.*

EASY SAUSAGE SWIRLS

Susan K. Yoder

2 (8 ounce) cans crescent rolls
2 tablespoons hot mustard

1 pound ham sausage

Separate rolls into 4 rectangles and spread with mustard. Spread with thin layer of sausage. Roll and chill until ready to serve. Thinly slice each roll (10 swirls per roll) and place on ungreased pan. Bake at 400° for 18-20 minutes. Makes 80 swirls.

Salvation is of the Lord, and God always finishes what he begins.

STROMBOLI

Miriam Yoder

1 loaf frozen bread dough
4 tablespoons pizza sauce
¼ pound boiled, cooked ham
¼ pound salami
¼ pound pepperoni

½ pound mozzarella cheese, grated
Parmesan cheese
Oregano
1 egg, beaten

Thaw bread dough, then roll out on greased cookie sheet. Spread pizza sauce on dough, then layer meats on top. Put grated cheese on top of meats. Sprinkle with Parmesan cheese and oregano. Roll up like jelly roll. Brush beaten egg on top of roll. Sprinkle Parmesan cheese on top. Bake at 350° for 30 minutes. Use an electric knife to cut.

TASSIES

Ruth Yoder

PASTRY:
1 (3 ounce) package cream
  cheese, softened

½ cup butter or margarine
1 cup all-purpose flour

FILLING:
¾ cup packed brown sugar
1 tablespoons butter, softened
1 egg
1 teaspoon vanilla extract

Dash of salt
⅔ cup finely chopped pecans,
  divided

For pastry, blend cream cheese and butter or margarine until smooth; stir in flour. Chill about 1 hour. Shape into 24 1-inch balls. Place in ungreased miniature muffin tins or small cookie tarts; press the dough against bottom and sides to form shell. Set aside.

For filling, in bowl, beat brown sugar, butter, and egg until combined. Add vanilla, salt, and half the pecans. Spoon into pastry. Top with remaining pecans. Bake at 375° for 20 minutes or until filling is set and pastry is light golden brown. Makes 24 tarts.

WEDDING MINTS

Laura K. Yoder

1 (3 ounce) package cream
  cheese, room temperature
2 or 3 drops food coloring

½ teaspoon lemon or mint extract
2½ cups powdered sugar

Beat cream cheese until soft; add food coloring and extract. Gradually add powdered sugar, mixing and kneading until it looks like pie dough. Roll into balls about the size of marbles. Place one side in small amount of sugar; place sugar side down into cavity of mold and press firmly to form design. Unmold onto waxed paper.

Pack between waxed paper in covered tins. You may wish to make several batches of different colors and flavors.

APPLE FRITTERS
Barbara Hershberger

1 cup sifted flour
½ teaspoon baking powder
½ teaspoon salt
¼ teaspoon apple pie spice
1 egg, beaten

½ teaspoon vanilla
½ cup sugar
Milk
1 apple, sliced thinly

Mix together dry ingredients and combine with egg, vanilla, and sugar stirred together. Add enough milk to make it the consistency of thick pancake batter. Add apples.

Drop into hot (375°-400°) oil or fat with a tablespoon dipped into oil to avoid sticking to the spoon. Turn fritters over in oil repeatedly to brown evenly. Fry about 9 or 10 minutes or until browned. (Over-frying can cause toughness). Makes several dozen.

Blessed are they which hunger and thirst after righteousness, for they shall be filled. — Matthew 5:6.

BROWN SUGAR BABIES
Mrs. Paul Yoder (Ruth), Martha Kauffman

PASTRY:
¼ pound butter (½ cup)
1 (3 ounce) package cream
  cheese, softened

1 cup flour
Dash of salt

FILLING:
1 egg, beaten
1 tablespoon butter
¾ cup brown sugar

1 teaspoon vanilla
Dash of salt
¾ cup chopped pecans

Mix butter and cream cheese. Add flour and salt. Refrigerate one hour. Shape into 1-inch balls and press into little muffin tins. Fill with remaining ingredients. Bake 25 minutes at 325°.

CHEESE WAFERS
Drusilla Beiler

1 (10 ounce) package extra sharp
  cheese, shredded
2 sticks butter
2 cups all-purpose flour

½ teaspoon cayenne pepper
¼ teaspoon salt
2 cups Rice Krispies cereal

Mix together everything except Rice Krispies. Stir in Rice Krispies by hand. Put spoon-size balls on cookie sheets. Flatten. Bake 15-18 minutes at 350°. Makes 4 dozen.

PETITE CHERRY CHEESE CAKE
Drusilla Beiler

24 vanilla wafers
2 (8 ounce) packages cream
 cheese
¾ cup sugar

2 eggs
1 tablespoon lemon juice
1 teaspoon vanilla
1 can cherry or blueberry pie filling

Place 1 vanilla wafer in the bottom of each paper-lined muffin cup. Beat together rest of ingredients until light and fluffy. Fill cups ⅔ full of cheese mixture. Bake at 350° for 15 or 20 minutes. Cool and top with pie filling.

EGGPLANT FINGERS
Mary Zook

1 large eggplant
1½ teaspoons salt, divided
1 cup flour
¼ teaspoon white pepper

1 egg, beaten
1 cup milk
1 tablespoon canola oil
Oil for frying

Peel eggplant and cut into finger-size strips. Sprinkle with 1 teaspoon salt. Place into colander and let sit for 1 hour. Drain well, rinse, and pat with paper towels.

Combine flour, ½ teaspoon salt, and pepper. Add egg, milk, and 1 table-spoon oil. Heat skillet to 360° with 1 inch canola oil. Dip eggplant fingers into batter and deep fry until golden brown. Drain well on paper towels. Serve at once with dill dip. Serves 6.

MOZZARELLA STICKS
Silla Yoder

2 eggs
1 tablespoon water
1 cup dry bread crumbs
2½ teaspoons Italian seasoning
½ teaspoon garlic powder
⅛ teaspoon pepper

12 sticks string cheese
3 tablespoons all-purpose flour
1 tablespoon butter or margarine,
 melted
1 cup spaghetti sauce, heated

In a small bowl, beat eggs and water. In a plastic bag, combine bread crumbs, Italian seasoning, garlic powder, and pepper. Coat cheese sticks in flour, then dip in egg mixture and bread crumb mixture. Repeat egg and bread crumb coating. Cover and chill for at least 4 hours or overnight.

Place on an ungreased baking sheet. Drizzle with butter. Bake uncovered at 400° for 6-8 minutes or until heated through. Allow to stand for 3-5 minutes before serving. Use spaghetti sauce for dipping. Serves 4-6.

HAM AND CHEESE PINWHEELS

Regina Overholt

1 (8 ounce) package cream
   cheese, softened
¾ package dry onion soup mix

2 tablespoons horseradish
10 slices square boiled ham
10 slices Swiss cheese

Mix cream cheese, soup mix, and horseradish. Cover one slice of ham with cheese and then spread with cream cheese mixture. Roll up from the short side of the ham and secure with several picks. Refrigerate until well-chilled, at least an hour. With a very sharp knife, slice into ¼-inch slices. Secure pinwheels with toothpicks.

HEAVENLY HASH

Mrs. Roger Helmuth, Sr.

2½ pounds white chocolate
10 cups Cap'n Crunch cereal
10 cups peanut butter Cap'n
   Crunch cereal

3 cups Cheerios cereal
5 cups miniature marshmallows

Melt white chocolate. Pour over cereals and marshmallows and mix. Scrumptiously delicious! Also good with some pretzels added.

JELLO ROLL-UPS

Merlyn Mullett

1 (3 ounce) package Jello (any
   flavor)
½ cup water

1½ cups miniature marshmallows
   (or 12 large)

Spray pan with Pam. Mix Jello and water. Microwave until completely dissolved. Add marshmallows to Jello. Microwave until almost melted. Stir until completely melted and smooth. Pour into 9x9-inch pan and refrigerate until set.

Loosen edges and roll up. Slice.

PARTY MEATBALLS

Judi Wagher

MEATBALLS:
2 pounds ground chuck
1 envelope Lipton's dry onion soup
  mix
1 egg

1 slice bread, crumbled
Milk to hold meatballs together
Salt and pepper to taste

SAUCE:
1 can cranberry sauce

1 bottle chili sauce

Mix together the meatball ingredients and form into the size meatballs desired. Brown lightly in a skillet and drain off the fat.

Mix together the sauce ingredients in an electric skillet. Heat to boiling, add meatballs, and simmer for at least 20 minutes. Makes 8-10 servings.

CHEESE BALL

Esther Mast

1 (8 ounce) package Philadelphia
  cream cheese
1 (4 ounce) package Cracker
  Barrel Cheddar cheese
½ teaspoon chopped onion (dry)

1 teaspoon Worcestershire sauce
½ teaspoon lemon juice
Chopped nuts
Crackers

Mix together first 5 ingredients and shape into a ball. Roll in chopped nuts. Serve with crackers.

ISLANDER CHEESE BALL

2 (8 ounce) packages cream
  cheese
8 ounces crushed pineapple,
  drained

2 tablespoons green onion,
  including tops, chopped
½ cup green pepper, chopped
2 teaspoons seasoned salt
2 cups pecans, chopped

Mix cheese and pineapple with mixer. Stir in rest of ingredients, leaving 1½ cups nuts. Roll into one large ball or fill a scooped out pineapple half. Roll ball in remaining pecans (or coat top of cheese ball with nuts if using scooped out pineapple half). Make 1-2 days ahead.

CALORIE LOVERS CHEESE BALL
Elsie Yoder

3 (8 ounce) packages cream
  cheese, softened
1 (8 ounce) jar Cheese Whiz
2 cups shredded Cheddar cheese
  (room temperature)
Dash of garlic powder, onion
  powder, seasoned salt, and
  celery salt

1 teaspoon liquid smoke
2 teaspoons Worcestershire sauce
½ cup fried, crumbled up bacon, or
  fried summer sausage, finely
  diced
Crushed pecans
Crackers

Mix up softened cream cheese until smooth, then add rest of ingredients except for pecans and crackers. Roll into a ball and put crushed pecans around it. Put in freezer for 1 hour and then keep in refrigerator. Serve with crackers.

LYNN'S CHEESE BALL
Naomi Yoder

2 (8 ounce) packages cream
  cheese, room temperature
1 package Good Season's Italian
  salad dressing mix (dry)

½ cup finely chopped pecans
Crackers

Mix cream cheese and Good Season's dressing mix. Mix well and form a ball. Cover with pecans. Chill and serve with crackers. Serves 12.

CITRUS-CHEESE SAUCE
Cynthia Helmuth

4 ounces Neufchâtel cheese,
  softened
3 tablespoons sugar
1 teaspoon finely shredded orange
  peel

½ teaspoon finely shredded lemon
  peel
1 tablespoon orange juice
1 tablespoon lemon juice
⅓ cup nonfat dry milk powder
⅓ cup ice water

In a small bowl, beat together first 6 ingredients on low speed until smooth. Cover and chill. To serve, in mixing bowl, combine dry milk powder and ice water; beat until stiff peaks form (tips stand straight). Fold into cheese mixture (do not overmix). Serve over cake or fruit. Makes about 2 cups.

CHEESE DIP

Mrs. Henry Overholt, Sr.,
Ramona Overholt, Wanda Steiner

2 packages cream cheese
1 (6 ounce) jar cheese
½ teaspoon garlic salt
1 teaspoon seasoning salt

2 teaspoons onion flakes
2 teaspoons Worcestershire sauce
1 package dried beef, cut up
Crackers

Mix first 7 ingredients together and serve with crackers. Best if chilled an hour or two before serving.

CHILI CON QUESO DIP

Mrs. Roger Helmuth, Sr.

1 pound ground beef
½ teaspoon salt
½ cup chopped green pepper
¾ cup chopped onion
1 (8 ounce) can tomato sauce
1 (4 ounce) can green chilies, chopped

1 tablespoon Worcestershire sauce
1 tablespoon brown sugar
1 pound cheese spread (cubed)
1 tablespoon red pepper
1 tablespoon paprika

Cook beef, salt, green pepper, onion, tomato sauce, green chilies, Worcestershire sauce, and brown sugar on low in crock pot for 2-3 hours. One hour before serving, add cubed cheese spread, red pepper, and paprika.

Stove top method: Simmer ½ hour.

CHIPPED BEEF DIP

Elva Miller

1 (8 ounce) package cream cheese, softened
2 tablespoons milk
2 teaspoons minced onions
2 teaspoons minced green peppers

2½ ounces dried beef (buy in jars)
½ cup sour cream
Chopped pecans
Chips or crackers

Stir together cream cheese and milk; mix well. Add onions, green peppers, dried beef, and sour cream; mix well. Pour into 8x8-inch baking dish and sprinkle chopped pecans on top. Bake at 350° for 30 minutes. Serve with favorite chips or crackers.

CUCUMBER DILL DIP
Sonia Hoffman

1 (8 ounce) package cream
  cheese, softened
1 cup mayonnaise
2 medium cucumbers, peeled,
  seeded and chopped

2 tablespoons sliced green onion
1 tablespoon lemon juice
2 teaspoons snipped fresh dill,
  or ½ teaspoon dried dill
½ teaspoon hot pepper sauce

Beat cream cheese until smooth. Stir in remaining ingredients until well mixed. Cover and chill. Makes 2½ cups. Serve with assorted raw vegetables.

*The measure of your usefulness is determined
by the measure of your consecration.*

DILL DIP
Mary Zook

1 cup light mayonnaise
¾ cup light sour cream
3 tablespoons dill weed
1 teaspoon finely chopped onion

½ teaspoon salt
¼ teaspoon black pepper
Few drops hot sauce

Combine everything and chill well before serving. Serve with Eggplant Fingers. (Would also be good with other vegetables.) Serves 4-6.

HOT CRAB DIP
Ruth Yoder

1 stick melted butter
8-12 ounces cream cheese,
  softened

1 pound crab meat (canned)
Paprika

Combine melted butter and softened cream cheese. Add crab meat. Sprinkle paprika on top and bake at 350° until bubbly.

HOT HAMBURGER DIP
Mrs. Shirley Yoder

2 pounds hamburger
1 medium onion, chopped
1 pound Velveeta cheese, cubed
1 can mushroom soup
1 can tomato soup

¼ green pepper, chopped
Red pepper
Chili powder
1 pint salsa

Fry hamburger and onion together; drain. Add remaining ingredients. Simmer 25-30 minutes. Serve with tortilla chips.

NACHO CHEESE DIP

Mrs. Merle Overholt

¼ pound bulk spicy pork sausage
2 tablespoons chopped green
  pepper
2 tablespoons chopped onion

1 pound processed American
  cheese, cubed
¾ cup salsa
Tortilla chips or raw vegetables

In a 1½-quart microwave-safe container, cook sausage, green pepper, and onion on high for 2-3 minutes or until sausage is fully cooked; drain. Add the cheese and salsa. Cover and microwave on high for 2-3 minutes, stirring frequently until cheese is melted and mixture is smooth. Serve with tortilla chips or vegetables. Yield: 3 cups.

RAW VEGETABLE DIP

Cissy Allen

1 package frozen chopped
  spinach, drained and cut up
  finely
½ cup fresh parsley, chopped
2 tablespoons grated onion

1 teaspoon salt
1 teaspoon black pepper
Enough mayonnaise to blend
  (3 or more tablespoons)

Blend together all ingredients, adding enough mayonnaise to reach desired consistency.

SHRIMP DIP

Cynthia Helmuth

2 (8 ounce) packages cream
  cheese
½ cup chopped onion
Seasoned salt
Garlic salt

2 cups ketchup
½ cup horseradish (or less)
1 small can shrimp
Oregano

Mix first 4 ingredients and spread on a serving platter. Mix ketchup, horseradish, and shrimp and spread over first layer. Sprinkle oregano over top and serve with crackers.

VELVEETA SALSA DIP

Ramona Overholt

1 pound Velveeta cheese, cubed
1 (8 ounce) jar chunky salsa or
  picante sauce

2 tablespoons chopped cilantro
  (optional)

Microwave Velveeta cheese and salsa or picante sauce in a 2-quart microwave bowl until cheese is melted; stir occasionally. Add cilantro if desired. Serve hot with tortilla chips.

EGG NOG SHAKE

Cynthia Helmuth

2 quarts commercial egg nog
1 quart egg nog ice cream
½ gallon vanilla ice cream
1 large container Cool Whip
  whipped topping

¼ teaspoon ground nutmeg
¼ teaspoon ground cloves
¼ teaspoon ground ginger
¼ teaspoon ground cinnamon

Mix all together with electric mixer and serve. Makes 20 servings.

CITRUS MINT COOLER

Merlyn Mullett

1 cup fresh lemon juice (about 6
  lemons)
1 cup fresh orange juice (about 3
  oranges)
2 cups sugar

2½ cups water
10 mint sprigs
1 (32 ounce) bottle ginger ale
Water

Place first 5 ingredients in a saucepan; bring to a boil, stirring until sugar dissolves. Cover and remove from heat; let steep until cool. Strain. Cover and refrigerate.

To serve, fill glasses or a pitcher with equal amounts of fruit juice, ginger ale and water. Add ice and serve immediately. Makes 15 servings.

HOT WASSAIL

Susan K. Yoder

4 cups pineapple juice
1½ cups apricot nectar
4 cups apple juice or cider

2 sticks cinnamon
2 teaspoons whole cloves
1 teaspoon ground nutmeg

Combine juices in a large saucepan. Tie spices in a cheesecloth bag; add to juice. Simmer mixture over medium heat for 30 minutes. Remove spice bag. Serve hot. Makes 2½ quarts.

No service in itself is small,
None great, though earth it fill;
But that is small that seeks its own,
And great that does God's will.

HOT APPLE PUNCH

Regina Overholt

8 cups apple juice
6 cups water
4 cups very strong brewed tea*
2 cups pineapple juice
¼ cup lemon juice

½ cup sugar
2 sticks cinnamon
½ teaspoon ground nutmeg
3 medium oranges
3 tablespoons whole cloves

Combine first 8 ingredients in large stockpot. Stud each orange with one tablespoon of the cloves. Place oranges in liquid mixture. Bring to a boil over medium heat; reduce heat and simmer 20 minutes. Serve hot. Makes 26 (6-ounce) servings.

*Note: For strong tea, steep 2 family-sized tea bags in 4 cups boiling water.

ICED TEA

Silla Beiler

4 cups water
4 family-size tea bags (I like JFG
  brand)

2 scant cups sugar
2 tablespoons frozen lemonade
  (optional)

Bring water to a boil. Take off burner and add tea bags; cover and brew for 3 minutes. Meanwhile, pour into a gallon jar 2 cups sugar and add enough hot water to dissolve sugar. Add ice, then pour tea brew over ice.

Never squeeze tea bags as it will make tea bitter. Add ice and water to make 1 gallon. Add 2 tablespoons frozen lemonade if desired. Makes 10 servings.

ORANGE PUNCH

Ruth Yoder

2 gallons orange Kool-Aid
4 cans pineapple juice

8 (2-liter) bottles 7-Up
1½ bags ice

Mix all together and serve.

PUNCH

Lela Brenneman

1 cup sugar
1 (4 ounce) packet tropical punch-
   flavored Kool-Aid
1 (12 ounce) can frozen orange
   juice concentrate

1 (12 ounce) can frozen lemon
   juice concentrate
1 (46 ounce) can unsweetened
   pineapple juice
Grapefruit juice, optional
1 (2 liter) bottle Sprite

In a 2½-gallon plastic container, dissolve sugar and Kool-Aid in warm water. Add juices and stir. Add water and ice, leaving enough room for Sprite. Add Sprite just before serving.

PARTY PUNCH

Ruth Yoder, Edna Schrock

2 cups sugar
6 cups water
1 (46 ounce) can orange juice
1 (46 ounce) can pineapple juice

6 ripe bananas, mashed
2 tablespoons lemon juice
1 liter ginger ale

Heat sugar and water until dissolved. Cool and add orange juice, pineapple juice, mashed bananas, and lemon juice. Stir everything together except ginger ale, and freeze.

Take out 2 hours before serving to make it slushy. Add ginger ale before serving. Ruth adds her mashed bananas just before serving. Um-m good! Serves 25 people.

MILK PUNCH

Miriam Yoder

1 quart cold milk
1 (6 ounce) can frozen lemonade
   concentrate

1 pint strawberry ice cream
2 quarts cold 7-Up

Mix together and serve. Makes 10 servings.

*We are God's showcase to the people around us
and to the evil forces as well.*

Breads

CINNAMON-RAISIN BREAD

Drusilla Beiler

2½ cups hot water
1 cup sugar
2 teaspoons salt
1 teaspoon ground cinnamon
½ cup shortening (melted)

2 eggs, beaten
7 cups flour
2 tablespoons instant yeast
2 cups raisins

Mix together hot water, sugar, salt, cinnamon, and melted shortening. Add eggs, flour, and instant yeast. (Mix yeast with part of flour). Then add remaining flour and raisins until no longer sticky. Knead with mixer for 15 minutes. Let rest for 10 minutes, and then form into loaves. Roll the top of loaf in a mixture of sugar and cinnamon. Put into sprayed pans and let rise until doubled in size. Bake at 375° for 35-40 minutes. Makes 4 or 5 loaves.

CINNAMON SWIRL BREAD

Judy Mullet

1½ cups milk
1 cup oatmeal, uncooked
1 cup raisins
½ cup sugar
½ cup oil
2 teaspoons salt

2 tablespoons yeast
½ cup warm water
1 egg
4½ cups bread flour
½ cup sugar
2 tablespoons cinnamon

GLAZE:
3 tablespoons sugar
5 tablespoons water

Powdered sugar

Scald milk; pour over oats, raisins, sugar, oil, and salt; stir and cool. Soften yeast in warm water; add to milk mixture along with beaten egg. Gradually add flour, mixing until soft dough. Knead until smooth; cover and let rise until double in bulk. Divide dough into 2 portions. Let rise 10 minutes; roll each portion into long rectangles. Brush on a little soft butter. Mix sugar and cinnamon and sprinkle over dough; roll up to form loaves. Place in pans and let rise until double. Bake at 350° for 40 minutes.

For glaze, cook sugar and water until slightly thickened. Add enough powdered sugar to make a thin glaze. Ice bread while still warm.

EASY BEGINNER'S WHEAT BREAD   Linda Zook

1½ cups whole wheat flour
1½ cups white flour
1 tablespoon salt
2 tablespoons yeast
3 cups water

½ cup honey
2 tablespoons oil
4 (additional) cups whole wheat
  flour

Combine 1½ cups whole wheat flour, 1½ cups white flour, salt, and yeast. Heat water, honey, and oil until warm. Pour warm water mixture over flour mixture. Beat until smooth. Stir in an additional 4 cups whole wheat flour. Knead 10 minutes. Cover and let rise twice before shaping into loaves. Bake at 350° for 25 minutes. Makes 4 loaves.

Let me no wrong or idle word
Unthinking say;
Set thou a seal upon my lips,
Just for today!

ENGLISH MUFFIN BREAD   Elva Miller

2 tablespoons yeast
6 cups flour, divided
1 tablespoon sugar
2 teaspoons salt

¼ teaspoon baking soda
2 cups milk
½ cup water
Cornmeal

Combine yeast, 3 cups flour, sugar, salt, and baking soda; set aside. Heat milk and water until lukewarm. Add milk and water mixture to dry ingredients. Beat well. Add 3 more cups flour to make a stiff dough.

Spoon into 3 *small* bread pans that have been greased and sprinkled with cornmeal. Sprinkle cornmeal on top. Cover and let rise in warm place for 45 minutes. Bake at 350° for 25 minutes. Remove from pans immediately and let cool.

FRENCH BREAD   Mrs. Vivian Miller

2 cups boiling water
2 tablespoons sugar
2 tablespoons salt
2 tablespoons lard or shortening

6-8 cups flour
½ cup warm water
2 tablespoons yeast
½ teaspoon sugar

Mix first 4 ingredients. When mixture cools to lukewarm, beat in 4 cups flour, then add yeast and ½ teaspoon sugar dissolved in warm water. Add remaining flour. Knead until smooth. Let rise. Divide in half and make two long rolls. Place side by side on a cookie sheet. Make several diagonal, ½-inch deep slashes on each loaf. Allow to rise. Bake at 375° for 15-20 minutes.

HILLBILLY BREAD

Mrs. David Wengerd

4 cups wheat flour
4 cups water
3 tablespoons yeast
6 teaspoons salt
2 tablespoons sugar

6-9 cups white flour
1 cup warm water
1 cup oil
1 cup brown sugar

Mix together the wheat flour, 4 cups water, yeast, salt, and 2 tablespoons sugar. Let stand 1 hour. Add white flour, 1 cup warm water, oil, and brown sugar. Mix thoroughly and let rise 45 minutes. Work out in pans. Bake at 325° for 30-35 minutes. Makes 6 small loaves.

HONEY WHEAT BREAD

Irene Yoder

2 cups lukewarm water
4 tablespoons yeast
4 cups lukewarm water
½ cup honey
1½ tablespoons salt

½ cup oil
2 tablespoons liquid lecithin
3 eggs
10 cups whole wheat flour
10 cups white flour (as needed)

Dissolve yeast in 2 cups water. Let set 10 minutes. Add remaining ingredients, kneading well. Let rise 1 hour, or until double in size. Form into 7 loaves and let rise. Bake at 350° for 25-30 minutes.

HONEY WHEAT BREAD

Barbara Hershberger

3 packages yeast
1 cup lukewarm water
1 teaspoon white sugar
3 cups whole wheat flour
2 cups boiling water
2 tablespoons molasses

½ cup honey
2 teaspoons salt
1 egg
⅓ cup margarine
3 cups white flour

Dissolve yeast in 1 cup lukewarm water. Add 1 teaspoon white sugar and allow to dissolve until bubbly. Add wheat flour to hot water along with other ingredients. By this time the mixture will have cooled; now add white flour slowly. Add enough flour to make dough soft and non-sticky. Allow to rise twice. Shape into loaves and bake at 350° for 30 minutes.

HONEY WHOLE WHEAT BREAD   Silla K. Yoder

10 cups lukewarm water
4 packages yeast
2 tablespoons salt
1 cup honey
1 cup dry powdered milk
1 cup instant potatoes

⅔ cup shortening
8 cups whole wheat flour (may
   replace 1 cup with cracked
   wheat, if desired)
5 pounds bread flour

Mix all ingredients and knead. Let rise half-way twice, double once, then put in pans to rise. It is ready to bake when dough springs back at touch. Bake at 325° for 15 minutes, then turn and bake until done. Makes 8 loaves.

LIGHT WHEAT BREAD   Mrs. Roger Helmuth, Sr.

5 cups warm water
4 tablespoons yeast
¾ cup sugar
¾ cup oil
2 tablespoons salt

3 eggs, beaten
4 cups wheat flour
12 cups bread flour
   (approximately)

Mix yeast in 1 cup warm water to dissolve. Add the other 4 cups warm water, sugar, salt, eggs, oil, and 4 cups wheat flour. Beat well, then add rest of flour. Allow to rise twice before putting in pans, then let rise and bake at 350° for 20-25 minutes. Makes 7 small (8½x4½-inch) loaves or 5 big loaves.

LIGHT WHEAT BREAD   Mrs. Eli Kauffman

½ cup oil
½ cup honey
4 teaspoons salt
2 tablespoons wheat gluten
2½ tablespoons vinegar

4 cups warm water
8-10 cups fresh ground wheat
   (preferably "Golden 86" spring
   white wheat)
3 tablespoons yeast (instant)

Mix oil, honey, salt, wheat gluten, vinegar, water, and 4 cups flour in bread mixer and mix for 1 minute. Gradually add remaining flour and instant yeast, just until sides of bowl begin to clean. (With a bread mixer you use less flour, which gives a lighter, fluffier bread.) When flour is added, knead dough for 8-10 minutes. Put a little oil on hands and counter and divide dough into 4 loaves. Let rise in pans. You may save a portion of the dough and roll it out to make cinnamon rolls. Bake at 325° for 30 minutes. Delicious. Makes 4 (4½x8½-inch) loaves.

RICH AND MOIST WHOLE WHEAT BREAD   Mrs. Eli Kauffman

6-8 cups fresh whole wheat flour
¼ cup dry potato flakes
¼ cup gluten flour
1½ tablespoons dry yeast
1½ cups warm (120°) water
1 cup yogurt or buttermilk

¼ cup oil
¼ cup honey
2 teaspoons salt
500 milligrams of vitamin C (you
   may use vitamin C tablets)

Mix 4 cups flour, potato flakes, gluten flour, and dry yeast in a mixer bowl. Add warm water and buttermilk or yogurt and mix for 1 minute. Turn off mixer. Let mixture sponge for 15 minutes. Add oil, honey, salt, and vitamin C. Mix until blended. Add remaining flour, 1 cup at a time until dough forms a ball and cleans the sides of the bowl. Knead 6 minutes with mixer or knead 10 minutes by hand. Oil hands and divide dough in two portions. Shape into loaves. Let rise. Bake at 325° for 30 minutes. Makes 2 (4½x8-inch) loaves.

WHEAT BREAD   Esther L. Miller

6 cups hot water
⅓ cup sorghum
6 cups whole wheat bread flour
2½ tablespoons salt
⅓ cup yeast
⅓ cup sugar

1½ cups warm water
5 eggs, well beaten
15½-16 cups white flour (better for
   bread)
½ cup melted lard

Combine first 4 ingredients in 13-quart bowl. Let stand 1 hour, stirring every 15 minutes. After 45 minutes, combine yeast and sugar. Add warm water and let stand 15 minutes. Stir into flour mixture; add eggs and stir thoroughly. Stir in 12 cups white flour 2 cups at a time. Add lard and knead in remaining 4 cups of flour. Let rise until double 3 times before putting in 6 bread pans. Bake at 350° for 10 minutes and at 300° for 15 minutes. Makes 6 loaves.

SOUR DOUGH STARTER AND BREAD   Ruth Yoder

STEP 1 (NEW STARTER):
1⅓ cups real slushy mashed potatoes

1⅓ tablespoons sugar
1⅓ cups flour

STEP 2:
1⅓ cups No. 1 starter
1⅓ cups warm water
1⅓ cups bread flour

⅔ cup sugar
⅓ cup potatoes

STEP 3:
2⅔ cups #2 mixture
1 cup oil
2⅔ cups hot tap water
3 tablespoons instant yeast

1 tablespoon salt
1 cup sugar
9½ cups bread flour

Step 1: Mix together, adding enough warm water to make thick pudding. Let sit in warm place to ferment until strong-smelling. Refrigerate 7 days.

Step 2: Mix together and let sit in warm place overnight.

Step 3: Mix all together adding yeast directly into liquids. Other yeast needs to be softened in small amount of water and a pinch of sugar before adding to liquid. Add flour a cup or two at a time, stirring well between each addition. When dough is too stiff to stir, knead with hands, working in last of flour. Knead very well. Leave dough a little sticky after all the flour is worked in. Place in a greased bowl. Cover and let rise until double in size. Divide into 6 equal parts. Shape into loaves. Place in greased loaf pans and let rise until nice and round above edge of pan. Bake for 25-30 minutes at 350°. Remove from oven and brush tops with butter. Cool.

WHOLE WHEAT BREAD   Lela Brenneman

4-4½ cups warm water
½ cup oil
½ cup honey
1 tablespoon salt

2 tablespoons dough enhancer
2 tablespoons wheat gluten
3 tablespoons yeast
9-10 cups flour (more if needed)

Knead 10 minutes with Bosch. Let rise 20 minutes. Shape into loaves. Let rise 30-40 minutes. Bake at 325°-350° for 20-30 minutes.

Dough enhancer makes bread softer and gives it a longer shelf life. Lecithin can be substituted.

WHOLE WHEAT BREAD

Martha Schrock

1 cup lukewarm water
1 teaspoon sugar
2 tablespoons yeast
1 tablespoon salt
½ cup sugar

½ cup Crisco oil
¼ cup honey
2 cups hot water
2 cups whole wheat flour
3 cups bread flour

Mix 1 cup lukewarm water, 1 teaspoon sugar, and yeast; set aside. Beat together salt, ½ cup sugar, oil, honey, and 2 cups hot water, then add 2 cups whole wheat flour. Now mix the two mixtures together. Mix well. Then add bread flour and mix by hand until it won't stick to the bowl much anymore. Let sit to rise until double in size and put in pans. Let dough rise in pans until about ½ inch higher than pan. Bake in 4 greased bread pans at 300° for 30-35 minutes. Brush with butter when baked.

You give little when you give of your possessions.
It is when you give of yourself that you truly give.

HAMBURGER BUNS

Drusilla Beiler

2 cups scalded milk
1 pound margarine
7 cups hot water
2 cups sugar
2 tablespoons salt
2 eggs

2 cups instant potatoes
3 cups wheat flour
3 cups oat bran
5 pounds bread flour
5 tablespoons instant yeast

½ BATCH:
1 cup scalded milk
½ pound margarine
3½ cups hot water
1 cup sugar
1½ tablespoons salt
1 egg

1 cup instant potatoes
1½ cups wheat flour
1½ cups oat bran
2½ pounds bread flour
3 tablespoons instant yeast

Scald milk and margarine. Add hot water, sugar, salt, eggs, and instant potatoes. Mix together, then add wheat flour, oat bran, and all the bread flour with the yeast mixed in. Knead with mixer for 10-15 minutes. If too sticky, add more bread flour. Let rest for 10 minutes. Then weigh out 3 ounce portions and form into hamburger buns. (2¼ ounces for hot dog buns). Also makes wonderful dinner rolls. Bake at 350° for 15 minutes. Makes 72 hamburger buns.

Man shall not live by bread alone, but by every word
that proceedeth out of the mouth of God. — Deuteronomy 8:3.

BUTTERHORNS
Judy Mullet

2 cups scalded milk
¾ cup sugar
2 teaspoons salt
1 cup butter
2 eggs

1 cup warm water
2 tablespoons yeast
6-7 cups flour
Brown sugar and cinnamon
   mixture

BUTTER CREAM ICING:
2 egg whites, beaten
4 tablespoons milk
4 tablespoons flour

1 cup Crisco shortening
4 cups powdered sugar

Scald milk. Pour over sugar, salt, and butter. Add eggs. Dissolve yeast in warm water. Add enough flour to make a soft dough. Let rise. Roll out half of dough as for pie (round circle). Spread with softened butter. Sprinkle with brown sugar and cinnamon. Cut up into crescent-shaped wedges. Roll up, starting at wide end. Let rise on greased cookie sheet 3 inches apart. Bake for 20 minutes at 350°. When cool, ice with Butter Cream Icing.

To make icing, beat all icing ingredients well until fluffy.

CLOVERLEAF ROLLS
Londa Kauffman

1½ cups lukewarm water
½ cup sugar
2 teaspoons salt
2 packages yeast
½ cup lukewarm water

1 egg
¼ cup oil
6-7 cups flour
Melted butter

Mix together water, sugar, and salt. Mix together the yeast and ½ cup water until dissolved. Add to sugar water. Add egg and oil and mix well. Stir in flour; add more or less until right consistency. Form 3 small 1-inch balls and place in greased muffin baking cups. Brush butter over top. Cover and let rise up to 3 hours. Bake at 350° for 12-15 minutes. After baking, brush with butter. Dough can be refrigerated up to a week. Makes 2 dozen rolls.

DINNER ROLLS
Viola Miller, Carol Petersheim

2 cups scalded milk
2 teaspoons salt
4 tablespoons sugar
4 tablespoons butter

2 beaten eggs
2 tablespoons yeast
6 cups bread flour

Mix first 4 ingredients, then add eggs. Add yeast and flour. Let rise until double in size, then shape into rolls. Let rise again. Bake at 375°-400° until a soft golden brown. Makes about 20 medium rolls.

DEBBIE'S FLAKY CRESCENT ROLLS
Debbie Graber

⅓ cup cornmeal
½ cup sugar
1 teaspoon salt
½ cup shortening
2 cups water

1 cup cool water
2 tablespoons yeast
2 eggs, beaten
4 cups flour (plus 2-3 more cups)

Cook first 5 ingredients on medium heat until slightly thickened. Cool slightly, and add 1 cup cool water to that mixture. Stir in next 3 ingredients and mix well. Add 2-3 more cups flour until a soft dough is formed. Let rise for 30 minutes. Roll out on oiled counter. Shave butter curls over surface. Fold dough over in half and roll out again. Repeat butter curls. Fold dough again and place in refrigerator for several hours, covered with a towel. Roll dough in 2 large circles cut into wedges and roll up in crescent shapes. Bake at 350° on well greased pans for 15-20 minutes.

GOLDEN CRESCENTS
Heidi Kauffman

2 packages yeast
¾ cup warm water
½ cup sugar
1 teaspoon salt

2 eggs
½ cup shortening
4 cups flour

Dissolve yeast in warm water. Add to sugar and salt. Add eggs, shortening, and flour. Let rise 1½ hours. Divide dough in half; roll each half into a 12-inch circle. Spread with butter; cut into 12 wedges. Roll up each wedge, beginning at rounded edge. Cover and let rise about 1 hour. Bake on a cookie sheet at 400° for 12-15 minutes.

DINNER ROLLS
Susan K. Yoder

2 packages dry yeast
1 cup warm water
½ cup sugar
1 teaspoon salt

1 cup milk
½ cup shortening
3 eggs, beaten
6-6½ cups bread flour

Soften yeast with water, sugar, and salt in a mixing bowl. Microwave milk and shortening until melted. Add to mixture along with eggs. Stir in flour a little at a time. Knead on lightly floured surface until smooth and elastic. Cover and let rise 1 hour. Punch down. Shape rolls, cover, and let rise 30 minutes. Bake at 375° for 15-18 minutes. Makes 3 dozen rolls.

DINNER ROLLS

Mrs. Eli Kauffman

2 tablespoons yeast
1 cup warm water
1 cup milk
½ cup sugar
7 cups flour

3 eggs, beaten
½ teaspoon salt
6 tablespoons shortening
Oat bran, wheat germ, optional
½ cup pumpkin, optional

Dissolve yeast in water. Heat milk and shortening until shortening dissolves; add sugar, salt, and eggs. Mix with yeast and water and optional ingredients. Beat well with mixer. Add flour and work until done. Let rise once or twice then shape into rolls. Bake at 350° for 15-20 minutes or until golden.

FEATHER ROLLS

Debbie Graber

5 cups bread flour
1 tablespoon instant yeast
½ cup mashed potatoes
½ cup warm water

¼ cup sugar
⅓ cup oil
1 teaspoon salt

In a mixer bowl, combine 2-3 cups of the flour and yeast. Combine rest of ingredients and add to flour and yeast mixture. Beat for 3 minutes then add remaining 2 cups of flour by hand. Can be refrigerated for several hours or overnight. Make little balls with oiled hands. Bake at 350° until golden.

SWEET POTATO DINNER ROLLS

Elva Miller

1 cup mashed cooked sweet
  potatoes
3 tablespoons melted butter
1 package yeast
½ cup warm water

1 egg
1 teaspoon salt
3 tablespoons sugar
5 cups all-purpose flour
¾ cup warm water

Combine potatoes and melted butter. Dissolve yeast in ½ cup warm water; add to potato mixture. Blend in egg, salt, and sugar. Add flour alternately with ¾ cup warm water to potato mixture. Knead well. Cover and let rise 2 hours. Shape into rolls and put on greased baking sheet. Bake at 425° for 15-20 minutes. These are very good and moist.

2 HOUR ROLLS
Denise Smith

½ cup sugar
½ cup shortening
2 eggs, beaten
1 teaspoon salt

1 cup boiling water
1 cup warm milk
2 packages yeast
6 cups bread flour

Cream sugar and shortening. Beat in eggs and salt. Warm water and milk together and mix with the above. Add yeast. Blend in flour and mix well. Let rise 1 hour. Shape into rolls and let rise 1 hour. Bake at 350° until light brown on top and bottom. Yields 3 dozen rolls.

DINNER ROLLS
Ruth Yoder

3 potatoes with enough water
  to cover
4 cups milk
3 sticks margarine
4 tablespoons yeast

1 cup water
2½ cups sugar
2 eggs
2 tablespoons salt
12-15 cups bread flour

Cook potatoes until tender; mash. Do not drain water. Scald milk and margarine. Dissolve yeast in a little water. Cool liquids before adding yeast. Mix together sugar, eggs, salt, and potatoes; add milk. Add 5 cups flour to make sponge. Let rest ½ hour, then add rest of flour until smooth and elastic. Knead. Let rise until light, about 30 minutes. Bake at 350° for 20-25 minutes. Makes 10-12 dozen rolls.

Jesus said, "I am the bread of life;
He who comes to me shall not hunger." — John 6:35

RAISED DINNER ROLLS
Mrs. Freeman Schlabach

1 package dry yeast
¼ cup sugar
1 teaspoon salt
3 cups white flour

1 cup warm water
1 egg
¼ cup vegetable oil

Place yeast, sugar, salt, and flour in a narrow bowl. Beat with electric mixer for a minute or two. Add water, egg, and oil and mix well. Knead until smooth and elastic.

Turn into greased bowl, cover, and let rise in a warm spot until doubled, about 45 minutes. Shape rolls as desired, place on greased baking sheet, and let rise. Bake about 15 minutes at 375°. Makes 12-16 rolls.

MILE HIGH BISCUITS
Celesta Miller

3 cups cake flour
4 teaspoons baking powder
½ teaspoon cream of tartar
¾ teaspoon salt

½ cup shortening
1 egg, beaten
1 cup milk

Combine dry ingredients in a mixing bowl. Cut in shortening until mixture resembles coarse crumbs. Add eggs and milk all at once. Mix until dough forms a ball. Turn dough out on a floured surface and knead 10-12 minutes. Roll out to ¾-inch thickness and cut with floured 2½-inch biscuit cutter. Place on greased baking sheet and bake at 425° for 10-12 minutes or until light brown.

CHEESE GARLIC BISCUITS
Mrs. Jonathan Yoder

2 cups Bisquick baking mix
⅔ cup milk
½ cup shredded Cheddar cheese

¼ cup butter
¼ teaspoon garlic powder

Mix Bisquick, milk, and cheese until soft dough forms; beat vigorously 30 seconds. Drop dough by spoonfuls onto ungreased pan. Bake at 425° for 8-10 minutes or until golden. Melt butter and garlic; brush over hot biscuits. Makes 10-12 biscuits.

There's a big difference between putting your nose in other people's business and putting your heart in other people's problems.

EMERGENCY BISCUITS
Ellen D. Miller

3 tablespoons soy flour
3 tablespoons oatmeal (quick)
3 tablespoons oat bran
Scant 1½ cups flour pastry

1 tablespoon baking powder
¼ teaspoon salt
3½ tablespoons shortening
⅞ cup milk

Combine dry ingredients with shortening. Add milk. Drop dough by teaspoon on greased 9-inch pan. Bake at 400°-425° for 15-20 minutes. Serve with sausage gravy. Makes 8-10 biscuits.

SALLY LUNN BREAD

Heidi Kauffman

1 package yeast
⅓ cup sugar
½ cup warm water
½ cup warm milk

1 stick melted butter
1 teaspoon salt
3 eggs, slightly beaten
3½-4 cups flour

Combine yeast, sugar, and water. Add milk, butter, and salt. Add eggs. Mix well with wooden spoon. Add 1 cup flour at a time. Place in buttered bowl, cover with damp cloth, and let rise. Beat dough hard with wooden spoon for 1 minute. Place in buttered angel food cake pan and let rise 45 minutes (covered). Bake at 350° for 45-50 minutes. This is a colonial recipe and a family favorite.

BANNOCK (SKILLET BREAD)

Jill Nussbaum

2 cups flour
¼ cup dry milk
1 tablespoon sugar

½ teaspoon salt
2 teaspoons baking powder
1 scant cup water

These are especially good for camping. Put dry ingredients together in plastic bag. At camp, add water and mix into stiff dough. If at home, 1¼ cups milk may be substituted for dry milk and water.

Roll egg-size chunks of batter into flattened patties. Fry in melted butter in iron skillet over campfire. Fun for all the family, and delicious, too! Makes 16 servings.

SOUTHERN RAISED BISCUITS

Mrs. Roger Helmuth, Sr.

2 packages dry yeast
¼ cup warm water
2 cups warm buttermilk
5 cups flour
⅓ cup sugar

1 tablespoon baking powder
1 teaspoon baking soda
1¼ teaspoons salt
1 cup shortening

Mix water and yeast, then add buttermilk. Mix dry ingredients. Cut in shortening, then add yeast mixture. Roll out ½-inch thick. Cut with biscuit cutter and place on greased pan. Let rise 1 hour. Bake in 375° oven for 10-12 minutes. To freeze, bake 5 minutes and wrap and freeze. Thaw and bake at 375° for 7-10 minutes.

UNLEAVENED BREAD

Ann Mast

2 cups flour
½ tablespoon sugar
½ cup butter

½ cup sweet milk
½ teaspoon salt

Mix all ingredients together. Beat for 20 minutes. Roll out on cookie sheet and mark in 1-inch squares. Prick with fork. Bake for 40 minutes at 250°.

GARLIC BUBBLE LOAF
Judy Mullet

1 tablespoon yeast
¼ cup warm water
2 cups scalded milk
¼ cup sugar
2 tablespoons shortening

2 teaspoons salt
6¼-6½ cups flour
½ cup butter, melted
1 tablespoon dried parsley flakes
1 tablespoon garlic powder

In a mixing bowl, dissolve yeast in warm water. Let stand for 5 minutes. Mix milk, sugar, shortening, salt, and 2 cups flour and beat until smooth. Add softened yeast. Stir in enough flour to make soft dough. Knead until smooth. Cover and let rise until double in size. Combine melted butter, parsley, and 1 tablespoon garlic powder. Punch dough down. Divide into fourths. Divide each portion into 12 pieces. Roll each piece into a ball, dip in butter mixture and place into 2 greased 9x5-inch loaf pans. Pour any remaining butter mixture over dough. Cover and let rise until doubled. Bake at 375° for 35 minutes or until golden brown. Cool for 10 minutes. Remove from pans and serve warm.

APPLE BANANA-NUT BREAD
Laura K. Yoder

½ cup applesauce
½ cup sugar
¼ cup plain nonfat yogurt
1 teaspoon vanilla
3 egg whites
2 cups all-purpose flour
½ teaspoon salt

1 teaspoon baking soda
½ teaspoon cinnamon
¼ teaspoon nutmeg
½ cup chopped pecans
1 cup peeled and chopped apples
1 cup ripe banana (mashed)

In a large bowl, cream applesauce and sugar. In a separate bowl, mix yogurt and vanilla. Add egg whites to yogurt and vanilla and beat thoroughly. Add to first mixture and mix well. Sift together the dry ingredients and combine with wet ingredients. Mix until well blended. Add fruit and nuts and mix well. Pour into well greased and floured 9x5-inch loaf pan. Bake at 350° for 1 hour. Let cool in pan 10-15 minutes. Makes 1 loaf, 16 slices.

BISQUICK MIX
Ruth Yoder, Sara Jean Yoder

9 cups all-purpose flour, sifted
⅓ cup baking powder
1 tablespoon salt

2 teaspoons cream of tartar
¼ cup sugar
2 cups shortening

Blend with pastry blender to the appearance of cornmeal. Store in cool, dry place. Use as commercial mix in recipes for biscuits, pancakes, etc. Makes 1 box.

BREAD IN A JAR

Ann Mast

6 wide-mouth pint-size canning jars
2⅔ cups sugar
⅔ cup vegetable shortening
4 eggs
⅔ cup water
2 cups fruit (grated apple, shredded carrots, mashed bananas, or applesauce)

3½ cups all-purpose flour
¼ teaspoon ground cloves
1 teaspoon cinnamon
1 teaspoon baking powder
2 teaspoons baking soda
1 teaspoon salt
⅔-1 cup raisins or nuts

Cream together the sugar and shortening. Beat in eggs and water. Add fruit or carrots. Add flour, cloves, cinnamon, baking powder, baking soda, and salt. Bake as directed:

Grease the inside, but not the rims, of 6 jars. Prepare quick bread batter above. Pour into the prepared jars 1 full cup of batter. Do not use more than 1 cup of batter or it will overflow. Place open jars evenly spaced on cookie sheet. Place in preheated 325° oven. Bake about 45 minutes or until toothpick inserted in center comes out clean. Remove jars one at a time. Wipe the rim top. Place the metal disk top in place, then twist on screw ring to secure. It will seal.

PEACH BREAD

Ruth Yoder

1½ cups sugar
½ cup shortening
2 eggs
2¼ cups peaches, blended
2 cups all-purpose flour
1 teaspoon cinnamon

1 teaspoon baking soda
1 teaspoon baking powder
¼ teaspoon salt
1 teaspoon vanilla
1 cup pecans

Cream sugar and shortening and add eggs. Mix well. Add peaches and dry ingredients. Mix well. Add vanilla and pecans and stir well. Pour in 2 bread pans that have been greased and floured. Bake at 325° for 55-60 minutes.

38

HUSH PUPPIES

Ruth Yoder

¾ cup cornmeal
¾ cup flour
1 teaspoon salt
2 tablespoons sugar
⅛ teaspoon baking soda

1 teaspoon baking powder
1 egg
1 tablespoon oil
1 onion, grated
½ cup buttermilk

Mix all ingredients together. Drop by tablespoon into hot oil. Serve with fish. These are very good hush puppies! Makes 12-15 hush puppies.

He knows, He loves, He cares,
Nothing this truth can dim
He gives the very best to those
who leave the choice to Him!

CORN BREAD

Barbara Hershberger

1 cup white flour
¾ cup yellow cornmeal
3½ teaspoons baking powder
1 teaspoon salt
2 tablespoons white sugar

2 eggs, beaten
2 tablespoons melted shortening,
   margarine, or butter
1 cup sweet milk

Sift flour and cornmeal. Measure and add baking powder, salt, and sugar. Sift again. Add beaten eggs and melted shortening, margarine, or butter, and milk. Beat thoroughly and pour into a well-greased, shallow 8x10-inch pan. Bake at 425° for 25 minutes.

CORN BREAD

Rose Yoder

1½ cups flour
1½ cups cornmeal
½ cup sugar
4 eggs, beaten

2¼ cups buttermilk
1 teaspoon salt
1 teaspoon baking soda
¾ cup oil

Mix all together and pour into a well-greased 9x13-inch baking pan. Bake at 350° for 25 minutes. Makes 16 servings.

MOM'S CORNBREAD

Silla Yoder

1 box Jiffy cornbread mix
1 cup flour
½ cup sugar
2 eggs

1 tablespoon baking powder
¼ cup oil
1 cup milk

Mix all above ingredients together and pour into greased 9x13-inch pan. Bake at 350° for 25 minutes.

BROCCOLI CORNBREAD

Rhoda Yoder

2 cups broccoli
1 large onion, diced
10 ounces cottage cheese
1 cup grated Cheddar cheese
4 eggs
1 stick butter

1½ cups cornmeal and 1½ cups
  flour (we use oat and wheat)
1½ teaspoons baking soda
1½ teaspoons baking powder
1 teaspoon salt

Mix wet ingredients. Measure dry ingredients and fold into first mixture. Put into oiled baking dish and bake at 400° for 25-30 minutes. This is very attractive baked in an iron skillet—you'll also need a bread pan.

HONEY CORN BREAD

Merlyn Mullett

1 cup yellow cornmeal
1 cup flour (can use whole wheat)
½ teaspoon salt
1 teaspoon baking powder
1 teaspoon baking soda

¼ cup honey
1 beaten egg
1⅞ cups buttermilk
1 teaspoon butter

Combine dry ingredients. Stir in liquid ingredients. Do not overmix! Cornbread batter *must* be a little lumpy. Pour batter into a well-buttered 8x8-inch pan. Bake in a 375° oven for ½ hour until toothpick inserted in center comes out clean. Cool slightly and cut into squares. Serves 9.

SARA MCKIE'S SOUR CREAM CORNBREAD

Martha Kauffman

1 cup cornmeal
1 cup sour cream
3 eggs
1 small can creamed corn

3 tablespoons baking powder
¼ teaspoon baking soda
½-1 teaspoon salt

Mix all ingredients in a medium bowl. Bake at 450° in an 8-inch iron skillet until done. Serves 6.

MEXICAN CORN BREAD

Mrs. Jonathan Yoder, Martha Kauffman, Rhoda Yoder, Mrs. Eli Kauffman

1 cup yellow cornmeal
⅓ cup all-purpose flour
2 tablespoons sugar
1 teaspoon salt
2 teaspoons baking powder
½ teaspoon baking soda
2 eggs, beaten
1 cup buttermilk

½ cup vegetable oil
1 (8¾ ounce) can cream-style corn
⅓ cup chopped onion
2 tablespoons chopped green pepper, or 2 tablespoons hot peppers
½ cup shredded Cheddar cheese

In mixing bowl, combine first 6 ingredients. Combine remaining ingredients and add to dry ingredients; stir only until moistened. Pour into a greased 9-inch square baking pan and bake at 350° for 25-30 minutes. Makes 8-10 servings.

A very thin man met a very fat man in the hotel lobby.
"From the looks of you," said the fat man,
"there must have been a famine."
"Yes," came the reply, "and from the looks of you,
you might have caused it."

STRAWBERRY NUT BREAD

Ruth Yoder

1 cup butter or margarine
1½ cups sugar
1 teaspoon vanilla
¼ teaspoon lemon extract
4 eggs
3 cups flour

1 teaspoon salt
1 teaspoon cream of tartar
½ teaspoon baking soda
1 cup strawberry jam
½ cup sour cream
1 cup chopped nuts

Cream butter or margarine, sugar, vanilla, and lemon extract until fluffy. Add eggs, one at a time. Add flour, salt, cream of tartar, and baking soda. Combine strawberry jam and sour cream. Add jam mixture alternately with dry ingredients until creamed. Stir in nuts. Bake at 350° for 50-55 minutes. Cool. Makes 3 loaf pans.

OATMEAL PONE
Ruth Yoder

1 pint whole wheat flour
1 pint oatmeal
1 pint sweet milk
1 tablespoon baking powder

1 teaspoon salt
¼ cup oil
¼ cup honey

Mix all ingredients together. Pour batter into a 9x13-inch baking pan and bake at 400° for 20-25 minutes. Serve with strawberries or peaches and milk.

CINNAMON STREUSEL SWIRL CAKE
Miriam Yoder

STREUSEL MIX:
½ cup flour
½ cup brown sugar

2 teaspoons cinnamon
2 tablespoons melted butter

CAKE:
1 package yellow cake mix
1 package vanilla instant pudding
3 tablespoons Crisco oil

1⅓ cups water
2 eggs

GLAZE:
¾ cup powdered sugar

2 tablespoons milk

Mix streusel mix together. Mix cake batter and pour ¾ of batter into tube pan, then put ⅔ of streusel mix on top. Add remaining batter; pour remaining streusel mix on top. Bake at 375° for 40-50 minutes. Cool and put glaze on top.

CREAM CHEESE DANISH
Ethelyn Stephens

2 cans Pillsbury crescent rolls
2 (8 ounce) packages cream
   cheese
⅔ cup sugar

1 egg yolk (reserve egg white for
   egg wash)
½ teaspoon vanilla
Sugar for sprinkling on top

Spread 1 can rolls in greased 9x13-inch pan. Mix all ingredients and pour over dough. Top with second can of rolls. Brush with frothy egg white and sprinkle with sugar. Bake at 325°-350° until bottom is brown (about 20-25 minutes). Cool before cutting.

CREAM CHEESE DANISH

Mrs. Jonathan Yoder

½ cup warm water
2 packages dry yeast
1 teaspoon sugar
1 cup commercial sour cream
½ cup butter

½ cup sugar
1 teaspoon salt
2 eggs, beaten
4 cups flour

CREAM CHEESE FILLING:
2 (8 ounce) packages cream
  cheese
¾ cup sugar

1 egg, beaten
⅛ teaspoon salt
2 teaspoons vanilla

GLAZE:
2 cups powdered sugar
4 tablespoons milk

2 teaspoons vanilla

Combine water, yeast, and sugar and set aside. Heat sour cream until barely bubbly; add butter, sugar, and salt, stirring until dissolved. Cool to lukewarm. Then add beaten eggs with the yeast mixture. Add 4 cups flour to all of the above. Cover and refrigerate overnight.

The next morning, make the Cream Cheese Filling by beating together cream cheese and sugar, then add egg, salt, and vanilla. Divide dough into 4 equal portions. Roll out on floured surface. Place on greased baking sheet. Make grooves down the middle in which to place the Cream Cheese Filling. Cover and let rise until double. Bake at 350° for 12-15 minutes. Do not overbake!

Mix together glaze ingredients and spread over loaves while they are still warm.

When you have nothing left but God,
you become aware that God is enough.

COFFEE CAKE
Denise Smith

1½ cups sugar
¾ cup butter, softened
3 eggs
1½ teaspoons vanilla
3 cups flour

1½ teaspoons baking powder
1½ teaspoons baking soda
¼ teaspoon salt
1½ cups buttermilk

FILLING:
½ cup brown sugar
1½ teaspoons cinnamon

½ cup finely chopped nuts

In a large mixing bowl, combine sugar, butter, eggs, and vanilla. Beat 2 minutes. Mix in flour, baking powder, baking soda, salt, and buttermilk. Put ¼ batter and about ¼ filling mixture in greased pan, alternating batter and filling. Bake at 350° for 45-50 minutes. Serve hot! (I also like to mix a little powdered sugar and milk together to a thin consistency and drizzle over top.) Delicious!

COFFEE CAKE
Barbara Ann Yoder, Emma Mae Yoder

1 box yellow cake mix
1 small box instant vanilla pudding
¾ cup Wesson oil
¾ cup water

4 eggs
1 teaspoon vanilla flavoring
1 teaspoon butter flavoring

SUGAR MIXTURE:
⅓ cup white sugar
2 tablespoons cinnamon

½ cup chopped pecans

GLAZE:
1 cup powdered sugar
2 tablespoons milk

½ teaspoon vanilla
½ teaspoon butter flavoring

Beat cake mix and remaining ingredients according to box directions. Grease bundt pan. Layer batter and sugar mixture. Bake in a 350° oven for 45-50 minutes. Cool 10 minutes. Remove and glaze.

DANISH COFFEE CAKE

Mrs. Jonathan Yoder

1 white cake mix
3 eggs

1½ cups sour cream
1 tablespoon butter

GLAZE:
⅔ cup powdered sugar

2-3 teaspoons water

FILLING:
Your choice of apple or cherry pie
  filling or cream cheese

Heat oven to 350°. Grease and flour jelly roll pan. Measure out ½ cup of the cake mix (dry) and reserve. Beat eggs slightly with fork and stir in sour cream. Mix in remaining cake mix (batter will be thick and slightly lumpy). Spread in pan. Make 15 shallow wells, evenly spaced, in batter with back of a spoon; put about 1 tablespoon of your choice of filling (apple or cherry pie filling or cream cheese) into each well. Cut butter into reserved ½ cup cake mix until crumbly. Sprinkle evenly over mixture in pan. Bake in a 15½x 10½x1-inch baking pan at 350° for 25-30 minutes. Makes 15 servings.

Clean Confession
Oh welcome cupboard sprucing time!
The time to toss away,
The bit of this, the mite of that
I've saved for many a day.
The bag that holds the pinch of rice,
The cloves that lost their zip
The crumb of cocoa, ages old
That wouldn't make a sip
The nearly empty box of starch
I arrange them on the floor
Then carefully return them as
I did the Spring before!

CREAM CHEESE COFFEE CAKE

Silla K. Yoder

1 box butter cake mix
1 stick butter, melted

1 egg

TOPPING:
3 eggs
1 (8 ounce) package cream
  cheese, softened

1 box powdered sugar

Mix cake mix, butter, and egg. Press into 9x13-inch pan. Mix and beat cream cheese, 3 eggs and powdered sugar. Pour over crust and bake at 350° for 45 minutes.

OVERNIGHT BLUEBERRY COFFEE CAKE   Silla Yoder

1 egg
½ cup plus 2 tablespoons sugar,
   divided
1¼ cups all-purpose flour
2 teaspoons baking powder

¾ teaspoon salt
⅓ cup milk
3 tablespoons butter or margarine,
   melted
1 cup *fresh* blueberries

In a mixing bowl, beat egg and ½ cup sugar. Combine flour, baking powder, and salt. Add alternately with milk to sugar mixture, beating well after each addition. Stir in melted butter or margarine. Fold in berries. Pour into a greased, 8-inch square baking pan. Sprinkle in the remaining sugar. Cover and chill overnight. Remove from the refrigerator 30 minutes before baking. Bake at 350° for 30-35 minutes. Serves 9.

CREAM FILLED COFFEE CAKE   Dorothy Schlabach

1 cup milk
1 stick margarine
½ cup sugar
1 teaspoon salt

2 eggs, beaten
1 tablespoon yeast,
   dissolved in ½ cup water
3½ cups flour

CRUMBS:
½ cup brown sugar
½ cup flour
3 tablespoons butter

1 teaspoon cinnamon
½ cup pecans, chopped (optional)

FILLING:
1 cup milk
3 tablespoons flour
1 cup shortening

2 teaspoons vanilla
2½ cups powdered sugar

Scald milk, then add margarine, sugar, and salt. When cooled, add eggs, dissolved yeast, and flour. Dough will be soft. Let rise until doubled, about 1 hour. Divide into 3 parts and put in 3 (8-inch) cake pans, putting crumbs on top. Let rise about 1 hour. Bake at 325° for 15 minutes.

To make filling, cook milk and flour to make a paste. After cooled, add shortening, vanilla, and powdered sugar.

After cake is cooled, split it and fill with filling. Makes 18 servings.

FINNISH COFFEE CAKE

Wanda Steiner

1¼ cups white sugar
1 teaspoon vanilla
1 cup Wesson oil
1 cup buttermilk or milk

2 cups flour
½ teaspoon baking soda
½ teaspoon salt
1 teaspoon baking powder

CINNAMON MIXTURE:
1 tablespoon cinnamon

4 tablespoons brown sugar

GLAZE:
1 cup powdered sugar
½ teaspoon vanilla

Enough hot water to make a thin
paste

Mix sugar, vanilla, oil, and buttermilk or milk together. Then add rest of ingredients and mix well. Put half the batter into a well greased 9x13-inch pan. Add half cinnamon and sugar mixture. Pour on the rest of the batter and top with remaining cinnamon and sugar mixture. Bake at 350° for 30 minutes.

Stir glaze ingredients together. Poke holes in hot cake with a fork. Drizzle still-hot cake with the glaze. Serves 12.

FRUIT SWIRL COFFEE CAKE

Esther Mast

4 cups Bisquick baking mix
½ cup sugar
¼ cup margarine or butter, melted
½ cup milk
1 teaspoon vanilla

1 teaspoon almond extract
3 eggs
1 (21 ounce) can cherry, apricot,
    or blueberry pie filling

GLAZE:
1 cup powdered sugar

1-2 tablespoons milk

Heat oven to 350°. Grease a 15½x10½x1-inch jelly roll pan or 2 (9x9x2-inch) square pans. Mix all ingredients except pie fillings and glaze; beat vigorously for 30 seconds. Spread ⅔ of the batter (about 2½ cups) in jelly roll pan or ⅓ of the batter (about 1¼ cups) in each square pan. Spread pie filling over batter (filling may not cover batter completely). Drop remaining batter by tablespoonfuls onto pie filling. Bake until light brown, 20-25 minutes.

To make glaze, beat powdered sugar and 1-2 tablespoons milk until smooth and of desired consistency. Drizzle with glaze while cake is still warm. Serve cake warm or cool. Makes 18 servings.

AUNT EBBIE'S
SOUR CREAM COFFEE CAKE

Roxanna L. Linneber

1½ cups sour cream
¾ stick butter, softened
2 eggs
1-1¼ cups white sugar
1 teaspoon vanilla

1 teaspoon baking powder
½ teaspoon baking soda
3 cups flour
Cinnamon and white sugar mixture
for sprinkling

Grease and flour bundt or tube pan. Mix together sour cream, softened butter, eggs, and white sugar and cream well. Add vanilla, baking powder, and baking soda. Mix, add flour 1 cup at a time. It will seem dry. Mix well. Put half of the batter in pan and sprinkle with the cinnamon and sugar mixture. Put the rest of the batter on top. Bake at 350° for 1 hour. Top with a cream cheese frosting.

SOUR CREAM COFFEE CAKE

Ruth Hershberger

1 stick plus 2 tablespoons
  margarine
1 cup sugar
2 eggs
1 cup sour cream
2 cups flour

½ teaspoon salt
1 teaspoon baking powder
1 teaspoon baking soda
½ cup water
1 teaspoon vanilla

CRUMBS:
½ cup brown sugar
½ cup white sugar

1 teaspoon cinnamon
½ cup chopped nuts

Cream margarine and sugar. Beat in eggs. Beat in sour cream. Sift dry ingredients. Beat into cake alternately with water and vanilla. Beat well. Place half of batter in bottom of greased and floured 9x13-inch pan.

Mix all crumb ingredients together. Add half of crumbs to top of batter. Put the rest of batter on top. Add the rest of crumb mixture. Bake at 350° for 20-25 minutes. Makes 16 servings.

He prayeth best, who lovest best
All things both great and small.
For the dear God who loveth us,
He made and loveth all. — Coleridge

BUTTERMILK DOUGHNUTS
Sara Jean Yoder

2 cups sugar
3 eggs, beaten
1½ cups warm mashed potatoes
⅓ cup butter, melted
1 cup buttermilk

6 cups sifted all-purpose flour
4 teaspoons baking powder
1½ teaspoons baking soda
1 teaspoon salt
1 teaspoon nutmeg

Add sugar to eggs. Beat until well mixed. Stir in potatoes, butter, and buttermilk. Add sifted dry ingredients and mix only until flour is completely moistened. Chill dough at least 1 hour. Roll ⅓ of dough at a time on lightly floured surface to ½-inch thickness. Cut with a floured cutter. Let rest 10-15 minutes. Fry in deep hot fat (370°). When doughnuts are golden brown, lift out and cool slightly. Roll in powdered sugar or frost with icing.

SIMPLE DOUGHNUTS
Silla K. Yoder

3½ cups flour
2 tablespoons oil
2 beaten eggs
1 cup white sugar

¾ cup milk
5 teaspoons baking powder
1 teaspoon nutmeg or vanilla

Mix above ingredients and turn out on floured surface. Cut with doughnut cutter and let dough rise 15 minutes. Fry in deep hot fat (375°) until brown. Roll in sugar. If you want a light glaze for doughnuts, mix powdered sugar and milk to a thin consistency.

HEALTHY APPLE WALNUT MUFFINS
Lydia Knox

2 cups flour
1 teaspoon baking powder
1½ teaspoons cinnamon
¼ teaspoon salt
2 large eggs
1 cup plus 2 tablespoons frozen,
    thawed, apple juice concentrate

⅔ cup buttermilk
2 tablespoons oat bran
2 apples, peeled, cored, and
    chopped
⅓ cup chopped walnuts

GARNISH:
1 small apple, peeled, cored, and
    cut into thin slices

Preheat oven to 375°. Mix together flour, baking powder, cinnamon, and salt. Mix together in separate bowl eggs, apple juice, and buttermilk. Stir flour mixture and oat bran into egg mixture until dry ingredients are just moistened. Do not overmix. Gently stir in chopped apples and nuts. Spoon batter into lined muffin pans, filling cups ⅔ full. Garnish each muffin with an apple slice. Bake muffins for 25 minutes or until lightly golden. Makes 18 muffins.

APPLE CORN MUFFINS
Ruth Yoder

1 (12 ounce) box corn muffin mix
⅔ cup milk
1 egg

2 apples, pared and shredded or
   finely chopped
2 tablespoons brown sugar

In a bowl, combine muffin mix, milk, and egg. Mix just until dry ingredients are moistened. Stir in apples. Spoon batter into 12 greased muffin cups. Sprinkle with brown sugar. Bake at 425° for 15-20 minutes or until golden brown. Makes 12 muffins.

BLUEBERRY BUTTERMILK MUFFINS
Esther L. Miller

⅓ cup soft shortening
⅓ cup sugar
1 egg, beaten
1¾ cups buttermilk
2 cups pastry flour
½ cup oat flour or quick oats

½ cup wheat germ
¼ cup whole wheat
4 teaspoons baking powder
1½ teaspoons baking soda
½ teaspoon salt
1 cup blueberries

Mix shortening and sugar; add egg and buttermilk. Mix dry ingredients together and add to liquid, stirring lightly; add blueberries. If using frozen blueberries, mix blueberries with 2 teaspoons flour before adding. Bake at 375° for 12-15 minutes. Makes 1 dozen large muffins.

BLUEBERRY MUFFINS
Heidi Kauffman

2 tablespoons butter or margarine
⅔ cup sugar
1 egg
½ cup milk

⅛ teaspoon salt
1½ cups flour
1 teaspoon baking powder
1 cup blueberries (fresh or frozen)

Cream butter or margarine, sugar, and egg. Add milk. Add dry ingredients and stir in blueberries. Gently spoon batter into lined cups of a muffin tin. Sprinkle a bit of sugar on top. Bake at 350° about 30 minutes. Makes 8-12 muffins.

BLUEBERRY STREUSEL MUFFINS

Linda Zook

⅓ cup sugar
¼ cup butter or margarine,
  softened
1 egg
2⅓ cups all-purpose flour
4 teaspoons baking powder

½ teaspoon salt
1 cup milk
1 teaspoon vanilla
1-1½ cups fresh or frozen
  blueberries

STREUSEL:
½ cup sugar
⅓ cup flour

½ teaspoon cinnamon
¼ cup margarine

In mixing bowl, cream sugar and butter or margarine. Add egg; mix well. Combine flour, baking powder, and salt; add to creamed mixture alternately with milk. Stir in vanilla. Fold in blueberries. Fill 12 greased or paper-lined muffin cups two-thirds full. In small bowl, combine sugar, flour, and cinnamon; cut in margarine until crumbly. Sprinkle over muffins. Bake at 375° for 25-30 minutes. Makes 1 dozen muffins.

The way to a friend's house is never long.

TERESA'S BLUEBERRY MUFFINS

Susan K. Yoder

½ cup butter
1 cup sugar
2 eggs
1 teaspoon vanilla
2 teaspoons baking powder
¼ teaspoon salt

2 cups flour
½ cup milk
2½ cups fresh blueberries
  (or 1 bag frozen unsweetened
  blueberries)

TOPPING:
¼ cup flour
¼ cup sugar

2 tablespoons butter
¼ teaspoon nutmeg

In mixing bowl, beat butter until creamy. Add sugar and beat until pale and fluffy. Add eggs one at a time. Beat in vanilla, baking powder, and salt. Add flour and milk alternately. Fold in blueberries. Spoon into muffin cups.

Rub together topping ingredients until crumbly. Sprinkle tops of muffins with topping mixture. Bake at 375° for 25-30 minutes until golden brown and top feels springy when pressed. Makes 18 regular size or 10 large size muffins.

SWEET BLUEBERRY MUFFINS   Laura K. Yoder

1 egg
½ cup milk
¼ cup salad oil
1½ cups all-purpose flour

½ cup sugar
2 teaspoons baking powder
½ teaspoon salt
1 cup blueberries

Beat egg, stir in milk and oil, and mix in remaining ingredients just until moistened. Batter should be lumpy. Fold in blueberries.

Fill greased muffin cups ⅔ full. Bake at 350° for 20-25 minutes or until golden brown. Remove immediately from pan. Makes 12 regular size or 30 small size muffins.

DELICIOUS BLUEBERRY MUFFINS   Drusilla Beiler

½ cup margarine
1 cup sugar
2 eggs
5 cups all-purpose flour
3 tablespoons baking powder

2 cups milk
2 teaspoons vanilla
3 cups blueberries
½ teaspoon salt
1 scant teaspoon cinnamon

STREUSEL TOPPING:
½ cup sugar
⅓ cup all-purpose flour

½ teaspoon cinnamon
¼ stick margarine

With electric mixer, cream together margarine and sugar until fluffy. Add eggs and mix well. Mix dry ingredients together and blend in milk and vanilla. Be careful to not overmix as muffins will become dry if overmixed. Just barely mix in flour, then add blueberries and mix in by hand. Place in muffin tins and put 1 teaspoon streusel topping on each muffin. Bake at 350° for 25-30 minutes or until golden brown. Makes 24 muffins.

BRAN MUFFINS   Mrs. Jonathan Yoder

2 cups shreds of whole bran cereal
2½ cups buttermilk
½ cup oil
2 eggs
2½ cups all-purpose flour

1½ cups sugar
1¼ teaspoons baking soda
1 teaspoon baking powder
½ teaspoon salt

In large bowl, combine cereal and buttermilk; let set 5 minutes. Add oil and eggs; blend well. Stir in remaining ingredients and mix well. Fill cupcake liners ¾ full and bake at 375° for 18-20 minutes.

Some people just can't count calories and have figures to prove it.

BRAN MUFFINS
Lela Brenneman

2 cups Nabisco Bran Buds cereal
2 cups boiling water
1 heaping cup Crisco shortening
3 cups sugar
4 eggs, beaten

1 quart buttermilk
5 cups flour
5 teaspoons baking soda
1 teaspoon salt
4 cups Kellogg's All Bran cereal

Add Bran Buds to boiling water. Set aside to cool. Cream shortening and sugar; add beaten eggs and buttermilk. Mix well and stir in Bran Buds mixture. Sift flour, baking soda, and salt and add to above mixture. Fold in All Bran until moist. Fill paper-lined muffin cups ⅔ full and bake at 400° for 18-20 minutes.

Batter keeps 6 weeks in refrigerator or can be frozen.

CORNMEAL MUFFINS
Ruth Yoder

1 cup sugar
⅓ cup yellow cornmeal
1⅓ cups plus 2 tablespoons flour
2¼ teaspoons baking powder
¼ teaspoon allspice
½ teaspoon salt

1 egg, beaten
1 cup plus 1 tablespoon melted
  butter (can substitute margarine
  or oil)
1 cup rich milk

Mix sugar and cornmeal. Add sifted dry ingredients. Add egg mixed with butter and milk. Mix together well. Grease muffin pans. Bake at 400° for 15-18 minutes. Makes 18 muffins.

HONEY DATE MUFFINS
Irene Yoder

1¼ cups flour
¼ cup sugar
3 teaspoons baking powder
¼ teaspoon salt
1 egg, slightly beaten

1 cup milk
⅓ cup honey
¼ cup oil
2 cups Bran Flakes cereal
½ cup snipped dates

Preheat oven to 400°. Grease 14 medium muffin cups. Stir together flour, sugar, baking powder, and salt. Combine egg, milk, honey, oil, and cereal. Let stand 2-3 minutes. (Stir to break up cereal.) Add dates. Add all at once to dry ingredients. Stir just until moistened. Fill muffin cups ⅔ full. Bake 18-20 minutes or until lightly browned. Makes 14 muffins.

EXCELLENT OAT MUFFINS

Rhoda Yoder

1 cup quick oats
1 cup buttermilk
3 tablespoons butter, melted
  (or oil)
2 eggs

3 tablespoons sugar
  (or Karo syrup)*
1 cup flour (whole wheat or other)
1 tablespoon baking powder
½ teaspoon baking soda
½ teaspoon salt

Combine oats with wet ingredients and let set for 1 hour. If you're in a hurry, just put in blender. Add dry ingredients and stir just enough to blend. Bake in greased muffin pan at 400° for 25 minutes.

Hint: Use an ice cream dipper (rinsed in hot water) to dip batter into muffin pan.

*If you need sugar free "cupcakes", use applesauce instead of buttermilk and add fruits and nuts according to taste. Makes 12 muffins.

OATMEAL MUFFINS

Ruth Hershberger

1½ cups oatmeal (blenderized)
1 cup buttermilk
½ cup brown sugar
½ cup vegetable oil
2 eggs

1 cup flour, sifted
1 teaspoon baking powder
½ teaspoon salt
½ teaspoon baking soda
1 teaspoon cinnamon

TOPPING:
¼ cup sugar

¾ teaspoon cinnamon

Blenderize oatmeal; stir in buttermilk, brown sugar, and oil. Beat eggs and stir in also. Sift all the dry ingredients, then stir into the buttermilk mixture by hand. Fill muffin cups ¾ full. Sprinkle cinnamon-sugar mixture on top. Bake at 400° for 12-15 minutes. Very moist and nutritious. Makes 15 regular sized muffins.

*How very happy I should be
for all these blessings given me,
A roof above, and love within,
To God and to my kith and kin.*

OATMEAL MUFFINS

Mrs. Gerald Lambright

1 cup quick oats
1 cup sour milk
½ cup brown sugar
½ scant cup oil
1 egg

1 cup flour
1 teaspoon baking powder
½ teaspoon salt
½ teaspoon baking soda

Mix oats and sour milk and let stand ½ hour. Add the rest of the ingredients. Put in muffin pans and bake at 400° for 25 minutes.

If muffins are too rich, use less oil.

GINGER RHUBARB MUFFINS

Sonia Hoffman

2¼ cups all-purpose flour
2 teaspoons baking powder
1 teaspoon baking soda
½ teaspoon salt
2 tablespoons finely chopped
  crystallized ginger

¾ cup sugar
½ cup milk
½ cup sour cream
⅓ cup vegetable oil
1 egg
1 cup finely chopped rhubarb

Preheat oven to 400°. In a large bowl, stir together flour, baking powder, baking soda, salt, and crystallized ginger. In a separate bowl, whisk together sugar, milk, sour cream, oil, and egg. Stir in rhubarb. Add to dry ingredients and stir until just blended. Fill each muffin cup ¾ full with batter. Bake until toothpick comes out clean, approximately 15 minutes. Cool in pan 5 minutes and then remove to cooling rack. Makes 16 standard size muffins.

SOUR CREAM APPLE MUFFINS

Mrs. Noah Yoder

2 cups sifted flour
2 teaspoons baking powder
½ teaspoon baking soda
½ teaspoon salt
3 tablespoons sugar
1 egg, beaten
1 cup sour cream

3 tablespoons oil or melted
  shortening
1 medium size apple, peeled and
  diced
1 teaspoon nutmeg
2 tablespoons sugar

Sift together flour, baking powder, baking soda, salt, and 3 tablespoons sugar. Combine egg, sour cream, and oil in bowl; pour into dry ingredients all at once. Stir partially, then add apples which have been peeled, diced, and sprinkled with nutmeg and 2 tablespoons sugar. Stir until all dry ingredients are moist but still lumpy, about 17-25 strokes. Spoon batter into greased muffin pans, filling pans only ⅔ full. Bake at 425° for 20-28 minutes. Makes about 18 muffins.

CINNAMON ROLLS

Ann Mast, Ruth Yoder

1½ cups shortening
2 cups sugar
4 teaspoons salt
4 packages yeast
5 cups warm water

4 eggs, beaten
12 cups flour
Butter
Brown sugar
Cinnamon

FROSTING:
4 cups powdered sugar
Water to mix well

1 teaspoon vanilla
2 tablespoons shortening

Melt shortening and add to sugar and salt. Put yeast in warm water. Let sit for 5 minutes, then add to sugar mixture. Add beaten eggs and flour. Let rise in warm place until double in bulk. Dough will be very soft. Divide and roll out. Put butter, brown sugar, and cinnamon on dough; roll up. Cut and put in pans. Let rise again and bake at 350° until brown.

Frost while still warm. Makes 30 rolls.

Ruth puts 1 (3 ounce) package instant vanilla pudding and 1 tablespoon nutmeg in the dough.

*If at first you don't succeed
take heart, you're running about average.*

CINNAMON ROLLS

Lela Brenneman

4 tablespoons yeast
4 teaspoons sugar
1 cup water
4 cups lukewarm buttermilk
1 cup sugar

4 teaspoons salt
2 teaspoons baking soda
4 eggs, beaten
11½-12 cups flour
1 cup melted shortening

Soak yeast and sugar in water for 5 minutes. Stir together lukewarm buttermilk, sugar, salt, baking soda, and eggs. Mix with yeast mixture. Add ½ of the flour (about 6 cups) and beat 2 minutes with electric mixer. Add melted shortening; beat. Stir in the rest of the flour (5½-6 cups) to make soft dough, and beat. Let rise and knead. Let rise again and turn out on floured board. Knead until smooth and elastic. Roll dough ¼-½-inch thick. Spread with melted butter, brown sugar, cinnamon, and nuts. Roll up as you would a jelly roll. Slice and put in prepared pans. Let rise. Bake at 325° for 15 minutes.

CINNAMON ROLLS

Ruth Yoder

4 tablespoons yeast
1 quart warm water
¾ cup sugar

3 tablespoons oil
8 cups doughnut mix
2 cups bread flour

Mix yeast in water. Mix all ingredients together and let rise. Roll out on a floured table, brush with melted butter, and sprinkle with brown sugar and cinnamon. Roll in jelly roll fashion. Cut and put in greased pans and bake at 350° for 10-12 minutes or until brown. Frost while still warm. You can find doughnut mix at bulk food stores. Makes around 30 rolls or 5 pans.

FRUIT CINNAMON ROLL

Elsie Brennamon

1 cup warm water
4 tablespoons yeast
4 teaspoons sugar
4 eggs, beaten
2 teaspoons baking soda
4 teaspoons salt

1 cup sugar
4 cups lukewarm buttermilk
1 cup melted shortening
Approximately 16 cups flour
Pie filling of your choice

Mix together water, yeast, and 4 teaspoons sugar and let sit a few minutes. Beat eggs. Next add baking soda, salt, 1 cup sugar, buttermilk, and shortening. To that add the yeast mixture, stirring in enough flour (about 16 cups) to make a soft dough (less than bread dough). Let rise. Divide dough in half and roll out into a rectangle. Spread with soft butter, brown sugar, and cinnamon. Roll up as you would a jelly roll. Slice and put in prepared pans. On each roll place 1 tablespoon pie filling of your choice, such as apple, blueberry, or raspberry. Let rise until light. Bake at 350° for 20 minutes or until light brown. Frost with cream cheese icing.

SMALL CINNAMON ROLLS

Elva Byler

1 cup scalded milk
2 eggs, separated
2 tablespoons yeast
4 cups bread flour

¼ cup sugar
1 teaspoon salt
1 cup margarine

Scald milk. Cool. Beat egg whites. Next add yolks and beat together. Add milk and yeast. Take all the dry ingredients and add margarine. Mix with fork until crumbly. Add to milk mixture and cool for 2 hours. Divide dough in 2 parts and roll mix. Sprinkle sugar and cinnamon on rolled dough. Roll up like jelly roll and cut in thin slices. Bake at 350° for 10-12 minutes.

ORANGE BLOSSOMS

Wanda Steiner

2 cups sugar
1 cup margarine
4 eggs
4 cups sifted flour (plain)

2 teaspoons baking powder
½ teaspoon salt
1 cup milk
1 teaspoon vanilla

GLAZE:
Juice of 2 lemons
Juice of 2 oranges

Grated rind of 2 lemons and 2
 oranges
1½ boxes powdered sugar

Cream sugar and margarine. Add eggs. Combine dry ingredients and add alternately with milk. Add vanilla. Bake in tiny muffin tins for 10 minutes at 375°. Do not overbake!

Make glaze by removing seeds from juices and mixing well with powdered sugar. Add grated rind. Keep mixture stirred. As tiny cakes come out of oven, dip in glaze while hot, coating well. Place on waxed paper to drain. Leftovers can be frozen. Makes 12 dozen tiny cakes.

POLISH SUGAR CAKE

Melody Helmuth

2 packages yeast
½ teaspoon sugar
½ cup warm water
¾ cup milk
½ cup butter, melted

2½-3 cups flour, divided
¼ cup instant potato flakes
½ cup sugar
½ teaspoon salt
2 eggs

TOPPING:
¾ cup brown sugar
1 cup nuts

1½ teaspoons sugar

GLAZE:
¾ cup powdered sugar

1 tablespoon milk

Dissolve yeast and sugar in warm water and let stand 5 minutes. Heat milk and butter until butter melts. Add yeast mixture, 1 cup flour, potatoes, sugar, salt, and eggs. Mix until smooth, then add remaining flour. Let rise 1 hour. Punch down and let rise ½ hour. Spread in greased 15x10-inch pan. Sprinkle evenly with topping. Make shallow indentations with wooden spoon handle and drizzle with ⅓ cup melted butter. Let rise ½ hour. Bake 12-15 minutes at 375°. Drizzle with glaze. Makes 15 servings.

PUMPKIN CINNAMON ROLLS
Faith Miller

2¾-3¼ cups flour, divided
1 package active dry yeast
½ cup solid-pack pumpkin
⅔ cup milk
2 tablespoons sugar

4 tablespoons butter or margarine,
  divided
½ teaspoon salt
1 egg, beaten
½ cup packed brown sugar
¾ teaspoon ground cinnamon

CARAMEL FROSTING:
2 tablespoons butter or margarine
¼ cup packed brown sugar
1 tablespoon milk

½ teaspoon vanilla extract
Dash salt
¼-⅓ cup powdered sugar

In a mixing bowl, combine 1½ cups flour and yeast; set aside. In a saucepan, heat and stir pumpkin, milk, sugar, 2 tablespoons butter, and salt until warm (120°-130°) and butter is almost melted. Add to flour/yeast mixture along with egg. Beat on low speed for 30 seconds. Beat on high speed for 3 minutes. Stir in enough remaining flour to make a moderately stiff dough. Knead on a lightly floured surface until smooth and elastic, about 6-8 minutes. Place in a greased bowl, turning once to grease top. Cover and let rise until doubled, about 1 hour. Roll out to a 12x10-inch rectangle. Melt remaining butter and brush on dough. Sprinkle brown sugar and cinnamon over butter. Roll into jelly roll style. Cut, and place in a greased 13x9-inch cake pan or in greased pie pans. Cover and let rise until doubled, about 30 minutes. Bake at 375° for 20-25 minutes, until golden brown. Cool.

To make frosting, melt butter in saucepan; stir in brown sugar and milk. Cook and stir over medium heat for 1 minute. Stir in vanilla, salt and ¼ cup powdered sugar. Beat until blended. Add more powdered sugar if necessary, to get desired consistency. Drizzle over rolls. Makes 1 dozen rolls.

PLUCKETS BUBBLE LOAF
Ruth Yoder

½ cup chopped nuts
1 package frozen roll dough
¾ cup brown sugar

1 package vanilla pudding mix
  (not instant)
1 teaspoon cinnamon
6 tablespoons butter

Grease bundt pans well. Sprinkle nuts in bottom of pan. Place frozen rolls in pan. Sprinkle brown sugar on rolls then pudding and cinnamon. Cut butter in small pieces and place evenly on top of other ingredients. Cover with waxed paper. Let stand overnight. Bake at 350° for 30 minutes. Turn upside down on plate.

PLUCKET

Heidi Kauffman

⅓ cup sugar
⅓ cup melted butter
½ teaspoon salt
1 cup scalded milk

1 package yeast,
   dissolved in ¼ cup water
3 eggs, well beaten
4 cups flour

TOPPING MIXTURE:
1 cup sugar
3 teaspoons cinnamon

½ cup chopped nuts

Add sugar, butter, and salt to scalded milk. When lukewarm, add dissolved yeast, eggs, and flour; beat thoroughly. Cover and let rise until doubled. Stir down and let rise again until doubled. Then take 1 teaspoon of dough and dip in melted butter. Roll in mixture of sugar, cinnamon, and nuts. Repeat process for rest of dough. Let rise 30 minutes. Bake in angel food cake pan at 325° for 30 minutes.

PULL BUNS OR PLUCKETS

Mrs. Robert Paul Yoder (Amanda)

2 tablespoons yeast
1 cup warm water
1 cup scalded milk
½ cup sugar

2 teaspoons salt
2 eggs
½ cup butter or margarine
7-7½ cups flour

DIPPING INGREDIENTS:
½ cup melted butter or margarine
Cinnamon and sugar mixture
   (1½ cups sugar and 3 teaspoons
   cinnamon)

¾ cup chopped pecans

Dissolve yeast in warm water. After dissolved, add milk, sugar, salt, eggs, butter or margarine, and about half the flour. Stir until smooth. Gradually add rest of flour. Knead until smooth and elastic. Cover. Let rise until doubled. Punch down and let rise again. Grease bread pan or angel food cake pan. Roll dough into teaspoon-sized balls. Roll in butter or margarine, then dip in sugar-cinnamon mixture. Sprinkle each layer with nuts. Fill pan about ½ full. Let rise until doubled (about 30 minutes). Bake at 350° for 30-40 minutes. When baked, turn pan upside down immediately. Serve warm. Each pulls or plucks off sections to eat.

The praise life wears out the self-life.

Breakfasts

BREAKFAST FRUIT

Judi Wagher

3 tablespoons Tang (dry)
2 large cans pineapple chunks
(drain and reserve juice)
1 small package instant French
vanilla pudding

2 cans mandarin orange slices
(drain and discard juice)
3 large bananas, sliced
Chopped maraschino cherries,
if desired
1 cup chopped pecans

Dissolve Tang in pineapple juice. Sprinkle pudding over fruit in medium-sized glass bowl. Add juice and toss. Refrigerate overnight. Add nuts just before serving. Serves 8-10.

BAKED OATMEAL

Ruth Yoder, Melody Helmuth

½ cup melted butter
¾ cup brown sugar
2 beaten eggs
3 cups oatmeal

2 teaspoons baking powder
1 teaspoon salt
1 cup milk

Mix butter, sugar, and eggs. Add remaining ingredients and stir until well blended. Pour batter into a 9x9-inch baking pan and bake 30 minutes at 350°. Good with cold canned peaches and milk. Makes 6-8 servings.

BREAKFAST CASSEROLE

Mrs. Shirley Yoder

8 slices bread
1 pound sausage, fried
2 cups shredded Velveeta cheese
6 beaten eggs
2 cups milk
½ teaspoon dry mustard

1 teaspoon onion salt
¼ teaspoon garlic powder
½ teaspoon salt
1 can cream of mushroom soup
½ can milk

Cube bread and put in bottom of 9x13-inch pan. Sprinkle sausage and cheese over bread cubes. Mix together eggs, milk, and seasonings and pour over sausage and cheese. Dot with butter. Mix soup and milk together and put on top. Bake at 350° for 45 minutes to 1 hour.

Only a word of anger,
But it wounded one sensitive heart;
Only a word of sharp reproach,
But it made the teardrops start;
Only a hasty, thoughtless word,
Sarcastic and unkind;
But it darkened the day before so bright
And left a sting behind.

BREAKFAST PIZZA

Carol Petersheim

CRUST:

2 cups flour
2½ teaspoons baking powder
¼ teaspoon baking soda
½ teaspoon salt

1 tablespoon sugar
⅓ cup oil
⅔ cup buttermilk

TOPPING:

10 eggs
1 cup milk
3 tablespoons flour
½ teaspoon salt
Pepper, if desired

1 pound sausage, browned
Shredded cheese
Chopped mushrooms (optional)
Diced green bell peppers (optional)

While you prepare crust, have 1 pound sausage (ham or bacon can be used, too) browning in a large skillet. Drain excess grease.

Sift together flour, baking powder, baking soda, salt, and sugar. Stir in oil and buttermilk. Press on regular size pizza pan. Bake at 400° until lightly browned, 8-10 minutes.

While this is baking, put the following into blender: eggs, milk, flour, salt, and pepper, if desired. Blend together. Pour into skillet with browned sausage. Stir over medium heat until eggs are done. Put on baked crust. Top with cheese. Return to oven just until cheese is melted. Mushrooms and bell peppers are good toppings, too. Serve with tomato gravy. Delicious!

BREAKFAST PIZZA

Ruth Yoder

1 biscuit recipe (for crust)
1 pound sausage, browned
1 cup shredded potatoes
1 cup shredded sharp Cheddar
  cheese

5 eggs
½ cup milk
½ teaspoon salt
⅛ teaspoon pepper

Take your favorite biscuit recipe and roll out for 12-inch pizza pan (can also use 10-inch pan). Place in pan, spoon meat on crust, sprinkle with potatoes, and top with cheese. In a bowl, beat eggs, milk, salt, and pepper. Pour into crust. Bake at 375° for 12 minutes or until lightly browned.

MARIE'S BREAKFAST PIZZA

Mrs. Freeman Schlabach

2 cups biscuit mix
Cream and milk
12 eggs, scrambled

1 can cream of mushroom soup or
  2 cups sausage and gravy
Shredded cheese

Mix biscuit mix, cream, and milk to the consistency of cake batter. Pour into greased medium size pizza pan and bake at 400° until lightly browned.

Meanwhile, scramble eggs and layer on crust, first gravy or mushroom soup, eggs, and cheese last. Set in 400° oven until cheese is melted. Serves 8.

BREAKFAST WAKE UP

Mrs. Freeman Schlabach

12 eggs, beaten
1 pound cooked sausage

1 can cream of mushroom soup
1 pound cheese

Layer in order given in a 13x9-inch greased pan. Bake for 30 minutes at 350°. This can be put together the night before. Refrigerate and bake the next morning. Serve with biscuits and juice. Delicious! Serves 8.

BRUNCH FRITTATA

Cynthia Helmuth

1 tablespoon butter
1½-2 cups hash brown potatoes,
  partially cooked
8 slices bacon, cooked and
  crumbled, or ½ cup cubed ham

8-10 eggs
¾ cup cream of mushroom or
  celery soup, optional
1½ cups shredded Cheddar
  cheese

Melt butter in skillet over moderate heat. Add hash browns and top with bacon or ham. Beat eggs and pour over ingredients in a 10-inch skillet. Cover pan and turn heat to low. Cook 10-12 minutes, until eggs are set. Top with cream soup, if desired, and add Cheddar cheese the last few minutes of cooking. Cut into wedges and serve. Makes 8 servings.

CREAMED EGGS

Elva Byler

3 tablespoons butter
3 tablespoons flour
2¼ cups milk
¼ teaspoon salt

Dash of pepper
4 hard boiled eggs
Fried sausage or bacon, broken up

Melt butter in skillet and add flour. Brown a little; gradually add milk and stir until smooth and thickened. Add salt and pepper to taste. Then add cut up hard boiled eggs and either fried sausage or bacon in small pieces. Serve over toasted bread and butter. Serves 4-6 people.

BLUEBERRY FRENCH TOAST   Silla Yoder

12 slices day old white bread, crusts removed

2 (8 ounce) packages cream cheese

1 cup fresh or frozen blueberries

12 eggs

2 cups milk

½ cup maple syrup or honey

SAUCE:

1 cup sugar

2 tablespoons cornstarch

1 cup water

1 cup fresh or frozen blueberries

1 tablespoon butter or margarine

Cut bread into 1-inch cubes; place half in greased 13x9x2-inch baking dish. Cut cream cheese in 1-inch cubes. Place over bread. Top with blueberries and remaining bread. In large bowl, beat eggs, milk, and syrup. Mix well. Pour over bread mixture. Cover and chill 8 hours or overnight. Remove from refrigerator 30 minutes before baking. Cover and bake at 350° for 30 minutes. Uncover and bake for 25-30 minutes more or until golden brown and center is set.

In saucepan, combine sugar and cornstarch. Add water. Bring to a boil over medium heat and boil 3 minutes, stirring constantly. Stir in blueberries. Reduce heat. Simmer for 8-10 minutes or until berries have burst. Stir in butter until melted. Serve over French toast. Makes 6-8 servings.

COUNTRY INN FRENCH TOAST   Elva Miller

25-30 slices raisin bread, cubed

10 eggs

2 cups half-and-half

1½ cups milk

½ teaspoon nutmeg

2 teaspoons cinnamon

¼ teaspoon salt

NEXT MORNING TOPPING:

1 cup brown sugar

½ cup butter

½ cup pecans

Fill a 9x13-inch pan with bread cubes. Blend eggs, milk, cream, and spices and pour over bread. Cover and refrigerate overnight. In the morning, sprinkle on topping mixed into crumbs. Cover. Bake at 350° for 1 hour or until set. Cut in squares and serve with syrup or plain.

FRENCH BREAKFAST PUFFS

Mrs. Ferlin L. Yoder

MUFFINS:
½ cup sugar
⅓ cup shortening
1 egg
1½ cups sifted flour

1½ teaspoons baking powder
½ teaspoon salt
¼ teaspoon nutmeg
½ cup milk

TOPPING:
½ cup white sugar
1 teaspoon cinnamon

6 tablespoons butter or margarine,
   melted

For muffins, cream together sugar, shortening, and egg. Sift together flour, baking powder, salt, and nutmeg. Add to creamed mixture alternately with milk, beating after each addition. Fill 12 greased muffin cups ⅔ full. Bake at 350° for 20-25 minutes.

Combine remaining sugar and cinnamon. After removing muffins from oven, immediately dip in melted butter, then in cinnamon/sugar mixture until coated. Serve warm. Makes 12 muffins.

GRAPE NUTS

David and Martha Wengerd

2 cups sour cream
2 teaspoons baking soda
1½ cups sugar

3½ cups wheat flour
1 teaspoon salt
1 tablespoon maple flavoring

Mix all together and put in a greased 13x9-inch cake pan. Bake at 325° until done. Crumble cake with hands while warm; when cool, run through food grinder or coarse sieve. Spread on trays and heat in 350° oven for 15-20 minutes until crisp. Store in airtight container.

GRAPENUTS

Mrs. David Wengerd, Mrs. John Nissley

3½ cups whole wheat flour
1 cup brown sugar
1 teaspoon baking soda

1 teaspoon salt
2 cups buttermilk or sour milk
½ cup oil

Mix flour, sugar, baking soda, and salt well. Add milk and oil. Mix well. Bake in 350° oven until done.

Variations: Leave out milk and oil and add 2½ cups light sour cream.

Leave out brown sugar and add ¾ cup white sugar and ¼ cup sorghum molasses.

When cake is cool, crumble and dry in warm oven.

GRANOLA CEREAL

Anna Mae Yoder

10 cups oatmeal
4 cups Rice Krispies cereal
¾ cup wheat germ
1 cup brown sugar
¼ cup water
1⅓ cups vegetable oil

1 cup honey
½ teaspoon salt
2 teaspoons maple flavoring
½ teaspoon vanilla
⅔ cup peanut butter

Combine oatmeal, Rice Krispies, and wheat germ. Mix remaining ingredients. Add to oatmeal mixture. Stir until well coated. Pour into shallow pan and bake at 300° until slightly toasted, about 25-30 minutes. Stir several times while in oven, also while cooling.

GRANOLA CEREAL

Elva Byler

10 cups oatmeal
1 cup coconut
¾ cup sunflower seeds
1 tablespoon vanilla
2 teaspoons salt

1⅓ cups brown sugar
1⅓ cups oil
¾ cup water
1 tablespoon maple flavoring

Mix all ingredients and toast in a 325° oven, stirring every 10 minutes (4 or 5 times).

Variation: Adding 1 cup applesauce or ¾ cup more water makes it more chunky.

Gross deceptions are easily discerned,
but there is not a greater or more dangerous lie than a half-truth.

GRANOLA

Judith Yoder

20 cups oats
4 cups wheat germ
5 cups coconut
5 cups nuts, chopped
2 cups brown sugar
1 pound butter

1 teaspoon salt
2 tablespoons vanilla
4 teaspoons cinnamon
1 cup water
Raisins, optional

In large bowl, mix first 5 ingredients. Melt butter and add salt, vanilla, cinnamon, and water. Stir well into granola mixture and toast at 250° until slightly browned. If desired, add raisins after toasting.

GOOD GRANOLA

Debbie Graber

7 cups oatmeal
2 cups coconut
1½ cups brown sugar
1 teaspoon salt

1 cup chopped pecans
1 cup melted butter
1½ teaspoons cinnamon

Mix all together and bake slowly at 250°-275° until golden brown.

MAY DAY BRUNCH

Martha Kauffman

1 (9-inch) deep dish pie shell
3 eggs
1½ cups lowfat milk
½ teaspoon Italian seasoning
⅓ teaspoon salt
⅛ teaspoon black pepper

1 small box frozen spinach
1 (9 ounce) package shredded
lowfat mozzarella cheese,
divided
2 small tomatoes, sliced
1 cup mushrooms, optional

Pierce pie shell and bake at 450° until pale golden color, about 8 minutes. Cool; reduce oven to 350°. Combine eggs, milk, and seasonings. Add spinach and 1 cup of cheese; pour into cooled pie shell. Top with tomato slices and sprinkle with remaining cheese. Bake at 350° until knife inserted in center comes out clean, about 50 minutes. Let stand 10 minutes before serving. Serves 6.

PEPPERONI BREAKFAST BAKE

Silla K. Yoder

8 ounces mozzarella cheese
½ cup pepperoni, thinly sliced
5 eggs

¼ teaspoon basil
¾ cup milk

Put cheese in pie plate, then put pepperoni on cheese. Beat eggs, basil, and milk. Pour over cheese and pepperoni. Bake at 400° for 20-25 minutes.

PEARL'S PRIZE WINNING PANCAKE MIX   Irene Yoder

6 cups whole wheat flour
4 cups cornmeal
2 cups oatmeal

¼ cup baking powder
2 tablespoons baking soda
½ cup sugar

Mix together. Store in airtight container.

To use: Per 1 cup of mix, add 1 tablespoon oil, 1 cup milk, and 1 egg (whip white separately) for correct consistency. Fruit, applesauce, or jams may be added to the mixture for variety.

APPLE WHEAT PANCAKES   Cynthia Helmuth

⅓ cup whole wheat flour
¼ cup plus 1 tablespoon powdered
   milk
1 tablespoon brown sugar
1½ teaspoons cinnamon
¼ teaspoon cardamom (optional)
¼ teaspoon baking soda

⅛ teaspoon baking powder
⅛ teaspoon salt
2 eggs, beaten
2 teaspoons vanilla
2 teaspoons water
2 small apples, cored and finely
   chopped

Sift together dry ingredients. Combine eggs, vanilla, water, and apples. Stir into dry ingredients. Mix well. Form pancakes by spooning batter onto hot skillet sprayed with non-stick spray. Cook over moderate heat until brown on each side. Makes 12 small pancakes, serving 3-4.

LIGHT PANCAKES   Jo Ann Inhulsen, Mrs. Roger Helmuth, Sr.

3 cups flour
3 tablespoons cornmeal
3 tablespoons sugar
1 teaspoon salt

5 teaspoons baking powder
2½ cups milk
2 eggs, separated
½ stick melted margarine

Mix together flour, cornmeal, sugar, salt, and baking powder. Set aside. Beat together milk, egg yolks, and melted margarine. Set aside. Beat egg whites. Set aside. Mix the dry and wet ingredients together, then fold in egg whites. Bake on hot griddle. Jo Ann uses whole wheat flour and likes to serve them with frozen peaches instead of syrup. Makes 10 pancakes.

MOTHER'S CLOUD LIGHT PANCAKES

Ruth Yoder

1 cup Pillsbury flour
1 tablespoon white sugar
2 tablespoons baking powder
½ teaspoon salt

1 egg
2 tablespoons melted shortening
1½ cups milk

Combine dry ingredients and mix well. Add egg and shortening and pour in milk while stirring. Mix lightly until foamy. Bake on greased griddle. Serve with syrup and butter. Serves 4.

RICE PUDDING PANCAKES

Sonia Hoffman

3 egg yolks
1⅔ cups buttermilk
1½ cups flour
⅓ cup sugar
1 teaspoon baking powder

1 teaspoon baking soda
½ teaspoon salt
3 tablespoons butter, softened
3 egg whites (stiffly beaten)
1 can rice pudding

Beat egg yolks well with beater. Beat in buttermilk. Add dry ingredients and mix. Mix in softened butter. Gently fold in beaten egg whites. Add rice pudding and mix. Fry by dropping batter on hot greased griddle. Serve with syrup. Serves 6-8.

WHOLE GRAIN PANCAKES

Rhoda Yoder

1½-2 cups buttermilk
2 tablespoons Karo syrup
2 eggs
¼ cup butter or oil
1 cup quick oats

1 cup flour (we like Golden 86
  whole wheat)
1 teaspoon baking soda
1 teaspoon baking powder
1 teaspoon salt

Mix buttermilk, syrup, eggs, and butter or oil together. Let oatmeal set in wet mixture for 10 minutes (or put in blender). Set aside. Mix oats, flour, baking soda, baking powder, and salt together. Add dry mixture to wet mixture and mix lightly. I like an ice cream dipper to "pour" pancakes onto griddle heated to 325°-350°. Makes 12-15 pancakes.

WHOLE WHEAT PANCAKES

Mary Zook, Mrs. Eli Kauffman

2 cups whole wheat flour
½ teaspoon salt
2 tablespoons sugar
2 teaspoons baking soda
1½ teaspoons baking powder
1 egg

2-3 cups sour milk or buttermilk
2 tablespoons shortening
1 ripe banana, mashed, optional
1 tablespoon potato flakes,
   optional

Mix dry ingredients. Beat egg and mix with sour milk or buttermilk and shortening. Add dry ingredients and mix well. Add mashed banana and potato flakes, if desired. Batter keeps for several days in refrigerator. Makes 3-4 servings.

Faults are thick where love is thin.

HASH BROWN QUICHE

Elsie Brenneman

3 cups frozen loose-packed
   shredded hash browns, thawed
⅓ cup butter or margarine, melted
1 cup diced fully-cooked ham
1 cup (4 ounces) shredded
   Cheddar cheese

¼ cup diced green pepper
2 eggs
½ cup milk
½ teaspoon salt
¼ teaspoon pepper

Press hash browns between paper towels to remove excess moisture. Press into the bottom and up the sides of an ungreased 9-inch pie pan. Drizzle with melted butter. Bake at 425° for 25 minutes. Combine the ham, cheese, and green pepper; spoon over crust. In a small bowl, beat eggs, milk, salt, and pepper. Pour over all. Reduce heat to 350° and bake for 25-30 minutes or until a knife inserted near the center comes out clean. Allow to stand for 10 minutes before cutting. Serves 6.

QUICK QUICHE
Edna Schrock

5 eggs, beaten
1 cup milk
1 teaspoon salt
½ teaspoon pepper
1 tablespoon Worcestershire sauce

1 cup crumbled cooked bacon
½ cup diced tomatoes
¼ cup chopped onion
¾ cup shredded cheese
1 (9-inch) unbaked pie crust

Beat eggs. Add milk and next 7 ingredients and pour in unbaked pie crust. Bake 45 minutes at 350°. Serves 8 people.

Variation: Omit bacon and add 1 cup finely chopped cooked broccoli.

SAUSAGE RING AND EGGS
Ramona Overholt

2 pounds mild sausage
1 cup milk
1 medium onion, chopped

2 eggs
1 cup oatmeal or bread crumbs
Eggs, scrambled

Combine all ingredients except eggs in a large bowl. Mix well. Place in ring mold sprayed with Pam. Bake at 350° for 45-60 minutes. Pour off liquid. Unmold on platter. Fill center cavity with scrambled eggs.

SCRAPPLE
Mrs. Roger Helmuth, Sr.

1 cup white or yellow cornmeal
2 tablespoons flour
1 teaspoon sugar
1 teaspoon salt
2¾ cups boiling water

1 cup milk
8 ounces bulk pork sausage, fried,
    drained, and crumbled
2 tablespoons margarine for frying

Combine dry ingredients. Gradually stir in water and milk. Cook until thickened and bubbly. Reduce heat and cook, covered, for 10 minutes longer or until very thick, stirring occasionally. Remove from heat. Stir in sausage. Pour into a greased 7½x3½x2-inch loaf pan (the pan will be very full). Cover with plastic wrap and refrigerate. To serve, unmold and cut ⅓-inch slices. Dip in flour and fry on both sides in melted margarine. Serve with tomato gravy. Delicious! Hubby's favorite breakfast. Makes 6 servings.

Canning
&
Freezing

APPLE BUTTER
Esther Mast

1½ cups apple juice concentrate
   or 6 cups apple juice
½ teaspoon allspice
2 tablespoons cinnamon

¼ teaspoon salt
6 cups thick unsweetened
   applesauce

Cook concentrate or juice with the spices and salt until there is about ¾ cup of liquid left in the pan. Add applesauce and cook slowly, stirring often. From time to time, put a teaspoon of the mixture on a cold saucer. The apple butter is done when no liquid runs from it. It won't take long because the cooking down is done before the applesauce is added.

MIRIAM'S APPLE BUTTER
Ruth Yoder

3 (#10) cans unsweetened
   applesauce
18 cups brown sugar

3 cups vinegar
3 cups crushed pineapple
6 tablespoons cinnamon

Mix all ingredients together and bake at 300° for 3 hours or longer.

MARY'S APPLE PIE FILLING
Barbara Kauffman

7 cups sugar
6 cups water
1¾ cups Clear Jell

1 cup cold water
1 tablespoon cinnamon
6 quarts peeled, sliced apples

CRUMBS FOR APPLE GOODIE:
½ cup oatmeal
½ cup brown sugar
½ cup flour

¼ cup butter
⅛ teaspoon baking soda
⅛ teaspoon baking powder

Bring sugar and 6 cups water to a boil in a large kettle. Mix Clear Jell with cold water and slowly add to sugar mixture as it's boiling. Stir and boil until thick and clear. Remove from heat and add cinnamon. Pour over apples and mix well. Fill clean quart jars. Leave *at least* 1 inch space in top of jars or they will run over. Put lids on and process 35 minutes in boiling water or in pressure canner for 13 minutes with 5 pounds pressure. Makes 8 quarts. Each quart makes 1 pie.

Also delicious used for Apple Goodie (by Irene Yoder). Just open jar and put in baking dish. Put crumbs on top. Bake at 375° for 35-40 minutes. Serve hot or cold. Handy and delicious with ice cream. Serves 6.

BEET JELLY

Mrs. Noah Yoder

6 cups beet juice
½ cup lemon juice
2 packages Sure-Jell

8 cups sugar
16 ounces raspberry Jello

Bring juices to a boil with Sure-Jell. Add sugar and Jello all at one time. Boil 5 minutes. Remove from heat, cool, pour into jars, and seal.

CANNING BLUEBERRIES

Ruth Hershberger

Clean, sort and wash blueberries. Fill quart or pint jars. Make a syrup with 50% sugar and 50% water. Bring to rolling boil. Pour over blueberries. Put lid and ring on and screw tightly. Place rack on bottom of canner. Place jars in canner. Fill canner up to necks with warm water. Bring to a rolling boil. Boil for 10 minutes. Turn burner off and leave the jars in canner until cool.

Blueberries can be used in many ways. Drain for blueberry muffins. When making blueberry pies or delight, drain blueberries, reserve juice. Bring blueberry juice to a boil, thicken with Clear Jell, and fold in the drained blueberries. One quart makes a 10-inch pie.

*Whosoever is kind to the poor lends to the Lord
and will be repaid in full. — Proverbs 19:17.*

BLUEBERRY PIE FILLING

Esther L. Miller

3½ quarts water
4 cups sugar
½ teaspoon salt
4 tablespoons lemon juice
2½ cups Perma Flo

1 quart water
2 cups Karo syrup
½ cup black raspberry Jello
¼ cup blueberry Jello
14 cups blueberries

Bring first 4 ingredients to a boil in 8-quart kettle. Mix Perma Flo with water and add to kettle just before boiling. Stir briskly to boiling point. Remove from heat and add Karo syrup, Jellos, and blueberries. Boil in hot water bath for 10 minutes. Yield: 7 quarts.

CHUNKY TOMATO KETCHUP

Mrs. James Mast

38 medium red tomatoes
  (some green may be used)
6 onions
6 sweet peppers
3 hot peppers

2 tablespoons salt
1½ teaspoons black pepper
7 cups sugar
1 pint vinegar

Grind tomatoes, onions, and peppers together. Add salt, pepper, sugar, and vinegar. Cook and stir until it thickens. Pour into sterilized jars and seal.

Use as a relish on meat sandwiches, add zip to your baked beans, or serve on cooked dried beans. Delicious! Yields 8-10 pints.

CHERRY PIE FILLING

Esther L. Miller

3½ quarts water
4½ cups sugar
½ teaspoon salt
2½ cups Perma Flo
1 quart water

¾ cup cherry Jello
2½ cups Karo syrup
1 package cherry Kool-Aid
14 cups sour cherries

Bring first 3 ingredients to boiling point. Mix Perma Flo and water together. Add to the near boiling ingredients in 8-quart kettle. Bring again to boiling point. Remove from heat and add Karo syrup. Mix Jello and Kool-Aid together and add to kettle. Put cherries in last. Put filling in 7 quart jars and put in hot water bath for 10 minutes.

FREEZER SLAW

Mrs. Ferlin L. Yoder

1 gallon shredded cabbage
1 tablespoon salt
½ cup water
2 cups sugar

1 cup vinegar
1 sweet pepper, grated
2 carrots, shredded
1 teaspoon celery seed

Add salt to cabbage. Stir and let set 1 hour. Drain water off real good.

Bring to a boil the water, sugar, and vinegar. Boil 1 minute. Cool. Add pepper, carrots, and celery seed. Pour over cabbage. Mix well. Let stand ½ hour. Package to freeze.

PICKLED OKRA

Mrs. Henry Overholt, Sr.

2 pints okra (small)
1 cup cider vinegar
¼ cup water
2 pods of hot pepper

1 tablespoon salt
2 teaspoons dill seed
4 garlic cloves

Wash okra. Bring the vinegar, water, and salt to a boil. Put okra in each jar. To each pint jar, add 1 teaspoon dill seed, 2 garlic cloves, and 1 pod of pepper. Pour boiling liquid mixture into jars and cover okra. Process in boiling water 5 minutes. Wait 1 month before using.

Have a set time to feed on the Word of God; not just a convenient time.

FROZEN PEACH JAM

Judith Yoder

4 cups peaches, chopped
20 ounces crushed pineapple

6 cups sugar
6 ounces orange Jello

In saucepan, mix first 3 ingredients. Boil 15 minutes. Remove from heat and add Jello. Mix well and freeze. Makes approximately 4 pints.

CANNING PECANS

Ruth Hershberger

Pecans, shelled, broken, or halves: Fill a clean, dry canning jar up to the neck with pecans. Put canning lid and ring on and screw tightly. Place in large canner; place a rack in bottom. Fill canner up to jar necks with water. Jars will float so weight them down with a large plate and brick or something to hold them down. Cold pack for 4 minutes. (In boiling water—begin counting when water is boiling.) Quart: 40 minutes. Pint: 35 minutes.

The canned nuts will keep for several years—and another benefit is that your freezer space is freed up for freezing other foods.

A very nice and unusual gift is to make a calico "cap" for a jar of pecans. Cut a round circle 2 inches wider all around. Sew a small edging of lace around outside, and zig-zag elastic 1 inch from outside (underside) or tie with contrasting ribbon around neck of jar.

Those who are generous are blessed,
for they share their bread with the poor. — Proverbs 22:9.

CANNING GREEN PEPPERS

Mrs. David Wengerd

1 cup vinegar
1 cup sugar
½ teaspoon salt
2 cups water

Red or green peppers, cut in half
 or chopped
Vegetable oil

Bring vinegar, sugar, salt, and water to a boil. Add peppers to mixture. Boil 10 minutes, then pack in hot, sterile jars. Add 1 teaspoon vegetable oil to top of jar before sealing.

CINNAMON CANDY PICKLE

Mrs. Henry Overholt, Sr.

2 gallons cucumbers
2 cups lime
2 gallons water
1 cup vinegar
1 tablespoon alum

2 cups vinegar
2 cups water
10 cups sugar
3 packages red hots candies

1st day: Prepare 2 gallons large cucumbers by peeling, scraping out insides, and cutting in ¼-inch slices. Soak overnight in a mixture of 2 cups lime and 2 gallons of water.

2nd day: Pour off and wash. Soak 2 hours in cold water, then mix 1 cup vinegar, 1 tablespoon alum, and enough water to cover cucumbers. Soak 2 hours and drain. After this, mix and boil 2 cups vinegar, 2 cups water, 10 cups sugar, and 3 packages of red hots candies and pour over cucumbers.

3rd and 4th days: Drain and bring liquid to rolling boil and pour over cucumbers.

5th day: Drain and pack in jars. Bring liquid to boil and pour over cucumbers. Process in hot water bath for 5 minutes.

If you want to feel rich,
just count all the things you have that money cannot buy.

FREEZER PICKLES

Mrs. Ferlin L. Yoder

3 quarts cucumbers, sliced
2 onions, thinly sliced
3 tablespoons salt

½ cup vinegar
2 cups sugar

Mix cucumbers and onions with salt. Let set 2 hours. Drain. Mix vinegar and sugar. Heat until dissolved. Mix with cucumber mixture. Package and freeze. Serve partially thawed.

BREAD 'N' BUTTER PICKLES
Dorothy Schlabach

8 pounds large cucumbers
(about 12)
8 large onions
4 large green peppers, sliced
⅔ cup canning salt

6 cups vinegar
6 cups sugar
2 teaspoons celery seed
2 teaspoons mustard seed
1 teaspoon ground turmeric

Cut cucumbers into ¼-inch slices and cut onions into ⅛-inch slices. In a large container, combine cucumbers, onions, green peppers, and salt. Add enough cold water to cover. Chill for 2 hours. Drain and rinse. In a large kettle, combine remaining ingredients; bring to a boil. Add cucumber mixture and return to a boil. Ladle hot mixture into hot jars, leaving ¼-inch head space. Adjust lids. Process for 10 minutes in a boiling water bath. Yield: 10 pints.

REFRIGERATOR PICKLES
Ann Mast

1 gallon sliced cucumbers
2 large onions, sliced
1 quart vinegar
3 cups sugar

¼ cup canning salt
1 teaspoon mustard seed
1 teaspoon celery seed
1 teaspoon turmeric

Mix cucumbers and onions in large bowl. Heat vinegar, sugar, and spices to boiling. Let simmer 5 minutes. Pour liquid over pickles. When cool, refrigerate. In 7 days, they are ready to use. Will keep for months.

SWEET GARLIC DILL PICKLES
Carol Petersheim

4 cups water
4 cups vinegar
6 cups sugar
1 tablespoon salt

1 tablespoon dill seed or 1 bunch
fresh dill
¼ teaspoon garlic powder

Stir together first 4 ingredients and bring to a good boil. Fill jars with unpeeled, fresh, sliced cucumbers. Add dill seed (or fresh dill) and garlic powder. Fill jars with hot syrup and seal immediately. This is enough syrup for about 7 quarts. For pint jars, use 1½ teaspoons dill seed and ⅛ teaspoon garlic powder.

A rejoicing Christian is one of God's best advertisements.

FOURTEEN DAY PICKLES

Jo Ann Inhulsen

2 gallons cucumbers, sliced
2 cups salt
3 gallons water, divided
1 tablespoon alum
5 pints vinegar

6 cups sugar
½ ounce celery seed
1 ounce cinnamon
3 cups sugar, divided

Into clean jars put 2 gallons of cucumbers. Dissolve 2 cups salt in a gallon of boiling water and pour over pickles while hot. Cover and weigh down pickles. Let stand 1 week. On the eighth day, drain and pour 1 gallon of boiling water over pickles and let stand 24 hours with 1 tablespoon alum added to water. On the tenth day, drain; pour 1 gallon of boiling water over pickles. Let stand 24 hours, then drain.

Combine vinegar, sugar, celery seed, and cinnamon. Pour over pickles while boiling hot.

Drain off for 3 mornings and reheat, adding 1 cup of sugar each morning.

With third and last heating, pack hot pickles into jars. Pour hot liquid over them and seal.

CUCUMBER RELISH

Barbara Ann Yoder

6 average sized cucumbers
4 large onions
2 large peppers
2 tablespoons pickling salt
2 cups vinegar

5 cups sugar
1 tablespoon celery seed
1 tablespoon mustard seed
1 teaspoon turmeric powder
Clear Jell or cornstarch to thicken

Grind together first 3 ingredients. Add pickling salt and let stand 4 hours or overnight. Drain, rinse, then add next 5 ingredients. Cook on low 20 minutes. Thicken with Clear Jell or cornstarch. Process in water bath for 10 minutes.

IOWA CORN RELISH

Lela Brenneman

2½ quarts corn kernels
1 cup each green and red peppers
1¼ cups chopped onion
1 cup chopped celery
1½ cups sugar
1½ tablespoons mustard seeds

1 tablespoon salt
1 teaspoon celery seeds
½ teaspoon turmeric
2⅔ cups vinegar
2 cups water

Combine all ingredients. Simmer for 20 minutes. Pack in clean hot pint jars. Process in boiling water bath (212°) for 15 minutes. Makes 6-7 pints.

ZUCCHINI RELISH

Melody Kauffman, Ruth Yoder,
Barbara Kauffman, Elsie Yoder

10 cups ground zucchini
4 cups ground onions
1 large green pepper
1 large red pepper
5 tablespoons salt
2½ cups vinegar

2 teaspoons celery seed
¼ teaspoon ground red pepper
 (scant)
1 teaspoon turmeric
4 teaspoons cornstarch
6 cups sugar

Combine first 5 ingredients into large stainless steel bowl. Let stand overnight. Rinse and drain well. Add rest of ingredients except cornstarch. Cook for 15 minutes. Mix cornstarch with a little water and slowly add to cooked mixture. Bring to a boil. Put into prepared canning jars. Seal. Boil jars for 10 minutes in hot water.

Elsie adds 1 (4 ounce) can green chilies and ½ teaspoon nutmeg.

SPANISH SAUCE

Sara Jean Yoder

6 green tomatoes
6 onions
6 red peppers
6 large cucumbers
1 large jar French's mustard

1 handful salt
6 cups sugar
1 quart vinegar
1 cup flour
1 pint vinegar

Grind through food chopper the tomatoes, onions, peppers, and cucumbers. Put in kettle. Add the mustard, salt, sugar, and 1 quart vinegar. Boil for 15 minutes. Stir the flour and 1 pint vinegar until creamy. Add this to vegetable mixture. Boil 5 minutes longer, then put in jars and seal. (A recipe from Grandmother.)

SALSA

Carolyn Eash

10-16 pounds ripe tomatoes
10 cloves garlic, peeled
6 bell peppers, seeded and
 chopped
4 chili or 5 jalapeño peppers,
 seeded
2 large onions

2 sticks celery
¾ cup sugar
¾ cup white vinegar
¼ cup salt
¾ cup Clear Jell
1½ tablespoons oregano
1 teaspoon cumin

Peel and chop tomatoes. Quarter small tomatoes and make large tomatoes in 16 pieces. Put cloves of garlic, peppers, onions, and celery through food processor. Put in large kettle with tomatoes. Bring to a boil. Cook for 15 minutes. Add rest of ingredients and bring to boil until thickened. Fill jars. Process for 20 minutes.

QUICK SALSA
Debbie Graber

2 cans Kuner's chili tomatoes
1 (4 ounce) can diced green chilies

1 teaspoon red pepper flakes
1 teaspoon salt

Blend ingredients for a few seconds in blender. Best if refrigerated for several hours before eating. (This is simple but one of the best-tasting salsas I've had!!)

SALSA
Melody Kauffman, Alta Kauffman, Debbie Graber

14 pounds tomatoes, peeled and
  quartered
5 cups chopped onions
10 green peppers, chopped
2 ounces jalapeño peppers
1 cup vinegar
½ cup sugar

¼ cup salt
2 teaspoons oregano leaves
3 teaspoons cumin
3 teaspoons chili powder
4 garlic cloves
Cornstarch or Clear Jell to thicken

Mix and cook for 45 minutes. Thicken slightly with cornstarch or Clear Jell to desired consistency. Pour into jars and seal. Process in boiling water bath for 20 minutes. Makes approximately 16 pints.

Debbie adds 1 (24 ounce) can chopped green chilies.

SALSA SAUCE
Paul and Ruth Yoder

1 peck Roma tomatoes
4 large onions
3 hot yellow peppers
3 jalapeño peppers
3 sweet peppers
½ cup vinegar

2 tablespoons salt
1 teaspoon garlic
5 tablespoons brown sugar
¼ cup parsley
18 ounces tomato paste
1 teaspoon ground cumin

Peel and chop tomatoes; grind or chop onions and peppers. Combine everything and cook for 2 hours. Put into jars. Cold pack for 10 minutes.

So easy to say what another should do,
So easy to settle his cares;
So easy to tell him what road to pursue
And dispose of the burden he bears.
It's easy to bid him be brave and be strong
And to make all his shortcomings known;
But, oh, it's so hard when the care and the wrong
And the dangers we face are our own.

MARIE'S SPECIAL PIZZA SAUCE   Mrs. Freeman Schlabach

3 pounds onions
1 pint oil
8 quarts tomato juice
11 (7 ounce) cans tomato paste

15 (4 ounce) cans mushroom
  stems and pieces
1½ cups white sugar
¼ cup salt
2 tablespoons Italian seasoning

Cook onions in oil until soft, and put in blender until very fine. Put onions and oil, juice, and all the rest of the ingredients in a large pot and simmer for 20 minutes. Taste and add more of this and that until it suits your taste. Cold pack 20 minutes. Makes 12 quart-size canning jars of sauce.

PIZZA SAUCE   Debbie Graber

2½ gallons tomato juice
8-10 onions
4 green peppers
2 tablespoons red pepper,
  crushed, or flakes
1 pint oil
1 cup sugar
2 tablespoons basil
2 tablespoons oregano

2 tablespoons parsley flakes
1 tablespoon Italian seasoning
3 tablespoons pizza seasoning
1 teaspoon garlic powder
2 teaspoons chili powder
6 bay leaves
½ cup salt
½ gallon tomato paste

Cook first 5 ingredients for 1 hour and put through strainer. Return to kettle and add the next 11 ingredients. Cook 1 hour. Cold pack for 10 minutes.

SANDWICH SPREAD   Judith Yoder

FIRST PART:
6 large cucumbers
6 large onions
6 large red peppers
6 large green peppers

6 large green tomatoes
⅛ cup salt
1 quart vinegar

SECOND PART:
5 cups sugar
2 tablespoons turmeric

1 cup mustard
1 pint vinegar

Grind together cucumbers, onions, red and green peppers, and green tomatoes. Stir in salt. Let stand one hour. Squeeze out juice; add 1 quart vinegar. Boil 15 minutes.

Mix second part together and cook for 15 minutes. Add liquid to vegetable mixture and cook until desired thickness. Put in jars and seal. Yields 8 pints.

SPAGHETTI SAUCE

Cissy Allen

1½ pounds ground beef
1 onion, chopped
2 cans whole tomatoes, drained
   and chopped
1 (15 ounce) can tomato sauce
1 (12 ounce) can tomato paste

2 tablespoons chopped parsley
2 teaspoons Italian seasoning
1 clove garlic
Chopped mushrooms, optional
Salt and pepper, optional

Brown hamburger and onions together. Mix all other ingredients and add to hamburger and onions. Also add mushrooms, salt, and pepper, if desired. Simmer for 30 minutes to an hour.

SPAGHETTI SAUCE

Debbie Graber

½ bushel tomatoes, peeled and
   quartered
1 cup oil
3 pounds onions, chopped
2-3 garlic buds
2 hot peppers, chopped

8 (12 ounce) cans tomato paste
1 tablespoon basil
1 tablespoon oregano
1½ cups sugar
¼-½ cup salt

Cook first 5 ingredients on low-medium heat for 3 hours, then add next 5 ingredients. Cook for 1 hour. Pour into jars and water bath process for 10 minutes.

TOMATO SOYA

Mrs. John Nissley

1 peck ripe tomatoes, peeled and
   sliced (8 quarts)
8 onions, sliced
½ cup salt
1 pint vinegar
1 teaspoon cinnamon

1 teaspoon cloves
1 teaspoon ginger
1 teaspoon mustard
½ teaspoon black pepper
2 pounds sugar

Layer tomatoes, onions, and salt and let stand overnight. Pour into colander and drain off juice. Pour water over it and drain again. Then add vinegar and spices. Cook slowly for 2 hours. When almost done, add 2 pounds sugar. Put into jars and seal.

V-8 VEGETABLE JUICE

Mrs. Henry Overholt, Sr.

10 pounds carrots
6 bunches celery
2 large onions
6 green peppers

28 quarts tomato juice
4 quarts beets
4 boxes spinach
Salt and pepper to taste

Cook each vegetable and put in blender. Pour into jars and seal. Hot water bath process at 5 pound cooker pressure for 10 minutes. Cold water bath process for 30 minutes. Makes 44 quarts.

Cakes
&
Frostings

TIPS ON USING CAKE MIXES

Paul and Ruth Yoder

To make a larger cake with a cake mix, make cake as directed on box then add:

1 egg
1 teaspoon baking powder
¾ cup flour
½ cup sugar

1 tablespoon cooking oil
⅓ cup water
Flavoring

Bake as directed.

You can also use milk instead of water when using only a cake mix.

ANGEL FOOD CAKE

Drusilla Beiler

1¼ cups flour
1⅓ cups sugar
1⅔ cups egg whites
1¼ teaspoons cream of tartar

¼ teaspoon salt
2 teaspoons vanilla flavoring
¼ teaspoon almond flavoring
½ cup sugar

Sift flour and 1⅓ cups sugar together 3 times. Beat egg whites until stiff peaks form, then add cream of tartar, salt, and flavorings. Gradually add ½ cup sugar and beat until very stiff. Stir in flour and sugar mixture with a large spoon. Mix well and bake at 375° in ungreased tube pan for 30-45 minutes.

ANGEL FOOD CAKE DESSERT

Ruth Yoder

1 medium size angel food cake
2 (3 ounce) packages instant
   vanilla pie filling

8 ounces non-dairy whipped
   topping
8 ounces sour cream
1 can blueberry pie filling

Break angel food cake into small pieces and place in a 9x13-inch glass pan. Mix pie filling according to package directions and spread over top of cake. Mix together whipped topping and sour cream and spread over other mixture like frosting on a cake. Drizzle filling over top and chill 3 hours or longer.

CHOCOLATE ANGEL FOOD CAKE

Elsie Brenneman

¾ cup sifted cake flour
1½ cups plus 2 tablespoons sugar, divided
¼ cup cocoa

1½ cups egg whites, room temperature
1½ teaspoons cream of tartar
¼ teaspoon salt
1½ teaspoons vanilla extract

CHOCOLATE FLUFF FROSTING:
2 cups whipping cream
1 cup confectioners sugar

½ cup cocoa
Dash of salt

Sift together flour, ¾ cup plus 2 tablespoons sugar, and cocoa three times. Set aside. In a large mixing bowl, beat egg whites, cream of tartar, salt, and vanilla until foamy. Slowly add remaining sugar, 2 tablespoons at a time, beating about 10 seconds after each addition. Continue beating until mixture holds stiff peaks. With a rubber scraper, stir in flour mixture, 5 tablespoons at a time. Mixture will be thick. Put into a 10-inch angel food pan. Cut through batter with a knife to remove air pockets. Bake at 350° for 40-45 minutes or until top of cake springs when touched. Immediately invert cake in pan. Cool. Run a knife around sides of cake and remove.

For frosting, combine all ingredients in a chilled bowl. Beat until thick enough to spread. Frost entire cake. Chill until ready to serve.

EAZY ANGEL FOOD CAKE

Mrs. John Nissley

5 eggs
Pinch salt
½ cup cold water
1½ cups sugar

1 cup flour
½ cup cornstarch
1 teaspoon baking powder
¾ teaspoon cream of tartar

Separate eggs. To yolks, add pinch of salt and cold water. Beat well. Add sugar and beat. Sift together flour, cornstarch, and baking powder. Stir into egg mixture. Beat egg whites with cream of tartar. Stir into first mixture. Pour into ungreased tube pan. Bake at 350° in preheated oven for 50-60 minutes.

APPLE CAKE

Ruth Yoder, Mrs. Ferlin L. Yoder

1 cup white sugar
½ cup shortening
1 egg, beaten
2 cups chopped apples
1½ cups flour

1 teaspoon baking soda
½ teaspoon baking powder
1 teaspoon vanilla
Salt
½ cup raisins

TOPPING:
½ cup brown sugar
2 teaspoons cinnamon
½ cup nuts, chopped

2 tablespoons flour
3 tablespoons butter

Cream together sugar and shortening. Add egg. Stir in apples. Add flour, soda, baking powder, vanilla, salt, and raisins. Pour into greased and floured pan.

Mix together topping ingredients. Sprinkle over cake. Bake in an 8x8-inch baking pan at 350° for 45 minutes. Serve with whipped cream or ice cream.

Ruth serves hers with cinnamon sauce and ice cream. Cinnamon sauce: 2 cups brown sugar, 1 teaspoon cinnamon, ¼ cup Clear Jell, and 2 cups water. Mix and cook until thick and clear. Remove from heat and mix in 2 tablespoons butter.

APPLE CAKE

Susan Yoder

2 cups sugar
⅔ cup shortening
2 eggs
2 cups all-purpose flour
1½ teaspoons baking soda

1½ teaspoons nutmeg
1 teaspoon cinnamon
½ teaspoon salt
4 cups peeled and diced apples
½ cup chopped nuts

SAUCE:
1 cup butter
1 cup cream

2 cups sugar
2 teaspoons vanilla

Cream together sugar, shortening, and eggs and set aside. Combine dry ingredients; add to creamed mixture. Mix in apples and nuts. Bake in a 9x13-inch baking pan at 350° for 40-45 minutes.

Mix sauce ingredients together; boil 1½ minutes. Serve with sauce and a dip of ice cream. Very good. Makes 12-15 servings.

Tell it again, tell it again,
Salvation's story repeat o'er and o'er;
Till none can say of the children of men
Nobody ever has told me before.

APPLE PECAN LAYER CAKE

Mrs. James Mast

2½ cups all-purpose flour
2 cups sugar
1 teaspoon baking soda
1 teaspoon baking powder
1 teaspoon salt

1 teaspoon cinnamon
1½ cups applesauce
¾ cup oil
2 eggs
½ cup chopped pecans

FROSTING:
½ cup butter (not margarine)
4½ cups powdered sugar

6-8 tablespoons apple juice
Chopped pecans for garnish

Grease and flour 2 (9-inch) round cake pans. In large bowl, combine flour, sugar, baking soda, baking powder, salt, and cinnamon. Add applesauce, oil, and eggs; blend at low speed until moistened. Beat 2 minutes at highest speed. Stir in pecans. Pour batter into pans and bake at 350° for 30-40 minutes.

Frosting: In heavy saucepan over medium heat, brown butter a light golden brown, stirring constantly. Remove from heat and cool. In large bowl, combine browned butter, powdered sugar, and 4 tablespoons apple juice; blend at low speed until moistened. Continue beating until well blended, adding more apple juice until mixture retains a spreading consistency. Fill and frost cake. Garnish with pecans as desired. Makes 12 servings.

FRESH APPLE CAKE

Esther L. Miller

3 cups pastry flour
1 teaspoon baking soda
½ teaspoon salt
½ teaspoon cinnamon
½ teaspoon ground nutmeg
¼ teaspoon ground cloves

1¾ cups sugar
1 cup vegetable oil
2 eggs
2 teaspoons vanilla
3 cups peeled, diced apples
1 cup chopped pecans

Combine first 6 ingredients; set aside. Combine sugar, oil, eggs, and vanilla in a large bowl and mix well. Add flour mixture, stirring well. Stir in apples and pecans. Batter will be stiff. Spoon batter into greased and floured 10-inch bundt pan. Bake at 325° for 1 hour and 15 minutes or until a wooden toothpick inserted in center comes out clean.

Cool cake in pan 10 minutes. Remove from pan and cool completely. Store in airtight container. Serves 16.

HARVEST APPLE CAKE

Mary Joyce Miller

3 cups flour
1 teaspoon baking soda
½ teaspoon salt
½ teaspoon cinnamon
½ teaspoon allspice
½ teaspoon nutmeg
½ teaspoon cloves

2 cups sugar
1 cup vegetable oil
2 eggs
2 tablespoons vanilla
3 cups peeled, shredded apples
1 cup chopped pecans

Combine dry ingredients; set aside. Combine sugar, oil, eggs, and vanilla; mix well. Add dry ingredients, stirring well. Add apples and pecans. Batter will be very stiff. Spoon batter into greased and floured 10-inch tube pan. Bake at 325° for 1 hour and 30 minutes or until toothpick comes out clean. Cool in pan 10 minutes. Remove from pan and cool completely. Store in airtight container. Makes 12-16 servings.

AUTUMN SURPRISE CAKE

Mrs. Merle Overholt, Pat Parker

2 cups unpeeled, chopped apples
1 cup sugar
1½ cups sifted flour
1 teaspoon baking soda
½ teaspoon salt

1 egg, beaten
½ cup cooking oil
1 teaspoon vanilla
½ cup chopped nuts
1 cup flaked coconut

Mix apples and sugar. Let stand until juice forms. Sift flour, baking soda, and salt together. Add apples and remaining ingredients; mix thoroughly. Pour into a greased and floured 8-inch square baking pan. Bake at 350° for 40-45 minutes. Frost with caramel frosting.

Pat puts ¾ cup brown sugar and 1 teaspoon cinnamon on and bakes at 350° for 30 or 40 minutes.

BANANA-NUT CAKE

Mrs. James Mast

2½ cups flour, sifted
1¼ teaspoons baking soda
1 teaspoon salt
1¼ teaspoons baking powder
1½ cups sugar
⅔ cup soft shortening

3 eggs
1 teaspoon vanilla
⅔ cup buttermilk
½ teaspoon nutmeg
1¼ cups mashed bananas
⅔ cup finely chopped nuts

Blend flour, baking soda, salt, and baking powder; set aside. Beat sugar and shortening 2 minutes, add eggs, and beat well. Add flour mixture, vanilla, buttermilk, and nutmeg. Beat mashed bananas well and fold in; add nuts. Pour into greased 13x9-inch pan and bake at 350° for 45-50 minutes. Frost as desired.

BANANA CAKE
Ruth Yoder

½ cup butter
1¾ cups sugar
2 eggs, lightly beaten
1 teaspoon baking soda
¼ cup sour cream

1 cup mashed banana pulp
1½ cups cake flour
¼ teaspoon salt
1 teaspoon vanilla

FROSTING:
2 tablespoons butter
1 cup confectioners sugar
2 tablespoons strong hot coffee

1 teaspoon cocoa powder
½ teaspoon vanilla

For cake, cream butter and sugar and add lightly beaten eggs. Dissolve the baking soda in the sour cream, then add to the creamed mixture. Beat well and add mashed bananas, then flour, salt, and vanilla. Beat well. Pour into greased and floured 9-inch square baking pan or tube pan and bake at 350° for 35-45 minutes.

For frosting, beat butter with sugar, then add coffee, cocoa, and vanilla. Beat until smooth and spread on cooled cake.

BRAN FLAKE CAKE
Celesta Miller

1½ cups bran flakes
1 cup vegetable oil
1½ cups pumpkin
4 eggs
1½ cups white sugar
2 teaspoons vanilla
2 cups pastry flour

2 teaspoons baking powder
1 teaspoon baking soda
½ teaspoon salt
½ teaspoon ginger
½ teaspoon cloves
½ cup nuts
1 cup chocolate chips

TOPPING:
3 tablespoons margarine
6 tablespoons sugar

½ cups chopped nuts

Crush bran flakes slightly. Add oil, pumpkin, eggs, sugar, and vanilla. Mix well with spoon or fork. Add dry ingredients. Mix well with fork. Add ½ cup nuts. Pour ¾ of batter in greased pan. Sprinkle chocolate chips on top. Dribble rest of batter over chips.

Combine topping ingredients, sprinkle over batter, and bake at 350° for 40-45 minutes.

THE BIBLE CAKE

Ruth Yoder

A. 1 cup Judges 5:25 (last clause)
B. 2 cups Jeremiah 6:20
C. 2 teaspoons I Samuel 14:25 (last clause)
D. 6 Jeremiah 17:11
E. ½ cup Judges 4:19 (last clause)
F. 4½ cups I Kings 4:22

G. 2 heaping teaspoons Amos 4:5
H. 1 cup I Samuel 30:12 (2nd phrase)
I. 1 cup Nahum 3:12
J. II Chronicles 9:9 (2nd phrase) (to taste)

Cream together A., B., and C. Beat well until frothy. Add E. to D. Add alternately to first mixture with F., G., and J., which have been mixed together. Chop H. and I.; add flour and add to mixture.

Bake in angel food cake pan at 375° for about 1 hour or until it tests done.

CARAMEL APPLE CAKE

Silla Yoder

1½ cups vegetable oil
1½ cups sugar
½ cup packed brown sugar
3 eggs
3 cups all-purpose flour
2 teaspoons ground cinnamon

1 teaspoon baking soda
½ teaspoon salt
3½ cups diced, peeled apples
1 cup chopped walnuts
2 teaspoons vanilla extract

CARAMEL ICING:
½ cup packed brown sugar
⅓ cup light cream
¼ cup butter

Dash of salt
1 cup confectioners sugar
Chopped nuts for garnish, optional

In mixing bowl, combine oil and sugars. Add eggs one at a time, beating well after each addition. Combine dry ingredients and add to batter. Stir well. Fold in apples, walnuts, and vanilla. Pour into greased and floured 10-inch tube pan and bake for 1½ hours at 325°. Cool in pan 10 minutes. Remove to wire rack to cool completely.

For icing, in top of double boiler over simmering water, heat brown sugar, cream, butter, and salt until sugar is dissolved. Cool to room temperature. Beat in confectioners sugar until smooth. Drizzle over cake. Sprinkle with chopped nuts, if desired. Makes 12-16 servings.

WEST VIRGINIA BLACKBERRY CAKE   Mrs. Freeman Schlabach

2 cups sugar
1 cup butter
4 eggs
3 cups flour
1 teaspoon cloves
1 teaspoon nutmeg

1 teaspoon cinnamon
1 teaspoon baking powder
1 teaspoon baking soda
1 cup buttermilk
1½ cups fresh or frozen
  blackberries or black raspberries

FROSTING:
1 cup butter
1 pound powdered sugar

1 teaspoon vanilla
3 tablespoons cold coffee

Cream sugar and butter. Add eggs and beat. Set aside. Mix together flour, spices, and baking powder. Add baking soda to buttermilk. Add these two mixtures alternately to first mixture. Stir berries in last. Pour into 3 (8-inch) greased and floured layer cake pans and bake for 30 minutes at 350°.

Frosting: Cream butter. Add powdered sugar, vanilla, and coffee. Beat until creamy. This cake is delicious! Makes one 3-layer cake.

BURNT SUGAR CAKE   Mrs. Merle Overholt

½ cup white sugar
½ cup water
1½ cups sugar
½ cup shortening
3 egg yolks
1 teaspoon baking soda

1 cup sour milk
2½ cups flour
½ teaspoon salt
1 teaspoon vanilla
2 beaten egg whites

Melt ½ cup sugar in heavy pan (without water) to a golden yellow, stirring continually. Add water and boil until all is dissolved. Cream 1½ cups sugar and shortening. Add egg yolks and beat well. Add burnt sugar syrup. Dissolve baking soda in milk and add to mixture. Then add flour, salt, and vanilla. Last add beaten egg whites. May be baked in either loaf or layers. Bake at 350° for 35 minutes. Makes 15 servings.

93

SPICED BUTTERNUT SQUASH CAKE   Laura Yoder

1 box French vanilla cake mix
1 cup cooked butternut squash
  (mashed)
½ cup brown sugar
¼ cup buttermilk

4 eggs, beaten
3 teaspoons grated orange peel
1½ teaspoons cinnamon
1 cup chopped pecans

FILLING:
1 (8 ounce) package cream cheese
½ teaspoon nutmeg

4 cups powdered sugar
⅓ cup butter, melted

Preheat oven to 350°. Combine all cake ingredients in a large bowl. Blend together with electric mixer for 2-3 minutes at high speed. Pour into 2 prepared 9-inch cake pans and bake for 35 minutes. Let cool.

Combine ingredients for filling; mix well and spread between layers and on top.

BUTTERSCOTCH CAKE   Mrs. Martha Wengerd

½ cup shortening
1¾ cups brown sugar
2 eggs
1 teaspoon vanilla

1 cup milk
2 cups flour
3 teaspoons baking powder
½ teaspoon salt

Mix shortening, margarine, and brown sugar. Add eggs, vanilla, and milk. Add flour, baking powder, and salt. Beat 2½ minutes. Put in a greased 13x9-inch cake pan and bake at 325° for 40 minutes.

A very simple and delicious cake that children can stir together. Makes 15 servings.

*Cling to God; count on God,
and move forward!*

CARROT PECAN CAKE

Ruth Yoder

3 cups flour
2 teaspoons baking powder
1 teaspoon baking soda
1 teaspoon cinnamon
½ teaspoon salt
1 cup butter, softened
1 cup packed light brown sugar
1 cup sugar

4 eggs
2 tablespoons grated lemon rind
2 tablespoons grated orange rind
2 tablespoons lemon juice
2 tablespoons orange juice
1 pound carrots, pared and grated
1 cup chopped pecans
1 cup raisins

Lightly grease and flour a 10x4-inch tube pan. Sift together flour, baking powder, baking soda, cinnamon, and salt; set aside. Beat butter and sugars until light, about 3 minutes. Add eggs, one at a time, beating well after each addition. Beat flour mixture in alternately with lemon rind, orange rind, lemon juice, and orange juice. Beat just until smooth, about 1 minute. Stir in carrots, pecans, and raisins. Pour in the prepared tube pan. Bake in a 350° oven for 60 or 70 minutes or until cake tests done. Cool completely in pan before removing. Wrap tightly in foil and age 2 days before frosting. Frost with cream cheese icing.

CARROT CAKE

Barbara Kauffman, Roxanna Linneber

2 cups sugar
4 eggs
¾ cup cooking oil
2 cups flour
2 teaspoons cinnamon

1 teaspoon salt
2 teaspoons baking soda
1 teaspoon mace, optional
3 cups grated carrots

FROSTING:
1 box powdered sugar
1 (8 ounce) package cream cheese
1 teaspoon vanilla

1 cup chopped nuts
A little milk, if desired

Beat sugar and eggs. Add oil and beat. Sift dry ingredients together and add to the rest. Add carrots and beat. Bake at 325°-350° in a 9x13-inch cake pan until toothpick inserted in center will come out clean. When cool, frost with cream cheese frosting. Makes 18-20 servings.

CHESS CAKE

Celesta Miller

1 box yellow cake mix
4 eggs
1 stick softened butter

1 box powdered sugar
1 (8 ounce) package softened
   cream cheese

Mix cake mix, 1 egg, and butter well to make a crust. Press into an 11½x 7¾-inch glass dish. Set aside. Mix powdered sugar, 3 eggs, and cream cheese. Pour into crust. Bake at 325° for about 15 minutes or until light golden brown.

MAHOGANY CHIFFON CAKE

Ellen D. Miller

¾ cup boiling water
¼ cup cocoa
2 cups pastry flour
1¼ cups sugar
1½ teaspoons baking soda
½ teaspoon salt

½ cup vegetable oil
7 egg yolks (medium)
2 teaspoons vanilla
1 cup egg whites (7 or 8)
½ teaspoon cream of tartar

Combine boiling water and cocoa. Let cool. Blend rest of dry ingredients in bowl. Make a well and add cocoa mixture, oil, egg yolks, and vanilla. Beat until smooth. Put egg whites and cream of tartar in large bowl. Beat until very stiff. Pour egg yolk mixture in thin stream over egg whites. Stir until blended. Pour in ungreased 10-inch tube pan. Bake at 325° for 45 minutes then 350° for 15 minutes. Makes 16 servings.

MAPLE CHIFFON CAKE

Mrs. Sol Yoder, Sr.

1½ cups all-purpose flour
1½ cups sugar
3 teaspoons baking powder
1 teaspoon salt
½ cup vegetable oil

7 egg yolks, unbeaten
¾ cup cold water
1 teaspoon maple extract
1 cup egg whites
½ teaspoon cream of tartar

Blend flour, sugar, baking powder, and salt thoroughly. Make a hollow and add in order the oil, egg yolks, cold water, and maple flavoring. Beat with electric mixer until smooth. Measure egg whites into large mixing bowl and add cream of tartar. Beat until *very* stiff peaks are formed. Pour egg yolk mixture over beaten egg whites folding in gently until blended. Pour into ungreased tube pan. Bake in slow oven (325°) for 55 minutes, then raise to 350° for 15 minutes. Turn pan upside down until cold before removing from pan.

SPICED CHIFFON CAKE

Elsie Brenneman

2½ cups sugar
2 cups all-purpose flour
1 tablespoon baking powder
1 teaspoon salt
1 teaspoon ground cinnamon
½ teaspoon ground allspice

½ teaspoon ground cloves
½ teaspoon ground nutmeg
¾ cup cold water
½ cup vegetable oil
7 eggs, separated
½ teaspoon cream of tartar

GLAZE:
2 tablespoons butter or margarine
1 tablespoon all-purpose flour
⅛ teaspoon salt
¼ cup packed brown sugar

¼ teaspoon vanilla extract
1 cup confectioners sugar
Chopped walnuts

In large mixing bowl, combine sugar, flour, baking powder, salt, cinnamon, allspice, cloves, and nutmeg. Add water, oil, and egg yolks. Beat on low speed just until combined. Increase speed and beat until smooth. Set aside. Whip egg whites and cream of tartar until still peaks form; fold into batter. Pour into an ungreased 10-inch tube pan. Bake at 325° for 70 minutes or until top springs back when lightly touched. Immediately invert pan; cool completely. Remove cake from pan.

For glaze, melt butter in a saucepan. Blend in flour and salt. Add milk all at once, stirring constantly. Bring to a boil; cook until thick and bubbly. Remove from the heat; beat in brown sugar and vanilla. Add confectioners sugar; mix until smooth. Drizzle over cake. Sprinkle with nuts. Serves 12.

CHOCOLATE CAKE

Ruth Hershberger

1¼ cups shortening or margarine
2¼ cups sugar
3 eggs
1 teaspoon vanilla
½ cup cocoa powder

3 cups flour
2 teaspoons baking soda
1 teaspoon salt
2 cups buttermilk

Beat shortening or margarine and sugar until well blended. Add eggs and vanilla. Sift dry ingredients and place with shortening mixture. Add 1 cup buttermilk and beat well. Add another cup buttermilk. Beat until blended. Pour into 3 greased and floured 9-inch round baking pans and bake at 350° for 25 minutes. A very moist 3-layer cake. Makes 16 large servings.

My God, I sit beneath Thee,
My little child upon my knee,
My little one looks up to me,
And I look up to Thee.

CHOCOLATE COCONUT CAKE   Ruth Yoder

1 box chocolate cake mix with
   pudding
1 cup sugar

1 cup milk
24 large marshmallows
1 (14 ounce) package coconut

FROSTING:
1 cup evaporated milk
1½ cups sugar
½ cup butter

2 cups semi-sweet chocolate chips
1 cup chopped almonds

Mix cake mix according to package directions. Grease 2 (9-inch) round baking pans and line bottoms of pans with wax paper. Spray with cooking spray. Divide batter into pans. Bake at 350° for 20 minutes.

In a saucepan, bring sugar and milk to a boil; reduce heat and stir in marshmallows until smooth. Add coconut. Spread filling mixture over one cake and place second cake on top of filling. In another saucepan, bring evaporated milk, sugar, and butter to a boil. Remove from heat and add chocolate chips. Stir until smooth. Add nuts and pour over cake. Chill overnight.

Waxed paper is good for any layer cakes. It prevents cake from sticking and falling apart.

CHOCOLATE MAYONNAISE CAKE   Rhoda Hilty

1½ cups sugar
1 cup mayonnaise or salad
   dressing
½ cup cocoa
3 teaspoons baking soda

1½ cups cold water
3 cups flour
¼ teaspoon salt
3 teaspoons vanilla

CREAM CHEESE FROSTING:
1 (8 ounce) package cream cheese
½ cup margarine, softened

1 teaspoon vanilla
4 cups powdered sugar

Cream sugar, mayonnaise, and cocoa. Mix baking soda with water and stir into mixture. Add rest of ingredients. Bake in 13x9-inch pan at 350° for 30-35 minutes. When cool, frost with Cream Cheese Frosting.

For frosting, cream together cream cheese and margarine. Add vanilla. Beat in sugar a little at a time until it is of spreading consistency. Makes 20 servings.

DELUXE CHOCOLATE CHERRY CAKE

Judy Mullet

1 box chocolate cake mix
1 can cherry pie filling

2 eggs

CREAM CHEESE ICING:
1 (8 ounce) package cream cheese
1 stick margarine

Enough powdered sugar to get
desired consistency

Mix cake mix, eggs, and pie filling together and bake in a 9x13-inch or a 15x10-inch cake pan at 350° for 25-30 minutes or until done. When cool, frost with Cream Cheese Frosting.

For icing, beat together cream cheese and margarine, slowly adding enough powdered sugar to spread easily.

LARGE CHOCOLATE CAKE

Elva Byler

2 cups sugar
¾ cup lard
2 eggs, beaten
2½ cups flour
½ cup cocoa (scant)

½ teaspoon salt
1 cup sour milk or buttermilk
1 teaspoon vanilla
2 teaspoons baking soda
1 cup boiling water

Mix sugar and lard; add beaten eggs and beat well. Add dry ingredients alternately with sour milk or buttermilk and vanilla. Add baking soda to boiling water. Add to mixture. Line bottom of 3 layer cake pans with wax paper and spray with cooking spray. Divide batter into pans and bake at 325° for 30 minutes.

MOIST CHOCOLATE CAKE

Dorothy Schlabach

3 cups all-purpose flour
¼ cup cocoa
1 teaspoon salt
2 teaspoons baking soda
2 cups sugar

2 cups cold water
2 teaspoons vanilla
2 teaspoons vinegar
⅔ cup oil

Sift together all dry ingredients two times. Add remaining ingredients and mix by hand. Pour into 13x9x2-inch cake pan and bake at 325° for 35 minutes.

MY FAVORITE CHOCOLATE CAKE   Ruth Yoder

1 cup butter, softened
3 cups packed brown sugar
4 eggs
2 teaspoons vanilla
2⅔ cups flour

¾ cup cocoa
1 tablespoon baking soda
½ teaspoon salt
1⅓ cups sour cream
1⅓ cups boiling water

FROSTING:
½ cup butter
3 squares sweet chocolate
3 squares semi-sweet chocolate

5 cups powdered sugar
1 cup sour cream
2 teaspoons vanilla

In mixing bowl, beat butter and sugar; add eggs one at a time, beating well after each addition. Beat until light and fluffy. Blend in vanilla. Combine flour, cocoa, baking soda, and salt and add to creamed mixture alternately with sour cream, beating well after each addition. Stir in water until well blended. Pour into 3 (9-inch) greased and floured round cake pans. Bake at 350° for 35 minutes.

Frosting: In saucepan, melt butter and chocolate over low heat. Cool. In mixing bowl, combine sugar, sour cream, and vanilla. Add chocolate mixture and beat until smooth. Frost cooled cake. Makes 15 servings.

SOUR CREAM CHOCOLATE CAKE   Rhoda Coblentz

3 cups all-purpose flour
1½ cups white sugar
¾ cup brown sugar
1½ teaspoons baking soda
1½ teaspoons baking powder
1 teaspoon salt

¾ cup cocoa
2 cups sour cream
½ cup canola oil
3 large eggs
1½ teaspoons vanilla

Heat oven to 350°. Measure all ingredients into large mixer bowl. Blend ½ minute on low speed, scraping bowl constantly. Beat 2½-3 minutes on high speed, scraping bowl occasionally. Pour batter into sheet cake size pan and bake for 35 minutes. This cake is good with caramel icing.

I often substitute 1 cup oat flour for 1 cup all-purpose flour. To make 2 cups oat flour, put 2 cups quick oats into the blender and blend on high speed until fine. This makes cake extra light.

SUPER MOIST CHOCOLATE CAKE   Judith Yoder

1 cup lard or butter
2 cups sugar
2 beaten eggs
1 cup sour milk
2½ cups flour

2 teaspoons baking soda
2 teaspoons baking powder
5 tablespoons cocoa
Pinch of salt
1 cup boiling water

Cream together lard or butter, sugar, and beaten eggs. Add sour milk, flour, baking soda, baking powder, cocoa, salt, and boiling water. Pour batter into a 13x9-inch baking pan and bake at 350° for 30-45 minutes.

CHOCOLATE SURPRISE CUPCAKES   Candace (Miller) Knepp

3 cups flour
2 cups white sugar
½ cup cocoa
1 teaspoon salt
2 teaspoons baking soda

⅔ cup oil
2 cups water
2 tablespoons vinegar
2 teaspoons vanilla

FILLING:
1 (8 ounce) package cream cheese
1 egg
⅓ cup white sugar

¼ teaspoon salt
1 (6 ounce) package chocolate
   chips

Mix together flour, 2 cups white sugar, cocoa, salt, and baking soda. Add oil, water, vinegar, and vanilla. Fill cupcake papers or muffin pan ⅔ full of the above mixture.

For filling, mix together cream cheese, egg, ⅓ cup white sugar, and salt until fluffy. Add chocolate chips. Drop one heaping teaspoonful of cream cheese-chocolate chip mixture into each cupcake. Bake 25 minutes at 350°. Makes 4 dozen cupcakes.

FRESH COCONUT CAKE   Lela Brennaman,
                                    Carol Petersheim, Ruth Yoder

1 box Duncan Hines butter recipe
   golden cake mix
1 container sour cream

1 box powdered sugar
4 packages fresh, frozen coconut

Make the cake according to directions, only making two layers. Let cool. Split each layer in half making 4 layers in all. Mix sour cream, powdered sugar, and coconut. Spread between layers and on top.

We like to make this cake several days ahead and let it age in the refrigerator. We also use the "lite" sour cream. This cake is a coconut lover's delight!

CLASSIC COCONUT CAKE

Ruth Yoder

1 cup butter, softened
2 cups sugar
3 cups all-purpose flour
1 tablespoon baking powder

1 cup milk
1 teaspoon vanilla
1 teaspoon coconut flavoring
8 egg whites

PINEAPPLE FILLING:
1 (15½ ounce) can crushed
   pineapple, undrained
1 cup sugar

3 tablespoons flour
¼ cup orange juice

Cream butter and gradually add sugar, beating until light and fluffy. Combine flour and baking powder and add to creamed mixture alternately with milk, beginning and ending with flour. Stir in flavoring. Beat egg whites until stiff peaks form. Fold into creamed mixture. Pour batter into 3 (9-inch) greased and floured cake pans. Bake at 350° for about 25 minutes. Cool about 10 minutes; remove from pans and cool.

Filling: Combine all ingredients in a saucepan and cook over medium heat until thickened. Let cool. Yields about 1½ cups filling mixture.

Spread Pineapple Filling between layers after cake has cooled.

Spread top and sides with Seven Minute Frosting. Sprinkle top and sides with coconut.

GRANDMA'S COCONUT CAKE

Martha Yoder

1 cup butter (room temperature)
2 cups sugar
4 eggs
3 cups flour
½ teaspoon salt

3 teaspoons baking powder
1 cup milk
1 teaspoon vanilla
¾ cup coconut

Cream butter and sugar. Add eggs. Mix well. Sift together flour, salt, and baking powder. Add alternately with milk and vanilla. Stir in ¾ cup coconut last. Pour batter into a 9x13-inch pan or 2 (9-inch) layer cake pans and bake at 350° for 25-30 minutes.

Variation: For a delicious nut cake, use nuts instead of coconut.

COWBOY CAKE

Carolyn Eash

NO. 1:
2 cups brown sugar
2 cups unsifted flour

½ cup shortening

NO. 2:
1 cup sour milk or buttermilk
1 teaspoon baking soda
1 egg

2 teaspoons vanilla
½ teaspoon salt
Chopped nuts, optional

Combine No. 1 until crumbly. Reserve ⅔ cup of crumbs. Add No. 2 to remainder of crumbs. Mix well. Pour mixture into greased 9x13-inch cake pan. Top with ⅔ cup crumbs. Chopped nuts may be added, if desired. Bake at 350° for 25-30 minutes.

Christianity is not a cloak put on, but Christ put in.

DATE NUT CHOCOLATE CHIP CAKE

Judi Wagher

1 cup hot water
1 cup dates, finely chopped
1 teaspoon baking soda
1 cup white sugar
1 cup shortening
2 eggs
1 tablespoon vanilla

1½ cups flour
2 tablespoons cocoa
¼ teaspoon salt
1 small bag chocolate chips
1 cup finely chopped nuts
½ cup sugar to sprinkle on top of
  hot cake

Combine hot water, dates, and baking soda. Let stand ½ hour. Mix sugar, shortening, eggs, and vanilla, and add to above ingredients. Sift flour, cocoa, and salt; add to mixture. Stir in ¼ cup chocolate chips and nuts. Pour into a greased 9x13-inch pan.

Sprinkle rest of small bag of chocolate chips on top and bake about 40 minutes in 350° oven. Remove from oven and sprinkle ½ cup sugar on top. Best when served warm! Makes 12-15 servings.

GERMAN CHOCOLATE CAKE

Mrs. Robert Paul Yoder

1 (4 ounce) bar German sweet
  chocolate
½ cup boiling water
2 cups sugar
1 cup butter or margarine
4 eggs, separated

1 teaspoon vanilla
2¼ cups all-purpose flour
1 teaspoon baking soda
½ teaspoon salt
1 cup buttermilk

COCONUT-PECAN FROSTING:
1 cup evaporated milk
1 cup sugar
3 egg yolks, slightly beaten
½ cup butter or margarine

1 teaspoon vanilla
1⅓ cups coconut
1 cup pecans

Melt chocolate in boiling water. Cool and set aside. Cream butter or margarine and sugar until fluffy. Add egg yolks one at a time, beating well after each. Add vanilla and melted chocolate. Sift flour with baking soda and salt. Add alternately with buttermilk to chocolate mixture. Fold in stiffly-beaten egg whites. Line bottom of 3 (9-inch) layer pans with wax paper. Bake at 350° for 30-35 minutes.

Frosting: Combine first 5 ingredients. Cook and stir over medium heat until thickened, about 12 minutes. Add coconut and pecans. Stir occasionally while cooling. When cool, spread on cake. Makes 2½ cups.

DO NOTHING CAKE

Ruth Yoder

2 cups flour
2 cups sugar
2 eggs
1 teaspoon vanilla

½ teaspoon salt
1 teaspoon baking soda
1 large can crushed pineapple,
  undrained

FROSTING:
1 stick margarine
1 cup sugar
1 small can evaporated milk

1 cup chopped nuts
1 cup coconut

Mix cake ingredients well by hand. Pour batter into well greased sheet pan. Bake at 350° for 30 minutes.

Frosting: Mix margarine, sugar, and milk in saucepan. Simmer for 5 minutes. Add nuts and coconut. Pour frosting over cake immediately after removing cake from oven. While it is still hot, cut into squares and serve.

EARTHQUAKE CAKE

Martha Kauffman, Alta Kauffman

1½ cups chopped pecans
1½ cups shredded coconut
1 box German chocolate cake mix

½ cup margarine
1 (8 ounce) package cream cheese
4 cups powdered sugar

Grease and flour a 9x13-inch pan. Combine pecans and coconut; sprinkle in bottom of pan. Prepare cake mix according to package directions and pour over pecan and coconut mixture. Melt margarine and cream cheese together in pan. Add powdered sugar; mix well. Pour mixture over cake batter. Bake at 350° for approximately 45 minutes or until cake tests done.

The Bible is meant to be bread for our daily use,
not cake for special occasions.

ELEGANT TORTE

Sara Jean Yoder

3 cups sifted cake flour
2 cups brown sugar, packed
½ teaspoon salt
½ cup nuts, finely chopped

1 cup shortening
1 egg, beaten
1 cup buttermilk or sour milk
1 teaspoon baking soda

Combine flour, sugar, salt, and nuts. Add shortening and blend until crumbly. Set aside 1 cup of mixture. Combine egg, milk, and baking soda. Add to dry ingredients and stir well.

Pour into greased 9-inch pans. Sprinkle nut and crumb mixture over top. Bake in moderate (375°) oven for 25-30 minutes.

FRUIT COCKTAIL CAKE

Mrs. Ferlin L. Yoder

1 can fruit cocktail
2 cups sugar
2 cups flour (more if needed)
2 eggs

2 teaspoons baking soda
1 teaspoon salt
1 teaspoon cinnamon
1 teaspoon vanilla

ICING:
½ cup margarine
¾ cup brown sugar

¾ cup evaporated milk
1 cup coconut or pineapple

Combine all ingredients in bowl. Mix 3 minutes. Pour batter into a 13x9-inch baking pan and bake 35 minutes at 350°.

Icing: Bring to a boil the margarine, sugar, and evaporated milk. Add coconut or pineapple. Pour over cake while it is still hot. Makes 15-20 servings.

STARTER FOR FRIENDSHIP CAKE
Elva Miller

1 (16 ounce) can sliced peaches, 2 cups sugar
  cut in ¼-inch slices

Stir peaches and sugar every day for 10 days.

16 ounces pineapple   2 cups sugar

Add pineapple and sugar to peaches and sugar mixture. Stir every day for 10 days.

2 small jars maraschino cherries, 2 cups sugar
  drained

Add cherries and sugar to peaches, pineapple, and sugar mixture. Stir every day for 10 days. Drain juice from fruit. Save juice. Divide fruit into 3 even portions. Makes 3 cakes. Recipe below.

FRIENDSHIP CAKE
Ruth Yoder

1 yellow cake mix   1 box instant pudding mix
⅔ cup oil   ⅓ of fruit from starter recipe
4 eggs   1 cup chopped nuts

Mix ingredients together and put in a tube pan or bread pans. Bake at 350° for 1 hour. Save juice to start another batch or share with a friend.

FRUIT CAKE
Ruth Yoder

¾ cup vegetable oil   1 cup raisins (yellow)
1 cup sugar   2 cups chopped dates
3 eggs   1 cup candied fruit
3 tablespoons molasses   2 cups pecans
½ cup flour   2 cups walnuts
¾ teaspoon baking powder 1 cup flour
1½ teaspoons cinnamon   ½ teaspoon lemon flavoring
¾ teaspoon nutmeg   1 teaspoon rum flavoring
1 cup orange juice

In bowl, mix together raisins, dates, and candied fruit; add flavorings to orange juice and pour over fruits. Let set a few hours. Mix together oil, sugar, eggs, and molasses; add ½ cup flour, baking powder, salt, and spices. Add fruit flavoring mixture. Refrigerate overnight.

On the following day, mix 1 cup flour with pecans and walnuts. Spray angel food cake pan thoroughly, pour batter into pan, and press in firmly. Decorate top with candied fruit and whole pecans. Bake in a slow oven at 275° for 1½ hours. It may take 2 hours. After cake is out of oven, mix a glaze of 2 tablespoons Karo and 1 tablespoon water; spoon over cake. A very good and attractive cake.

FRIENDSHIP FRUIT CAKE   Ruth Yoder

This cake involves a step-by-step process taking 31 days to complete.

Day 1: Get 1 pint starter from a friend. Pour starter into gallon size glass jar. Add 1 (16 ounce) can sliced peaches and juice (cut slices). Add 2½ cups white sugar. Cover jar loosely with dish and stir each day for 10 days. Keep at room temperature.

Day 10: Add 1 (16 ounce) can crushed pineapple and juice; add 2½ cups white sugar. Stir each day for 10 days.

Day 20: Add 3 small cans maraschino cherries (cut up); don't add juice. Add 2½ cups white sugar and stir each day for 10 days. You now have enough mixture for 3 cakes.

Day 31: Time to bake with ingredients listed below. Makes 1 cake.

FRIENDSHIP CAKE

1 box Duncan Hines golden butter
  cake mix
1 (3 ounce) box instant vanilla
  pudding mix
4 eggs
⅔ cup Crisco or Wesson oil

1¼ cups drained fruit from
  your 30 day mix
2 cups chopped pecans
1 cup raisins
1 cup flaked coconut

Preheat oven to 275°-300°. Grease and dust with flour 2 bread pans or 1 bundt pan. Hand-mix ingredients in large bowl and pour in pan(s). Bake for 1½ hours.

Drain balance of fruit for 2 more cakes. Save juice for starter, but process must be started in 3 or 4 days, or starter will spoil.

HANDY MADE CAKE   Mrs. Paul Yoder (Ruth)

2 cups sugar
½ cup margarine
3 eggs
3 cups flour

3 teaspoons baking powder
Pinch of salt
1 cup milk

Cream sugar and margarine, then add eggs. Sift flour, baking powder, and salt. Add alternately to creamed mixture with milk. Bake at 350° in a 9x13x2-inch baking pan for 20-30 minutes.

Note: Is delicious warm with strawberries and milk.

JAPANESE FRUIT CAKE

Ruth Yoder

1 cup Crisco shortening
2 cups sugar
4 eggs
3 cups flour
1 cup sweet milk
1 teaspoon vanilla
3 teaspoons baking powder

1 teaspoon allspice
1 teaspoon cinnamon
½ teaspoon cloves
2 teaspoons nutmeg
½ cup raisins
1½ cups nuts (or less)

ICING:
Juice of 2 large lemons
Grated rind of 1 lemon
1 cup coconut
2 cups sugar

1 cup boiling water
½ cup water
3 tablespoons cornstarch
2 tablespoons flour

Cream shortening and sugar. Add eggs and rest of ingredients except spices, raisins, and nuts. Divide in two equal parts. Pour 1 part into 2 (9-inch) pans. Add all spices, nuts, and raisins to other half and pour into 4 (9-inch) greased and floured pans. Bake at 350° for about 20 minutes. Do not overbake.

Icing: Mix together lemon juice, lemon rind, coconut, sugar, and 1 cup boiling water. Bring to a boil and thicken with ½ cup water, cornstarch, and flour. Cook until thick and clear. Ice cake, sprinkling nuts between layers and on top.

GRAHAM STREUSEL CAKE

Silla K. Yoder

2 cups graham cracker crumbs
¾ cup chopped nuts
¾ cup brown sugar
1¼ teaspoons cinnamon
½ cup margarine, melted

1 package butter pecan or yellow
  cake mix
1 cup water
¼ cup vegetable oil
3 eggs
Vanilla flavoring

VANILLA GLAZE:
1 cup powdered sugar
1-2 tablespoons water

1 teaspoon vanilla

Mix crumbs, nuts, brown sugar, cinnamon, and margarine. Reserve. Blend cake mix, water, oil, eggs, and vanilla. Pour ½ of batter into a 9x13-inch pan. Sprinkle with ½ of crumb mixture. Spread remaining batter evenly over crumbs. Bake at 350° for about 30 minutes or until wooden pick inserted comes out clean. Cool and drizzle with Vanilla Glaze.

Vanilla Glaze: Mix powdered sugar with water.

GRAHAM CRACKER CAKE   Naomi Yoder

1 cup butter or margarine
1½ cups sugar
5 eggs
1 teaspoon vanilla
1 pound graham crackers, finely
  crushed

1 cup milk
1 (8 ounce) can crushed, drained
  pineapple
1 cup coconut
1 cup chopped pecans

Cream butter and sugar; beat in eggs one at a time. Add vanilla and mix well. Add cracker crumbs alternately with milk. Fold in pineapple, coconut, and nuts. Turn into greased and floured tube or bundt pan. Bake at 350° for 45-60 minutes or until done.

Best flavored when stored in cool place several days before eating. Makes 12-15 servings.

HAWAIIAN LOAF   Deborah Kauffman

1 cup butter
2 cups sugar
4 eggs
1 cup mashed ripe bananas
4 cups flour

2 teaspoons baking powder
¾ teaspoon salt
1 (20 ounce) can undrained
  crushed pineapple
1 cup flaked coconut

Preheat oven to 350°. In medium bowl, beat butter with electric mixer until light and fluffy, gradually beat in sugar until light. Add eggs; beat well. Stir in mashed bananas. In medium bowl, combine the dry ingredients. Add to butter mixture, mixing just until smooth. Stir in pineapple and coconut. Spoon batter into 2 greased and floured 9x5-inch loaf pans. Bake at 350° for 60-70 minutes or until toothpick inserted comes out clean.

KENTUCKY PECAN CAKE   Ellen D. Miller

2½ cups flour
1 cup white sugar
⅔ cup brown sugar
1½ cups vegetable oil
1 cup applesauce
¾ teaspoon cinnamon
¾ teaspoon nutmeg
4 egg yolks

2 tablespoons hot water
¼ teaspoon baking powder
1½ teaspoons baking soda
1 teaspoon salt
1 cup chopped pecans
2 teaspoons vanilla
⅛ teaspoon cloves
4 egg whites

Mix all ingredients except egg whites together until smooth. Beat egg whites until stiff. Fold into batter. Pour in ungreased tube pan and bake at 350° for 1 hour and 30 minutes. Makes 16-20 servings.

HONEY BUN CAKE

Ramona Overholt

STEP 1:
1 box yellow cake mix
4 eggs

⅔ cup oil
1 cup sour cream

STEP 2:
1 cup brown sugar

3 teaspoons cinnamon

GLAZE:
3 cups powdered sugar
¾ cup milk

2 teaspoons vanilla

Mix cake mix, eggs, oil, and sour cream and beat for 3 minutes. Pour ½ of this mixture into a 9x13-inch pan. Mix brown sugar and cinnamon together and sprinkle over mixture in pan. Drizzle second half of mixture over this.

Bake at 350° 45-60 minutes. Punch holes in cake with fork. Mix glaze ingredients together and pour over cake while still warm.

HO-HO CAKE

Dorothy Schlabach

*1 box chocolate cake mix
  (your choice)

TOPPING NO. 1:
5 tablespoons flour
1¼ cups milk
1 cup sugar

½ cup margarine
1 cup Crisco shortening

TOPPING NO. 2:
½ cup margarine
½ cup cocoa
1 egg

1 teaspoon vanilla
2½ tablespoons hot water
1¼-1½ cups powdered sugar

Bake cake as directed in 10x15-inch jelly roll pan. Cool.

Topping No. 1: Mix flour and milk in saucepan. Cook until thick, stirring constantly. Cool. Cream together sugar, margarine, and shortening. Add to flour mixture and beat well. Spread over cooled cake.

Topping No. 2: Melt margarine and cool. Add cocoa. Beat egg, vanilla, and hot water. Add powdered sugar. Blend in well. Pour this over first topping. Refrigerate.

*I use the moist chocolate cake recipe in this book.

LAZY DAISY CAKE   Celesta Miller

4 eggs
1¾ cups sugar
1 cup milk
2 tablespoons butter

2 cups flour
2 teaspoons baking powder
½ teaspoon salt
2 teaspoons vanilla

Beat eggs until thick and light. Add sugar. Beat until blended. Heat milk and butter until scalded. Beat quickly into egg mixture. Add dry ingredients alternately with milk and vanilla. Pour batter into a greased 9x13-inch pan. Bake at 350° for 30 minutes.

LEMON BUTTERMILK CAKE   Donna Stephens

3 sticks margarine
2 cups sugar
4 eggs
1 cup buttermilk
½ teaspoon baking soda dissolved
   in 1 tablespoon water

½ teaspoon salt
1 tablespoon lemon flavoring
   (or 2 teaspoons lemon flavoring
   and 1 teaspoon almond
   flavoring)
3⅓ cups flour

TOPPING:
Juice and rind of 2 lemons and 1
   orange

1½ cups sugar

Cream together margarine and sugar. Add eggs, buttermilk, baking soda dissolved in water, salt, and flavoring and beat until fluffy. Add flour. Bake in greased angel food cake pan at 300° for 1 hour and 15 minutes.

Topping: Combine juices and rinds with sugar. Pour over cake while hot.

LEMON ORANGE CAKE

Elsie Brenneman

1 cup butter or margarine, softened
1/4 cup shortening
2 cups sugar
5 eggs
3 cups all-purpose flour
1 teaspoon baking powder

1/2 teaspoon baking soda
1/2 teaspoon salt
1 cup buttermilk
1 teaspoon vanilla extract
1/2 teaspoon lemon extract

FROSTING:
1/2 cup butter or margarine,
  softened
3 tablespoons orange juice
3 tablespoons lemon juice

1-2 tablespoons grated orange
  peel
1-2 tablespoons grated lemon peel
1 teaspoon lemon extract
5 1/2-6 cups confectioners sugar

In a mixing bowl, cream butter or margarine, shortening, and sugar until light and fluffy. Add eggs, one at a time, beating well after each addition. Combine dry ingredients; add to creamed mixture alternately with buttermilk, beginning and ending with dry ingredients. Stir in extracts. Pour into 3 greased and floured 9-inch cake pans. Bake at 350° for 25-30 minutes or until cakes test done. Cool in pans for 10 minutes before removing to wire racks to cool completely.

For frosting, beat butter in a mixing bowl until fluffy; add the next 5 ingredients and mix well. Gradually add confectioners sugar; beat until frosting has desired spreading consistency. Spread between layers and over the top and sides of cake. Serves 10-12.

LOVELIGHT TEA CAKES

Barbara Kanagy

2 egg whites, unbeaten
1/2 cup white sugar
2 1/4 cups cake flour
1 cup white sugar
3 teaspoons baking powder

1 teaspoon salt
1/3 cup salad oil
1 1/2 teaspoons vanilla
1 cup milk
2 egg yolks

Beat egg whites until frothy, then slowly add 1/2 cup sugar, beating until very stiff and glossy. Sift flour, 1 cup sugar, baking powder, and salt. Add salad oil, vanilla, and half of milk. Beat at medium speed 1 minute. Add rest of milk and egg yolks. Beat 1 minute. Fold in meringue. Fill muffin tins a little over half full and bake at 400° for 15 minutes. Makes 3 1/2 dozen cakes.

Variation: 1/2 teaspoon lemon flavoring may be added instead of vanilla.

OATMEAL CAKE

Ruth Yoder

1 cup rolled oats
1¼ cups boiling water
1 cup sugar
1 cup brown sugar
½ cup margarine
2 eggs

1⅓ cups flour, unsifted
1 teaspoon baking soda
½ teaspoon salt
½ teaspoon cinnamon
½ cup broken nutmeats
1 teaspoon vanilla

TOPPING:
6 tablespoons butter
1 cup brown sugar
¼ cup canned milk

½ cup coconut
½ cup broken nutmeats

Stir oats in water. Remove from heat; cover and let stand for 20 minutes. Cream sugar, brown sugar, margarine, and eggs. Add sifted dry ingredients and nutmeats. Add vanilla and bake at 350° for 30-40 minutes in a 9x13-inch pan.

Topping: Mix topping ingredients and cook over low heat until it bubbles. Spread on baked cake. Return to oven until it boils again. Makes 15-20 servings.

OATMEAL-CHIP CAKE

Faith Miller

1¾ cups boiling water
1 cup uncooked oatmeal
1 cup packed brown sugar
1 cup sugar
½ cup margarine, softened
3 eggs
1¾ cups flour

1 teaspoon baking soda
1 teaspoon baking cocoa
¼ teaspoon salt
1 (12 ounce) package chocolate
  chips, divided
½ cup pecans, chopped

In a mixing bowl, pour water over oatmeal. Allow to stand 10 minutes. Add sugars and margarine, stirring until the margarine melts. Add eggs, one at a time, mixing well after each addition. Sift flour, baking soda, cocoa, and salt together. Add to batter. Mix well. Stir in half the chocolate chips. Pour in a greased 13x9-inch baking pan. Sprinkle top of cake with pecans and rest of chocolate chips. Bake at 350° for about 40 minutes. Serves 12.

Many of God's greatest blessings
come to us in rough wrappings,
but there is gold inside.

ORANGE CAKE ROLL
Cynthia Helmuth

Reduced calorie — 135 calories per serving.

4 egg yolks
1 tablespoon frozen orange juice
  concentrate, thawed
½ teaspoon finely shredded
  orange peel
¼ cup sugar
4 egg whites
⅓ cup sugar
½ cup flour
1 teaspoon baking powder

¼ teaspoon salt
Sifted powdered sugar
1 (1½ ounce) envelope dessert
  topping mix
1 medium orange, peeled,
  sectioned, and cut up
Orange slices (optional)
Finely shredded orange peel
  (optional)

In small bowl, beat egg yolks at high speed until thick and lemon-colored. Add orange juice concentrate and ½ teaspoon orange peel; beat at low speed until blended and then at medium speed until thick. Gradually add the ¼ cup sugar, beating until sugar is dissolved. Wash beaters thoroughly. In large mixer bowl, beat egg whites at medium speed until soft peaks form. Gradually add the ⅓ cup sugar; continue beating until stiff peaks form. Fold yolks into whites. Mix flour, baking powder, and salt; sprinkle over egg mixture. Gently fold in just until blended. Spread batter evenly in a greased and floured 15x10x1-inch pan. Bake at 375° for 12-15 minutes. Immediately turn out onto towel sprinkled with sifted powdered sugar. Starting with narrow end, roll the warm cake and towel together. Cool on wire rack. Prepare topping mix according to directions, using skim milk. Fold in cut up orange. Unroll cake; spread topping over cake leaving 1-inch rim. Roll up cake. If desired, garnish with orange slices and peel. Makes 10 servings.

MAMA'S ORANGE ICE BOX CAKE
Sonia Hoffman

1 angel food cake mix
1 package plain gelatin
¼ cup cold water
½ cup boiling water

1 small can frozen orange juice
  concentrate, thawed
½ cup sugar
2 tablespoons lemon juice
½ pint whipping cream, whipped

Prepare angel food cake according to directions. Let cool.

Soak gelatin in cold water for a few minutes. Add boiling water to dissolve. Mix concentrated orange juice, sugar, and lemon juice. Add gelatin. Place in refrigerator until almost set. Whip cream and add to gelatin mixture. Slice cake in half crosswise. Place one layer on a plate and cover with half of the orange juice mixture, top layer of cake, and the rest of the orange juice mixture. Refrigerate to set and keep in refrigerator until ready to eat.

ORANGE CLOUD CAKE

Mary Joyce Miller

1 box yellow cake mix   Orange juice

FILLING:
1¼ cups sugar   3½ cups orange juice
½ cup cornstarch   1 teaspoon vanilla flavoring

TOPPING:
2 tablespoons instant vanilla   1 cup filling mixture
   pudding mix   8 ounces whipped topping
1 teaspoon vanilla

Mix cake according to directions on package, using orange juice instead of water. Bake in 3 (8-inch) round cake pans at 350° for 20-25 minutes or until done. Cool.

Meanwhile, combine sugar and cornstarch. Slowly stir in orange juice. Bring to boil. Stirring constantly, cook 1 minute. Remove from heat and stir in vanilla. Chill.

For topping, beat pudding mix, vanilla, and 1 cup of cooled filling mixture into whipped topping. Spread filling between layers, on top of, and around cake. Chill several hours or overnight before serving. Makes 12-16 servings.

ORANGE JUICE CAKE

Mrs. Gerald Lambright

1 box yellow cake mix   1 cup orange juice
4 eggs   ½ cup flour
½ cup vegetable oil   1 small box vanilla instant pudding

GLAZE:
1 cup orange juice   1 stick margarine
1 cup sugar

Grease and flour a bundt pan well. Mix ingredients. Add instant pudding last. Beat well and immediately pour into pan. Bake at 325° for 50 minutes or until done.

Make glaze of orange juice, sugar, and margarine. Boil 2-3 minutes. Put on cake immediately, as it comes out of the oven. Serves 12-15.

PEACH CAKE

Cynthia Helmuth

3 eggs, well beaten
1¾ cups sugar
1 cup oil
2 cups flour
1 teaspoon salt

1 teaspoon cinnamon
2 cups chopped peaches
½ cup chopped nuts
1 teaspoon baking soda

Mix thoroughly by hand. This is delicious when made with freshly ground soft wheat flour. Bake in a 9x13-inch pan at 375° for 50 minutes.

PEACH PECAN CAKE

Elva Miller, Pat Parker, Ruth Yoder

1 box white cake mix
1 (3 ounce) box peach gelatin
4 eggs
½ cup milk

1 cup chopped peaches, drained
1 cup cooking oil
1 cup coconut
1 cup pecans, chopped

PEACH FROSTING:
1 box confectioners sugar
1 stick butter or margarine
½ cup chopped peaches, drained

½ cup coconut
½ cup pecans

For cake: Mix dry gelatin and cake mix together. Add remaining ingredients, adding eggs one at a time. Bake cake according to cake mix directions in 3 greased 8-inch layer pans.

For frosting: Cream sugar and butter or margarine. Add remaining ingredients.

Note: Strawberry gelatin and fresh strawberries may be substituted for peach gelatin and peaches.

BLUEBERRY POUND CAKE

Laura K. Yoder

1 cup plus 2 teaspoons butter
2¼ cups sugar
4 eggs
1 teaspoon vanilla

3 cups all-purpose flour
1 teaspoon baking powder
½ teaspoon salt
2 cups blueberries

Grease tube pan with 2 teaspoons butter, then sprinkle with ¼ cup sugar. Cream 1 cup butter, gradually adding 2 cups sugar. Add eggs, one at a time, beating well between each. Add vanilla. Combine 2¾ cups flour, baking powder, and salt. Gradually add to creamed mixture.

Dredge blueberries in ¼ cup flour, then stir berries into batter. Pour into prepared pan and bake at 325° for 1 hour and 10 minutes. Cool in pan for 10 minutes before removing.

POPPY SEED CAKE

Melody Helmuth

3 large eggs
1½ cups milk
1 cup oil
1½ teaspoons vanilla
1½ teaspoons butter flavoring
1½ teaspoons almond flavoring

3 cups flour
1½ teaspoons baking powder
1½ teaspoons salt
2¼ cups sugar
2 tablespoons poppy seeds

GLAZE:
¾ cup sugar
¼ cup orange juice
½ teaspoon vanilla

¼ teaspoon butter flavoring
¼ teaspoon almond flavoring

Combine first 6 ingredients. Add remaining ingredients and beat 1-2 minutes. Pour into greased bundt pan and bake at 350° for 1 hour. Remove from pan.

For glaze: Mix all ingredients and bring to a boil. Pour glaze over top of cake.

POUND CAKE

Rose Yoder

1 stick butter
2 cups sugar
½ cup shortening
3 eggs

1 cup flour
⅓ cup oil
1 tablespoon vanilla

Grease and flour tube pan. Cream butter with sugar and shortening. Add eggs, flour, oil, and vanilla. Pour batter in tube pan. Put in cold oven and bake at 325° for 1 hour. Makes 16 servings.

For a different taste, put in lemon flavoring and omit the vanilla.

CREAM CHEESE POUND CAKE

Drusilla Beiler, Laura Yoder

1 (8 ounce) package cream cheese
1 stick butter
2 sticks margarine
3 cups sugar

3 cups sifted flour
6 eggs
1 tablespoon vanilla or lemon
   flavoring

Combine softened cream cheese, butter, and margarine. Add sugar. Alternately add flour and eggs, mixing well after each addition. Add vanilla or lemon flavoring. Bake in greased and floured tube pan at 350° for 1 hour and 15 minutes.

Laura adds ¼ teaspoon lemon, coconut, almond, and rum flavorings to her cake.

117

FRESH COCONUT POUND CAKE

Marialice Yoder

1 cup butter, softened
3 cups sugar
5 eggs
3 cups all-purpose flour
1 cup fresh coconut (or frozen)

¼ teaspoon salt
¼ teaspoon baking soda
8 ounces dairy sour cream
1 teaspoon vanilla extract
1 teaspoon coconut extract

ICING:
½ cup vegetable shortening
1 (1 pound) box powdered sugar
¼ cup water

⅛ teaspoon salt
1 teaspoon vanilla (preferably
   clear)

Cream butter for cake, gradually adding sugar. Beat until mixture is light and fluffy. Add one egg at a time, beating well after each addition. In separate bowls, combine flour, salt, and baking soda. Mix well. Add alternately to creamed mixture, with sour cream, starting with flour and ending with flour. Add coconut. Stir in vanilla and coconut extracts. Pour batter into greased and floured 10-inch tube pan. Bake at 350° for 1 hour and 20 minutes. Cool 10-15 minutes before removing from pan. Cool completely before frosting or cutting.

To make icing: Combine all ingredients in large bowl of electric mixer. Mix on high speed until fluffy. Makes 16 servings.

LEMON POPPY SEED POUND CAKE

Deborah Kauffman

2 cups sugar
1 cup butter, softened
1 cup buttermilk
4 eggs
3 cups all-purpose flour
¼ cup poppy seeds

½ teaspoon baking powder
½ teaspoon baking soda
½ teaspoon salt
4 teaspoons grated lemon peel
½ teaspoon vanilla

GLAZE:
1 cup powdered sugar

2 tablespoons lemon juice

Heat oven to 325°. In large bowl, combine sugar, butter, buttermilk, and eggs. Mix at medium speed with an electric mixer until smooth. In separate bowl, combine flour, poppy seed, baking powder, baking soda, and salt. Add flour mixture to liquid ingredients, beating on high until thoroughly mixed. Add lemon peel and vanilla and beat 1 minute more or until mixture is smooth. Pour batter into greased 10-inch bundt pan. Bake 60 minutes or until cake tests done. Allow cake to cool in pan. Invert cake onto plate.

Glaze: Mix powdered sugar and lemon juice together. Top cake with glaze. Makes 20 servings.

GEORGIA PEACH POUND CAKE   Deborah Kauffman

1 cup plus 2 tablespoons butter
2¼ cups sugar, divided
4 eggs
1 teaspoon vanilla

3 cups all-purpose flour, divided
1 teaspoon baking powder
½ teaspoon salt
2 cups chopped fresh peaches

Grease a 10-inch tube pan with 2 tablespoons of butter. Sprinkle pan with ¼ cup sugar. Cream remaining butter; gradually add remaining sugar, beating well. Add eggs, one at a time, beating well after each addition. Add vanilla and mix well. Combine 2¾ cups flour, baking powder, and salt. Gradually add to creamed mixture, beating until well-blended. Dredge peaches with remaining ¼ cup flour. Stir peaches into batter. Pour batter into prepared pan. Bake at 325° for 1 hour and 10 minutes. Remove from pan and cool completely. Serves 16.

5 FLAVOR POUND CAKE   Alta Kauffman

2 sticks butter
½ cup shortening
3 cups sugar
5 eggs, well beaten
3 cups flour
½ teaspoon baking powder

½ teaspoon salt
1 cup milk
1 teaspoon each of coconut,
    almond, butter, lemon, and
    vanilla flavoring

GLAZE:
1 cup sugar
½ cup water

1 teaspoon each of coconut,
    almond, butter, lemon, and
    vanilla flavoring

Cream butter, shortening, and sugar until light and fluffy. Add well beaten eggs and blend. Combine flour, baking powder, and salt and add to creamed mixture, alternately with milk. Stir in the flavorings. Spoon into a 10-inch tube pan which has been greased and floured. Bake at 325° for 1½ hours or until done. Leave in pan to cool.

Glaze: Mix all ingredients. Bring to a boil. Spoon over cake in pan.

Faith is the vision of the heart!
It sees God in the dark, as in the day!

MILLION DOLLAR POUND CAKE

Ruth Yoder

1 pound butter, softened
3 cups sugar
6 eggs
4 cups all-purpose flour

¾ cup milk
½ teaspoon salt
1 teaspoon vanilla extract
1 teaspoon almond extract

Cream butter. Gradually add sugar, beating well at medium speed of electric mixer. Add eggs one at a time, beating after each addition. Add flour and salt to creamed mixture alternately with milk, beginning and ending with flour. Mix just until blended after each addition. Stir in flavorings. Pour batter into a greased and floured 10-inch tube pan. Bake for 1 hour and 40 minutes at 325°. Remove from pan and let cool on wire rack.

PRINCE OF WALES CAKE

Mrs. Gerald Lambright

1 cup sugar
½ cup shortening
1 egg
½ cup maple syrup
2 cups flour
1 teaspoon baking soda
1 teaspoon vanilla

½ teaspoon cinnamon
½ teaspoon cloves
½ teaspoon nutmeg
1 cup sour milk
Raisins, optional
Nuts, optional

Cream sugar, shortening, and egg. Add maple syrup. Sift dry ingredients and add alternately with sour milk and vanilla. If raisins and/or nuts are desired, add last. Pour into a 13x9-inch pan and bake at 350° for 30 minutes.

PUMPKIN CAKE

Martha Yoder

½ cup shortening
1 cup white sugar
1 cup brown sugar
2 eggs, beaten
1 cup cooked, mashed pumpkin
3 cups sifted cake flour

4 teaspoons baking powder
¼ teaspoon baking soda
½ teaspoon salt
½ cup milk
1 cup chopped nuts
1 teaspoon maple extract

Cream shortening. Add sugars, eggs, and pumpkin. Sift together dry ingredients. Add alternately with milk to mixture. Fold in nuts and extract. Pour into 3 greased 8-inch layer pans or a 9x13-inch baking pan and bake at 350° for 30 minutes. Frost with cream cheese frosting.

PUMPKIN CAKE

Martha Yoder, Rhoda Hilty

3 cups flour
2 cups white sugar
2 teaspoons pumpkin pie spice
2 teaspoons baking powder
2 teaspoons baking soda
1 teaspoon salt

2 cups pumpkin
1½ cups oil
4 eggs
1 teaspoon vanilla
½ cup chopped nuts

COFFEE FROSTING:
1 tablespoon instant coffee
1 tablespoon hot water
½ cup margarine, melted

3⅓ cups powdered sugar
1 teaspoon vanilla
3-5 teaspoons milk

For cake, mix all ingredients except nuts; beat well. Stir in nuts. Bake at 350° in a 13x9-inch pan or 3 round layer pans for 45 minutes. (If round pans are used, shorten baking time.)

When cool, frost with Coffee Frosting. Dissolve coffee in hot water, add margarine, powdered sugar, vanilla, and milk until mixture reaches right consistency. Makes about 20 servings.

PUMPKIN CRUNCH CAKE

Mrs. Noah Yoder

1 box yellow cake mix
1 cup mashed pumpkin
½ cup water

3 eggs
1 teaspoon pumpkin spice

TOPPING:
1 cup brown sugar
1 cup chopped nuts
2 teaspoons cinnamon

2 tablespoons flour
2 tablespoons melted butter

Mix yellow cake mix, pumpkin, water, eggs, and pumpkin spice. Pour half of batter in greased and floured 9x13-inch pan. Combine topping mixture. Sprinkle half of mixture over cake batter. Add the rest of cake batter on top and the remaining crumbs on top of batter. Bake at 350° for 45-50 minutes. Makes 15-20 servings.

PUMPKIN ROLL

Mrs. Jonas Schrock (Kathy)

3 eggs
1 cup sugar
⅔ cup mashed pumpkin
1 teaspoon baking soda
¾ cup flour

½ teaspoon cinnamon
½ teaspoon nutmeg
1 teaspoon ginger
½ cup chopped nuts (optional)

FILLING:
1 (8 ounce) package cream cheese
2 teaspoons margarine

1 cup powdered sugar
1 teaspoon vanilla

Beat eggs and sugar for several minutes until very light. Beat in the pumpkin. Fold in the dry ingredients. Spread on a well greased and floured cookie sheet. Bake at 350° for about 15 minutes. Remove from pan and roll up in a towel that has been sprinkled with powdered sugar.

Filling: Combine cream cheese, margarine, powdered sugar, and vanilla. Mix well. After cooling the cake, open it and spread with filling. Roll up again. Makes 10 servings.

RANCH CAKE

Linda Kauffman

1 stick butter or margarine
1½ cups boiling water
1 cup uncooked quick oatmeal
1½ cups flour
1 teaspoon baking soda

1½ teaspoons cinnamon
½ teaspoon salt
1 cup granulated sugar
1 cup brown sugar
2 beaten eggs

TOPPING:
¾ cup packed brown sugar
2 tablespoons milk
6 tablespoons butter or margarine

½ cup pecans
1 cup coconut

Break butter into chunks and pour boiling water over oatmeal and butter. Stir until butter melts. Set aside. Sift flour, baking soda, cinnamon, and salt, and add to oat mixture. Mix well. Add both sugars. Add eggs. Mix thoroughly. Bake in greased 9x13-inch pan at 350° for 30 minutes.

Topping: Combine sugar, milk, and butter in saucepan and heat until boiling. Remove from heat and blend in pecans and coconut. Spread on warm cake. Place under broiler long enough to slightly brown. Makes 15 servings.

RASPBERRY SNACK CAKE
Celesta Miller

1 cup margarine, softened
1½ cups sugar
4 eggs
3 cups all-purpose flour
½ teaspoon salt

4 teaspoons baking powder
1 cup milk
1 teaspoon vanilla
3½ cups raspberries

GLAZE:
1¼ cups confectioners sugar
2 tablespoons melted butter

1 teaspoon vanilla

Cream softened margarine and sugar. Add eggs and beat well. Add dry ingredients alternately with milk and vanilla. Beat well. Spread cake batter in 13x9x2-inch baking pan. Spread berries over top of batter. Sprinkle 2 tablespoons sugar over top of berries. Bake at 350° for 30-35 minutes. Let cool.

Combine glaze ingredients and spread over cake. If glaze is too thick, a small amount of milk or hot water may be added.

RED DEVIL'S FOOD CAKE
Barbara Kanagy

½ cup cold water
1½ teaspoons baking soda
½ cup cocoa
⅔ cup shortening
1 teaspoon vanilla

1¾ cups sugar
2 eggs
1½ cups flour
½ teaspoon salt
¾ cup sour milk

Grease and flour an oblong 13x9-inch or 2 layer pans and set aside. Preheat oven to 350°. Mix cold water, baking soda, cocoa and let set. Combining cocoa and soda makes it red. Cream shortening, vanilla, and sugar. Add eggs and beat until light. Sift together flour and salt. Add alternately with sour milk to creamed mixture. Stir in cocoa mixture. Pour batter into prepared pans and bake at 350° for 45-50 minutes. Makes 15 servings.

RED VELVET CAKE
Naomi Yoder

1 box yellow cake mix
2 tablespoons cocoa
1 (3 ounce) package instant vanilla
    pudding

2 (1 ounce) bottles red food
    coloring, with enough water
    added to make 1 cup liquid
½ cup vegetable oil
4 eggs

Mix all ingredients together. Beat well. Bake at 350° in 3 (8-inch) round pans or loaf pans for 25-30 minutes. Frost with fluffy frosting or cream cheese frosting. Makes 12-15 servings.

STRAWBERRY SHORTCAKE   Elva Byler

2¼ cups cake flour
4 teaspoons baking powder
½ teaspoon salt
2 tablespoons sugar

⅓ cup shortening
1 egg, slightly beaten
⅔ cup milk

Sift flour, baking powder, salt, and sugar together. Add shortening, cutting in with pastry blender until crumbly. Stir in egg and milk and spread in greased cake pan. Bake at 425° for 15 minutes. Serve with fresh or frozen strawberries and milk. Makes 6 servings. Very good.

SHORTCAKE   Ruth Yoder

⅓ cup butter
¼ cup sugar
2 cups all-purpose flour

3 teaspoons baking powder
½ teaspoon salt
¾-1 cup milk

Cream sugar and butter with a pastry knife. Add rest of ingredients and mix lightly. Bake in a 9-inch pan at 450° for 15-20 minutes. Serve with fresh fruit and whipped cream. Serves 9.

SILVER WHITE CAKE   Rachel Swarey

2¼ cups flour
1½ cups sugar
3½ teaspoons baking powder
1 teaspoon salt

½ cup soft shortening
1 cup milk
1 teaspoon flavoring
4 egg whites, unbeaten

Sift together dry ingredients. Add shortening, ⅔ cup milk and flavoring. Beat 2 minutes at medium speed. Keep sides and bottom scraped. Add rest of milk and egg whites. Beat 2 more minutes. Bake in greased and floured 13x9-inch pan at 350° for 35-40 minutes or until done. This is a beautiful, light cake.

QUICK CARAMEL FROSTING   Ruth Yoder

1 cup brown sugar
½ cup butter
¼ cup milk or cream

2 cups powdered sugar
Pinch of salt

Stir together sugar, butter, and milk or cream in heavy saucepan. Boil for 2 minutes. Add powdered sugar and beat well. Spread on cake while still hot.

Note: Caramel icing will turn out much better if sugar is completely dissolved in butter before adding other ingredients.

CREAM CHEESE FROSTING

Roxanna Linneber

1 (3 ounce) package cream cheese
¼ cup butter
2 tablespoons cream or milk

1 teaspoon vanilla
2 cups powdered sugar

Beat all together until smooth and creamy.

FLUFFY FROSTING

Naomi Yoder

1 cup sugar
¼ teaspoon cream of tartar
⅓ cup water

¼ teaspoon salt
2 egg whites
1 teaspoon vanilla

In saucepan, combine sugar, cream of tartar, water, and salt; cook and stir until bubbly and sugar is dissolved. With electric mixer on high speed, beat egg whites, slowly adding cooked syrup. Beat on high for 7 minutes, add vanilla and spread on Red Velvet Cake.

The guess-so Christians are never found among the soul-winners.

FROSTING

Martha Yoder

3 cups powdered sugar
⅔ cup Crisco shortening
½ teaspoon salt
⅓ cup boiling water

1 teaspoon vanilla
Butter flavoring (or just a little
    butter)

Mix together powdered sugar, shortening, and salt. Add boiling water and rest of ingredients. Mix until nice and smooth.

CREAMY BROWNIE FROSTING

Rachel Swarey

3 tablespoons butter
1½-2 tablespoons cocoa
1 tablespoon light corn syrup

½ teaspoon vanilla
1 cup confectioners sugar
1-2 tablespoons milk

Cream butter, cocoa, corn syrup, and vanilla in bowl. Add sugar and milk. Beat to spreading consistency. Makes about 1 cup frosting.

DECORATING ICING

Ruth Yoder

½ cup Crisco shortening
1 egg white
1 ounce water

1 teaspoon vanilla
1 box powdered sugar

Beat shortening, egg white, water, and vanilla real well. Add powdered sugar and beat until well blended.

NUT CAKE FROSTING
Rachel Swarey

3 cups powdered sugar
¼ cup boiling water
¼ teaspoon salt

Vanilla to taste
¾ cup Crisco shortening

Beat until nice and fluffy. Also called Wedding Frosting.

7 MINUTE ICING
Ruth Yoder

1½ cups sugar
2 egg whites
1 tablespoon light corn syrup

Dash salt
⅓ cup cold water
1 teaspoon vanilla extract

Combine sugar, egg whites (at room temperature), corn syrup, and salt in top of large double boiler. Add cold water and beat on low speed with an electric mixer for 30 seconds. Place over boiling water. Beat on high speed with an electric hand mixer 7 minutes or until stiff peaks form. Remove from heat and add vanilla. Beat 2 additional minutes or until frosting is thick. Yields enough for 1 (3-layer) cake.

WHITE FROSTING
Ruth Yoder

3 tablespoons flour
1 cup milk
1 cup white sugar

1 cup butter
1 teaspoon vanilla
½ box powdered sugar

Cook flour and milk until thickened (like a thick white sauce). Let cool. Cream together sugar and butter, then add the cooled flour and milk mixture. Add vanilla and cream well. Gradually add powdered sugar and mix until spreading consistency.

CHOCOLATE FROSTING
Ruth Yoder

½ cup butter
3 (1 ounce) squares unsweetened
  chocolate
3 (1 ounce) squares semi-sweet chocolate

5 cups confectioners sugar
1 cup sour cream
2 teaspoons vanilla extract

In a medium saucepan, melt butter and chocolate over low heat. Cool several minutes in a mixing bowl. Combine sugar, sour cream, and vanilla. Add chocolate mixture and beat until smooth. Frost cooled cake.

BUTTER FROSTING
Jonas and Kathy Schrock

2¾ cups confectioners sugar
½ teaspoon salt
1 egg

½ cup Crisco shortening or butter
2 teaspoons vanilla
¼ cup dark Karo or pancake syrup

Beat all together on high speed until smooth.

Cookies,
Bars,
&
Candy

APPLE COOKIES

Mrs. David Wengerd

2 cups white sugar
2 cups brown sugar
1 cup shortening
4 eggs
2 teaspoons vanilla
4 teaspoons baking powder
2 teaspoons soda

2 teaspoons salt
6 cups flour
1 cup sour cream
4 cups diced apples
2 cups nuts
2 cups raisins

Cream together sugars and shortening. Add eggs and vanilla. Stir in dry ingredients alternately with sour cream. Last add apples, nuts, and raisins. Drop by tablespoonfuls onto cookie sheet. Bake at 325° about 8-10 minutes or until light brown. Makes 5½ dozen.

BIG TOLL HOUSE COOKIES

Mrs. Freeman Schlabach

1 cup butter, melted
¾ cup sugar
¾ cup brown sugar
1 teaspoon vanilla
2 eggs

2¼ cups flour
1 teaspoon baking soda
1 teaspoon salt
2 cups chocolate chips
1 cup chopped nuts

In large mixer bowl, beat butter, sugars, and vanilla until creamy. Add eggs and beat again. Add flour, baking powder and salt. Stir in chips and nuts. Spread in greased 15-inch round pizza pan. Bake in a 375° oven for 20-25 minutes. Cool and cut in wedges. Makes 35 cookies.

BOYFRIEND COOKIES

Mrs. Vivian Miller

1 cup butter or margarine
1⅓ cups white sugar
1⅓ cups brown sugar
2 eggs
1 teaspoon vanilla
1½ cups flour

1 teaspoon baking soda
3 cups cooking oats
1 (6 ounce) package chocolate
  chips
1½ cups pecans or peanuts

Cream butter or margarine and sugars in large bowl. Add eggs and vanilla; beat until fluffy. Sift flour and baking soda and mix alternately with oats. Stir in chips and nuts. Batter will be stiff. Drop by tablespoonfuls on cookie sheet and bake at 375° for 8-10 minutes. Makes 3 dozen cookies.

BUTTERSCOTCH COOKIES

Mrs. Jonathan Yoder

2¾ cups all-purpose flour
1 teaspoon cream of tartar
1 teaspoon baking soda
¼ teaspoon salt

½ cup shortening
2 cups brown sugar
2 eggs
¼ teaspoon vanilla

Sift together flour, cream of tartar, baking soda, and salt. Set aside. Cream shortening, sugar, and eggs. Add vanilla, then the flour mixture. Form into rolls about 2 inches in diameter and wrap in wax paper. Chill in refrigerator. When ready to bake, slice and place on ungreased baking sheet. Bake at 350° for about 10 minutes. Makes 2½ dozen cookies.

*Anyone who is too busy for prayer
is busier than God ever intended they should be.*

CHOCOLATE COOKIES

Judith Yoder

2 cups brown sugar
1 cup shortening
1 cup milk
1 teaspoon baking soda
2 eggs

3 cups flour
2 teaspoons baking powder
½ cup cocoa
¼ teaspoon salt
1 teaspoon vanilla

FROSTING:
6 tablespoons butter (browned)
3 tablespoons hot water

1 teaspoon vanilla
Powdered sugar as needed

Mix in order listed and drop by teaspoonfuls on cookie sheet. Bake at 375° for 8-10 minutes. Cream frosting ingredients and frost cookies while still warm. Makes 3 dozen.

CHOCOLATE CHIP MELTAWAYS

Debbie Graber

1 cup butter or margarine, softened
1 cup vegetable oil
1 cup white sugar
1 cup powdered sugar
2 eggs
4 cups flour

½ teaspoon salt
1 teaspoon baking soda
1 teaspoon cream of tartar
1 teaspoon vanilla
1 (12 ounce) package chocolate
  chips

Combine first 5 ingredients. Beat until smooth. Combine flour, baking soda, cream of tartar, and salt. Add to butter or margarine mixture. Beat until smooth. Stir in vanilla and chocolate chips. Shape into balls. Roll into white sugar. Bake at 375° for 10-12 minutes. Makes 3 dozen.

CHOCOLATE DROP COOKIES
Heidi Kauffman

½ cup margarine
2½ squares unsweetened
chocolate
1 cup sugar
1 teaspoon vanilla

2 eggs
2 cups flour
1 teaspoon baking powder
½ teaspoon baking soda
½ cup sour milk

FROSTING:
1 tablespoon margarine
1½ squares unsweetened
chocolate

1½ cups powdered sugar
2 tablespoons milk

Melt margarine and chocolate. Remove from heat. Add sugar and mix. Add vanilla and eggs and beat well. Sift together flour, baking powder, and baking soda. Add dry ingredients alternately with milk. Bake at 350° for 8-12 minutes. Makes 3 dozen cookies.

For icing, melt margarine and chocolate. Blend in sugar and milk. Frost cooled cookies.

DOUBLE-CHOCOLATE SUGAR COOKIES
Deborah Kauffman

1 (12 ounce) package semi-sweet
chocolate morsels, divided
1 cup butter or margarine, softened
1 cup sugar
1 large egg
2 tablespoons milk

1 teaspoon vanilla extract
3 cups all-purpose flour
1 teaspoon baking powder
½ teaspoon baking soda
½ teaspoon salt
½ cup sugar

Melt 1 cup semi-sweet chocolate morsels in a heavy saucepan over low heat, reserving remaining morsels. Set melted morsels aside.

Beat butter or margarine at medium speed with an electric mixer until fluffy; gradually add sugar, beating well. Add egg, milk, and vanilla, mixing well. Add melted morsels, mixing until blended. Combine flour and next 3 ingredients; gradually add to butter or margarine mixture, mixing well. Stir in remaining chocolate morsels. Roll dough into balls 1 tablespoon at a time; roll balls in ½ cup sugar. Bake at 400° for 8-10 minutes. (Cookies will be soft and will firm up as they cool). Remove to wire racks to cool. Makes 4½ dozen.

CLASSIC CHOCOLATE CHIP COOKIES

Ruth Yoder, Alta Kauffman, Barbara Ann Yoder, Londa Kauffman

2¼ cups flour
1 teaspoon baking soda
1 cup butter or margarine, softened
¼ cup granulated sugar
¾ cup brown sugar
1 teaspoon vanilla

1 (3½ ounce) package instant vanilla pudding
2 eggs
½ teaspoon salt
1 (12 ounce) package semi-sweet chocolate chips
1 cup nuts, optional

Combine flour, baking soda, and salt; set aside. Combine butter or margarine, sugars, vanilla, and pudding mix in large mixer bowl. Beat until smooth and creamy. Beat in eggs; gradually add flour mixture. Stir in chocolate chips (and nuts, if desired). Batter will be stiff. Drop on ungreased cookie sheets. Bake at 375° for 9-10 minutes or until browned. Yield: 4½ dozen cookies 2½ inches in diameter.

FAVORITE CHOCOLATE CHIP COOKIES

Mrs. Paul Yoder, Dorothy Schlabach

1¼ cups firmly packed brown sugar
½ pound or 1 cup butter or Crisco shortening
2 eggs
1½ teaspoons vanilla

2¼ cups flour
¼ teaspoon baking soda
1 teaspoon salt
1 (6 ounce) package chocolate chips
1 cup nuts

Mix together sugar and butter or shortening, then add eggs and vanilla. Add to mixture of flour, baking soda, and salt. Add chips and nuts. Bake at 350°-375° for 10-12 minutes. Makes 2½ dozen cookies.

GRANDMA'S CHOCOLATE CHIP COOKIES

Kathy Schrock, Rose Yoder, Wanda Steiner, Carolyn Eash

½ cup butter
½ cup brown sugar
½ cup granulated sugar
1 egg
1½ cups flour
½ teaspoon salt

½ teaspoon baking soda
1 (7 ounce) package chocolate chips
1 teaspoon hot water
1 teaspoon vanilla
½ cup chopped nuts (optional)

Cream butter and sugars together. Add egg and mix well. Add remaining ingredients (except chocolate chips) and mix well. Stir in chocolate chips and nuts. Bake at 350° for 10-15 minutes. Makes 2½ dozen.

LO-FAT CHOCOLATE CHIP COOKIES   Pat Parker

1 cup canola oil
2 cups brown sugar
1⅓ cups sugar
4 eggs
4 teaspoons vanilla

2½ cups whole wheat flour
2½ cups white flour
2 teaspoons baking soda
2 teaspoons salt
2 cups chocolate or white chips

Cream oil, sugars, eggs, and vanilla. Add flours, baking soda, and salt. Mix well. Add chips and mix gently. Bake on ungreased sheet for 9 minutes at 350°. Remove to rack to cool. Makes 6 dozen.

SOFT CHOCOLATE CHIP COOKIES   Debbie Graber

2 cups brown sugar
1 cup shortening
1 teaspoon vanilla
2 eggs
2 teaspoons baking powder
4 cups flour

Dash of salt
2 teaspoons baking soda
1 cup buttermilk
1 (12 ounce) package chocolate
   chips

Mix sugar and shortening; add vanilla and eggs. Beat well. Add baking powder to the flour and salt. Mix baking soda with buttermilk. Add liquid and dry ingredients alternately to sugar mixture. Stir in chocolate chips and drop by teaspoonfuls on cookie sheet. Bake at 350° for 8-10 minutes. Makes 3½ dozen.

CHRISTMAS FRUIT COOKIES   Carol Petersheim

½ cup Crisco shortening
½ cup butter
2 cups white sugar
3 eggs
1 teaspoon lemon extract
1½ teaspoons vanilla
3¼ cups flour
½ teaspoon salt
¼ teaspoon cloves

1 teaspoon baking soda
¼ cup orange juice concentrate
½ pound chopped dates
½ pound raisins
¼ pound candied cherries
¼ pound candied pineapple
¼ pound candied orange peel
¾ pound pecans

Cream shortening, butter, and sugar; add eggs and beat until fluffy. Add flavorings and beat again. Sift flour. Add salt, spices, and baking soda. Sift again. Add dry ingredients with concentrate. Add chopped fruits and nuts. Blend well. Drop by teaspoonful on greased cookie sheet 2-3 inches apart. Bake at 350° until lightly browned. Very tasty!

COWBOY COOKIES

Mrs. John Nissley

2 cups shortening
2 cups white sugar
2 cups brown sugar
4 eggs
2 teaspoons vanilla
1 teaspoon baking powder
1 teaspoon salt

2 teaspoons baking soda
4 cups flour
4 cups oats
2 medium packages chocolate
  chips
Nuts, if desired

Beat together shortening, sugars, and eggs. Add vanilla. Blend in dry ingredients and chips (and nuts if desired). May have to mix by hand. Drop by tablespoonful on cookie sheet and bake at 350° for 8-10 minutes. Makes 5 dozen.

CREAM CHEESE COOKIES

Drusilla Beiler

2 sticks butter
2 (3 ounce) packages cream
  cheese
2 tablespoons milk

2 cups sugar
1 teaspoon vanilla
2 cups all-purpose flour
1 cup pecans

Cream butter, cream cheese, and milk in large mixer bowl at medium speed until well blended. Beat in sugar and vanilla. Mix in flour and nuts. Drop by tablespoon of dough 2 inches apart onto ungreased cookie sheets and bake at 375° for 10 minutes. Makes 6 dozen cookies.

Apply thyself wholly to the scriptures and the scriptures wholly to thyself.

EVERYTHING COOKIES

Mrs. Paul Yoder

1 cup margarine
1 cup brown sugar
1 cup white sugar
1 egg, beaten
1 teaspoon cream of tartar
1 cup oatmeal
1 cup coconut

1 cup salad oil
2 tablespoons vanilla
3¼ cups flour
1 teaspoon baking soda
1 cup Rice Krispies cereal
1 cup chocolate chips
1 teaspoon salt

Mix in order given and drop by teaspoonfuls on ungreased cookie sheet. Bake at 350° until lightly browned, around 12 minutes. Makes 4-5 dozen cookies.

FUDGE-MARSHMALLOW COOKIES

Donna Stephens,
Ellen D. Miller

½ cup shortening
⅔ cup sugar
1 egg
1 teaspoon vanilla
¼ cup milk

1¾ cups cake flour
¼ teaspoon salt
½ teaspoon baking soda
⅓ cup cocoa
18 large marshmallows, halved

FROSTING:
2 cups powdered sugar
5 tablespoons cocoa
3 tablespoons margarine

4-5 tablespoons light cream
½ cup chopped pecans for
  sprinkling on top

Cream shortening and sugar. Add egg, vanilla, and milk. Add dry ingredients and mix well. Drop on greased cookie sheet. Bake at 350° for 8-10 minutes. Do not overbake. Remove cookies from oven and top each with a marshmallow half. Return to oven for 2 minutes. Makes 3 dozen.

Beat all frosting ingredients together. Spread frosting on each cookie and sprinkle with chopped pecans.

GINGER SNAPS COOKIES

Mrs. Roger Helmuth, Sr.

2 cups shortening
4 cups sugar
4 eggs, beaten
1 cup sorghum or regular syrup
8½-9 cups flour

8 teaspoons baking soda
1 teaspoon salt
1½ teaspoons cinnamon
1½ teaspoons cloves
1½ teaspoons ginger

Mix shortening, sugar, and eggs. Add rest of ingredients. Shape into balls and roll in white sugar. Press a little flat with base of a greased and sugared coffee cup. Bake at 350° for about 12 minutes. Do not overbake — only until a very light brown. Makes 7-8 dozen.

HOLIDAY CREAM CHEESE DROPS

Ruth Yoder

½ cup butter or margarine
1 (3 ounce) package cream cheese
½ cup sugar
½ teaspoon vanilla
1 egg yolk

1 cup sifted flour
¼ teaspoon salt
Maraschino cherries, halved, or
  pecans, halved

In a mixing bowl, thoroughly cream together butter or margarine and cream cheese. Add sugar, vanilla, and unbeaten egg yolk. Beat until light. Add flour and salt, then mix well. Drop by teaspoonfuls onto an ungreased cookie sheet. Top each cookie with a cherry or pecan. Bake at 350° for 10-12 minutes or until a *very* light brown. Makes 2 dozen.

IMAGINATION COOKIES   Mrs. Ferlin L. Yoder

1 box cake mix, any flavor   ½ cup vegetable oil
2 eggs

Combine all ingredients in a mixer bowl. Mix well. Add 1 tablespoon water
if necessary to have desired consistency. Drop by spoonful onto greased
cookie sheet. Bake at 350° for 10 minutes. Makes 2-3 dozen cookies.

VARIATIONS:
Oatmeal Cookies: Add ¾ cup oats, 1 egg, and ¼ cup brown sugar to
original recipe.

Double Chocolate: Use chocolate cake mix with original recipe and add 1
cup chocolate chips.

Chocolate Chip: Use yellow cake mix and add 1 package chocolate chips.

Coconut-Almond: Use white cake mix and add 1 cup coconut and 1
teaspoon almond extract.

Banana Spice: Use spice cake mix. Add ½ cup mashed bananas and ½
cup chopped nuts.

LEBKUEN   Mrs. Martha Wengerd

1 pound lard   1 teaspoon nutmeg
1 quart brown sugar   1 teaspoon ginger
1 quart molasses   ½ tablespoon salt
2½ tablespoons baking soda   13 cups flour
1 quart buttermilk   1 quart walnuts or pecans
1 tablespoon cinnamon   1 pound raisins, chopped

Mix together lard, sugar, and molasses until creamy. Add baking soda to
buttermilk and add alternately with dry ingredients to creamed mixture.
Last add nuts and raisins.

Mix and let sit in a cool place for several days. Bake at 350° for 20-25
minutes and then store for several days in a cool place.

LITTLE DEBBIES

Ruth Yoder, Mrs. Gerald Lambright

1 cup margarine
4 eggs
1½ teaspoons nutmeg
3 cups brown sugar
2 teaspoons cinnamon

1 teaspoon baking soda
½ teaspoon baking powder
3 cups flour
3 cups oatmeal

FILLING:
2 egg whites
2 teaspoons vanilla
4 tablespoons milk

4 cups powdered sugar, divided
1 cup Crisco shortening (scant)

Cream first 7 ingredients. Add flour and oatmeal last. Bake at 350° for 8-10 minutes until done. Do not overbake.

Make filling by beating egg whites, then add vanilla, milk, and 2 cups powdered sugar. Beat thoroughly, then add remaining 2 cups powdered sugar and the shortening.

Place filling on cookie and place another cookie on top, sandwich-style. Makes 5-6 dozen.

MAPLE DROP COOKIES

Mrs. Sol Yoder, Sr.

1 cup shortening or butter
2 cups brown sugar
3 eggs
½ teaspoon salt

1 teaspoon baking soda
4 cups flour
¾ cup milk
¾ cup nuts

ICING:
¼ cup butter
1 teaspoon maple flavoring
1 beaten egg

2 cups powdered sugar
2 tablespoons water

Cream shortening or butter and sugar; add eggs and beat well. Add salt and soda to flour, and mix. Add dry ingredients alternately with milk. Add nuts and mix well. Drop by teaspoonful on cookie sheet. Bake at 350° for 8-10 minutes. Makes 4 dozen.

Icing: Brown butter. Let cool. Add flavoring, egg, and powdered sugar. Add water last to desired consistency, and spread on cookies.

MOLASSES CRINKLES

Betty Yoder

1 cup brown sugar
¾ cup shortening
1 egg
⅓ cup molasses
2¼ cups flour

½ teaspoon salt
2 teaspoons baking soda
1 teaspoon cinnamon
1 teaspoon ginger
½ teaspoon cloves

Cream sugar and shortening. Add egg and molasses and beat well. Sift flour, salt, baking soda, and spices. Add dry ingredients to creamed mixture and mix thoroughly. Shape in balls and roll in white sugar. Bake for 12-15 minutes at 350°.

MONSTER COOKIES

Rhoda Hilty

3 eggs, beaten
1 cup brown sugar
1 cup white sugar
1 teaspoon vanilla
1 teaspoon pancake syrup
2 teaspoons baking soda

½ cup butter
1½ cups peanut butter
4½ cups oatmeal
½ cup chocolate chips
½ cup M&M's candy

Cream first 8 ingredients. Add oatmeal, chocolate chips, and M&M's last. Bake at 350° for about 12 minutes. Do not overbake. Makes 4½ dozen.

AMISH OATMEAL COOKIES

Mrs. Eli Kauffman

1½ cups raisins
1 cup salted peanuts
6 cups sifted flour
3 teaspoons baking powder
1 teaspoon salt
1 teaspoon each nutmeg and
    cinnamon

1½ cups shortening
3 cups sugar
2 cups quick-cooking oats
3 teaspoons baking soda
1 cup buttermilk
½ cup dark molasses
4 eggs, divided

Grind raisins and peanuts. Sift flour, baking powder, salt, nutmeg, and cinnamon. Stir in shortening with pastry blender until mixture forms fine crumbs. Add raisins, nuts, sugar, and oats; mix well. Dissolve baking soda in buttermilk; add molasses and 3 eggs. Beat well. Add to flour mixture and mix well with spoon. Drop by heaping tablespoon about 3 inches apart. Flatten each with floured bottom of glass to 2½-inch round. Beat 1 egg and brush tops of unbaked cookies. Bake at 375° for 8-10 minutes. Makes 4½ dozen.

JULIA'S OATMEAL COOKIES   Barbara Kauffman

2 cups brown sugar
1 cup shortening
2 eggs
1½ cups sifted flour
½ teaspoon salt

1 teaspoon baking powder
1 teaspoon baking soda
1 teaspoon vanilla
3 cups oatmeal

Cream sugar, shortening, and eggs. Add flour, salt, baking powder, and baking soda. Add vanilla and oatmeal. Chill, then form into 1-inch balls. Roll in powdered sugar and place on greased cookie sheets. Bake at 350° for 8 minutes. Makes 3 dozen.

Sometimes I add chocolate chips or butterscotch chips to the batter—then I don't roll the balls in powdered sugar.

Only this hour is mine, Lord;
May it be used for Thee;
May every passing moment
Count for eternity.

OATMEAL-PEANUT BUTTER   Deborah Kauffman
CHOCOLATE CHIP COOKIES

½ cup butter or margarine,
    softened
1 (18 ounce) jar chunky peanut
    butter
1½ cups sugar
1½ cups firmly packed brown
    sugar

4 large eggs
1 teaspoon vanilla extract
6 cups quick-cooking oats
    (uncooked)
2½ teaspoons baking soda
1 cup semi-sweet chocolate
    morsels

Beat butter or margarine and peanut butter at medium speed with an electric mixer until fluffy; gradually add sugars, beating well. Add eggs and vanilla, mixing well.

Combine oats and baking soda; add to butter mixture, mixing well. Stir in chocolate morsels and drop by tablespoonfuls onto ungreased cookie sheets. Bake at 350° for 9-10 minutes. Cool on cookie sheets 5 minutes before removing. Makes 7 dozen cookies.

OATMEAL DROP COOKIES
Debbie Graber

½ cup oil
½ cup margarine
1 cup white sugar
1 cup brown sugar
1 teaspoon vanilla
2 cups all-purpose flour

1 teaspoon baking soda
½ teaspoon baking powder
½ teaspoon salt
2 cups oatmeal
2 cups raisins (or chocolate chips)

Cream together first 5 ingredients. Next add flour, baking soda, baking powder, and salt. Stir in oats (old fashion oats are best) and raisins or chocolate chips. Bake for 12-15 minutes at 350°. Take out of oven before they look done. Makes 3-4 dozen cookies.

PEANUT BUTTER COOKIES
Miriam Yoder

5 sticks margarine
2½ cups white sugar
2½ cups brown sugar
5 eggs
2½ cups peanut butter

2½ teaspoons baking powder
3¾ teaspoons baking soda
1 teaspoon salt
5 cups flour

Cream together margarine, sugars, and eggs. Add peanut butter and mix well. Add dry ingredients. Drop by teaspoonful on cookie sheet and bake at 350° for 8-10 minutes. Makes 8 or 9 dozen.

PEANUT BUTTER COOKIES
Rose Yoder

¾ cup peanut butter
½ cup Crisco shortening
1¼ cups brown sugar
3 tablespoons milk
1 tablespoon vanilla

1 egg
1¾ cups flour
¾ teaspoon salt
¾ teaspoon baking soda

Combine the first 5 ingredients and mix well. Add egg and mix until well blended. Add flour, salt, and baking soda and mix until well blended. Drop by heaping teaspoonfuls on cookie sheet. Flatten slightly with fork. Bake at 375° for 7-8 minutes. Makes 3 dozen.

PEANUT BUTTER CHEWS
Betty Yoder

1 quart Karo syrup
1 quart sugar

1 quart peanut butter
5 quarts corn flakes

Bring the syrup and sugar to a boil. Stir in peanut butter and pour over corn flakes. Drop by teaspoon onto waxed paper and allow to cool.

PEANUT BUTTER SANDWICH COOKIES   Rhoda Hilty

3 cups butter
3 cups white sugar
3 cups brown sugar
6 eggs
3 cups peanut butter

3 teaspoons vanilla
9 cups flour
6 teaspoons baking soda
1½ teaspoons salt

PEANUT BUTTER FILLING:
1½ cups peanut butter
3 teaspoons vanilla

12 tablespoons milk
9 cups powdered sugar

Cream butter and sugars; add eggs one at a time. Add peanut butter and vanilla; stir in flour, baking soda, and salt. Bake at 350° for 12 minutes. Fill cookies with Peanut Butter Filling.

Beat peanut butter, vanilla, and milk. Add powdered sugar. Put filling on one cookie and top with another and enjoy your peanut butter sandwich cookie! Makes about 3 dozen.

PINEAPPLE DROP COOKIES   Rhoda Yoder

2 cups flour
¼ teaspoon salt
¼ teaspoon baking soda
1 teaspoon baking powder
½ cup shortening
½ cup brown sugar

½ cup white sugar
1 egg
1 teaspoon vanilla
½ cup crushed pineapple, drained
½ cup chopped nuts

Measure dry ingredients. Add to creamed shortening, sugars, egg, and vanilla. Mix well and add pineapple and nuts. Drop by teaspoonfuls onto a cookie sheet. Bake at 350° for 8-10 minutes. Makes 2-3 dozen.

POINSETTIA COOKIES   Debbie Graber

2 cups powdered sugar
1 cup margarine
2 eggs
1 teaspoon vanilla
½ teaspoon rum extract

3 cups flour
1 teaspoon salt
1 cup coconut
1 cup butterscotch chips, divided
½ cup candied red cherries

Beat together sugar and margarine. Add eggs and extracts. Mix in flour and salt. Stir in coconut and ¾ cup butterscotch chips. Chill dough. Roll into 1-inch balls and place on cookie sheet. Flatten with a glass dipped in sugar. Place a butterscotch chip in middle. Cut cherries in wedges and place around chip. Bake at 375° for 15 minutes. Makes 3 dozen.

POTATO CHIP COOKIES

Mrs. Merle Overholt

1 cup shortening
1 cup brown sugar
1 cup granulated sugar
2 well-beaten eggs
2 cups flour

1 teaspoon baking soda
2 cups potato chip, crushed
1 small package butterscotch
  morsels
1 teaspoon vanilla

Cream shortening and sugars. Add eggs, then flour and baking soda which have been sifted together. Add potato chips, butterscotch morsels, and vanilla. Shape into walnut-sized balls and bake on ungreased cookie sheet at 325° for 10-12 minutes. Makes 2½-3 dozen.

QUICK AND EASY COOKIES

Alta Kauffman, Ruth Yoder

1 box cake mix, any flavor
2 eggs

⅔ cup oil

Mix and drop on greased cookie sheet. Bake at 350° until done, 10-12 minutes. Simple, but delicious.

RAISIN COOKIES

Mrs. Amanda Yoder,
Alta Kauffman, Mrs. David Wengerd

1½ cups raisins
1 cup water
1 cup shortening
1½ cups sugar
2 eggs

3½ cups flour
½ teaspoon salt
1 teaspoon baking soda
1 teaspoon vanilla

Boil raisins in water until water is absorbed. Set aside until cool. Cream shortening and add sugar. Add eggs and vanilla and beat well. Add dry ingredients and raisins. Make dough into small balls and roll in sugar. Place on baking sheets but do not flatten. Bake at 325°-350° for 8-10 minutes until light brown. Makes 2½-3 dozen.

Tip: To keep thread from twisting and knotting, pull through a fabric softener sheet.

SOUR CREAM REFRIGERATOR COOKIES   Donna Stephens

1 cup butter or margarine
1 cup sugar
2½ cups sifted plain flour
¼ teaspoon salt
¼ teaspoon baking soda

2 teaspoons cinnamon
½ teaspoon cloves
½ teaspoon nutmeg
¼ cup sour cream
1 cup chopped nuts

Cream sugar and butter until well blended. Set aside. Sift together dry ingredients and spices. Beat into butter or margarine mixture alternately with sour cream. Beat in chopped nuts. Form into bars and freeze. Slice thin and bake at 375° for about 8 minutes.

Wrapped in plastic wrap and aluminum foil, these will keep in the freezer about 1 year.

Cover my eyes to make me blind
To the petty faults I should not find
Open my eyes and let me see
The friend my neighbor tries to be.

SNICKERDOODLES   Judi Wagher, Heidi Kauffman

1 stick butter
1 stick margarine
1½ cups sugar
2 eggs

2¾ cups flour
2 teaspoons cream of tartar
1 teaspoon baking soda
¼ teaspoon salt

Heat oven to 400°. Mix butter, margarine, sugar, and eggs thoroughly. Blend all dry ingredients; stir into egg mixture. Roll into balls the size of small walnuts. Roll in a mixture of 2 tablespoons sugar and 2 teaspoons cinnamon. Place on ungreased baking sheet. Bake at 400° for 8-10 minutes. These cookies puff up at first, then flatten out. Don't overbake — bottom should be lightly browned. Makes about 5 dozen 2-inch cookies.

GOLDEN SUGAR COOKIES   Drusilla Beiler

1 cup butter
2 cups sugar
½ teaspoon vanilla
½ teaspoon lemon flavoring
3 egg yolks

2½ cups flour
1 teaspoon baking soda
¼ teaspoon salt
1 teaspoon cream of tartar

Cream butter, sugar, and flavorings together until fluffy. Add egg yolks one at a time, beating well after each addition. Combine dry ingredients gradually to creamed mixture. Roll into 1-inch balls. Place in a container with sugar. Coat well and place on ungreased cookie sheets. Bake at 350° for 10 minutes. Makes 3 dozen.

FAVORITE TEA CAKES

Ruth Yoder

½ cup butter or margarine,
    softened
1 cup sugar
1 egg
1 teaspoon vanilla extract
1 teaspoon grated lemon rind

2¾ cups all-purpose flour
½ teaspoon baking soda
½ teaspoon salt
¼ cup buttermilk
Sugar

Cream butter and gradually add sugar, beating well at medium speed of electric mixer. Add egg, vanilla, and lemon rind; beat well. Combine flour, baking soda, and salt in medium bowl; add to creamed mixture alternately with buttermilk, beginning and ending with flour mixture. Cover dough and refrigerate 2 hours. Roll dough to ¼-inch thickness on a lightly floured surface. Cut with 2-inch cookie cutter and place on lightly greased baking sheets; sprinkle with sugar. Bake at 375° for 6-8 minutes or until edges are lightly brown. Cool on wire racks. No tea party is complete without these light, soft, delicious tea cakes. Makes 3-4 dozen.

WHOO-PIE PIES

Barbara Hershberger

1 cup margarine
2 cups white sugar
1 teaspoon vanilla
4 eggs (separate 2 and
    reserve the whites)
2 teaspoons baking soda

1 cup hot water
4½ cups flour
⅔ cup cocoa
2 teaspoons baking powder
1 cup sour milk or buttermilk

FILLING:
2 egg whites (reserved from above
    recipe)
2 cups Crisco shortening
6 cups powdered sugar

8 teaspoons milk
8 teaspoons flour
4 teaspoons vanilla

Mix together margarine, sugar, vanilla, and eggs (except 2 whites). Add baking soda to water and add to sugar mixture. Add dry ingredients alternately with sour milk or buttermilk. Drop by teaspoonfuls on cookie sheet. Bake at 400° for 6-7 minutes.

Filling: Beat the 2 reserved egg whites until stiff. In another bowl, mix shortening, powdered sugar, milk, flour, and vanilla. Add whipped egg whites and beat until real fluffy. Put filling between 2 cookies. Makes 2-3 dozen.

PUMPKIN WHOOPIES

Linda Zook

1 pound brown sugar
1 cup Crisco shortening
2 cups pumpkin
2 eggs
3½ cups flour
1 teaspoon cinnamon

1 teaspoon cloves
1 teaspoon ginger
1 teaspoon salt
1 teaspoon baking powder
1 teaspoon baking soda
1 teaspoon vanilla

Mix sugar and shortening. Add pumpkin and eggs. Add dry ingredients. Bake at 350° for 12 minutes.

VANILLA WHOOPIE PIES

Linda Zook

1 cup shortening
2 cups sugar
¾ teaspoon salt
2 whole eggs plus 2 egg yolks
2 teaspoons baking soda

½ cup hot water
5 cups flour
1 teaspoon baking powder
½ cup buttermilk
1 tablespoon vanilla

FILLING:
2 egg whites
1 tablespoon vanilla

2 cups confectioners sugar
1½ cups Crisco shortening

Cream first 4 ingredients until smooth. Dissolve soda in hot water. Add dry ingredients alternately with buttermilk. Add water and vanilla. Drop on cookie sheet. Bake at 400° for 8-10 minutes.

Filling: Beat egg whites until foamy. Add remaining ingredients, and beat on high speed until fluffy. Spread on cookie and top with another cookie. Makes 2 or 3 dozen filled cookies.

BROWNIES

Miriam Yoder

1½ sticks margarine
1½ cups sugar
½ cup water
2 cups chocolate chips
2 teaspoons vanilla

4 eggs
1½ cups flour
½ teaspoon soda
½ teaspoon salt
1 cup chopped nuts

Melt margarine in saucepan. Add sugar and water; bring to a boil. Pour boiling mixture into bowl and add chocolate chips and vanilla. Stir until chips are dissolved. Add beaten eggs and mix well, then add flour, baking soda, salt, and nuts. Mix together. Pour into a greased 11x15-inch pan Bake at 350° for 20-25 minutes. These brownies are good without frosting.

BLONDE BROWNIES

Debbie Graber

⅔ cup margarine
2½ cups brown sugar
3 eggs
2¾ cups flour
1½ teaspoons baking powder
½ teaspoon salt

1 teaspoon vanilla
½ cup chopped nuts
2 teaspoons milk
Chocolate chips, optional
Butterscotch chips

Melt margarine over low heat. Remove from heat and add brown sugar. Stir until blended. Cool, then stir in eggs. Sift flour, baking powder, and salt together and stir into mixture. Add milk, vanilla, nuts, and butterscotch chips. Spread in well greased 9x13-inch pan and bake at 350° for 20 minutes, until when lightly touched with finger, only slight imprint remains. Don't overbake. Cut in squares while warm. Makes 25 servings.

FUDGE BROWNIES

Mrs. Shirley Yoder

1⅓ cups flour
2 cups sugar
¾ cup baking cocoa
1 teaspoon baking powder
½ teaspoon salt

½ cup chopped nuts
⅔ cup oil
4 eggs, slightly beaten
2 teaspoons vanilla

Combine flour, sugar, cocoa, baking powder, salt, and nuts. Set aside. Combine oil, eggs, and vanilla and add to dry ingredients. Do not overmix. Spread in 9x13-inch pan and bake at 350° for 20-25 minutes. Makes 24.

*Those are most valuable sermons where one man
is both the preacher and the congregation.*

FRUIT BARS OR COOKIES

Rhoda Yoder

½ cup dates
½ cup prunes
½ cup raisins
1 cup water
½ cup butter

2 eggs, beaten
1 cup flour (or ½ cup each
   of flour and oatmeal)
1 teaspoon baking soda
Nuts (as desired)

Cook dates, prunes, raisins, and water for 3-5 minutes. Add butter and cool. Add rest of ingredients, mixing well. Bake at 350° as bars or drop cookies.

BLUEBERRY BARS
Heidi Kauffman

1¾ cups sugar
1 cup margarine
4 eggs
1 teaspoon vanilla

3 cups flour
1½ teaspoons baking powder
½ teaspoon salt
2 cans blueberry pie filling

Mix first 7 ingredients together. Press ¾ of dough into large greased cookie sheet. Spread blueberry pie filling on top. Add the rest of the dough by small spoonful drops on top. Bake at 350° for 30-35 minutes. *Do not overbake.* Makes 15-20 bars.

CARAMEL SQUARES
Mrs. John Nissley

½ cup butter
½ cup sugar
2 egg yolks
1 teaspoon baking powder .
1½ cups flour

1 teaspoon vanilla
2 egg whites
1 cup light brown sugar
1 cup nuts

Cream butter and sugar; add egg yolks. Sift dry ingredients and add, stirring well. Last add vanilla. Spread on a buttered 8-inch square pan.

Beat 2 egg whites. Add brown sugar and nuts. Blend and spread over first mixture. Bake 30 minutes or until brown in 350° oven. When cool, cut into squares. Makes 16.

CHEESE CAKE BARS
Ruth Yoder

1 cup flour
⅓ cup brown sugar
6 tablespoons butter, softened
1 (8 ounce) package cream
  cheese, softened
¼ cup sugar

1 egg
2 tablespoons milk
¼ teaspoon fresh lemon zest
¼ teaspoon lemon juice
½ teaspoon vanilla
2 tablespoons chopped walnuts

In large mixing bowl, combine flour and brown sugar. Cut in butter until mixture forms fine crumbs. Reserve 1 cup for topping. Press remainder of crumbs over bottom of ungreased 8x8-inch pan. Bake for 12 minutes or until lightly browned. In mixer bowl, thoroughly cream together cream cheese and granulated sugar. Add egg, milk, lemon peel, lemon juice, and vanilla. Beat well and spread batter over partially baked crust. Combine walnuts with reserved crumb mixture and sprinkle over all. Bake for 20-25 minutes at 350°. Cool and cut in squares. Makes 9-12 squares.

FUDGY MINT CHEESECAKE BARS

Mrs. Eli Kauffman

4 (1 ounce) bars Hershey's unsweetened baking chocolate
10 tablespoons margarine
2 cups sugar
4 eggs
2 teaspoons vanilla extract
1 cup unsifted flour

1 (8 ounce) package cream cheese, softened
1 tablespoon cornstarch
1 (14 ounce) can Eagle brand sweetened condensed milk
1 teaspoon peppermint extract
Green food coloring, optional

GLAZE:
1 cup semi-sweet chocolate chips   ½ cup unwhipped whipping cream

Preheat oven to 350°. Melt chocolate with ½ cup margarine. In bowl, combine chocolate mixture with sugar, 3 eggs, vanilla, and flour. Spread in greased 13x9-inch baking pan. Bake 12 minutes. In mixer bowl, beat cheese, 2 tablespoons margarine, and cornstarch until fluffy. Gradually beat in sweetened condensed milk, then remaining ingredients. Pour over brownie layer. Bake 30 minutes or until set. Top with glaze. Makes 24-36 bars.

Glaze: Melt chocolate chips with whipping cream. Cook and stir until thickened.

CHOCOLATE CHIP BARS

Mrs. Vivian Miller, Carolyn Eash

2 cups flour
2 cups sugar
2 teaspoons baking powder
1½ teaspoons salt

2 cups chocolate chips
4 eggs, beaten
½ cup butter, melted
1 teaspoon vanilla

PEANUT BUTTER ICING:
¼ cup peanut butter   ¼-⅓ cup milk
3 cups sifted confectioners sugar

Combine dry ingredients with chocolate chips in large mixing bowl. Beat eggs until light and fluffy, 1-2 minutes. Add eggs, melted butter, and vanilla to dry ingredients. Stir to mix. Pour into 9x13-inch cake pan. Bake at 350° for 25-30 minutes. Do not overbake. Cool, and ice with peanut butter icing and cut into bars. Makes 3 dozen.

Peanut Butter Icing: Stir peanut butter, sugar, and milk together until creamy.

CHOCOROONS
Mrs. Ferlin L. Yoder

½ cup butter or margarine
⅓ cup white sugar
⅓ cup brown sugar, packed
1 egg
1 teaspoon vanilla

½ teaspoon salt
½ teaspoon baking soda
1 cup flour
1 cup chocolate chips
½ cup coconut

Cream together first 7 ingredients. Blend in flour. Add chocolate chips and coconut. Spread in greased pan. Bake at 375° for 15-20 minutes or until lightly brown. Makes 3 dozen.

COCONUT BARS
Rhoda Yoder

½ cup margarine or butter
½ cup brown sugar
1 cup flour
¾ cup brown sugar

½ cup flour
Dash salt
1 cup coconut flakes
2 eggs, beaten

Cream first 3 ingredients. Press into 9x13-inch pan. Bake 10 minutes at 350°. Mix remaining ingredients and spread over top. Bake 18-20 minutes at 350°. Makes 3 dozen.

COCONUT CHOCOLATE MERINGUE BITS
Esther Mast

¾ cup margarine
½ cup brown sugar
½ cup granulated sugar
3 eggs, separated
1 teaspoon vanilla
2 cups flour
1 teaspoon baking powder

1 teaspoon baking soda
¼ teaspoon salt
1 cup chocolate chips
1 cup coconut
¾ cup chopped nuts, optional
1 cup brown sugar

Mix margarine, ½ cup brown sugar, granulated sugar, egg yolks, and vanilla. Beat 2 minutes. Blend flour, baking powder, baking soda, and salt together. Mix in thoroughly with first mixture. Spread or pat dough in 13x9½x2-inch pan. Sprinkle chocolate chips, coconut, and nuts on top of dough in layers.

Beat egg whites until frothy. Add 1 cup brown sugar gradually, beating until stiff. Spread this over top layer.

Bake 35-40 minutes at 350°. Cool and cut into bars. Makes 40-60 bars.

EASY CHOCOLATE ÉCLAIR SQUARES
Judi Wagher

1 (14 ounce) box graham crackers
2 (4 ounce) packages French vanilla pudding
3 cups milk
12 ounces Cool Whip whipped topping

3 ounces semi-sweet chocolate chips
2 teaspoons light corn syrup
3 teaspoons butter
1 teaspoon vanilla extract
3 tablespoons milk
1½ cups powdered sugar

Line a 9x13-inch glass casserole dish with whole graham crackers. Whip the pudding mixes and milk together. Mixture will be thick. Fold in Cool Whip. Spread half the mixture over the graham crackers. Repeat the cracker and pudding mixture layers. Top with a layer of crackers. Prepare icing by melting the chocolate chips, syrup, and butter together in the microwave. Stir in vanilla, sugar, and milk. Spread over top layer of graham crackers. Refrigerate overnight. Makes 12-16 servings.

FRUIT BARS
Ellen D. Miller

2 cups flour
1¾ cups oatmeal
1 teaspoon baking soda
1 teaspoon vanilla

½ cup brown sugar, packed
1 cup margarine
1 quart pie filling

Combine all ingredients but pie filling. Put ½ of dry ingredients in a 13x9-inch pan. Spread on filling. Put rest of crumbs on top. Bake at 350° for 30-45 minutes. Serves 15.

*The doctrine of grace humbles a man without degrading him
and exalts him without inflating him.*

GOOEY BUTTER CAKE BARS
Silla Yoder

1 box yellow cake mix
1 stick butter

1 egg

TOPPING:
2 eggs
1 (8 ounce) package cream cheese

1 pound powdered sugar

Mix first 3 ingredients and press into greased 9x13-inch pan. Beat topping ingredients and pour over bottom layer. Bake at 350° for 40-45 minutes. Makes 15 servings.

GRAHAM CRACKER BARS

Lena Schrock

2 sticks margarine, melted
1 cup sugar
1 egg
½ cup milk

1 cup graham cracker crumbs
1 cup coconut
1 cup chopped nuts (any kind)

ICING:
1 stick soft margarine
1 box confectioners sugar

1 teaspoon vanilla
2 teaspoons milk

Cream margarine and sugar. Beat egg into milk and add to sugar mixture. Stir in cracker crumbs, coconut, and nuts. Heat to bubbling, about 5 minutes. Line pan (oblong works best) with whole graham crackers. Spread cooked mixture over crackers. Add another layer of crackers. Cool before icing.

Icing: Mix all ingredients well. Spread on top of crackers. Chill or freeze. Cut into approximately 20 bars.

GRANOLA BARS

Melody Kauffman

7 cups baby oats
1 cup sunflower seeds
1 cup coconut
1 cup oat bran
1 cup wheat germ
1 cup almonds or pecans
1 cup walnuts
½ cup powdered milk
2 cups crispy rice

2 cups raisins
2 cups chocolate chips
1 cup honey
1 cup corn syrup
2 cups sugar
2 tablespoons vanilla
4 tablespoons molasses
2 cups peanut butter

Mix all dry ingredients. Boil together the honey, corn syrup, and sugar. Remove from heat and add vanilla, molasses, and peanut butter. Pour over dry ingredients and mix thoroughly. With greased fingers, press mixture into 2 (9x13-inch) pans. Cool completely and cut into approximately 48 bars.

LEMON BARS

Ruth Yoder

1 cup flour
¼ cup powdered sugar
½ cup butter
2 tablespoons flour
½ teaspoon baking powder

2 eggs, beaten
1 cup sugar
Rind of 1 lemon, grated
3 tablespoons lemon juice
Powdered sugar

Combine 1 cup flour, ¼ cup powdered sugar, and butter. Mix well. Press into 9-inch square pan and bake at 350° for 20 minutes. Combine 2 tablespoons flour and baking powder. Set aside. Combine eggs, sugar, rind, and lemon juice and beat well. Stir dry ingredients into egg mixture. Pour over baked crust. Bake at 350° for 25 minutes or until browned. Sprinkle powdered sugar on top. Cool and cut into squares. Makes 12 squares.

PEANUT BUTTER FINGERS

Heidi Kauffman

1 cup flour
½ cup sugar
½ cup brown sugar
½ teaspoon baking soda
¼ teaspoon salt

1 egg
½ teaspoon vanilla
⅓ cup creamy peanut butter
1 cup quick rolled oats
1 cup chocolate chips

PEANUT BUTTER DRIZZLE:
¼ cup creamy peanut butter
2-4 tablespoons milk

½ cup powdered sugar

Press mixture of flour, sugars, baking soda, salt, egg, vanilla, ⅓ cup creamy peanut butter, and oats into a greased 9x13-inch pan. Bake at 350° for 20 minutes. Sprinkle immediately with chocolate chips. Let stand 5 minutes. Spread evenly.

Mix Peanut Butter Drizzle ingredients. Spread over bars. Cool and cut into 24-28 bars.

Once His gifts I wanted,
now the Giver own;
Once I sought for blessings,
now Himself alone. — A.B. Simpson

CHEWY PEANUT BUTTER BARS
Carolyn Eash

1 cup all-purpose flour
⅓ cup sugar

½ cup butter or margarine

FILLING:
2 eggs
½ corn syrup
½ cup sugar
¼ cup crunchy peanut butter

¼ teaspoon salt
½ cup flaked coconut
½ cup semi-sweet chocolate chips

In a bowl, combine flour and sugar; cut in the butter or margarine until crumbly. Press into a greased 13x9-inch baking pan. Bake at 350° for 14-16 minutes or until lightly browned. In a mixing bowl, mix eggs, corn syrup, sugar, peanut butter, and salt until smooth. Fold in coconut and chocolate chips. Pour over crust. Return to oven for 15-20 minutes or until golden. Makes 3 dozen.

PECAN DELIGHTS
Alta Kauffman

2¼ cups packed brown sugar
1 cup butter or margarine
1 cup light corn syrup
⅛ teaspoon salt
1 (14 ounce) can sweetened
  condensed milk

1 teaspoon vanilla
1½ pounds whole pecans
1 cup milk chocolate chips
1 cup semi-sweet chocolate chips
2 tablespoons shortening

In a large saucepan, combine the first 4 ingredients. Cook over medium heat until all sugar is dissolved. Gradually add milk and mix well. Continue cooking until candy thermometer reads 248° (firm ball stage). Remove from heat; stir in vanilla. Stir in the pecans. Drop by tablespoonfuls onto waxed paper. Chill until firm. Melt chocolate chips and shortening in microwave or double boiler. Drizzle over each cluster. Cool.

RICE KRISPIE DELUXE
Ellen D. Miller, Mrs. Ferlin L. Yoder

1½ pounds white chocolate or
  almond bark
1 cup peanut butter

3 cups marshmallows
9 cups Rice Krispies cereal

Melt together white chocolate and peanut butter. Pour over marshmallows and Rice Krispies. Mix well and press in 13x9-inch pan. Chill and cut to desired size.

PECAN SQUARES
Denise Smith

CRUST:
3 cups all-purpose flour
½ cup sugar

1 cup softened butter
½ teaspoon salt

FILLING:
4 eggs
1½ cups corn syrup
1½ cups sugar

3 tablespoons melted butter
1½ teaspoons vanilla extract
2½ cups chopped pecans

Using large mixing bowl, blend flour, sugar, butter, and salt until crumbly. Press firmly and evenly into a pre-greased 15x10-inch baking pan. Bake at 350° for 20 minutes. Meanwhile, in another bowl, combine filling ingredients (except pecans). Mix well, then stir in pecans. Spread evenly over hot crust. Bake at 350° for 25 minutes or until set. Cool on wire rack. Makes 4 dozen.

EASY PUMPKIN BARS
Barbara Kauffman, Faith Miller, Elva Byler

2 cups flour
2 teaspoons baking powder
½ teaspoon salt
2 teaspoons cinnamon
4 eggs

2 cups pumpkin, mashed and
  cooked
1 teaspoon baking soda
2 cups sugar
1 cup oil

ICING:
1 (3 ounce) package cream cheese
¾ stick margarine, melted
1 tablespoon cream or milk

1 teaspoon vanilla
1⅓ cups powdered sugar

Mix flour, baking powder, salt, cinnamon, eggs, pumpkin, baking soda, sugar, and oil very well, and pour into a 13x9-inch cake pan. Bake at 350° for 25 minutes. Cool.

Cream together icing ingredients; spread on cake when cool. This is a nice recipe for a child to mix together and is delicious! Makes 24 bars.

Barbara Kauffman adds 1 cup nuts or raisins to hers, and no icing.

If we want an increase of Christ, there must be a decrease of self.

FROSTED PUMPKIN BARS
Miriam Yoder

4 eggs, beaten
1 cup salad oil
2 cups sugar
1 cup pumpkin
½ teaspoon salt

2 teaspoons cinnamon
1 teaspoon baking soda
1 teaspoon baking powder
2 cups flour
1 cup nuts or raisins (optional)

Combine all ingredients well and pour into a greased and floured cookie sheet. Bake at 350° for 20-25 minutes. Frost with cream cheese frosting. Makes 36 bars.

PUMPKIN CAKE BARS
Carolyn Eash

4 eggs, well beaten
2 cups pumpkin
1½ cups sugar
¼ teaspoon salt
1 teaspoon ginger

1 teaspoon cinnamon
½ teaspoon cloves
1 box yellow cake mix
½ cup butter, melted
1 cup chopped pecans

Mix eggs, pumpkin, sugar, salt, ginger, cinnamon, and cloves. Pour into greased 9x13-inch cake pan. Sprinkle dry cake mix on top. Drizzle melted butter over cake mix. Spread chopped nuts over all. Bake at 325° for 1 hour and 20 minutes. Makes 24-28 bars.

ROYAL ROMANCE BARS
Mrs. Roger Helmuth, Sr.

CRUST:
1 cup flour
½ cup butter

2 tablespoons white sugar

FILLING:
2 eggs, beaten
1¼ cups brown sugar
½ cup chopped nuts
½ cup coconut

2 tablespoons flour
¼ teaspoon salt
½ teaspoon baking powder

Blend flour, butter, and sugar. Stir until crumbly. Press firmly into 8x8-inch pan. Bake at 400° for 8 minutes, or until very light brown.

Combine and mix filling ingredients and spread into baked crust. Bake at 325° for 20-30 minutes until golden brown. Should be very moist. (Be careful not to overbake). Makes 12 bars.

ROCKY ROAD FUDGE BARS

Drusilla Beiler

½ cup margarine
1 square unsweetened chocolate
1 cup sugar
1 cup all-purpose flour

½ cup pecans
1 teaspoon baking powder
1 teaspoon vanilla
2 eggs

FILLING:
1 (8 ounce) package cream cheese
  (reserve 2 ounces for frosting)
½ cup sugar
2 tablespoons flour

¼ cup margarine
1 egg
½ cup pecans
3 tablespoons marshmallow creme

FROSTING:
¼ cup margarine
1 square unsweetened chocolate
2 ounces cream cheese (reserved
  from filling ingredients)

¼ cup milk
3 cups powdered sugar
1 teaspoon vanilla

In glass bowl on low heat of microwave, melt chocolate and margarine. Add remaining bar ingredients. Mix well. Spread in a 9x13-inch Pam-sprayed pan.

Mix cream cheese and add the rest of filling ingredients except for marshmallow creme. Spread over first layer and bake at 350° for 25-30 minutes, or until toothpick comes out clean. Remove from oven and spread marshmallow creme over bars.

In glass bowl, melt margarine, chocolate, cream cheese, and milk in microwave on low heat. Add 3 cups powdered sugar and vanilla. Pour bars and swirl with marshmallow creme. Makes 3 or 4 dozen bars.

TOFFEE NUT BARS

Edna Schrock

1 cup butter
1 cup brown sugar
1 egg yolk
2 cups flour

1 teaspoon vanilla
6 ounces chocolate chips
1 cup chopped pecans

Cream butter and sugar until light. Add egg yolk and mix well. Add flour, stirring until well blended. Add vanilla. Press in 9x13-inch pan. Bake 20-25 minutes at 350°. While in oven, distribute chocolate chips on top and spread gently. Sprinkle pecans on top. Cut while warm. Makes 2 dozen bars.

TWINKIES

Martha Schrock, Ruth Yoder

1 box chocolate or yellow cake mix
  with pudding
½ cup oil

4 eggs
1 cup water

FILLING:
1 cup milk
4 tablespoons flour
1 cup granulated sugar
½ cup margarine

½ cup Crisco shortening
1 teaspoon vanilla
Pinch of salt

Beat cake mix and other ingredients together. Divide in 2 greased and floured cookie sheets lined with wax paper. Bake at 350° for 15 minutes.

Filling: Blend and shake milk and flour together. Cook milk and flour until paste-consistency. Set aside and cool (refrigerator cold). Beat other ingredients together. Add flour and milk mixture. Beat until fluffy. Remove cake from pan onto a large tray. Discard paper. Spread filling over first layer and put second layer on top. (Cut in 1x3-inch pieces).

YUM YUM BROWNIES

Rachel Swarey

2 cups white sugar
¾ cup margarine
4 eggs
1 teaspoon vanilla

½ cup chopped nuts
1 cup all-purpose flour
½ teaspoon salt
½ cup cocoa

Cream sugar and margarine well. Add eggs, vanilla, and nuts. Sift together dry ingredients. Add to sugar mixture and stir well. Bake in greased and floured 8x14-inch pan at 350° until it shrinks from edges of pan. *Do not overbake.*

> *Man may whitewash himself,*
> *but only God can wash him white.*

UNCOOKED FUDGE

Merlyn Mullett

1 pound confectioners sugar
½ cup cocoa powder
½ cup chunky peanut butter

1 teaspoon vanilla
Pinch of salt
1 cup melted butter

Combine sugar, cocoa powder, peanut butter, vanilla, and salt. Pour butter over ingredients and stir.

Spread in pan or dish and refrigerate. When cool, cut and enjoy. So easy to make!

MY MOTHER'S BEST EVER FUDGE
Ruth Yoder

1 can evaporated milk
4 cups white sugar
2 large Hershey bars
2 small packages chocolate chips

1 (7 ounce) jar marshmallow
 creme
½ cup butter
2 cups nuts
2 teaspoons vanilla

First put milk and sugar in saucepan and boil hard for 6 minutes. Stir constantly to keep from scorching. Have rest of ingredients in large mixing bowl and pour boiling mixture over it and stir or mix well. Pour on greased cookie sheet or waxed paper. Cool and cut into squares.

PEANUT BUTTER FUDGE
Silla Yoder

2 cups white sugar
2 tablespoons light corn syrup
⅛ teaspoon salt

¾ cup milk
4 tablespoons peanut butter
1 teaspoon vanilla

Combine sugar, syrup, salt, and milk in saucepan. Heat to 234°. Add peanut butter and vanilla and beat until creamy. Pour into lightly buttered pan and cut into squares. Makes 1 pound.

PEPPERMINT PATTIES
Mrs. Ferlin L. Yoder

⅓ cup light corn syrup
⅓ cup butter
1 box powdered sugar

Peppermint flavoring
Coating chocolate, melted

Mix together syrup, butter, sugar, and flavoring. Shape in a roll and freeze. Slice while still frozen, then dip in melted chocolate.

HEATH BARS
Judy Mullet

1½ cups white sugar
½ cup real butter
½-¾ pound slivered almonds

Milk chocolate chips
Chopped pecans

Melt butter and sugar in heavy skillet. Cook to golden brown. Add almonds and cook until almonds start popping or until creamy. Spread on ungreased cookie sheet real thin. Sprinkle milk chocolate chips over while hot. Before chocolate sets, sprinkle chopped pecans over top. Set until hard. Twist cookie sheet and break into small pieces.

HOLIDAY DIVINITY

Mary (Mrs. Paul) Miller

3 cups sugar
1 cup Karo light corn syrup
2 egg whites
¼ teaspoon salt

½ cup water
1 teaspoon vanilla
1 cup finely chopped pecans

Combine sugar, corn syrup, water, and salt and cook over low heat, stirring constantly until sugar dissolves. Increase heat to high and cook without stirring until mixture reaches hard ball stage (260°). Beat egg whites (at room temperature) in a large mixing bowl until stiff peaks form. (Now you need 2 more hands). Pour hot sugar mixture in a thin stream over egg whites while beating constantly at high speed. Add vanilla and continue beating 5 to 10 minutes until mixture holds its shape. Stir in pecans. Drop by teaspoonfuls onto waxed paper. Makes 3½ dozen.

JUNE BUGS & FISH WORMS

Heidi Kauffman

1 large package butterscotch chips
½ cup creamy peanut butter

2 cups marshmallows
1 small can chow mein noodles

Melt chips in heavy kettle. Mix in peanut butter and stir well. Then add other ingredients and stir well. Drop by teaspoon on waxed paper and cool.

NUT CRUNCH

Judy Mullet

1 cup white sugar
½ teaspoon salt
¼ cup water

½ cup butter
1 cup nuts (peanuts or pecans)
Coating chocolate

Combine sugar, salt, water, and butter. Heat to boiling. Cook to crack stage (285°). Remove from stove and add nuts. Spread real thin on greased cookie sheet. Cool and spread with coating chocolate. Turn over and cover on other side with chocolate also. Break in pieces. Do not stir syrup while cooking. Do not scrape your syrup out of pan into cookie sheet. Only pour out what comes out. If you scrape it, it may become sugary.

PEANUT BUTTER REESE

Ruth Yoder

1 pound butter
3 pounds powdered sugar
1 quart peanut butter

2 large packages chocolate chips
1 (2-inch) square paraffin

Mix butter, sugar, and peanut butter until smooth and creamy. Shape into balls and chill overnight. Melt chocolate chips and paraffin in double boiler. Dip balls into chocolate mixture using toothpicks.

Desserts

ALMOND DELIGHT BLIZZARDS   Regina Overholt, Debbie Graber

1 box Almond Delight cereal (I also
   use Honey Bunches of Oats)
2 cups milk chocolate chips

½ cup peanut butter
1 (5-quart) container vanilla ice
   cream, softened

Crush cereal slightly. Melt chocolate chips and peanut butter together and pour over cereal until combined. Cool slightly. Stir cereal mixture into ice cream and freeze. (This is a yummy dessert.) Very good.

SUGARFREE ALMOND FRUIT FLAN   Mary Zook

CRUST:
1½ cups almonds
3 eggs

½ cup maple syrup
1 teaspoon almond extract

TOPPING:
16 ounces blueberries
¼ cup maple syrup

2½ tablespoons Clear Jell
1 cup water

FRUIT FOR GLAZE:
2 kiwi

Several strawberries (other fruits
   may be used)

GLAZE:
1 cup water or apple juice
Several drops lemon juice

1 tablespoon Clear Jell

If almonds have skins, blanch and rub together to remove them. Dry well, and put in food processor to make a flour. Add rest of crust ingredients and process several minutes. Pour in 8- or 10-inch springform pan. Bake 20 minutes at 350°. Cool.

Topping: Cook blueberries and maple syrup 8 minutes. Add Clear Jell and water and cook until thick. Cool. Put topping over crust and make a glaze.

Glaze: Cook together water or apple juice, several drops lemon juice, and Clear Jell. Arrange fruit slices on top of topping, and pour glaze over top. Chill well, then remove from springform pan. Serves 8-10.

DANISH DESSERT   Esther Mast

4 cups water
½ cup Clear Jell
1¼ cups white sugar

Raw fruit of your choice
1 package orange, strawberry,
   raspberry, or cherry Kool-Aid

Combine water, Clear Jell, sugar, and Kool-Aid in saucepan and bring to a boil. Cook, then add raw fruit.

AMBROSIA DESSERT BOWL

Silla Yoder

20 large marshmallows
2 cups heavy cream, divided
2 tablespoons sugar
2 teaspoons vanilla extract
½ teaspoon almond extract
1 (20 ounce) can pineapple
   wedges, drained

1 cup flaked coconut
4 cups pound cake, cubed
5-6 large navel oranges, peeled
   and sectioned
¼ cup slivered almonds, toasted

Place marshmallows and ¼ cup cream in the top of a double boiler. Heat over boiling water until the marshmallows are melted and mixture is smooth. Cool completely. Meanwhile, whip the remaining cream until thick, add sugar, fold in marshmallow mixture, fold in extracts, pineapple, and coconut. Place half of the pound cake cubes in the bottom of a 2½- to 3-quart clear glass bowl and top with ½ of orange sections. Top with half of cream mixture. Repeat layers. Sprinkle with almonds. Chill until serving time. Serves 10-12.

APPLE-CHEESE CASSEROLE

Donna Stephens

½ cup all-purpose flour
½ cup sugar
¼ teaspoon salt
¼ cup butter or margarine

7 apples, peeled, cored, and sliced
⅓ cup water
1 tablespoon lemon juice
1 cup shredded Cheddar cheese

Combine flour, sugar, and salt; mix well. Cut in butter or margarine until mixture resembles coarse meal. Toss apples with water and lemon juice, spoon into greased 8-inch casserole, and sprinkle with flour mixture. Bake, covered, at 350° for 30 minutes. Top with cheese and bake an additional 5 minutes. Serves 8.

BAKED APPLE SLICES

Silla Yoder

3 large baking apples, peeled and
   sliced
¾ cup sugar
1 tablespoon ground cinnamon
¼ teaspoon nutmeg

¼ teaspoon ginger
¼ cup apple cider
½ cup butter
½ cup chopped nuts or raisins
Vanilla ice cream

Place apples in greased 1-quart baking dish. Combine sugar, cinnamon, nutmeg, ginger, and apple cider. Pour over apples. Dot with butter. Sprinkle with nuts or raisins. Bake uncovered at 350° for 45-60 minutes or until apples are tender. Serve warm over ice cream. Serves 4.

APPLE DANISH
Denise Smith

PASTRY:
3 cups all-purpose flour
½ teaspoon salt
1 cup shortening

1 egg yolk
½ cup milk

FILLING:
6 cups sliced, peeled apples
1½ cups sugar
¼ cup butter, melted

2 tablespoons flour
1 teaspoon cinnamon

In a mixing bowl, combine flour and salt. Cut in shortening until mixture resembles coarse crumbs. Combine egg yolk and milk and add to flour mixture. Stir just until dough clings together. Divide dough in half. On a lightly floured surface, roll ½ of dough into a 15x10-inch rectangle. Transfer to a greased pan and set aside.

In a bowl, toss together filling ingredients. Spoon over pastry in pan. Roll out rest of dough and put on top. Spoon glaze on top and bake at 375°.

To make glaze, take 2 cups powdered sugar and enough water to make a thin paste. Makes 20-24 servings.

APPLE ROLL UPS
Silla Kay Yoder

PASTRY:
2 cups flour
2½ teaspoons baking powder
½ teaspoon salt

⅔ cup shortening
⅔ cup milk

FILLING:
½ stick melted butter
½ cup brown sugar

1 teaspoon cinnamon
6 baking apples, chopped

SAUCE:
2 cups brown sugar
2 cups water
¼ cup butter

¼ teaspoon cinnamon
¼ teaspoon nutmeg

To make pastry, sift flour, baking powder, and salt together. Cut in shortening until particles are about the size of small peas. Sprinkle milk over mixture. Press together lightly, working dough only enough to hold together. Roll pastry into 1 large piece, ¼-inch thick.

Spread with melted butter, brown sugar, and cinnamon. Add chopped apples and roll as a jelly roll. Cut in slices 1¼ inches thick. Place in a greased baking pan. Make sauce by cooking brown sugar, water, butter, cinnamon, and nutmeg over low heat for 10 minutes. Cover rolled dough slices with sauce and bake in oblong cake pan at 375° for 35-40 minutes. Serve warm with whipped cream or milk. Delicious. Serves 8.

APPLE DUMPLINGS
Tina Nussbaum

SYRUP:
2 cups sugar   ¼ teaspoon nutmeg
2 cups water   ¼ cup butter
¼ teaspoon cinnamon

6 apples

DOUGH:
2 cups flour   ¼ cup shortening
1 teaspoon salt   ½ cup milk
2 teaspoons baking powder

Mix first 4 ingredients in saucepan and bring to a boil. Remove from heat and add butter. Pare apples and quarter.

For the dough, mix dry ingredients and add shortening and milk. Roll out ¼-inch thick in 5-inch squares on floured surface. Put apples in dough. Dot with butter, brown sugar, and cinnamon on each square. Bring corners of dough up and close. Place in 8-inch cake pan and pour syrup over them. Bake at 375° for 35 minutes. DELICIOUS! Makes 6.

APPLE GOODIE
Silla K. Yoder

1 tablespoon flour   ½ teaspoon cinnamon
¾ cup sugar   2 cups sliced apples
⅓ teaspoon salt

TOPPING:
½ cup oatmeal   ⅛ teaspoon baking soda
½ cup brown sugar   ⅛ teaspoon baking powder
½ cup flour   ¼ cup margarine

Sift flour, sugar, salt, and cinnamon together and combine with apples. Mix together well and place in the bottom of a greased casserole dish.

To make topping, combine dry ingredients and rub in margarine to make crumbs. Put crumbs on top of apple mixture. Bake at 350° until brown and apples are tender. Makes 6 servings.

CREAM CHEESE DANISH
Ruth Yoder

2 packages cream cheese
½ cup sugar
1 egg yolk
1 teaspoon vanilla flavoring

2 cans dinner rolls
1 teaspoon cinnamon
1 teaspoon sugar
½ cup chopped pecans

Mix cream cheese, sugar, egg yolk, and vanilla flavoring in bowl. Set aside. Place 1 can of dinner rolls in Pyrex oblong dish. Pinch holes together, then put cream cheese mixture on top of rolls. Put 1 can of rolls on top of that. Mix cinnamon and sugar together, and sprinkle cinnamon-sugar and nuts on top. Bake at 350° for 10-15 minutes.

BAKED ALASKA
Betty Yoder

6 large egg whites
½ teaspoon cream of tartar
1 cup sugar

½ gallon vanilla ice cream
1 (9-inch) square baked chocolate
   cake (or any flavor)

Beat egg whites and cream of tartar until frothy. Add sugar and beat until stiff peaks form. Put ice cream over baked cake then top with egg whites. Make sure it is sealed to pan. Bake at 500° for 3-5 minutes. Freeze until ready to serve.

What you do with your money tells what it has done to you.

BANANA SPLIT DESSERT
Silla K. Yoder, Melody Kauffman

2 packages graham crackers,
   coarsely crushed
3 bananas, sliced
½ gallon 3-flavored ice cream
1 cup nuts
½ cup chocolate chips

¼ cup butter
1 cup confectioners sugar
¾ cup evaporated milk
1 teaspoon vanilla
2 cups whipped cream (or 8
   ounces frozen whipped topping)

Press crumbs in 9x12-inch pan. Reserve 1 cup for topping. Arrange banana slices on crumbs. Slice ice cream in approximately 1½-inch slices and put over bananas. Sprinkle nuts over ice cream; freeze until firm. Melt chocolate chips and butter. Add sugar and milk. Cook until thick and smooth, stirring constantly. Remove from heat and add vanilla. Cool and pour over ice cream; freeze until firm. Spread whipped cream over chocolate and sprinkle with reserved cracker crumbs. Remove from freezer about 15 minutes before serving. Makes approximately 20 servings.

HEAVENLY BANANA DELIGHT
Ruth Yoder

1 (3½ ounce) package instant
  vanilla pudding
1 can condensed milk
1 cup sweet milk
1 half-pint whipping cream

1 (8 ounce) container sour cream
1 box vanilla wafers
3 or 4 bananas
3 tablespoons chocolate syrup

Use large mixing bowl. Mix instant pudding, condensed milk, and sweet milk together for 2 minutes or until well blended. Refrigerate 10 minutes. Whip the whipping cream. Add whipped cream and sour cream to the chilled milk and pudding mixture. In a large dish, place layer of vanilla wafers, a layer of sliced bananas, half of mixture and stream a bit of chocolate syrup on top. Repeat next layer same and garnish top with chocolate syrup. Makes 10-12 servings.

BLUEBERRY CRISP
Elva Miller

1 (16 ounce) can crushed
  pineapple
3 cups blueberries
¾ cup sugar

1 box yellow cake mix
1 stick melted butter
1 cup chopped nuts

Mix first 3 ingredients and put into a 9x13-inch pan. Next put dry cake mix on blueberry mixture. Melt butter and drizzle on cake. Add nuts and bake at 350° for 1 hour.

BLUEBERRY CRUNCH
Judith Yoder

CRUMBS:
1 cup flour
1 cup oatmeal
1 cup brown sugar

⅛ teaspoon salt
½ cup soft butter

FILLING:
½ cup sugar
2 tablespoons cornstarch

1 cup boiling water
3 cups blueberries

Mix first 5 ingredients until crumbly. Put ½ of crumbs in bottom of 9x9-inch pan.

Stir together sugar and cornstarch. Add to boiling water and cook until thickened. Add blueberries to filling and pour in pan on top of crumbs. Add remaining crumbs and bake at 350° for 30 minutes. Cherries, apples, or other fruit may be used. Makes 6-10 servings.

BLUEBERRY BUCKLE

Mrs. Kathy Schrock, Laura K. Yoder

BATTER:

2 cups all-purpose flour
¾ cup sugar
2½ teaspoons baking powder
¾ teaspoons salt

¼ cup shortening
¾ cup milk
1 egg
2 cups blueberries

TOPPING:

½ cup sugar
⅓ cup flour

½ teaspoon cinnamon
¼ cup softened butter

Blend all batter ingredients except berries. Then carefully fold in berries. Spread in prepared 10-inch round pan.

Prepare topping: Mix topping ingredients and sprinkle over batter and bake 45-50 minutes in a 375° oven.

BOILED CUSTARD

Rhoda Hilty

6 egg yolks
½ cup sugar
¼ teaspoon salt

2 cups scalded milk, slightly cooled
1 teaspoon vanilla

Combine egg yolks, sugar, and salt. Beat slowly and stir in milk and vanilla. Cook in double boiler, stirring constantly, until mixture coats a metal spoon. Cool in cold water; stir 1-2 minutes then chill. This is good with angel food cake.

CHEESE CAKE

Rose Yoder

CRUST:

3 cups graham crackers
½ cup butter

¼ cup sugar

FILLING:

1 (3 ounce) package lemon Jello
1 cup boiling water
1 (8 ounce) package cream cheese
1 cup sugar

1 teaspoon lemon juice
1 (16 ounce) container Cool Whip
  whipped topping

For crust, mix graham crackers, butter, and sugar together and press in bottom and up sides of a 9x13-inch pan.

Dissolve Jello in boiling water. Cool until it begins to gel. Cream the cream cheese and sugar and add lemon juice, Jello, and Cool Whip. Whip all together and pour over crust.

CHEESECAKE
Barbara Kauffman

1 box yellow cake mix
2 tablespoons oil
2 (8 ounce) packages cream
  cheese, softened
½ cup sugar

4 eggs
1½ cups milk
3 tablespoons lemon juice
3 teaspoons vanilla

Reserve 1 cup dry cake mix. In large mixing bowl, combine remaining cake mix, 1 egg, and oil. Mixture will be crumbly. Press crust mixture evenly into bottom and ¾ way up the sides of a greased 13x9x2-inch cake pan. Set aside.

In same bowl, blend cream cheese and sugar. Add 3 eggs and reserved cake mix; beat 1 minute at medium speed. At low speed, slowly add milk and flavorings; mix until smooth. Pour into crust. Bake at 300° for 45-55 minutes until center if firm. (If made in 2 (9-inch) pans, bake at 300° for 40-50 minutes).

Cool and refrigerate until ready to serve. Top with your choice of fruit pie filling, such as cherry, strawberry, blueberry, or peach. This can be covered with foil and frozen. Makes 18-20 servings.

TURTLE CHEESECAKE
Ruth Yoder

CRUST:
2 cups vanilla wafer crumbs

½ cup butter or margarine, melted

FILLING:
1 (14 ounce) package caramels
1 (5 ounce) can evaporated milk
2 cans chopped pecans, toasted,
  divided
4 (8 ounce) packages cream
  cheese, softened
1 cup sugar

2 teaspoons vanilla extract
4 eggs
1 cup (6 ounces) semi-sweet
  chocolate chips, melted and
  slightly cooled
Whipped cream, optional

Combine crumbs and butter or margarine. Blend well and press in the bottom and 2 inches up the sides of a 10-inch springform pan. Bake for 8-10 minutes at 350° or until set.

In a saucepan over low heat, melt caramels in milk, stirring until smooth. Cool 5 minutes. Pour into crust and top with 1½ cups chopped pecans. In a mixing bowl, beat cream cheese until smooth. Add sugar and vanilla. Mix well. Add eggs, one at a time, beating well after each addition. Add chocolate and mix just until blended. Carefully spread over pecans. Bake at 350° for 55-65 minutes or until filling is almost set. Cool to room temperature. Chill overnight. Garnish with whipped cream and nuts. Makes 16 servings.

CHERRY BLOSSOM CHEESECAKE   Ruth Yoder

CRUST:

1 cup graham cracker crumbs   2 tablespoons granulated sugar
½ cup chocolate wafer crumbs   4 tablespoons butter, melted
½ cup pecan meal

TOPPING:

16 ounces sour cream   4 tablespoons sugar
1 tablespoon Kirsch liqueur*

FILLING:

6 ounces white chocolate, melted   1 teaspoon vanilla extract
3 (8 ounce) packages cream   2 tablespoons Kirsch or cherry
  cheese, room temperature   flavoring
2 tablespoons flour   ½ cup sour cream
¾ cup sugar   6 ounces cherry preserves
4 large eggs, room temperature

To make crust, mix crumbs, pecan meal, sugar, and butter and press in bottom and up sides of pan.

Melt white chocolate until smooth; cool to lukewarm. Using electric mixer, beat cream cheese until smooth; add flour and sugar. Blend eggs one at a time. Add vanilla and Kirsch or cherry flavoring. While mixer is running, add melted white chocolate. Fold in sour cream. Pour filling over cooled crust. Warm cherry preserves enough to drizzle over the top of your filling, cut through the batter with knife to create a marble effect. Bake at 325° until cheesecake is firm around edges but still moves slightly in center, about 45-55 minutes. Have topping mixture ready when you take the cake out of the oven.

Topping: Mix all ingredients in bowl then pour mixture over cake. Using a spatula, spread to edges. Return cake to oven and continue cooking 5-7 minutes. Cool to room temperature 1 hour and refrigerate.

Garnish with cherry preserves and toasted almonds.

*Kirsch cherry liqueur can be substituted with cherry flavoring.

*The Lord is a friend
To the person who is honest. — Proverbs 3:32*

CHOCOLATE-GLAZED TRIPLE-LAYER CHEESECAKE

Ruth Yoder

CRUST:

1 (8½ ounce) package chocolate wafer cookies, crushed
¾ cup sugar, divided

¼ cup plus 1 tablespoon butter, melted

FILLING:

2 (8 ounce) packages cream cheese, softened and divided
3 eggs
1 teaspoon vanilla extract, divided
2 (1 ounce) squares semi-sweet chocolate, melted

1⅓ cups sour cream, divided
⅓ cup firmly packed brown sugar
1 tablespoon all-purpose flour
¼ cup chopped pecans
5 ounces cream cheese, softened
¼ teaspoon almond extract

CHOCOLATE GLAZE:

6 (1 ounce) squares semi-sweet chocolate
¼ cup butter or margarine

¾ cup sifted powdered sugar
2 tablespoons water
1 teaspoon vanilla

Combine cookie crumbs, ¼ cup sugar, and butter; blend well. Press onto bottom and 2 inches up sides of a 9-inch springform pan. Set aside.

Combine 1 (8 ounce) package cream cheese and ¼ cup sugar; beat at medium speed of an electric mixer until fluffy. Add 1 egg and ¼ teaspoon vanilla; beat well. Stir in melted chocolate and ⅓ cup sour cream. Spoon over chocolate crust. Combine remaining (8 ounce) package cream cheese, brown sugar, and flour; beat until fluffy. Add 1 egg and ½ teaspoon vanilla; beat well. Stir in pecans and spoon over chocolate layer. Combine 5 ounces cream cheese and remaining ¼ cup sugar; beat until fluffy. Add remaining egg and beat well. Stir in remaining 1 cup sour cream, ¼ teaspoon vanilla, and almond extract. Spoon over pecan layer.

Bake at 325° for 1 hour. Turn oven off and leave cheesecake in oven 30 minutes; open door of oven, and leave cheesecake in oven an additional 30 minutes. Cool. Cover and chill at least 8 hours. Remove from pan. Spread with warm chocolate glaze. Garnish with chocolate leaves if desired.

Glaze: Combine chocolate and butter or margarine in top of a double boiler. Bring water to a boil. Reduce heat to low; cook until chocolate melts. Remove from heat; stir in remaining ingredients. Stir until smooth. Spread over cheesecake while glaze is warm. Serves 10-12.

PEACH CHEESECAKE

Sara Jean Yoder

4 ounces cream cheese
1 teaspoon vanilla
⅓ cup powdered sugar
¼ teaspoon salt

1 (8 or 9 ounce) container Cool
  Whip whipped topping
1 (9x9-inch) graham cracker pie
  crust

PEACH TOPPING:
2 (3 ounce) packages peach Jello
¼ cup sugar
2 tablespoons lemon juice

1 large can peaches, drained
2½ cups boiling water

Mix together cream cheese, vanilla, powdered sugar, salt, and Cool Whip and place on graham cracker crust in 9x9-inch pan. Let set until firm.

Mix together the Peach Topping ingredients. Cool slightly and put on top of the cream cheese mixture.

This is good made with *fresh* peaches. Recipe following:

PEACH TOPPING NO. 2:
1 cup water
½ cup white sugar
3 tablespoons Clear Jell

1 tablespoon peach Jello
1 scant tablespoon lemon juice
Dash of salt

Boil water, sugar, and Clear Jell. Add peach Jello, lemon juice, and salt. Cool slightly. Stir in sliced sweetened peaches and put on cheesecake. Serves 10.

GOURMET CHEESECAKE

Martha Kauffman

CRUST:
1 box Zwieback toast, crushed
3 tablespoons sugar

3 tablespoons butter, melted
2 teaspoons cinnamon

FILLING:
4 egg whites
¾ cup sugar
3 (8 ounce) packages cream
  cheese

2 tablespoons flour
1½ cups sour cream
1 teaspoon lemon flavoring
1 teaspoon vanilla flavoring

Grease springform pan. Mix Zwieback toast with sugar, butter, and cinnamon. Mix well and press in bottom and up sides of springform pan.

Beat egg whites until frothy. Add sugar, cream cheese, flour, sour cream, and lemon and vanilla flavorings. Beat until smooth. Fold egg whites into cream cheese mixture and pour into pan. Top with remaining Zwieback crumbs. Bake in preheated 350° oven for 1 hour. Let cool in oven 1 more hour.

SOUTHERN PECAN CHEESECAKE   Ruth Yoder

CRUST:
1½ cups quick oats   ½ cup brown sugar
½ cup finely chopped pecans

FILLING:
5 (8 ounce) packages cream   5 eggs
   cheese, softened   1 teaspoon vanilla
1⅔ cups light brown sugar   2 cups chopped pecans, divided

To make crust, place oats in food processor or blender; process to consistency of flour. Combine oats with remaining crust ingredients; press into bottom of 10-inch springform pan. Chill.

To make filling, beat cream cheese with mixer until fluffy. Slowly add brown sugar and mix well. Add eggs, one at a time, mixing after each one. Stir in vanilla and half of nuts. Mix and pour over crust. Bake at 350° for 1 hour. Turn off oven but leave cake in for 30 minutes more. To reduce chance of cracks on top surface, run a knife around edge of cheesecake as soon as you remove from oven. Let cool to room temperature; chill 8 hours. Remove sides of pan. Press additional chopped pecans around sides and dollop with whipped cream. Makes 20-24 servings.

ORANGE CHEESECAKE   Mary Joyce Miller

CRUST:
1 cup chocolate wafer crumbs   3 tablespoons butter, melted

FILLING:
½ cup orange juice   1¼ cups sugar
1 envelope unflavored gelatin   1 cup heavy cream, whipped
3 (8 ounce) packages cream   1½ tablespoons grated orange
   cheese, softened   peel

Combine crumbs and butter. Press into bottom of a 9-inch springform pan. Bake at 350° for 10 minutes.

Combine orange juice and gelatin. Let stand 5 minutes. Beat until gelatin dissolves. Cool 10 minutes. Meanwhile, beat cream cheese and sugar until light and fluffy. Gradually add to gelatin mixture. Mix well; chill until partially set, 3-5 minutes. Stir in whipping cream and orange peel. Spoon into crust and chill overnight. Garnish with chocolate chips and orange wedges. Makes 8-10 servings.

WHITE CHOCOLATE CHEESECAKE

Ruth Yoder

CRUST:

¾ cup blanched almonds, ground
¾ cup quick-cooking oats, uncooked
¾ cup graham cracker crumbs

¼ cup sugar
¼ cup plus 2 tablespoons butter, melted

FILLING:

2 (8 ounce) packages softened cream cheese
1 cup sugar
1 (16 ounce) container regular sour cream

1 teaspoon vanilla extract
8 ounces melted white chocolate
4 egg whites
⅛ teaspoon cream of tartar
1 tablespoon powdered sugar

Combine first 5 ingredients in a medium bowl; blend well. Press onto bottom and 2 inches up sides of a 10-inch springform pan. Bake at 350° for 5 minutes. Cool on wire rack.

For filling, combine cream cheese and sugar in a large mixing bowl; beat at medium speed of electric mixer until fluffy. Add sour cream and vanilla; mix well. Stir in white chocolate. Beat egg whites (at room temperature) in a large bowl at high speed until foamy; add cream of tartar, beating until soft peaks form. Add powdered sugar and continue beating until stiff peaks form. Fold egg whites into cream cheese mixture. Spoon mixture into crumb crust and bake at 325° for 55 minutes; turn oven off. Leave cheesecake in oven 30 minutes. Partially open door of oven an additional 30 minutes. Cool. Chill 8 hours. Remove from pan. Makes 10-12 servings.

CHOCOLATE CHIP DESSERT

Sharon Miller

2 (10 ounce) packages marshmallows
1 cup milk
3 cups chocolate chips

2 cups heavy cream, whipped
1 package graham crackers, crushed
½ cup nuts

Melt marshmallows and milk together in double boiler. Add chocolate chips. Cool. Put all crushed crackers except ½ cup into a 9x13-inch pan. Stir cream into pudding mixture and pour over crackers in pan. Combine nuts and remaining cracker crumbs. Sprinkle over pudding and refrigerate overnight. Makes 12-16 servings.

CHERRY COBBLER
Rachel Swarey

BATTER:

1 cup sugar	¼ cup shortening
1½ cups flour	1 egg
½ teaspoon salt	⅓ cup milk
2 teaspoons baking powder	

FILLING:

2 cups cherries, sweetened	1 tablespoon lemon juice
1-2 tablespoons Minute tapioca	2 tablespoons butter

Sift together dry ingredients and cut in shortening. Beat egg and add milk. Combine with flour mixture.

Pour cherries into greased 13x9-inch pan. Sprinkle with tapioca, add lemon juice, and dot with the butter. Put batter on top and bake at 375° for 30 minutes or until toothpick inserted in center comes out clean.

The best place to prepare for the duties of life is, like Mary...
at Jesus' feet!

CHERRY CRUNCH
Tina Nussbaum

1 can cherry pie filling	1 package white cake mix
1 teaspoon lemon juice	1 stick margarine, melted

Spread pie filling in bottom of 9x9-inch pan. Sprinkle with lemon juice. Set aside. Combine dry cake mix with melted margarine. Mixture will be crumbly. Sprinkle over filling. Bake at 350° for 40-50 minutes until golden brown. Makes 6 servings.

RHUBARB COBBLER
Sara Jean Yoder

1 cup sugar	1 teaspoon vanilla
3 cups rhubarb, cut up	2 tablespoons butter
1 cup flour	1 teaspoon baking powder
2 tablespoons sugar	½ cup milk
¼ teaspoon salt	

Pour 1 cup sugar over rhubarb. Make dough with flour, 2 tablespoons sugar, salt, vanilla, butter, and baking powder, and crumble this together. Add milk. Spread dough over rhubarb in 8x11-inch pan and bake at 350° for 45 minutes. Makes 8 servings.

MY FAVORITE PEACH COBBLER

Ruth Yoder

CAKE MIXTURE:
2 cups flour
1½ cups sugar
½ teaspoons salt

4 teaspoons baking powder
1½ cups milk
1 teaspoon vanilla

FILLING:
2 quarts peaches
½ stick butter
2 teaspoons lemon juice
½ cup sugar

3 tablespoons cornstarch or Clear
  Jell
¾ cup water
1 teaspoon ground cloves

TOPPING:
1 stick margarine
¼ cup sugar

1 teaspoon cinnamon

Combine flour, sugar, salt, and baking powder. Stir in milk and vanilla and set aside.

In saucepan, put first 4 filling ingredients. Add cloves. Bring to a boil. Mix together cornstarch or Clear Jell and water to make paste. Gradually add to filling mixture. Pour into pan and put cake mixture on peach filling.

For topping: Melt 1 stick butter and drizzle on top. Mix together sugar and cinnamon and sprinkle over top. Bake in 9x13-inch (3-quart) baking dish at 350° for 40 minutes. Serve warm with milk. Also great with a slice of cheese. Makes 10 servings.

PEACH COBBLER

Jo Ann Inhulsen

4 cups sliced peaches
1½ cups sugar
½ stick butter or margarine
¾ cup flour

2 teaspoons baking powder
Pinch of salt
¾ cup milk

Prepare peaches and mix with 1 cup sugar. Set oven temperature to 350°. Put butter or margarine in small loaf pan and set in oven to melt.

Stir up batter of ½ cup sugar, flour, baking powder, salt, and milk. Pour over melted butter. Do not stir. Put the sweetened peaches on top and again do not stir. Bake 1 hour or until golden brown.

CHOCOLATE MARSHMALLOW CREAM — Viola Miller

½ cup sugar
1 envelope unflavored gelatin
  (tablespoon)
2¼ cups milk
1 (1 ounce) square unsweetened
  chocolate
¼ pound marshmallows (11-16),
  cut up
¼ cup ground nuts, if desired
2 egg whites, stiffly beaten
1 cup whipping cream, whipped
  stiff

Blend first 4 ingredients in saucepan thoroughly. Cook over medium heat, stirring constantly, just until mixture comes to a boil. Place pan in cold water; cool until mixture mounds slightly when dropped from spoon. Stir in marshmallows and nuts. Fold in egg whites and cream. Chill 4 hours. Makes 8 servings.

CREAM PUFF DESSERT — Silla K. Yoder, Barbara Ann Yoder

1 stick margarine
1 cup boiling water
1 cup flour
4 eggs
1 (8 ounce) package cream cheese
4-4½ cups milk
3 boxes instant vanilla pudding
1 (8 ounce) container Cool Whip
  whipped topping
Fresh fruit or chocolate syrup for
  garnish

Melt margarine in water and bring to boil. Remove from heat and add flour; stir until it forms a ball. Beat eggs and add to first mixture. Spread into a 9x13-inch pan and bake at 375° until lightly browned. Cool.

Beat cream cheese until soft. Very gradually add milk. Add pudding. Spread over cooled crust.

Top with Cool Whip and any kind of fresh fruit, or drizzle chocolate syrup on top.

CHOCOLATE UPSIDE DOWN CAKE — Martha Kauffman, Denise Smith

1 cup self-rising flour
½ teaspoon salt
1½ tablespoons cocoa
2 teaspoons baking powder
¾ cup milk
1 teaspoon vanilla
¾ cup nuts
½ cup chocolate syrup
1 cup hot water

Mix first 7 ingredients and put in a greased 8-inch square pan. Mix chocolate syrup and hot water. Pour over top of first ingredients and bake at 350° for 35 minutes.

CHOCOLATE PEANUT BUTTER LOAF

Elsie Brenneman,
Ruth Yoder

1½ cups vanilla wafers, crushed
½ cup peanuts
2 tablespoons powdered sugar
3 tablespoons melted butter
3 cups vanilla ice cream
1 (3 ounce) package cream cheese

¾ cup powdered sugar
⅓ cup peanut butter
⅓ cup milk
½ cup whipped cream
3 cups chocolate ice cream

Mix together first 4 ingredients, reserving ½ cup crumbs. Press in bottom of a 9x13-inch pan. Freeze 15 minutes. Soften vanilla ice cream and spread on crust. Freeze ½ hour.

Combine cream cheese, powdered sugar, and peanut butter. Beat cream cheese mixture, adding milk gradually. Fold in whipped cream. Put on top of ice cream and return to freezer until firm. Put chocolate ice cream on top. Put remaining crust crumbs on top and freeze. Makes 12-15 servings.

COOL AND CRUNCHY

Judi Wagher

1 stick margarine
2½ cups Rice Krispies cereal
1 cup broken pecans

1 cup flaked coconut
¾ cup brown sugar
½ gallon vanilla ice cream

In 300° oven, melt margarine; stir in Rice Krispies, pecans, and coconut. Return to oven and bake for 30 minutes, stirring occasionally. Remove and add brown sugar. Put half of mixture in 9x13-inch pan. Top with ice cream which has been cut in 1-inch slices. Sprinkle remaining mixture over top. Cover tightly and freeze. Makes 8-10 servings.

CREAM PUFF DESSERT

Barbara Ann Yoder, Alta Kauffman

1 stick margarine
1 cup boiling water
1 cup flour
¼ teaspoon salt
4 eggs
1 (8 ounce) package cream cheese

3 cups milk
2 packages vanilla instant pudding
1 (8 ounce) container whipped
    topping
Fresh fruit or chocolate syrup for
    garnish

Melt margarine in water and bring to a boil. Remove from heat and add flour and salt, stirring until you can form a ball. Beat eggs into mixture one at a time. Spread into a greased pan. Bake in a 9x13-inch pan at 400°-425° for 25 minutes or until done. Cool completely. Beat cream cheese to soften. Gradually add milk to get a smooth consistency. Stir in instant pudding and beat mixture together for 2 minutes. Spread pudding mixture over cooled puff. Top with a layer of whipped topping and fresh fruit or drizzle with chocolate syrup.

JIMMY CARTER DELIGHT

Mrs. Shirley Yoder

1ST LAYER:
1 cup flour
1 stick margarine

⅔ cup chopped peanuts

2ND LAYER:
1 (8 ounce) package cream cheese
⅓ cup peanut butter

1 cup powdered sugar
1 cup Cool Whip whipped topping

3RD LAYER:
1 small box instant chocolate
  pudding
2 small boxes instant vanilla
  pudding

4 cups milk
1 cup Cool Whip whipped topping
1 grated Hershey bar
⅓ cup chopped peanuts

Mix ingredients for first layer and press into a 9x13-inch pan. Bake at 375° for 20 minutes. Cool. Mix together second layer and spread over cooled crust.

For third layer, mix together puddings and milk until it begins to thicken. Spread over second layer. Top with Cool Whip, grated Hershey bar, and chopped peanuts. Makes 15 servings.

EARTHQUAKE DESSERT

Rhoda Hilty

Coconut
1 cup chopped nuts
1 box German chocolate cake mix
½ cup margarine

4 cups powdered sugar
1 (8 ounce) package cream
  cheese, at room temperature

Grease a 9x13x3-inch (not 9x13x2-inch) pan. Cover bottom with coconut and sprinkle with nuts. Prepare cake mix according to directions on box and pour into pan. Combine margarine, powdered sugar, and cream cheese until smooth. Spoon over cake mix; do not stir. Bake at 350° for 1 hour. Makes 12-15 servings.

FRUIT DANISH

Jonas and Kathy Schrock

1½ cups sugar
1 cup margarine
4 eggs
3 cups flour

1½ teaspoons baking powder
1 teaspoon vanilla
1 teaspoon almond extract
1 can pie filling

Beat sugar, margarine, and eggs until light and fluffy. Add flour, baking powder, and flavorings. Spread ¾ of batter on cookie sheet. Spread pie filling on top. Drop rest of batter on top of filling by teaspoons. Bake at 325° for 30-35 minutes.

LEMON DELIGHT

Emma Mae Yoder

½ cup melted margarine
1 tablespoon sugar
½ cup nuts
1 cup self-rising flour
1 cup powdered sugar
1 (8 ounce) package cream cheese

1½ cups whipped topping
2 small boxes lemon instant
   pudding
3 cups milk
1½ tablespoons lemon juice
1 large carton whipped topping

Mix margarine, sugar, nuts, and flour and spread out in an 11x13-inch pan. Bake at 350° for 15 minutes.

Blend powdered sugar, cream cheese, and 1½ cups whipped topping; spread on cooled crust.

Mix lemon pudding, milk, and lemon juice together. Pour over cream cheese mixture and top with whipped topping. Serves 12.

I have a lesson learned
My life is but a field
Stretched out beneath God's sky,
Some harvest rich to yield.

GINGERBREAD

Jill Nussbaum

½ cup Crisco oil
¼ cup sugar
1 egg
½ cup dark molasses or Karo
   syrup
1¾ cups flour

1 teaspoon baking soda
½ teaspoon cinnamon
1 teaspoon ginger
½ teaspoon salt
½ cup milk

SAUCE:
1½ cups brown sugar
1 cup water

2 tablespoons flour
Lump of butter

Cream oil and sugar. Add egg and beat well. Add molasses or Karo syrup. Sift together dry ingredients; add alternately with milk to creamed mixture. Pour into greased 8x8-inch pan and bake at 350° for 45 minutes.

Sauce: Combine ingredients. Heat and serve over warm gingerbread. Delicious. Serves 9.

Our afflictions are not designed to break us, but to bend us toward God.

GINGERBREAD

Barbara Ann Yoder, Mrs. Sol Yoder, Sr.

½ cup white sugar
½ cup shortening
1 egg, beaten
1 cup molasses
2½ cups flour
1½ teaspoons baking soda

1 teaspoon cinnamon
1 teaspoon ginger
½ teaspoon cloves
½ teaspoon salt
1 cup hot water

Cream shortening and sugar; add beaten egg, molasses, then dry ingredients which have been sifted together. Add hot water last and beat until smooth. The batter is soft but it makes a fine cake. Bake in greased 9x13-inch pan in 350° oven for 35 minutes. Serve warm or cold with whipped cream.

Barbara Ann uses 2 cups flour and 2 eggs.

FROSTIES

Emma Mae Yoder

1 small box vanilla pudding
2 small boxes milk chocolate
   pudding*
1½ cups sugar

3 eggs
¾ teaspoon salt
8 cups milk
4 cups cream

Beat eggs, salt, and sugar until smooth. Add milk. Stir in puddings and mix thoroughly. Add the cream and freeze in 6-quart ice cream freezer until firm.

*Note: If you can't get milk chocolate pudding, use 2 small vanilla and 1 small chocolate.

VANILLA ICE CREAM

Martha Yoder

FOR 6-QUART FREEZER:
7½ cups milk
3½ cups sugar
9 tablespoons flour
¾ teaspoon salt

9 eggs
6 cups heavy cream
6-7 teaspoons vanilla

FOR 4-QUART FREEZER:
5 cups milk
2¼ cups sugar
6 tablespoons flour
½ teaspoon salt

6 eggs
4 cups heavy cream
4½ teaspoons vanilla

Scald milk. Combine sugar, flour, and salt in saucepan. Slowly stir in hot milk. Cook over low heat for about 10 minutes, stirring constantly until mixture is thickened. Mix small amount of hot mixture into beaten eggs. Add to hot mixture and cook 1 minute longer. Chill in refrigerator. Add cream and vanilla. Pour into ice cream freezer and freeze.

BUTTER BRICKLE ICE CREAM   Debbie Graber

1 cup brown sugar
½ cup white sugar
4 tablespoons cornstarch or Clear
   Jell
4 eggs, beaten

⅔ cup pancake syrup
5 cups milk
2 cups whipping cream
3 teaspoons vanilla
1 bag Heath Bits-O-Brickle chips

Combine sugars, cornstarch or Clear Jell, eggs, and syrup in pan. Gradually add milk and cook over low heat until thickened. Remove from heat and chill for several hours. Stir in cream, vanilla, and Bits-O-Brickle. Freeze in ice cream container.

JAKE CLARK'S PEACH ICE CREAM   Ruth Yoder

8 cups finely chopped peaches
4 cups sugar
¾ teaspoon almond flavoring
¾ teaspoon vanilla extract

1 teaspoon lemon juice
¾ teaspoon salt
2½ quarts half-and-half
1 drop red food coloring

Blend all ingredients with half-and-half and pour into ice cream churn tank. Start churn and pour ice well laced with salt into churn bucket. Allow to churn until firm or motor pulls down. Makes 1 gallon.

ICE CREAM   Viola Miller

4 eggs
½ can Eagle brand milk
Scant 1 cup brown sugar
Scant 1 cup white sugar

1 large box instant pudding
¾ cup whipped topping
Milk

Beat eggs and Eagle brand milk together and add sugars. Make instant pudding as directed on box and add to first mixture. Add whipped topping and enough milk to make 2 gallons finished ice cream.

STRAWBERRY ICE CREAM   Emma Mae Yoder

2 pints strawberries
8 cups milk
3 small boxes vanilla pudding
1⅛ cups sugar

3 eggs
½ teaspoon salt
4 cups cream

Put strawberries and some milk in blender. Beat the rest of the ingredients with remaining milk. Mix all together and put in a 6-quart ice cream freezer.

VANILLA ICE CREAM
Cynthia Helmuth

⅓ cup boiling water
3 tablespoons melted butter
1-2 eggs
½ cup sugar
1 cup powdered milk
¼ teaspoon salt

1½ teaspoons vanilla
Milk
½ package instant vanilla pudding mix
1 cup Cool Whip whipped topping, optional

Put boiling water and melted butter in 5-cup blender. While blending, add eggs, sugar, and powdered milk. Blend for 5 minutes. Add salt, vanilla, enough milk to fill blender, and pudding mix. Blend until smooth. Chill. Pour into Donvier ice cream maker and freeze. Recipe can be doubled for larger freezers.

Option: For a low-cal version, omit butter and sugar and sweeten with Sweet-n-Low or Equal.

BUTTERSCOTCH ICE CREAM DESSERT
Dorothy Schlabach

50 Ritz crackers, crushed
1 stick margarine
1 box instant butterscotch pudding*
1 box instant vanilla pudding

1½ quarts soft vanilla ice cream
1 (8 ounce) container Cool Whip whipped topping
1½ cups cold milk

Mix together crushed crackers and margarine; press in 9x13-inch pan. Save ¼ cup to sprinkle on top.

Mix 2 boxes pudding in milk until thick, then add the softened ice cream. Put in pan. Top with Cool Whip and cracker crumbs. Makes 12-14 servings.

*Other flavors of pudding may be used.

BUTTERSCOTCH ICE CREAM TOPPING
Silla K. Yoder

1 cup white Karo syrup
1 cup brown sugar
1 teaspoon vanilla

½ teaspoon salt
3 teaspoons butter
½ cup milk

Cook together 5 minutes stirring constantly. Serve over ice cream.

ICE CREAM SANDWICHES

Silla K. Yoder

1 (3.4 ounce) package instant
  vanilla pudding
2 cups cold milk
2 cups whipped topping

1 cup (6 ounces) miniature semi-
  sweet chocolate chips
48 graham cracker squares

Mix pudding and milk according to package directions and refrigerate until set. Fold in whipped topping and chocolate chips. Place 24 graham crackers on a baking sheet. Top each with about 3 tablespoons filling. Place another graham cracker on top of each. Freeze for 1 hour or until firm. Wrap individually in plastic wrap. Freeze. Serve sandwiches frozen. Yield: 2 dozen.

CHOCOLATE ICE CREAM BARS

Mrs. James Mast

1ST PART:
⅛ cup cocoa
½ cup sugar

1½ cups milk

2ND PART:
6 egg yolks

⅓ cup sugar

3RD PART:
6 egg whites
¼ teaspoon salt

1 cup sugar

4TH PART:
2 cups cream

2 teaspoons vanilla

GRAHAM CRACKER CRUST:
¼ cup brown sugar
½ cup margarine

2 cups graham cracker crumbs

Mix 1st part all together in saucepan, and bring to scalding. Beat 2nd part together until light and fluffy; add to milk mixture and cook until thickened. Cool.

Beat 3rd part all together until stiff.

Whip 4th part until fluffy. Fold all ingredients together, and pour into graham cracker crust. Cover and freeze overnight. Serves 12.

Crust: Mix ingredients all together and sprinkle into a 9x13-inch or 2 (9-inch) pans. Save some to garnish top.

OREO DESSERT
Elsie Yoder

½ box yellow or white cake mix
1 (16 ounce) package Oreo
  cookies, crushed
¼-½ cup chocolate syrup

1 box instant vanilla or chocolate
  pudding
2 cups Cool Whip whipped topping

Bake cake mix according to directions and bake in 9x11-inch pan after Oreos are crushed. Reserve 1 cup for topping. Put in bottom of 9x12-inch pan. Pour chocolate syrup on crushed Oreos then place baked cake on. Next, mix the pudding and poke holes in cake with wooden spoon. Pour pudding on cake immediately, then top with 2 cups Cool Whip. Sprinkle with rest of crushed Oreos.

PEANUT CHOCOLATE PARFAIT DESSERT
Regina Overholt

BASE:
1 box devil's food cake mix
¼ cup milk
½ cup butter, melted

1 egg
¾ cup peanuts or other nuts
  (optional)

FILLING:
¾ cup peanut butter
1½ cups powdered sugar
1 (8 ounce) package cream cheese
2½ cups milk

1 (5½ ounce) package instant
  vanilla pudding
1 (8 ounce) container whipped
  topping

TOPPING:
1 (1½ ounce) milk chocolate bar,
  chilled and grated

½ cup nuts

Base: Mix ingredients and put in a 9x13-inch pan. Bake at 350° for 20-25 minutes. Cool.

Mix peanut butter and powdered sugar until crumbly. In a large bowl, mix cream cheese until smooth and add milk, pudding, and whipped topping. Pour ½ of cream cheese mixture over baked base. Sprinkle ½ of peanut butter mixture over cream cheese mixture. Repeat.

Sprinkle grated chocolate and nuts on dessert and chill or freeze.

(FROZEN) PEANUT BUTTER DESSERT Janet Showalter Miller

1 (8 ounce) package cream cheese
3 cups confectioners sugar
1 cup peanut butter
1 cup milk

1 large carton Cool Whip whipped
  topping
1 stick butter, melted
2½ cups graham cracker crumbs

Whip cream cheese at low speed until soft and fluffy. Beat in sugar and peanut butter. Slowly beat in milk. Stir in Cool Whip.

Mix melted butter with graham crackers crumbs and line 9x13-inch pan (do not bake). Pour peanut butter mixture over crumbs and freeze. Remove from freezer approximately ½ hour before serving. Makes 16 servings.

*Afflictions are blessings to us
when we bless God for the affliction!*

FRUIT PIZZA Debbie Graber, Martha Yoder, Melody Kauffman, Dorothy Schlabach

½ cup margarine
½ cup sugar
1 egg
½ cup flour
1 teaspoon baking powder
¼ teaspoon salt
1 (8 ounce) package cream cheese
½ cup powdered sugar
1 teaspoon vanilla

4 ounces Cool Whip whipped
  topping (approximately)
1 cup fruit juice
¾ cup sugar
1 tablespoon lemon juice
2 tablespoons Clear Jell
Fresh fruit (strawberries, seedless
  grapes, bananas, apples,
  peaches, etc.)

Beat together margarine, sugar, and egg. Sift flour, baking powder, and salt; add to first mixture and mix well. Press into a greased medium pizza pan and bake at 350° until golden brown. Cool.

Whip cream cheese and powdered sugar until smooth. Add vanilla and Cool Whip. Spread over crust. Combine next 4 ingredients and cook until thickened, stirring constantly. Cool. Arrange sliced fruit on crust and pour cooked sauce over all. Keep refrigerated.

Debbie Graber puts ¾ cup chocolate chips in crust.

STRAWBERRY PIZZA
Silla Yoder

CRUST:
1 cup self-rising flour
½ cup powdered sugar

½ cup melted butter

TOPPING:
1 (8 ounce) package cream
cheese, softened
1 (14 ounce) can sweetened
condensed milk

⅓ cup lemon juice
Vanilla extract

GLAZE:
¼ cup powdered sugar
2 tablespoons cornstarch
½ cup water

2 pints fresh strawberries, halved
Few drops red food coloring

Combine flour, powdered sugar, and butter, mixing well. Pat dough out into a 14-inch pizza pan. Bake for 10 minutes at 325° or until lightly browned.

Combine cream cheese, condensed milk, lemon juice, and vanilla. Mix well and spread on cooled crust. Chill thoroughly.

Combine powdered sugar and cornstarch in a large saucepan. Add water, mixing until smooth. Cook over medium heat until thickened, about 5 minutes, stirring constantly. Add strawberries and stir in food coloring. Cool completely. Spread strawberry glaze mixture over cream cheese layer and chill.

You can use peach slices in place of strawberries and almond flavoring in place of vanilla.

Outward circumstances have nothing to do with our joy in the Lord.

EASY PINEAPPLE DESSERT
Mrs. Roger Helmuth, Sr.

1 can crushed pineapple
1 (8 ounce) container Cool Whip
whipped topping

1 box vanilla instant pudding mix

Mix all together and top with whipped cream or Cool Whip. May also be put in graham cracker crust for pie.

ICE CREAM PISTACHIO PUDDING
Faith Miller

BOTTOM LAYER:
30 Ritz crackers, crushed

1 stick margarine, melted

FILLING:
2 packages pistachio instant
   pudding mix
1½ cups milk
1 quart vanilla ice cream, softened

Cool Whip whipped topping for
   garnish
1 or 2 Heath bars, crushed, for
   garnish

Mix together crackers and margarine and press in 8x8-inch cake pan. Bake at 350° for 10 minutes. Cool.

Beat together pudding mix and milk, then add softened ice cream at low speed. Pour on top of crust. Cool. Put Cool Whip on top and sprinkle with 1 or 2 crushed Heath bars. Serves 4.

STRAWBERRY VANILLA PUDDING
Silla K. Yoder

4½ cups (6 ounces) angel food
   cake cubes
1 (3 or 3¾ ounce) package vanilla
   instant pudding mix
1 cup cold milk
1 pint vanilla ice cream

1 (3 ounce) package strawberry
   Jello
1½ cups boiling water
1 (10 ounce) package frozen
   strawberry slices
Whipped cream

Place cake cubes in a 9x9x1½-inch baking dish. In mixing bowl, combine instant pudding and milk. Add ice cream. Beat at low speed until well blended. Pour over cake cubes. Set aside until firm. Dissolve Jello in boiling water. Add frozen strawberries. Stir until Jello begins to thicken. Pour over pudding (do not stir) until set. Serve with whipped cream. Serves 8-9.

PUMPKIN WHIP
Mrs. Merle Overholt

1 package butterscotch instant
   pudding mix
1½ cups cold milk
1 cup canned pumpkin

1 teaspoon pumpkin pie spice
1½ cups whipped topping
Gingersnaps, optional

In a mixing bowl, beat pudding mix and milk until well blended, about 1-2 minutes. Blend in pumpkin and pie spice. Fold in whipped topping. Spoon into dessert dishes. Chill. Garnish with gingersnaps, if desired. Serves 6.

FRUIT AND NUT BREAD PUDDING
Ruth Yoder

16 slices day-old bread,
  torn into 1-inch pieces
2 cups sugar
4 eggs
3 cups milk or 3 cups egg nog
2 teaspoons ground cinnamon
½ teaspoon salt

2 tablespoons vanilla extract
1 (21 ounce) can apple pie filling,
  slices cut in half
2 cups coarsely chopped pecans
1 cup golden raisins
¾ cup butter or margarine, melted
Whipped cream, optional

In a large bowl, combine bread and sugar. Set aside. In another bowl, beat eggs, milk or egg nog, cinnamon, salt, and vanilla until foamy. Pour over bread and sugar; mix well. Cover and refrigerate 2 hours. Stir in all remaining ingredients except cream. Pour into greased 13x9x2-inch baking pan. Bake at 350° for 45-50 minutes or until firm. Cut into squares. Serve warm or cold with whipped cream if desired. Serves 12-15.

GRAPE NUT PUDDING
Alta Kauffman

1 teaspoon lemon rind
4 tablespoons butter
¾ cup sugar
2 egg yolks, well beaten
3 tablespoons lemon juice

2 tablespoons flour
Dash of salt
4 tablespoons Grape Nuts cereal
1 cup milk
2 stiffly beaten egg whites

Mix lemon rind with butter and cream well. Add sugar gradually and beat well. Add egg yolks, lemon juice, flour, salt, Grape Nuts, and milk; mix well. Fold in egg whites. Pour into greased baking dish and put into a pan of hot water. Bake at 300° for 1 hour and 15 minutes.

Our strength is shown in the things we stand for.
Our weakness is shown in the things we fall for.

PUMPKIN DELIGHT
Esther L. Miller

1½ cups pumpkin
2 cups milk
3 beaten eggs
½ cup white sugar
½ cup dark brown sugar

1½ teaspoons cinnamon
¾ teaspoon nutmeg
1 box yellow cake mix
½ cup melted margarine

Mix pumpkin, milk, eggs, sugars, cinnamon, and nutmeg and pour in greased 9x13-inch cake pan. Top with cake mix and drizzle with melted margarine. Bake at 350° for 30-50 minutes. Serves 12-16.

FROZEN PUMPKIN DESSERT

Heidi Kauffman

CRUST:
3 cups crushed graham crackers
⅔ cup melted margarine

½ cup sugar

FILLING:
2 cups cooked pumpkin, or 1 (16 ounce) can Libby's pumpkin
1 cup brown sugar
½ teaspoon salt

½ teaspoon nutmeg
2 teaspoons cinnamon
2 quarts vanilla ice cream, softened

Mix crust ingredients and press into a 9x13-inch pan. Blend filling ingredients and put on top. Put in freezer. Take out and cut about 5-10 minutes before serving. Nice summer snack!

RHUBARB CUSTARD CRUNCH

Rhoda Coblentz

4 cups rhubarb, cut up
1 cup sugar
2 tablespoons flour

1 egg
1 cup milk
2 tablespoons butter

TOPPING:
1 cup sugar
1 teaspoon baking powder
1 cup flour

¼ teaspoon salt
1 egg, beaten

Mix together rhubarb, sugar, and flour in a greased 8x11-inch cake pan. Beat egg and add milk. Pour over first mixture. Dot butter over rhubarb.

Mix together topping ingredients. Will be crumbly. Sprinkle over rhubarb. Bake at 350° for 40 minutes or until crust is golden brown. Makes 8 servings.

CHOCOLATE FUDGE SAUCE

Ruth Yoder

¼ cup cocoa
1 cup sugar
½ cup whipping cream
2 tablespoons light corn syrup

3 tablespoons butter
¼ teaspoon salt
1 teaspoon vanilla

In a medium saucepan, combine all ingredients except vanilla over moderate heat. Bring to a boil. Boil for 1 minute, stirring constantly. Remove from heat and add vanilla. Reheat. Stir over low heat. Spoon over ice cream and top with nuts.

FRUIT SLUSH

Ruth Yoder, Mrs. Ferlin L. Yoder

1 (6 ounce) can frozen orange
 juice concentrate
3 cups water
1½ cups sugar, if desired

6 bananas, partially mashed
1 (20 ounce) can crushed
 pineapple

Mix concentrate, water, and sugar. Add bananas and pineapple. Freeze.
Partially thaw and serve with pretzels or snack crackers.

Note: 7-Up or strawberries may be added.

FROZEN STRAWBERRY DESSERT

Lena Schrock

1 can strawberry pie filling
1 small can pineapple
1 can Eagle brand milk

1 container Cool Whip whipped
 topping

Mix all ingredients together and put in a 9x12-inch cake pan. Freeze.
Soften a little before serving. Makes approximately 20 servings.

STRAWBERRY DELITE FOR A CROWD

Silla Beiler

CRUST:
3 cups flour
2 sticks margarine

½ cup nuts

MIDDLE LAYER:
1½ pounds cream cheese
2 cups Cool Whip whipped topping

1½ cups confectioners sugar

GLAZE:
3 cups Sprite
2 cups sugar
6 tablespoons tapioca starch

10 tablespoons strawberry Jello
1 quart fresh strawberries, sliced

Crust: Press dough in bottom of 2 (9x13-inch) pans and bake at 350° for 20
minutes. Combine middle layer ingredients and spread over cooled crust.

Cook the first 3 glaze ingredients, then mix Jello and sliced strawberries
into glaze. Spread over cream cheese layer.

VANILLA PUDDING

Ellen D. Miller

11 cups milk
2 cups sugar, divided
1 teaspoon salt
1½ cups Perma Flo

1 cup milk
12 egg yolks
1½ tablespoons vanilla
1 stick margarine, optional

Bring 11 cups milk and ½ cup sugar to a boil. Mix rest of sugar, salt, Perma Flo, 1 cup milk, and egg yolks together. Boil until thick. Add vanilla and margarine. Cool. Makes 16 servings.

A Bible in hand is worth two in the shelf.

SWEETHEART PUDDING

Judith Yoder

1 quart milk
½ cup flour
¾ cup sugar

4 egg yolks
1 cup milk
½ teaspoon vanilla

CRUST:
26 graham crackers
¾ cup sugar

1½ sticks margarine

Heat 1 quart milk. Mix together flour, sugar, egg yolks, and 1 cup milk and add to hot milk. Cook until thickened. Add vanilla and pour into crust.

Crust: Crush graham crackers and mix well with sugar and margarine. Press into 9x13-inch pan. Pour filling on top. Meringue or whipped topping may also be used on top.

TAPIOCA PUDDING

Rhoda Yoder

2¾ cups milk
⅓ cup sugar
3 tablespoons tapioca

2 eggs, beaten
1 teaspoon vanilla

Combine milk, sugar, and tapioca. Let set a few minutes. Bring to a boil on low heat. Add eggs, beaten with a little of the milk. Stir until thickened (do not cook after adding eggs). Add vanilla. Cool 20 minutes, then stir.

GRAPE JUICE TAPIOCA

Elva Miller

¾ cup sugar
2½ cups water
⅔ cup Minute tapioca
Juice of 1 lemon

1 cup grape juice
1 (8 ounce) container Cool Whip
 whipped topping

Combine sugar and water and boil together until sugar is dissolved. Add tapioca and cook until clear. Add lemon juice and grape juice and continue to cook for 3 minutes. Let cool. Fold in Cool Whip. Serves 6.

MINUTE TAPIOCA

Mrs. James Mast

2½ quarts water
1½ cups Minute tapioca
1 teaspoon salt
2 cups sugar

2 small boxes Jello
1 teaspoon vanilla
Your choice of fruit
1-2 cups whipping cream

Bring water to a boil; add tapioca and salt. Cook for 6 minutes. Stir in sugar, Jello, and vanilla; stir until dissolved. Cool. When cold, add pineapple, strawberries, bananas, or whatever you prefer. Whip the cream and fold in. Yields 5 quarts.

When using orange Jello, add a few tablespoons frozen orange juice concentrate. Delicious!

STRAWBERRY TAPIOCA

Mrs. Sol Yoder, Sr.

½ cup pearl tapioca
Dash salt
4 cups boiling water
1 small box strawberry Jello

¾ cup sugar
1 quart strawberries, frozen
Whipped cream or Cool Whip
 whipped topping

Boil tapioca, salt, and water for 20 minutes. Add Jello and sugar. Stir until dissolved. Add frozen strawberries and stir occasionally until dissolved. Cool. When ready to serve, add lots of whipped cream or Cool Whip.

CHERRY TORTE

Mrs. Freeman Schlabach

½ cup egg whites
¼ teaspoon cream of tartar

¾ cup white sugar

FILLING:
1 (3 ounce) package cream cheese
½ cup sugar
½ teaspoon vanilla

1 (8 ounce) container whipped
 topping
1 cup miniature marshmallows
Cherry pie filling

Cover cookie sheet with brown paper bag. Beat egg whites and cream of tartar until foamy. Beat in sugar until very stiff and glossy. Shape on sheet and make a dip in center with spoon. Bake 1½ hours at 275°. Turn oven off and leave in oven for 1 hour.

Mix cream cheese, ½ cup sugar, vanilla, whipped topping and marshmallows. Chill 12 hours, then spoon into meringue crust and top with pie filling. Makes 6 or 8 servings.

I like to make a big heart-shape tart and fill with ice cream and topping for Valentine's Day!

PUMPKIN TORTE

Mrs. Sol Yoder, Sr.

CRUST:
30 graham crackers, crushed to
 crumbs

½ cup sugar
½ cup melted butter

2ND LAYER:
2 eggs, beaten
¾ cup sugar

1 (8 ounce) package cream cheese

FILLING:
1 package gelatin
¼ cup water
2 cups pumpkin
3 egg yolks
½ cup sugar
½ cup milk

½ teaspoon salt
1 tablespoon cinnamon
3 egg whites
¼ cup sugar
Whipped topping

Mix crust ingredients and press into a 9x13-inch pan. Beat 2nd layer ingredients together and put on crust. Bake for 20 minutes at 350°.

For filling, dissolve gelatin in water. Set aside. Boil together pumpkin, egg yolks, sugar, milk, salt, and cinnamon until thick. Add gelatin to hot mixture. Cool, then add well-beaten egg whites and ¼ cup sugar and fold into boiled mixture. Put on top of crust and chill. Serve with whipped topping.

CHOCOLATE TORTE   Linda Zook

½ cup butter
3 ounces unsweetened chocolate
1½ cups whipping cream
4 eggs, well beaten
1 teaspoon vanilla

1½ cups sugar
2 cups flour
2 teaspoons baking powder
½ teaspoon salt

FILLING:
1 cup cream, whipped to soft
  peaks
1 (8 ounce) package cream cheese

1 cup powdered sugar
1 teaspoon vanilla

FROSTING:
2 ounces chocolate (or less)
¼ cup butter
3 cups powdered sugar

½ cup cream
1 teaspoon vanilla

Melt butter and chocolate. Cool and set aside. Beat cream until soft peaks form. Add butter mixture, beaten eggs, and vanilla. Mix only until blended. Sift dry ingredients and add to mixture. Mix on low just until mixed. Pour into 3 well-greased 8- or 9-inch pans and bake at 350° for 20-25 minutes. Cool completely, then wrap each layer in plastic wrap and chill well. Split each layer and fill with filling. Refrigerate or freeze before frosting.

Filling: Whip cream; add cream cheese and powdered sugar. Beat until smooth. Add vanilla.

Frosting: Melt chocolate and butter. Cool. Add remaining ingredients.

WEDDING FRUIT   Carol Petersheim

3 dozen oranges, peeled, cut up,
  and sugar added to desired
  sweetness
4 pounds grapes
1 gallon fruit cocktail

1 gallon pineapple rings
1 quart cherries, optional
12 quarts peaches
Instant lemon pudding

Mix fruit together in a large container, then add instant lemon pudding to thicken the juice. Add to suit your taste. Some like more, some less. Guests heartily enjoy it! One batch equals 6 gallons.

YOGURT

Esther Mast

1 gallon milk
2 tablespoons unflavored gelatin
½ cup cold water
½ cup plain yogurt
1-2 cups sugar (or more for making vanilla-flavored yogurt)

1-2 packages pie filling or ½ cup or desired amount of Jello, flavor of your choice
2 tablespoons vanilla (if making vanilla-flavored yogurt)

Heat milk to 180° then cool to 130°. While milk is cooling, soak gelatin in cold water. When milk has cooled, add gelatin, plain yogurt and sugar. Beat all together and set on top of pilot light for 8 hours or overnight. Skim off top skin. Or if desired, put yogurt through strainer. Beat well. Then add pie filling or Jello. Beat well again. Always beat well before serving.

This is very smooth. If vanilla yogurt is desired, add more sugar and 2 tablespoons vanilla.

Salvation is a GIFT;
it is grace plus NOTHING!

KATHRYN'S YOGURT

Rachel Swarey

1 gallon milk
2 tablespoons sugar
1½ tablespoons plain gelatin

1 cup powdered milk
1-2 cups plain yogurt

FILLING:
4 cups water
1 cup Perma Flo
½-¾ cup sugar

¾ cup of your choice flavor of Jello

Heat milk to 180°. (Put a little sugar in bottom of bowl to prevent scorched milk.) Remove from heat and add sugar and gelatin which has been softened in a little water. Cool to 112°. Put 2 cups 112° milk, the powdered milk, and yogurt into blender and blend well. Stir into milk mixture and keep the temperature close to 112° until set. Set under desk lamp or wrap in blanket. Refrigerate when set.

Cook together first 3 filling ingredients until very thick and clear. Remove from heat and add Jello. Fold this into the yogurt when yogurt has cooled completely.

Meats

HAM CROQUETTES

Elsie Yoder

2 pounds chopped ham
2 pounds hamburger
2 eggs
1½ cups milk
½ teaspoon liquid smoke

1½ cups bread crumbs or oatmeal
1 teaspoon salt
1 teaspoon pepper
2 teaspoons Worcestershire sauce
½ teaspoon onion powder

TOPPING:
1 cup brown sugar
1 teaspoon dry mustard
½ cup water

½ cup vinegar or 1 tablespoon
   prepared mustard

Mix all meatball ingredients and shape into walnut sized balls. Bring topping ingredients to a boil. Pour over meatballs and bake at 350°, covered, for 1 hour, and about 10 minutes uncovered. Makes about 50 meatballs.

MOCK HAM LOAF

Mrs. Sol Yoder, Sr., Miriam Yoder

2 pounds hamburger
1 pound hot dogs, ground

2 cups cracker crumbs
2 eggs, beaten

SYRUP:
1½ cups brown sugar
2 cups water
2 tablespoons vinegar

1 teaspoon dry mustard
1 teaspoon salt
Dash of pepper

Mix hamburger and hot dogs with cracker crumbs and eggs thoroughly. Prepare ingredients for syrup an add 1 cup syrup to meat and mix. Form into a loaf shape and pour the rest of syrup over loaf. Bake at 350° for 1½ hours. Makes 6-8 servings.

GRAVY BAKED PORK CHOPS

Mrs. Shirley Yoder

4 pork chops
¼ teaspoon salt
⅛ teaspoon pepper
1 tablespoon shortening

1 can cream of mushroom soup
⅔ cup evaporated milk
⅓ cup water

Sprinkle pork chops with salt and pepper and brown in skillet with shortening. Pour off excess drippings. Mix soup with milk and water and pour over pork chops. Bake at 350° for 45 minutes to 1 hour. Makes 4 servings.

PINEAPPLE GLAZED HAM BALLS
Linda Zook

3 pounds ground ham
2½ pounds ground pork
2 cups milk

3 eggs
2 cups cracker crumbs
2 tablespoons parsley

PINEAPPLE GLAZE:
1 cup crushed pineapple
1 cup brown sugar
3 tablespoons honey

2 tablespoons vinegar
Clear Jell
8 ounces Sprite

Mix all meatball ingredients well and shape into balls. Place in a single layer on baking sheet and bake at 300° until nicely browned. Remove from baking sheet and place in casserole.

Make glaze by combining pineapple, sugar, honey, and vinegar. Bring to boil and thicken with Clear Jell. Add Sprite after thickening. Pour glaze over top and bake 1 hour.

SAVORY HAM CASSEROLE
Cynthia Helmuth

2 tablespoons margarine, melted
¼ teaspoon thyme, crushed
3 cups Rice Chex cereal
1 (10¾ ounce) can cream of
  mushroom soup
½ cup sour cream

1 (10 ounce) package frozen lima
  beans or green beans, cooked
  and drained
1 cup cooked ham strips
Shredded cheese, optional

Combine margarine and thyme. Add Rice Chex and mix until evenly coated. Set aside. Combine soup and sour cream. Stir in beans, ham, ½ cup seasoned Chex, slightly crushed. Spread in shallow 1½-quart casserole. Crumble remaining Chex over top. Sprinkle shredded cheese over crumbs if desired. Bake at 350° for 25 minutes or until bubbly and crumbs are toasted. Makes 6 servings.

It is not success, but faithfulness that God rewards.

ASPARAGUS HAM QUICHE
Sonia Hoffman

1 package frozen asparagus cuts,
  thawed
½ pound cooked ham, chopped
1 cup shredded Swiss cheese
¼ cup chopped onion

3 eggs
1 cup milk
¾ cup buttermilk baking mix
⅛ teaspoon pepper
⅛ teaspoon nutmeg

Grease 9-inch pie plate. Layer asparagus, ham, cheese, and onion. In a bowl, beat eggs. Add remaining ingredients and mix well. Pour mixture over ham and asparagus mixture. Bake at 375° for 30 minutes. Makes 6 servings.

UNDERGROUND HAM CASSEROLE

Linda Kauffman

4 cups chunked or chopped ham
4 tablespoons butter or margarine
½ cup chopped onion
2 tablespoons Worcestershire
 sauce
2 cans cream of mushroom soup

1 cup milk
2 cups cheese, grated or cubed
4 quarts mashed potatoes
1 pint sour cream
8-10 strips bacon, fried

Combine and sauté first 4 ingredients. Pour in medium roaster. In medium saucepan, heat soup, milk, and cheese until cheese melts. Spread on ham mixture. Mash potatoes. Do not add salt or milk, but mix with sour cream. Spread potatoes over top, and sprinkle with crumbled bacon. Bake at 350° for 20 minutes or until slightly browned. Serves 6-8.

SAUSAGE CASSEROLE

Mrs. Jonathan Yoder

2 pounds pork sausage
2 tablespoons chopped green
 peppers (optional)
8 ounces noodles
1 (10 ounce) can cream of chicken
 soup

½ cup milk
½ teaspoon salt
¼ teaspoon Accent
1 cup grated cheese
Cornflake crumbs to garnish

Sauté sausage and green peppers in skillet. Cook noodles until tender; drain. Mix together soup, milk, and seasonings and cheese. Mix all together and pour into 2-quart casserole dish. Sprinkle crumbs over top and bake at 350° for 30-35 minutes. Makes 6-8 servings.

You can't rid yourself of a bad temper by losing it.
When you are right no one remembers;
when you are wrong no one forgets.

SAUSAGE & RYE

Barbara Kauffman

1 pound ground beef
1 pound ground sausage
1 teaspoon oregano
½ teaspoon garlic salt

1 pound Velveeta cheese, cut in
 small pieces
1½ -2 loaves rye bread (about 48
 slices of the small loaves)

Brown and drain meat. Add oregano, garlic salt, and cheese. Stir until cheese is melted. Spread on rye slices and freeze on cookie sheets. Place in plastic bag when frozen. When ready to use, place on cookie sheets and put under broiler until lightly browned.

QUICK SAUSAGE SUPPER
Silla K. Yoder

¾ cup water
1 package smoked beef sausage
4 or 5 medium potatoes, quartered

2 medium onions, quartered
Salt and pepper to taste
Cabbage, about 6 wedges

Place water in large frying pan on medium heat. Cut sausage in serving pieces. Add sausage, potatoes, and onion to the water. Sprinkle with salt and pepper mostly on potatoes. Simmer covered about 8 minutes, then place cabbage wedges on top. Sprinkle salt and pepper on top of cabbage. *Do not stir.* Cover and simmer about 10 minutes or until potatoes are tender. Serve with cornbread.

SPICY RICE CASSEROLE
Mrs. Vivian Miller

1 pound mild pork sausage
1 teaspoon ground cumin
½ teaspoon garlic powder
2 medium onions, chopped
2 medium green peppers, chopped

2 beef bouillon cubes
2 cups boiling water
1 (6.25 ounce) package long grain
  & wild rice

In a large skillet, cook sausage, cumin, and garlic powder, stirring often. Drain. Add onions and green peppers; sauté until tender. Dissolve bouillon in water; add to sausage mixture. Stir in rice and seasoning packets. Bring to a boil. Reduce heat and simmer, uncovered, 5-10 minutes or until the water is absorbed. Serves 8.

WIENER BEAN CASSEROLE
Alta Kauffman

4 medium potatoes, diced
1½ cups milk
¾ cup mayonnaise
3 tablespoons flour
1 teaspoon salt
¾ teaspoon dry mustard

¼ teaspoon black pepper
1 medium onion, chopped
6 wieners, sliced
2 cups cooked or canned green
  beans, drained
Bread crumbs for topping

Cook potatoes until just tender; drain. Meanwhile, put milk, mayonnaise, flour, salt, mustard, pepper, and onion in blender. Blend until mixed. Place potatoes, wieners, and beans into a casserole dish. Pour milk mixture over all. Top with bread crumbs. Bake at 350° for 45 minutes. Serves 6-8.

SUGAR CURED HAM

Mrs. Noah Yoder

Freshly butchered pork before
  cooling
2 cups coarse salt
1 cup brown sugar

2 teaspoons black pepper
1 teaspoon red pepper
1 ham from 200-pound hog

Mix ingredients. Provide brown wrap paper large enough to wrap ham. Lay ham on it, skin up, and rub in mix in small amounts as it melts. Lift ham and sprinkle paper with mix. Turn cut side up.

Pack rest of mix on cut side and as much as possible under skin around knee joint. Hold mix directly on joint while wrapping tightly in the brown paper. Try not to disturb mix. Tie tight as possible and sew muslin tightly around the ham. Lay skin side down for 24 hours at room temperature. Turn over and leave laying for another 24 hours. Insert into cloth bag knee down and hang in dark, well-ventilated room, for 6 months.

To fry, simply slice. To bake, wash well and place in kettle. Fill with water and soak overnight. Drain and add fresh water. Simmer, covered, until tender, approximately 25 minutes per pound. Take off skin and place fat side up on rack in baking pan. Sprinkle with brown sugar and stud with whole cloves. Preheat oven to 350° and bake 35 minutes.

SHRIMP AND WILD RICE CASSEROLE

Ruth Hershberger

1 cup melted butter, divided
½ cup flour
4 cups chicken broth
1 cup finely chopped onion
½ cup finely chopped mushrooms
2 pounds cooked, peeled, and
  deveined shrimp

2 tablespoons Worcestershire
  sauce
4 cups cooked rice
1 teaspoon salt
¼ teaspoon white pepper

Make a thin white sauce with ½ cup butter, flour, and broth. Sauté veggies in remaining butter. Drain. Stir together with remaining ingredients and bake at 300° for 45-50 minutes in shallow 4-quart casserole dish.

Hearts, like doors, will open with ease
To very, very little keys.
And don't forget that two of these,
Are "Thank you, sir" and "if you please."

SEAFOOD CASSEROLE
Jo Ann Inhulsen

2 cups bread crumbs
2 cups cream
3 small cans crab
1½ pounds fresh shrimp (medium)
2 cups mayonnaise
6 hard boiled eggs (pushed
  through a sieve)

2 tablespoons fresh chopped
  parsley
2 teaspoons onion
Red pepper
Salt and pepper to taste
Extra bread crumbs and paprika
  for topping

Soften bread crumbs with cream and mix with rest of ingredients. Top with extra bread crumbs and paprika. Bake at 350° for 35 minutes.

IMPOSSIBLE SEAFOOD PIE
Elva Miller

1 (6 ounce) package frozen
  crabmeat (can also use fresh)
1 cup shredded Cheddar cheese
1 (3 ounce) package cream
  cheese, cut in cubes

2 tablespoons minced onion
2 cups milk
1 cup Bisquick baking mix
4 eggs
¾ teaspoon salt

Grease pie plate. Mix meat, cheeses, and onion in plate. Beat remaining ingredients until smooth. Pour over meat mixture and bake at 400° for 35-40 minutes.

TARTAR SAUCE
Judith Yoder

1 cup salad dressing
1 teaspoon grated onion
2 tablespoons minced dill pickle

1 teaspoon parsley flakes
½ teaspoon parsley seed
Dash red pepper

Combine ingredients. Yields 1 cup sauce.

LONG JOHN SILVER FISH BATTER
Mary Zook,
Naomi Yoder, Elsie Brenneman

¾ cup flour
½ teaspoon baking powder
¼ cup cornstarch
Pinch of salt

1 egg
1 cup water
2-3 pounds fish

Mix dry ingredients. Mix egg and water separately. Gradually stir into flour mixture. Flour fish and dip into batter. Deep fry.

I like to salt my fish before battering.

MARINADE FOR GRILLED MEATS

Mrs. Vivian Miller

1 pint water
1 quart vinegar
1 pound margarine, melted

½ cup salt
½ cup black pepper
1 tablespoon Worcestershire sauce

Heat all ingredients in large kettle. Add meat and marinate for several hours. Excellent for chicken, pork chops, spare ribs, etc.

DEER STEAK MARINADE

Mrs. Roger Helmuth, Sr.

½ cup water
1 cup vegetable oil
10 tablespoons soy sauce

1 clove garlic or minced onion
1 tablespoon parsley flakes
1 tablespoon black pepper

Marinate steaks in refrigerator overnight or 4 hours at room temperature. Grill.

These steaks stay very moist after grilling.

STEAK SAUCE

Denise Smith

1½ cups ketchup
¾ cup brown sugar
1 tablespoon mustard
1 tablespoon vinegar
⅓ cup Worcestershire sauce
½ teaspoon smoked flavoring
½ teaspoon onion powder

½ teaspoon garlic powder
1 teaspoon paprika
2 teaspoons BBQ seasoning
1 teaspoon seasoned salt
1 teaspoon meat tenderizer
½ teaspoon Nature's Seasoning

Mix well and serve. I like to add as many different seasonings as I can. It helps to give it a better flavor. Try some of your own and see how you like it. (Fantastic on steaks!)

BAR-B-QUE

Viola Miller

A pork or beef roast
2 small onions
⅔ bottle chili sauce

½ cup ketchup
1 teaspoon lemon juice

Cook roast several hours until it falls apart. Add onions which have been cut into small pieces. Add the other 3 ingredients and cook another 30 minutes. Serves 10.

CALOCHIES
Debbie Graber

1½ pounds hamburger, fried
1 cup pizza sauce
1 recipe feather roll dough

Pepperoni, cut in pieces
Grated cheese

Mix hamburger and pizza sauce together. Make balls of the roll dough and roll out onto greased counter top. They should be 6 inches in diameter. Spoon 3 tablespoons of meat mixture in center. Top with pepperoni and a few sprinkles of cheese. Fold in 4 sides of dough and pinch top to seal. Sprinkle more cheese on top. Place on greased cookie sheets. Repeat with remaining dough. Bake at 400° until golden brown, 20-25 minutes. To serve, top with additional pizza sauce.

CHOP SUEY
Tina Nussbaum

1 pound hamburger

2 onions

SAUCE:
1 tablespoon soy sauce
½ teaspoon salt
2 tablespoons cornstarch

1 tablespoon molasses (or Karo syrup)
1 (4 ounce) can mushrooms
2 cups water

Brown hamburger and drain. Add onions and mushrooms. Make sauce by mixing soy sauce, salt, cornstarch, molasses or Karo syrup, and mushrooms and add to hamburger. Add 2 cups water and bring to a boil. Simmer 15 minutes. Serve over rice. Serves 4.

BRAN & BEEF STROGANOFF
Silla Beiler

1 egg
⅓ cup milk
1¼ cups 40% Bran Flakes cereal
½ teaspoon garlic salt
¼ teaspoon pepper
¼ teaspoon paprika
¾ pound hamburger
1 medium onion, chopped

1 tablespoon margarine
½ cup hot water
1 can mushrooms, drained
1 beef bouillon cube
1 can mushroom soup
1 (8 ounce) carton sour cream
Buttered noodles

Beat egg, milk, Bran Flakes, garlic salt, pepper, and paprika. Let set for 5 minutes. Add hamburger and shape into balls. Place in oven at 400° for 12 minutes or until browned. Meanwhile, in large frying pan, cook onion in margarine until tender. Stir in water, mushrooms, and bouillon cube. Simmer several minutes. Add to meatballs and continue simmering 15 minutes. Combine soup and sour cream and pour over meatballs. Just before serving, pour over noodles.

AUNT LOU'S MEATBALLS

Roxanna Linneber

2 pounds hamburger
1 pound Italian sausage
2 eggs

Diced celery
Diced onion
Real fine Progresso bread crumbs

SAUCE:
1 large can tomato sauce

1 packet spaghetti sauce mix

Combine all ingredients and make into small balls. Brown them. Put in crock pot and cover with tomato sauce and spaghetti sauce.

BARBECUED MEAT BALLS

Martha Yoder

1½ pounds ground beef
¾ cup quick oats or bread crumbs
2 tablespoons minced onion

1½ teaspoons salt
¼ teaspoon pepper
1 cup milk

SAUCE:
2 tablespoons brown sugar
1 tablespoon Worcestershire sauce
1 cup ketchup

¼ cup water
¼ cup vinegar
¼ cup minced onions

Mix meat mixture well and form into balls. Roll in flour then fry in skillet until nicely browned. Put in roaster. Mix together sauce ingredients. Pour over meatballs and bake at 250° for 1 hour.

BARBECUED MEATBALLS

Linda Kauffman

MEATBALLS:
3 pounds ground beef
1 (12 ounce) can evaporated milk
1 cup oatmeal
1 cup cracker crumbs
2 eggs

½ cup chopped onion
½ teaspoon garlic powder
2 teaspoons salt
½ teaspoon pepper
2 teaspoons chili powder

SAUCE:
2 cups ketchup
1 cup brown sugar
½ teaspoon liquid smoke

½ teaspoon garlic powder
¼ cup chopped onion

To make meatballs, combine all ingredients (mixture will be soft) and shape into walnut-size balls. Place meatballs in a single layer on wax paper-lined cookie sheets; freeze until solid. Store frozen meatballs in freezer bags until ready to cook.

To make sauce, combine all ingredients and stir until sugar is dissolved. Place frozen meatballs in 9x13-inch baking pan and pour on sauce. Bake at 350 for 1 hour. Makes 80 meatballs.

"CHRISTMAS" MEATBALLS
Lydia Knox

2 pounds ground beef
2 eggs
1 cup shredded mozzarella cheese
½ cup bread crumbs
¼ cup finely chopped onion
2 tablespoons Parmesan cheese

1 tablespoon ketchup
2 teaspoons Worcestershire sauce
1 teaspoon Italian seasoning
1 teaspoon salt
¼ teaspoon pepper

SAUCE:
1 (14 ounce) bottle ketchup
2 tablespoons cornstarch

1 (12 ounce) jar apple jelly
1 (12 ounce) jar currant jelly

In a bowl, combine the first 11 ingredients; mix well. Shape into 1-inch balls. Place on rack on large cookie sheet and bake at 350° for 10-15 minutes. Remove rack and drain meatballs.

Combine ketchup and cornstarch in roasting pan, stir in jellies, and add meatballs. Cover and bake at 350° for 30 minutes. Makes 8 dozen meatballs.

Remember, you are not only the salt of the earth, but the sugar.

VOLCANO MEATBALLS WITH BARBECUE SAUCE
Faith Miller

2 pounds hamburger
2 eggs
1 cup cracker crumbs
1 medium onion, chopped

½-¾ cup milk or water to moisten
Salt and pepper
Cubes of Swiss or desired type of
    cheese (enough for each meatball)

SAUCE:
2 onions, chopped
4 tablespoons sugar
2 tablespoons vinegar

3 tablespoons Worcestershire sauce
1 cup ketchup
1 can mushroom soup

Mix together the first 6 ingredients, and shape into balls. Place a cube of cheese into the center of the meatball, leaving a cavity in the top with a little of the cheese showing in it.

Mix sauce ingredients together, cook for ½ hour, then put over the meatballs and bake for an hour at 350°.

SWEET & SOUR MEATBALLS

Melody Helmuth

MEATBALLS:
2 pounds hamburger
1 cup finely crushed cracker crumbs
¼ cup milk

Salt and pepper
1 tablespoon grated onion
(if desired)

SAUCE:
1½ cups pineapple juice
⅓ cup vinegar
⅓ cup brown sugar

¼ cup soy sauce
2 tablespoons cornstarch
1½ cups pineapple chunks

For meatballs, mix all ingredients well. Shape into balls and brown in skillet. Remove meatballs and add all sauce ingredients except pineapple chunks. Stir until thick and smooth. Add meatballs and simmer 15-20 minutes or until meatballs are done in center. Add pineapple chunks and simmer a few minutes longer. Serve over rice. Makes 4-6 servings.

SAUCE FOR SWEDISH MEATBALLS

Ruth Yoder

1 jar cherry preserves
1 can cranberry sauce
2 tablespoons brown sugar
½ cup ketchup

2 teaspoons lemon juice
Black pepper
2 tablespoons soy sauce

Cook all together at low temperature until smooth.

COUNTRY MEATLOAF

Mrs. Jonathan Yoder

1½ pounds hamburger
2-4 tablespoons chopped onion
1 teaspoon salt
⅛ teaspoon garlic powder
¼ teaspoon poultry seasoning
⅛ teaspoon dried mustard
⅛ teaspoon black pepper

1½ teaspoons Worcestershire
sauce
3 slices bread, cubed
1 cup warm milk
2 eggs
Pinch of red pepper (optional)

SAUCE:
⅓ cup ketchup
1½ tablespoons brown sugar

1½ teaspoons mustard

Mix together hamburger, chopped onion, salt, garlic powder, poultry seasoning, dry mustard, black pepper, and Worcestershire sauce. Then soak bread in a mixture of the warm milk and eggs. Mix thoroughly all of the above. Make into loaf and bake at 350° for 45 minutes to 1 hour. Pour sauce over meatloaf about last 10 minutes of baking. Makes 6 servings.

HAMBURGER PATTIES

Ann Mast

1½ pounds ground beef
½ cup cracker crumbs
¾ teaspoon salt
½ teaspoon pepper

1 egg, beaten
6 slices onion
6 slices cheese
¾ cup tomato sauce

Combine meat, crumbs, salt, pepper, and egg. Shape into patties. Place in oblong 9x13-inch pan. Place onion slice and cheese on patties. Pour tomato sauce over top. Bake at 375° for 35-40 minutes. Makes 6 patties.

SALISBURY STEAK

Rhoda Hilty

¾ cup saltine crackers, crushed
1 pound ground beef
¼ cup ketchup
1 teaspoon chopped onions
1 egg
½ teaspoon Worcestershire sauce
¾ teaspoon salt

¼ teaspoon pepper
1 (10½ ounce) can cream of
  mushroom soup
½ cup milk
1 tablespoon butter
¼ teaspoon garlic salt
1 (4 ounce) can mushroom stems
  and pieces

Mix first 8 ingredients and make oval patties and put in a deep dish or casserole. Then mix cream of mushroom soup, milk, butter, and garlic salt and beat. Pour over meat and bake at 350° for 45 minutes. During the last 10 minutes, top with mushrooms. Makes 8 servings.

SALISBURY STEAK

Sara Jean Yoder

2 beef bouillon cubes
½ cup hot water
1½ pounds hamburger
½ cup fine bread crumbs
1 small onion, chopped
Garlic or celery salt

Salt according to taste
1 tablespoon Worcestershire
  sauce
1 large egg
1 can mushroom soup
1 soup can milk

Dissolve bouillon cubes hot water. Mix this in with meat, crumbs, onion, seasonings, and egg. Make patties. Preheat oven to 350°. Bake patties about 15 minutes. Cover with soup and milk gravy. This can be topped with biscuits and baked 20 minutes. Makes 8 servings.

HAWAIIAN STEAK

Mrs. Roger Helmuth, Sr.

Steak
1 can mushroom soup
1 medium size bottle soy sauce
2 teaspoons ginger

3 tablespoons brown sugar
1 tablespoon vinegar
Garlic to taste (optional)

Fry the steak. Mix rest of ingredients and pour over fried steaks. Bake at 275°-300° for 3½-4 hours.

POOR MAN'S STEAK

Mrs. Sol Yoder, Sr., Ruth Yoder

1 pound hamburger
1 cup milk
1 onion, chopped fine

1 cup soda crackers, crushed
1 teaspoon salt
½ teaspoon pepper

SAUCE:
1 can cream of mushroom soup

½ soup can milk

Mix well and shape in narrow loaf. Let set in refrigerator 8 hours, and slice and fry until brown. Put slices in layers in roaster, then pour a sauce made with soup and milk over meat. Bake at 350° for 1 hour. Makes 10 servings.

Do you know why mountain climbers rope themselves together?
To prevent the sensible ones from going home.

HARK'S DELICIOUS
CHICKEN & DUMPLINGS

Mrs. Freeman Schlabach

1 quart canned chicken and broth
1 stick margarine

Self-rising flour
1 can cream of mushroom soup

Heat chicken and broth with margarine in a 3-quart pot. Take out 1 cup broth and mix it with the flour for drop biscuits. Add cream of mushroom soup to the chicken and broth. Have it simmering, then drop biscuits on top. Cover and simmer about 20 minutes. Check with a fork to see if it's done. Serves 8.

EASY CHICKEN POT PIE

Cece Allen

2 pie crusts
2 cans Veg-All
Onion powder to taste

2 cans cream of chicken soup
4 cooked chicken breasts in bite-
   size pieces

Mix all ingredients and put in pie shell. Cover with other pie shell and bake at 350° until pie shell is done.

GRANDMA SLAPPEN GOOD CHICKEN

Drusilla Kay Yoder,
Donna Kauffman

1 (3 pound) fryer, cut up
Salt
Minced onion
1 (8 ounce) package Pepperidge
   Farm cornbread stuffing mix

1 stick butter, melted
2 cups chicken broth, divided
2 cans cream of celery soup
4 ounces sour cream

Cook chicken and debone it. Season with salt and small amount of minced onion. Toss stuffing mix with melted butter. Put ½ in bottom of a 9x13-inch pan. Place deboned chicken over stuffing. Pour 1 cup broth over chicken. Mix soup and sour cream. Spread over chicken. Cover with remaining stuffing mix. Pour 1 cup broth over all. Bake at 375° for 1 hour. Serves 10.

The smile on your face is the light in the window
that tells people you are at home.

MELT IN YOUR MOUTH CHICKEN PIE   Sara Jean Yoder

1 (16 ounce) can peas and carrots,
   drained
2 cups chicken, cooked and
   chopped
2 cups chicken broth

1 can cream of chicken soup
1 stick melted butter or margarine
2 cups self-rising flour
2 cups buttermilk

Place peas, carrots, and chicken in a 9x12-inch glass baking dish. Mix chicken broth with undiluted soup to a smooth consistency and pour over chicken/vegetable mixture. Mix melted butter, flour, and buttermilk. Pour over chicken mixture. Do not stir. Bake at 350° for 30 minutes. Brown at 450° for 10 more minutes. Makes 8 servings.

MICROWAVE ORIENTAL   Martha Kauffman
CHICKEN AND CASHEWS

5 tablespoons oil
4 boneless chicken breasts,
   skinned and thinly sliced
   in 1-inch strips
2 cloves garlic, minced
4 tablespoons soy sauce

2 tablespoons sherry or cooking
   wine
2 tablespoons cornstarch
½ teaspoon ginger
1½ medium green peppers, cut up
½-1 cup cashews

Place oil in 4-quart baking dish. Microwave on *high* for 1 minute. Combine chicken, garlic, soy sauce, sherry, cornstarch, and ginger. Add to oil and microwave on *high* for 3-4 minutes, stirring after each minute. Add green peppers and cashews, cover with plastic wrap, and microwave on *high* 3-5 minutes, or until chicken is done and green pepper is crisp-tender. Stir after 1 minute. Let stand 3 minutes before serving. Serve over rice. Makes 8 servings.

TACO CHIP MAIN DISH   Judi Wagher

1 medium-sized bag nacho Doritos
1 cup sour cream
1 can cream of chicken soup
¼ pound grated Cheddar or
   Monterey Jack cheese

1½-2 cups cooked chicken,
   chopped
A few drops hot sauce, if desired

Crush Doritos and spread ⅔ of them in the bottom of an 8x10-inch casserole dish. Mix remaining ingredients. Spread over Doritos. Sprinkle the remaining Doritos over the top. Bake at 375° for 30 minutes. Makes 4-6 servings.

STIR-FRIED LAOS FOOD

Ramona Overholt

STEP 1:

3 pounds boneless, skinless chicken, cubed
3 tablespoons soy sauce
2 teaspoons salt
½ teaspoon black pepper and red pepper

Oil for frying
About 1½ tablespoons Clear Jell or cornstarch
2 cups water

STEP 2:

2 teaspoons salt
½ teaspoon black pepper
1½ teaspoons Accent
½ teaspoon garlic salt
1 teaspoon seasoned salt

1 bundle broccoli, stemmed and shaved
1 head cauliflower, chopped fine
4 medium squash, thinly sliced
1 large sweet onion, finely shaved
½ head cabbage, finely shaved

Step 1: Marinate meat in soy sauce, salt, and peppers for 1 hour or overnight. Then fry in small amount of very hot grease. When meat is tender, mix Clear Jell or cornstarch with water and add to meat to make gravy.

Step 2: Mix together all the seasonings and sprinkle over prepared vegetables. Let set 1 hour or overnight. Then stir-fry on high heat in very hot oil (about 2 tablespoons) until tender-crisp.

Optional: French-cut green beans may be used instead of squash. Mix two dishes together and serve with sticky or regular rice or fine noodles.

BROCCOLI AND CHICKEN STIR-FRY

Silla K. Yoder

2 (1 pound) bags frozen broccoli, cooked until tender
Dash of pepper
Dash Louisiana hot sauce
3 teaspoons soy sauce
Dash salt
1½ teaspoons Dale's seasoning

3 teaspoons dried diced onions
2 cups cooked chicken sautéed in ½ cup Italian dressing
½ teaspoon hickory smoke salt
1½ teaspoons ginger
½ teaspoon red pepper
¼ stick butter

Mix all above ingredients together and let simmer at medium-high for 15 minutes or until thoroughly heated. Serve over rice.

You may also add your own seasonings or add more hot sauce, according to your taste.

CHICKEN STIR-FRY

Tina Nussbaum

1 tablespoon soy sauce
1 tablespoon cornstarch
½ cup water
¾ cup mushrooms
¾ cup onions
¾ cup peppers

1 tablespoon soy sauce
1 tablespoon cornstarch
½ teaspoon salt
½ teaspoon sugar
1 tablespoon water
1½-2 cups chicken, cut up

Mix first 3 ingredients and add to cut-up mushrooms, onions, and peppers. Fry. Mix next 5 ingredients and add to cut-up chicken. Fry. When chicken is browned, add the vegetable mixture and simmer on low for 15-20 minutes. Serve over rice. Makes 4 servings.

GROUND TURKEY GOULASH

Carolyn Eash

1 pound ground turkey (or ground beef)
Salt, pepper, onion powder, and garlic powder, to taste
4 cups canned chopped tomatoes
½ cup chopped green pepper

1 tablespoon instant minced onion
1 (4 ounce) can mushrooms with liquid
2 cubes beef or chicken bouillon
3 ounces elbow macaroni

Brown ground turkey or beef in a large skillet. Add rest of ingredients except macaroni. Bring to boil, then add macaroni. Continue to boil, uncovered, until macaroni absorbs all of liquid and is tender, about 20 minutes. Serves 4-5.

TURKEY-VEGETABLE BAKE

Cynthia Helmuth

1 cup chopped carrots
1 cup sliced celery
½ cup chopped onion
½ cup chopped green pepper
1½ cups chopped, cooked turkey or chicken
1 (4 ounce) can sliced mushrooms, drained

½ teaspoon dried marjoram, crushed
¼ teaspoon ground sage
¼ teaspoon salt
Dash pepper
2 beaten eggs
½ cup skim milk
¼ cup shredded Cheddar cheese

Cook vegetables 10 minutes or until tender. Drain. Combine vegetables, turkey or chicken, and seasonings in 8x8x2-inch pan. Combine eggs and milk. Pour over turkey mixture. Sprinkle cheese atop. Bake at 325° for 30-35 minutes or until set. Let stand 5 minutes. Cut into squares and serve. Makes 6 servings.

BAKED CHICKEN
Denise Smith

12 pieces of chicken
Salt water to cover
¼ cup Worcestershire sauce
½ cup vinegar
Onion
Salt

Paprika
Seasoned salt
Lemon pepper
BBQ seasoning
Meat tenderizer
Chicken seasoning

Soak chicken for approximately 30 minutes in salt water, then lay out on cookie sheet. Pour vinegar and Worcestershire sauce over chicken. Sprinkle onion, salt, paprika, seasoned salt, lemon pepper, BBQ seasoning, meat tenderizer, and chicken seasoning on top to your liking.

Bake at 300° for 2 hours or until done. I like to put tin foil on the bottom of the cookie sheet so nothing gets stuck to the pan. Virtually fat-free!

BAKED CHICKEN
Ruth Yoder

1 cup Worcestershire sauce
1 tablespoon liquid smoke
1 tablespoon garlic salt
1 tablespoon paprika

1 tablespoon curry powder
1 tablespoon poultry seasoning
1 (16 ounce) bottle Italian dressing
1 tablespoon seasoning salt

Mix all ingredients together and pour over chicken. Marinate chicken in refrigerator overnight. Bake for about 1½ hours at 350°.

BAKED CHICKEN BREASTS
Edna Schrock

2 cups all-purpose flour
4 teaspoons lemon-pepper
   marinade seasoning
1 teaspoon garlic powder
4 teaspoons parsley flakes
2 teaspoons salt
1 teaspoon pepper

8 chicken breasts
Accent
4 tablespoons butter-flavored
   Crisco shortening
Parsley and lemon wedges for
   garnish

Mix first 6 ingredients and put in a gallon-size plastic bag. Coat chicken breasts real good. Fry in Crisco until golden brown. Place in 13x17-inch baking dish and sprinkle Accent over top. Bake 1 hour at 325°.

Garnish with parsley and lemon wedges. Serves 8.

Suggestion: Serve with rice, buttered peas and carrots, and homemade dinner rolls.

BAKING AND FRYING CHICKEN MIXTURE

Ruth Yoder

2 cups flour
2 teaspoons baking powder
2 teaspoons paprika
½ cup instant potato powder

½ cup seasoning salt
2 tablespoons salt
2 tablespoons pepper
1 tablespoon garlic salt

Put all ingredients in a plastic or paper bag and shake well.

For baking: Cover chicken with mixture. Place in a baking pan and add ½ cup water into dish. Cover loosely with tin foil. Bake at 300° for 1½ hours. Uncover and bake for 15 more minutes.

For frying: Dip chicken into egg and milk mixture and then roll in chicken mixture. Fry chicken partially and bake for 1½-2 hours.

BAKED CHICKEN

Jill Nussbaum

Chicken
2-3 eggs
Flour
Salt

Morton's seasoning blend
Butter
Basil leaves

Skin chicken and set aside. Beat eggs with a fork. Dip chicken pieces in the egg. Roll the chicken in flour. Season with salt and Morton's seasoning blend. Melt butter in baking dish. Place chicken in dish. Add basil leaves. Bake at 400° until golden brown, about 1 hour. Be sure to turn chicken while baking. Simple and tasty.

The mighty oak was once a little nut that stood its ground.

BARBECUED CHICKEN

Mrs. Noah Yoder

2 (2 pound) chickens
Oil or other shortening for
  browning
½ cup chopped celery
1 onion, chopped
2 tablespoons brown sugar
2 tablespoons vinegar
1 cup water

1 teaspoon lemon juice
1 cup ketchup
Dash red pepper
½ tablespoon prepared mustard
3 tablespoons Worcestershire
  sauce
1 tablespoon hickory smoked liquid
2 cloves garlic, or garlic powder

Cut chicken and brown in fat. Place in large, 3- to 4-quart baking dish. Brown onion and celery in same fat. Add remaining ingredients to onion and celery and simmer for 15 minutes. Pour over chicken and bake for 1½ hours, uncovered, at 325°. There should be plenty of gravy to serve with rice. Serves 10-12.

SAUCE FOR BBQ CHICKEN

Paul and Ruth Yoder

½ pound margarine and ½ pound
  butter
1 small can Accent
1 pint vinegar

4 tablespoons salt
1 teaspoon pepper
4 tablespoons Worcestershire
  sauce

Cook until all is well mixed together. Dip chicken and put on grill. Dip very often in sauce while grilling. Makes enough sauce for 6 chickens.

SAUCE FOR GRILLED CHICKEN

Ruth Yoder

1 cup vinegar
1 cup water
¼ pound butter

7 teaspoons salt
1 teaspoon pepper
¼ cup Worcestershire sauce

Put all ingredients in saucepan and heat until hot. Dip chicken in sauce and put on grill. Keep dipping chicken in sauce every few minutes until chicken is done. Steam chicken in oven on low heat for ½-1 hour.

BAR-B-Q SAUCE FOR CHICKEN

Carolyn Eash

1 cup ketchup
1 cup margarine
¾ cup vinegar
3 tablespoons salt
½ cup brown sugar
2 tablespoons Tabasco sauce

½ cup onion
¾ teaspoon poultry seasoning
⅓ teaspoon pepper
2 teaspoons liquid smoke
5 tablespoons Worcestershire
  sauce

Combine all ingredients in saucepan. Bring to a boil and cook for 5 minutes. Cool. Pour over chicken pieces and marinate for 6 hours. Baste chicken with this sauce every 5-10 minutes while grilling. Will do approximately 7 pounds of leg quarters.

BARBEQUE MARINADE SAUCE

Ruth Yoder

1 gallon vinegar
1 pound butter
4 whole lemons, cut into fourths
1 (8 ounce) bottle Tabasco sauce

1 (8 ounce) bottle Worcestershire
  sauce
4 ounces red pepper
8 ounces salt

Bring to a boil and simmer 30 minutes. Can be reheated and frozen.

BAR-B-Q OVEN CHICKEN
Pat Parker

6 chicken leg/thigh pieces

⅓ stick butter

MARINADE:
1 clove garlic, crushed
1 teaspoon salt
½ teaspoon thyme
¼ cup oil

½ cup lemon juice
2 tablespoons chopped onion
1 teaspoon pepper

Mix marinade ingredients well.

Coat chicken pieces in marinade mixture. In oven at 400°, melt butter in 13x9-inch pan. Add chicken, skin side down, and brown for 30 minutes, uncovered. Turn chicken and cook, covered, for 30 more minutes. Makes 6-8 servings.

CHICKEN CACCIATORE
Ramona Overholt

4 pieces boneless, skinless
    chicken thighs
⅓ cup flour
¼ cup butter

2 bell peppers, sliced or chopped
4 ounces drained mushrooms
2 cups spaghetti sauce
Swiss or Monterey Jack cheese

Rinse chicken. Coat chicken with flour. In large skillet, heat butter over medium heat. Fry chicken in butter, turning occasionally until lightly browned. Add bell peppers to skillet and cook about 1 minute. Add mushrooms. Pour spaghetti sauce over all and cover and simmer 25-30 minutes or until done. Sprinkle with cheese before serving.

CHICKEN PARMESAN
Wanda Steiner

2 pounds boneless chicken breasts
2 eggs, beaten
1½ cups Italian seasoned bread
    crumbs
Vegetable oil

1 (30 ounce) jar Ragu pizza sauce
Grated Parmesan cheese
1½ cups mozzarella cheese,
    shredded

Preheat oven to 350°. Pound chicken thin. Dip chicken in eggs, then into bread crumbs to coat thoroughly. In skillet, brown chicken on both sides in oil. Drain on paper towels. Pour 1 cup pizza sauce in a 9x13-inch baking dish. Layer chicken and top with remaining pizza sauce. Sprinkle with cheeses. Bake for 30 minutes at 350°, or until done. Makes 8 servings.

CHICKEN SOUFFLÉ

Mrs. Freeman Schlabach

3 cups cooked, diced chicken
3 cups grated Cheddar cheese
2 cups bread crumbs
4 beaten eggs

1 can cream of chicken soup
1 can cream of mushroom soup
1 cup milk

Blend all ingredients well and turn into greased 9x13-inch pan. Save 1 cup cheese to sprinkle over top. Bake 1 hour at 350°. Serves 10.

I love to put this on time bake for Sunday dinner, and 300° for 2 hours is perfect.

CORN CRISP CHICKEN

Mrs. Henry Overholt, Sr., Rose Yoder

1 fryer chicken
½ cup evaporated milk (thin milk
   just won't do)
1 cup Kellogg's corn flake crumbs

1 teaspoon Accent
1 teaspoon salt
½ teaspoon pepper

Dip chicken in evaporated milk, then in crumbs mixed with seasoning. Bake at 350° in shallow pan lined with foil for 1 hour or until tender. Makes 8 servings.

A kind deed is never lost, even though you may not be able to see results.

EASY BAKED CHICKEN

Rhoda Yoder

Chicken pieces
Seasoning salt
Salt

Pepper
Onions, peppers, carrots, and/or
   potatoes, optional

Skin chicken pieces. Sprinkle with seasonings of your choice, and bake, covered, at 350° for 1-1½ hours. If you like BarBQ, add BarBQ sauce.

We like baked chicken so well that we hardly every fry chicken anymore. You can also place chicken on top of uncooked rice (and water and salt, of course) and have some tasty rice with your chicken.

FANCY FAST CHICKEN

Ramona Overholt

8 boneless, skinless chicken
  breasts
8 ounces Swiss cheese
1¼ cups mushrooms

1 can cream of mushroom soup
¼ cup dry white wine or water
2 cups herb stuffing
¼ cup butter, melted

Spray a 9x13-inch pan. Lay chicken breasts in pan. Slice cheese and put over chicken. Then place mushrooms on top of cheese. Mix cream of mushroom soup and wine or water and spread over mushrooms. Sprinkle stuffing over chicken and drizzle the butter on top. Bake, uncovered, at 350° for 45 minutes, or at 250° for 1½ hours.

FIERY CHICKEN

Melody Kauffman

3 pounds frying chicken pieces
2 tablespoons vegetable oil
1 medium onion, chopped
¼ cup soy sauce
2 cloves garlic, pressed
2 teaspoons paprika

½ teaspoon ground cumin
¼ teaspoon ground red pepper
  (cayenne)
¼ teaspoon oregano, crumbled
2 tablespoons cornstarch
Hot, cooked noodles or rice

Brown chicken in oil in large skillet. Remove chicken and drain off fat. Mix next 7 ingredients and 1 cup water in skillet. Return chicken. Cover and simmer 25 minutes. Turn and simmer 20 minutes or until done. Thicken 2 cups of pan drippings with cornstarch and ¼ cup water. Coat chicken with sauce. Serve over noodles or rice.

GOLDEN PARMESAN CHICKEN

Drusilla K. Yoder

1¼ cups grated Parmesan cheese
1 teaspoon salt
¼ teaspoon pepper

4 boneless chicken breasts
⅓ cup butter, melted

Heat oven to 425°. Grease a 13x9x2-inch baking pan. Mix cheese, salt, and pepper. Dip chicken in butter, then coat with cheese mixture. Arrange chicken in pan and pour remaining butter on chicken. Bake, uncovered, for 30 minutes. Turn chicken and continue baking 20 minutes longer or until done. Makes 4 servings.

HAWAIIAN CHICKEN

Alta Kauffman

5-6 cups (or 2 pounds) chicken,
   cut into 1-inch cubes

MARINADE:
½ cup cooking wine   12 tablespoons sugar
½ cup soy sauce

SAUCE:
½ cup ketchup   10 tablespoons brown sugar
½ cup oyster sauce   2-4 tablespoons chopped garlic
6 tablespoons soy sauce   1 cup water
½ cup chopped onions   1 tablespoon cornstarch
4 tablespoons vinegar

Mix marinade ingredients; add chicken and let set for 15 minutes. After 15 minutes, drain and coat meat with flour, then fry in hot oil. Remove meat from skillet. Set aside.

Combine sauce ingredients except water and cornstarch. Wipe skillet, add sauce, and simmer a few minutes. Mix 1 cup water and 1 tablespoon cornstarch and slowly add to sauce. Stir until thickened. Add meat and stir gently to coat. Serve with steamed rice.

If you can't sleep, don't count sheep.
Talk to the Shepherd.

HEART SMART BAKED CHICKEN

Naomi Yoder

6-8 pieces fryer chicken, skinned   2 cloves garlic, minced
1 cup uncooked oatmeal   ⅓ cup milk
⅓ cup grated Parmesan cheese   ¼ cup margarine, melted
½ teaspoon salt   Parsley and cherry tomatoes for
½ teaspoon paprika   garnish
⅛ teaspoon pepper

Mix together oatmeal, cheese, and seasonings. In separate dish, mix garlic and milk. Place chicken 1 piece at a time in oatmeal mixture, then in milk mixture, and then in oatmeal mixture again. Place coated chicken in large shallow baking dish. Drizzle melted margarine over chicken and bake at 375° for 1 hour or until fork-tender. Garnish with parsley and cherry tomatoes. Serves 4.

HONEY-GLAZED CHICKEN

Ruth Yoder

½ cup all-purpose flour
1 teaspoon salt
½ teaspoon cayenne pepper
1 (about 3 pound) broiler/fryer
   chicken, cut up
½ cup butter, melted and divided

½ cup packed brown sugar
½ cup honey
¼ cup lemon juice
1 tablespoon soy sauce
1½ teaspoons curry powder

In a bowl or bag, combine flour, salt, and cayenne pepper; add chicken pieces and dredge or shake to coat. Pour 4 tablespoons butter in pan. Place chicken in 13x9x2-inch pan, turning pieces once to coat. Bake at 350°, uncovered, for 30 minutes. Combine brown sugar, honey, lemon juice, soy sauce, curry powder, and remaining butter. Pour over chicken. Bake 45 minutes more or until chicken is tender, basting several times with pan drippings. Makes 4-6 servings.

HONEY MUSTARD CHICKEN

Marialice Yoder

½ cup salad dressing
2 tablespoons Dijon mustard
1 tablespoon honey

4 boneless, skinless chicken
   breast halves

Stir salad dressing, mustard, and honey. Place chicken on grill or rack of broiler pan. Brush with ½ of sauce. Grill or broil 8-10 minutes. Turn and brush with remaining sauce. Continue grilling or broiling 8-10 more minutes, or until tender. Makes 4 servings.

ITALIAN CHICKEN

Pat Parker

1 pound sweet Italian sausage,
   cut up
1 pound chicken breasts
2 bell peppers, diced
3 onions, diced

2-3 fresh tomatoes, or 1 large can
   tomatoes, chopped
3-5 garlic cloves, minced
4-6 tablespoons basil

Cook sausage in fry pan until well done, then layer all ingredients in large pot. Heat on medium-high until boiling, then lower temperature, cover pot, and simmer 60 minutes. Debone chicken and serve with crusty Italian bread and lettuce salad. Serves 6-8.

ITALIAN DRESSING CHICKEN

Silla K. Yoder

2 chickens, cut up
1 (8 ounce) bottle Italian dressing

1 stick margarine
Salt and pepper to taste

Place chicken in Pyrex dish. Pour dressing over chicken. Dot with margarine. Season with salt and pepper. Bake in oven for 1 hour at 350° or until done. Remove chicken from dressing mixture. Thicken with a little cornstarch and water. Bring to a boil. Serve with rice.

LYNFORD'S GOOD CHICKEN

Debbie Graber

Whole young fryers

Lawry's seasoning salt

Liberally season whole young fryers with Lawry's seasoning salt. Let set overnight in refrigerator. On gas grill, place 2 pie pans or small cake pans directly on lava rocks. Fill one with mesquite chips and the other one with water. Pour 1 cup water over chips. Light burner *under chips* only. Replace grill rack. Place chicken above the water pan. Cover and let cook for 3½ hours. I usually turn the chicken once or so during cooking. Keep burner on low the whole time.

SCALLOPED CHICKEN

Ruth Yoder

16 slices white bread, cubed and
    dried
4 cups cooked chicken
1 cup chopped onion
1 cup chopped celery
1 cup mayonnaise
½ teaspoon salt

⅛ teaspoon pepper
¼ teaspoon curry powder
3 eggs
3 cups milk
1 can cream of mushroom soup
1 cup shredded cheese

Mix all ingredients except mushroom soup and cheese. Put in a 9x13-inch baking dish. Before baking, spread mushroom soup on top. Bake at 325° for 1 hour and 20 minutes. Sprinkle cheese over the top for the last 10 minutes of baking. This may be fixed the day before and put in the refrigerator overnight. Serves 15.

*Keep your face toward the sunshine of His love,
and the shadows will fall behind you.*

SOUR CREAM CHICKEN

Silla Kay Yoder, Barbara Ann Yoder

½ cup celery
½ cup onions
½ cup peppers
½ cup butter

16 ounces sour cream
1 can cream of mushroom soup
1 (4 ounce) can mushrooms
2 cups deboned chicken

Sauté celery, onions, and pepper in butter until soft. Add the rest of the ingredients and simmer for a few minutes. Let stand 15 minutes to let flavor get through. Put this over rice.

SWEET AND SOUR CHICKEN

Ramona Overholt

1 onion, chopped
2 tablespoons butter
3 tablespoons ketchup
3 tablespoons brown sugar
2 tablespoons soy sauce

2 tablespoons lemon juice
⅛ teaspoon black pepper
4 boneless, skinless chicken thighs
  or breasts
1 tablespoon cornstarch

In a large frying pan over medium heat, sauté chopped onion in butter until soft. In small bowl, combine ketchup, sugar, soy sauce, lemon juice, and black pepper. Add to pan with onion. Add chicken to pan. Bring to a boil; cover and simmer 25-35 minutes or until chicken is done. Remove chicken and add cornstarch mixed with a little water to sauce. Bring sauce to a boil, stirring constantly until thickened. Pour sauce over chicken.

Before serving, I like to make a double recipe of sauce and then serve chicken over rice.

TACO CHICKEN

Silla Yoder

1 chicken
1 bell pepper, chopped
1 onion, chopped
¼ cup butter
1 can cream of mushroom soup
1 can cream of chicken soup

¼-½ cup picante sauce
1 bag taco-flavored Dorito chips,
  divided
8 ounces Cheddar cheese, grated,
  divided

Cook chicken in water until tender. Sauté bell pepper and onion in butter. Add mushroom and chicken soups, picante sauce, and chicken. Layer bottom of casserole dish with ½ bag crushed Dorito chips. Top with ½ chicken mixture. Add 4 ounces cheese. Layer rest of Doritos, chicken mixture, and top with remaining cheese. Bake at 350° for 30 minutes.

YUMMY CHICKEN
Faith Miller

Chicken, cut up
24 Ritz crackers
¼ cup Parmesan cheese

Melted butter
Seasoning salt
Garlic salt

Skin chicken pieces. Mix Ritz crackers and Parmesan cheese together. Roll chicken in melted butter, and then into crackers and cheese mixture. Season with seasoning salt and a little garlic salt. Place in a covered baking dish for 2 hours at 250°. Uncover the last half hour.

AMISH DRESSING
Dorothy Schlabach

1 loaf bread
Butter
6 eggs, well beaten
2 cups milk
½ cup shredded carrots
½ cup celery, chopped fine

1 cup cubed potatoes, cooked
1 quart chicken bits and broth
2 teaspoons chicken base
½ cup chopped onion
Salt and pepper to taste

Cube bread; toast in butter. Mix remaining ingredients. Fry in butter until slightly browned. Put in oven and bake at 350° until heated through.

MOM'S CORNBREAD DRESSING
Cece Allen

1 chicken
1 recipe muffin bread (using hot rise cornmeal recipe on bag of Martha White cornmeal)
4-5 slices bread

½ small onion
1 stalk celery
1 teaspoon sage, optional
Salt and pepper to taste, optional

Boil chicken. Pour off stock and let cool. Skim fat. Bake muffin bread according to recipe on the back of the cornmeal bag. Let oven cool a little, then put 4-5 slices bread in oven to dry. Put muffin bread and dried bread in food processor and crumble up. Chop up the onion and celery. Put with bread crumbs in lasagna pan.

Heat chicken stock and pour over bread mixture until it is the consistency of cake batter. May add a little more chicken broth if not enough. Sage, salt, and black pepper may be added, if needed, to taste. Stir all ingredients together and place in 8x8-inch casserole dish. Bake for 1 hour at 350°.

CHICKEN DRESSING

Mrs. Freeman Schlabach

1 cup butter
1 loaf white bread, toasted
1 quart canned chicken and broth
⅓ chopped onion
2 stalks celery, chopped

3 beaten eggs
Dash parsley
Pinch of salt and pepper
¼ teaspoon poultry seasoning
Water

Place cubed, toasted bread and browned butter in large bowl. Mix in next 7 ingredients. Add water until a bit sloppy. Turn into greased, medium-sized casserole dish and bake at 350° until brown on top. Serves 8-10.

The secret to this Virginia-style dressing is to use white bread and water. (No milk).

CHICKEN COATING

Carol Petersheim

2½ pounds cracker crumbs (white)
2½ cups Bisquick baking mix

20 ounces Potato Buds
12 ounces Season-All

Cracker crumbs should be crushed very fine. Mix all ingredients together. Store in airtight containers or freezer.

When ready to use, dip chicken in oil or butter, then in coating. Bake or fry. This is also good on pork chops, meat patties, and fried squash.

DEVILED TURKEY SEASONING MIX

Ruth Yoder

½ teaspoon salt for each pound of turkey
2 tablespoons black pepper
2 tablespoons sage
2 teaspoons curry powder
2 teaspoons garlic powder

2 teaspoons dried parsley
2 teaspoons celery seed
1 teaspoon paprika
½ teaspoon dry mustard
¼ teaspoon allspice
3-4 bay leaves (crumbled)

Mix all ingredients together well.

To use, rub turkey inside and outside with vegetable oil. Use sharp knife and carve small pockets in breast. Rub mix all over turkey, in pockets, inside and out. Should set in refrigerator overnight or equivalent to allow meat time to absorb the seasoning. Bake at 375° until golden brown. Check baking time on turkey bag according to the weight. Will have terrific flavor!

Casseroles

BARBEQUED BEANS
Ramona Overholt

1 pound ground beef
½ cup chopped onion
1 (1 pound, 12 ounce) can pork
  and beans
½ cup ketchup

1 tablespoon Worcestershire
  sauce
1 tablespoon vinegar
A little brown sugar

Fry hamburger and onions together; drain. Add remaining ingredients and place in casserole dish. Bake at 250° or 300° for 1 hour.

BEEF ON RICE
Rose Yoder

2 pounds stew beef
2 teaspoons dry onion flakes
Salt and pepper
2 teaspoons Worcestershire sauce

1 can cream of mushroom soup
1 can cream of celery soup
3 cups cooked rice

Brown meat in skillet; add remaining ingredients except rice. Simmer 1 hour, adding additional water if needed. Serve over hot rice. Serves 8.

CALICO BEANS
Merlyn Mullett, Wanda Steiner, Elsie Yoder

1 (2 pound) can pork and beans
1 (1 pound) can green lima beans
  or butter beans
1 (1 pound) can red kidney beans
¼-½ pound bacon, cut up
1 pound ground beef

1 medium onion, chopped
½ cup brown sugar
½ cup ketchup
½ teaspoon salt
2 tablespoons vinegar
1 tablespoon prepared mustard

Brown ground beef. Mix all ingredients in large casserole dish and bake at 350° for 1 hour.

Note: This is a very versatile dish and can be changed to suit your taste. Substitute chopped hot dogs for beef, or use no meat. Almost any beans, peas, or cooked dried beans can be used. This is an excellent crock pot recipe: Cook on low all day or high for 5-6 hours.

*Seeing Jesus only is the sovereign remedy
against fault-finding, doubt and spiritual defeat.*

CONNECTICUT BEEF SUPPER

Judith Yoder

2 pounds ground beef
2 large onions, chopped
1 cup water
4 large potatoes, cooked and diced
1 can mushroom soup
1 cup sour cream

1¼ cups milk
1 teaspoon salt
¼ teaspoon pepper
1 cup shredded cheese
1¼ cups Wheaties cereal, crushed

Brown meat and onions. Add water; heat to boiling. Pour meat mixture into 3-quart casserole. Stir together soup, sour cream, milk, salt, and pepper. Add to potatoes. Pour on top of meat. Sprinkle with cheese and Wheaties. Bake at 350° for 1½ hours. Serves 10.

GROUND BEEF CASSEROLE

Mrs. James Mast

1 pound ground beef
1 small onion
1 pint fresh or frozen peas and
  carrots

1 cup uncooked macaroni
Cubed cheese
Buttered bread crumbs

Fry beef with onion; add seasonings as desired. When browned, add vegetables with a little water. Cover and cook until veggies are tender.

Cook macaroni in salt water until tender, then drain and mix with meat mixture. Stir in some cubed cheese. Pour into buttered 2-quart casserole and top with bread crumbs. Bake at 350° for 30-40 minutes. Serves 6.

HAMBURGER CABBAGE CASSEROLE

Ruth Yoder

1 pound hamburger
1 small onion, chopped
½ head cabbage

1 cup spaghetti sauce (or more)
Velveeta cheese

Fry hamburger mixed with chopped onion. Put in medium size casserole dish. Cut cabbage in wedges and place on top. Pour spaghetti sauce (as much as you want) on top. Bake at 325° for 45 minutes. Top with sliced strips of cheese and serve on rice.

HAMBURGER COBBLER

Mrs. Shirley Yoder

PART 1:
2 pounds hamburger
¾ cup chopped onions
¼ cup chopped green pepper

1 teaspoon salt
1¼ teaspoons pepper
Cheese to cover

PART 2:
1 cup pizza sauce
3 tablespoons ketchup

2 teaspoons Worcestershire sauce

PART 3 (BISCUIT MIX):
1½ cups flour
1¼ cups shortening
1½ teaspoons baking powder

1½ cups milk
1½ teaspoons salt

Brown hamburger, onions, and green peppers. Add salt and pepper. Put in a 9x9-inch pan and cover with cheese. Mix part 2 and pour over cheese. Mix biscuits and drop by teaspoon on top. Bake at 375° for 15 minutes. Serves 9-10.

HAMBURGER RICE DISH

Mrs. David E. Wengerd

2 pounds hamburger, cooked
¼ cup brown sugar
2 teaspoons salt
3 tablespoons flour
3 cups ketchup
1 teaspoon oregano
1 chopped onion
1 or 2 cans pork & beans

2½ cups rice
5 cups water
1 tablespoon butter
1½ teaspoons salt
1 cup whole milk
Cheese, to put in between layers
3 cups rich milk

Mix together in large saucepan the hamburger and the next 7 ingredients. Cook until hot. Set aside while cooking rice.

Cook rice with water, butter, and salt. Cook until rice is soft and fluffy. Stir in 1 cup whole milk.

Put in layers in a medium sized roaster. Start with hamburger mix, then rice and cheese. Pour all 3 cups rich milk over mixture and put cheese on top. Bake 1 hour at 350° or until bubbly. Serves 12.

PAUL'S HAMBURGER DELIGHT   Mrs. R. Paul Yoder (Amanda)

3-4 pounds hamburger	3 large onions
Garlic powder	5-6 medium potatoes, sliced
Salt	5-6 large carrots, sliced
Pepper	Cabbage (optional)

Press hamburger in skillet. Sprinkle with garlic powder, salt, and pepper. Slice onions over hamburger. Add sliced potatoes next; sprinkle again with garlic powder, salt, and pepper. Next put on sliced carrots; sprinkle again with seasonings. Next put on cabbage, if desired. Cover with Lectro Maid cover. If you don't have Lectro Maid skillet, you may use smaller skillet and make on stove, then adjust ingredients according to size of skillet. Cook on high for 30-45 minutes. Serves 8-10.

HUSBAND'S DELIGHT   Carol Petersheim

1 pound hamburger	1 tablespoon Worcestershire
2 cans tomato sauce	sauce
1 teaspoon salt	½ carton sour cream
¼ teaspoon garlic salt	1 (8 ounce) package cream cheese
1 tablespoon sugar	1 onion, chopped
1 teaspoon pepper	1 (12 ounce) package noodles

Brown hamburger in skillet; drain. Add tomato sauce. Stir in salt, garlic salt, sugar, pepper, and Worcestershire sauce.

Blend sour cream with cheese and onion. Cook noodles and drain. Place in layers in casserole dish. Bake at 350° for 25-30 minutes until heated through.

HUSBAND'S DELIGHT   Dorothy Schlabach

1½ pounds ground beef	24 ounces tomato sauce
¼ cup bell pepper, chopped	½ cup sour cream
2 cloves garlic, chopped	1 cup cottage cheese
1 (8 ounce) package wide noodles,	1 (8 ounce) package cream cheese
cooked as directed	1 medium onion, chopped fine
1 tablespoon sugar	1 cup grated Cheddar cheese

Brown ground beef, bell peppers, and garlic together and drain. Cook noodles as directed then drain. Add noodles, sugar, and tomato sauce to ground beef. Stir.

Combine sour cream, cottage cheese, cream cheese, and chopped onion. Put into a 3-quart casserole dish a layer of noodles and meat, then a layer of cheese mixture; add the last of meat and noodle mixture. Last of all add grated cheese. Bake at 350° for 25-30 minutes. Makes 10-12 servings.

LASAGNA
Cece Allen

3 pounds hamburger
2 large onions, chopped
4 small cans tomato paste
8 cans water
4 teaspoons garlic powder
6 teaspoons basil

Salt
4 packages mild Cheddar cheese
2 large containers cottage cheese
Parmesan cheese
Lasagna noodles, uncooked

Brown hamburger and onions together. Mix together next 5 ingredients and bring to a boil. Reduce heat to simmer for 1 hour.

Meanwhile, mix Cheddar, cottage cheese and Parmesan cheese together. In lasagna pan put small amount of hamburger mixture then a layer of noodles, then a layer of cheese mixture. Next put a large amount of sauce, a layer of noodles, a little more sauce, and cheese. Bake at 350° for 1 hour.

EASY LASAGNA
Mrs. Freeman Schlabach

1½ pounds hamburger
1 quart pizza sauce
9 lasagna noodles, uncooked

15 ounces drained cottage cheese
12 ounces grated cheese of your
   choice

Brown hamburger, add pizza sauce, and stir. In greased 13x9-inch pan, layer in 3 layers, hamburger, noodles, hamburger, cottage cheese, cheese, noodles, etc., with cheese last. Bake at 375° covered for 30 minutes, uncovered 30 minutes. Let stand before serving. Serves 10-12.

LAZY DAY LASAGNA
Irene Yoder

1 (12 ounce) container cottage
   cheese
2 cups shredded mozzarella cheese
2 eggs
⅓ cup chopped parsley
1 teaspoon onion powder

½ teaspoon dried basil leaves
⅛ teaspoon pepper
1 (32 ounce) jar spaghetti sauce
¾ pound cooked hamburger
9 uncooked lasagna noodles
Grated Parmesan cheese

In large bowl, mix first 7 ingredients until well blended; set aside. In another bowl, mix spaghetti sauce and cooked hamburger. In a 12x8x2-inch baking dish, spread ¾ cup meat sauce. Layer three uncooked noodles on top of meat sauce. Spread with half of cottage cheese mixture and 1½ cups meat sauce. Layer three more uncooked noodles on top of meat mixture. Spread with remaining cottage cheese mixture. Top with remaining three un-cooked noodles and remaining meat sauce. Pour ⅓ cup water around edges of dish. Cover tightly with foil. Bake 45 minutes at 375°. Uncover and bake 15 minutes more or until noodles are tender. Let stand 15 minutes before serving. Serve with Parmesan cheese. Makes 10 servings.

"SOME-MORE"   Linda Kauffman, Jill Nussbaum

2 pounds hamburger
1½ cups onions, chopped
2 cups celery, chopped
6 tablespoons ketchup

2 cans cream of chicken soup
2 cans cream of mushroom soup
1 cup rice (uncooked)
Chow mein noodles

Brown hamburger with onions and celery. Add ketchup and both soups (undiluted). Cook rice and add to mixture. Sprinkle with noodles. Spread evenly in a 9x13-inch pan and bake at 350° for 15-20 minutes. Serves 8.

Real friends are those who, when you've made a fool of yourself, don't feel you've done a permanent job.

SPAGHETTI PIZZA DELUXE   Elsie King Horst

1 (16 ounce) package spaghetti
1 cup skim milk
2 eggs, beaten
1 pound lean ground beef
2 medium onions, chopped
2 medium green peppers, chopped
4 cloves garlic, minced

4 cups sliced fresh mushrooms
2 (15 ounce) cans tomato sauce
2 teaspoons Italian seasoning
2 teaspoons salt-free herb
  seasoning
½ teaspoon pepper
4 cups shredded mozzarella cheese

Prepare spaghetti as package directs; drain. Blend milk and eggs; add spaghetti and toss to coat. Spray 2 (15x10-inch) pans with vegetable cooking spray. Spread spaghetti mixture evenly in prepared pans. In large skillet, cook beef, onion, green pepper, garlic, and mushrooms until beef is no longer pink; drain. Add tomato sauce and seasonings. Simmer 5 minutes. Spoon meat mixture evenly over spaghetti. Top with cheese. Bake at 350° for 20 minutes. Let stand 5 minutes more before cutting. Makes 12 plus servings.

MICROWAVE TACO CASSEROLE   Cece Allen

1 pound hamburger
1 (15 ounce) can tomato sauce
1 (1⅓ ounce) envelope taco sauce
  mix

1 (16 ounce) can refried beans
¼ cup chopped green olives
2½ cups Fritos corn chips
½ cup Cheddar cheese, shredded

Place meat in 1½-quart casserole dish. Cook on full power 3-4 minutes or until beef is no longer pink. Stir and chop up meat every minute while cooking. Combine all ingredients with meat except corn chips and cheese. Spoon mixture over 2 cups crushed Fritos in 1½-quart casserole dish. Cook on high for 5 minutes. Crush remaining Fritos and put over casserole. Put cheese over casserole and heat on high for 30 seconds-1½ minutes or until cheese is melted.

SUPPER IN A DISH
Ramona Overholt

1 pound hamburger
1 pound sausage
Salt
Pepper
Garlic salt
Seasoning salt
Sliced raw potatoes
Sliced carrots

Peas
Chopped onion
Chopped celery
Chopped green pepper
2 (10 ounce) cans cream of
   mushroom soup
½ cup milk
Grated cheese

Brown hamburger and sausage; drain. Put hamburger mixture in bottom of pan. Sprinkle some of all the seasonings on top. Layer vegetables on top of meat in order given. Sprinkle each layer with seasonings. Mix soup and milk together and pour over top. Bake at 350° for 1½ hours. Sprinkle cheese on top and return to oven until cheese is melted.

ONE-DISH MEAL
Miriam Yoder

½ pound spaghetti
1 cup cheese, divided
2 tablespoons butter
1 small onion, chopped
1 pound ground beef
Salt and pepper

3 cups milk
3 tablespoons flour
1½ cups peas
1 cup carrots
1 cup tomato chunks

Cook spaghetti until tender; drain off excess water. Mix ½ of cheese with spaghetti. Melt butter in skillet; add onions and brown. Add the meat. Salt and pepper to suit taste; brown lightly.

Put milk and flour in blender; blend until smooth. Put spaghetti in a 4-quart roaster. Next add meat. Then add the peas and carrots. Top with milk sauce and mix until blended, then add tomatoes. Top with cheese. Bake at 350° for 1 hour. Serves 6-8.

PLANTATION SUPPER
Mrs. Shirley Yoder

1 pound ground beef
½ cup onion
¾ cup milk
1 can cream of mushroom soup
1 (8 ounce) package cream cheese

1½ cups whole kernel corn, drained
¼ cup chopped pimiento
1½ teaspoons salt
⅛ teaspoon pepper
8 ounces cooked noodles

Brown meat and add onion; cook until tender. Stir in milk, soup, and cream cheese until well blended. Add remaining ingredients; heat either on stove top or bake in oven until hot.

POCKET PIZZA
Londa Kauffman

PIZZA DOUGH:
2 cups flour
⅔ cup milk
4 tablespoons oil

2 teaspoons baking powder
1 teaspoon salt

TOPPING:
2 tablespoons oil
½ cup pizza sauce
1 cup shredded mozzarella cheese
1 pound cooked Italian sausage or
    ground beef

2 tablespoons finely chopped onion
½ teaspoon garlic powder
1 (3 ounce) package pepperoni
⅓ cup pizza sauce
1 cup shredded American cheese

Preheat oven to 375°. Beat together flour, milk, oil, baking powder, and salt. Gather into a ball and knead 10 times. Cover and let stand for 15 minutes.

Lightly grease 2 cookie sheets with shortening. Prepare pizza dough and roll into 2 (12-inch) circles. Fold loosely in half and place on cookie sheets and unfold. Brush lightly with oil.

Layer remaining ingredients on half of each circle in order listed. Fold dough over filling. Turn edge of the lower dough over edge of the top dough and pinch edge to seal. Prick top with fork and bake at 375° until golden brown, 20-25 minutes. Makes 6-8 servings.

POP UP PIZZA CASSEROLE
Rhoda Coblentz,
Ramona Overholt, Faith Miller

1½ pounds ground beef
1 cup chopped onion
½ teaspoon ground oregano

1½ cups pizza sauce
Dash of salt
6-8 ounces cheese of your choice

POPOVER BATTER:
1 cup milk
1 tablespoon oil
2 eggs

1 cup flour
½ teaspoon salt

In skillet, cook together beef, onion, oregano, pizza sauce, and salt. Pour hot meat mixture in ungreased 9x13-inch pan; top with cheese. Mix batter ingredients together and pour batter over cheese, covering filling completely. Sprinkle with Parmesan cheese. Bake at 400° for 20-30 minutes or until puffed and deep golden brown. Serve immediately. Serves 10.

Faith also adds cream of mushroom soup to the hamburger mixture.

233

PIZZA BAKE

Rhoda Coblentz

1 pound hamburger
½ cup chopped onions
1 pint pizza sauce
2 tablespoons flour

Cheese
2 eggs, beaten
1 cup milk
1 cup Bisquick baking mix

Brown hamburger and onions; season meat as for pizza. Add pizza sauce and flour. Pour into 9x13-inch pan and top with cheese.

Beat eggs, milk, and Bisquick. Pour on top of hamburger. Bake at 350° for 30 minutes or until nicely browned. Serves 6-8.

MY FAVORITE PIZZA

Mrs. Milton Yoder

1 pound hamburger
1 pound sausage
¼ teaspoon taco seasoning
¼ teaspoon chili powder
Salt and pepper
1 teaspoon Italian seasoning
1 (8½ ounce) can pizza sauce
½ cup Parmesan cheese

1 small onion, chopped
1 diced pepper
1 small jar mushrooms
¾ cup chopped ham
1 package grated mozzarella
  cheese
Pepperoni

Fry hamburger and sausage. Add taco seasoning, chili powder, salt, pepper, and Italian seasoning. Bake a pizza crust until partially baked. Put on crust in this order: Pizza sauce, ¼ cup Parmesan cheese, hamburger and sausage with seasonings mixture, chopped onions, diced peppers, mushrooms (or substitute 1 can cream of mushroom soup), ham, mozzarella cheese, ¼ cup Parmesan cheese, and pepperoni. Bake 20 minutes at 350°. Serves 4-6.

QUICK HAMBURGER CASSEROLE

Debbie Graber

1½ pounds hamburger, fried
3 cups cooked rice
1 quart green beans
Salt and pepper to taste

Onion powder to taste
2 cans cream of mushroom soup
Shredded cheese

Mix all together and top with shredded cheese. Bake for 1 hour at 350°. Serves 12-15.

The parent's life is the child's copy-book.

QUICK CHEESEBURGER PIE

Londa Kauffman

PASTRY:
1⅓ cups flour	½ cup shortening
½ teaspoon salt	3-4 tablespoons cold water

MEAT FILLING:
1 pound ground beef	⅓ cup dill pickle liquid
½-¾ cup chopped onion	⅓ cup milk
1 clove garlic, finely chopped	½ cup chopped dill pickles
½ teaspoon salt	2 cups shredded American or
¼ cup flour	Swiss cheese

Heat oven to 400°. Prepare pastry by mixing flour and salt, then cut in shortening until mixture looks like tiny peas. Sprinkle in cold water, and stir with fork. (Add more water if necessary.) Pat pastry in bottom and up sides of an 8-inch quiche dish or any 8-inch round pan. Bake at 400° for 15 minutes.

Brown together beef, onion, and garlic in skillet. Drain. Sprinkle with salt and flour. Stir in pickle liquid, milk, pickles, and cheese. Spoon into crust and bake until crust is golden brown, about 5 minutes. Makes 4-6 servings.

ZUCCHINI SUPREME SURPRISE

Naomi Yoder

2 pounds ground beef	1 small carton cottage cheese
1 medium onion, chopped	1 can cream of mushroom soup
Salt and pepper to taste	2 cups shredded sharp Cheddar
1½ pounds zucchini squash	cheese
2 cups cooked rice	

Brown ground beef and onion, adding salt and pepper to taste. Place thinly sliced squash on bottom of greased 9x13-inch casserole dish. Layer rice, ground beef and onion mixture, cottage cheese, soup, and Cheddar cheese. Bake at 325° for 45 minutes. Serves 8.

CHILI FOR HOT DOGS

Ruth Yoder

4 pounds hamburger	1 box chili powder
3 onions, chopped	Sugar to taste
3 small jars spaghetti sauce	

Fry hamburger and onions; add remaining ingredients. Simmer for 1 hour.

YUMM-E-SETTI
Esther Mast

2 pounds ground beef, browned
1 (12 ounce) package noodles
1 can cream of tomato soup
1 can cream of celery soup

1 can cream of chicken or
  mushroom soup
Salt to taste
Velveeta cheese

Fry hamburger in skillet, stirring occasionally. Cook noodles in hot water until tender but not soft. Mix tomato soup with hamburger, and celery and chicken or mushroom soups with noodles. Put in layers in casserole dish. Cover with Velveeta cheese. Bake for 1 hour at 250°. Serves 8.

ALMOND CHICKEN CASSEROLE
Susan K. Yoder

3 cups rice
1 can chicken broth
Water
1 medium onion, chopped
1 green pepper, diced
6 pieces celery, chopped
1 (5 pound) hen, cooked and
  deboned

Pepper
2 cans cream of mushroom soup
1½ cups grated Cheddar cheese
1 small can chopped pimiento
1 (4 ounce) package slivered
  almonds
1 medium size can mushrooms (or
  use fresh and sauté them)

Cook rice in broth, adding enough water to cover. Sauté onion, green pepper, and celery. Place layer of rice in the bottom of 2 large well greased casserole dishes. Combine chicken with the sautéed vegetable mixture. Place 1 layer over rice. Add pepper to taste. Spread on a layer of soup. Sprinkle with cheese, pimiento, almonds, and mushrooms. Repeat layers. Bake at 325°-350° for 20 minutes. Makes enough for 10-12 people.

BBQ CHICKEN AND RICE
Marialice Yoder

2½ pounds chicken pieces
2 tablespoons oil
1¼ cups barbecue sauce
¾ cup water

1½ cups Minute rice
1 cup corn
Green and red peppers as desired
  for garnish

Brown chicken in hot oil in large skillet. Stir in barbecue sauce and water. Cover; cook over medium heat 20 minutes or until tender. Stir in rice and corn. Cover; reduce heat and simmer 5 minutes. Makes 4 servings.

Where souls are being tried,
there God is hewing out pillars for His Temple.

BAKED CHICKEN DINNER   Debbie Graber

4-5 pounds chicken pieces
6 potatoes, peeled and chunked
6 carrots, chunked
1 pound fresh mushrooms, sliced

Lawry's seasoning salt to taste
Pepper to taste
1 can cream of chicken soup

Sprinkle meat and vegetables with lots of Lawry's seasoning salt and pepper. Place in roaster pan. Spoon soup over all and cover and bake at 250° for 3½ hours. Serves 12.

CHICKEN BAKE   Mrs. John Nissley

2 cups broccoli
2 cups cauliflower
2 cups carrots (cooked)
2 cups chopped cooked chicken

½ cup chopped onion
2 tablespoons chicken fat
1 recipe biscuit dough

Combine vegetables and meat. Fry onion in chicken fat until softened and add to vegetables. Make approximately 1 quart thin chicken gravy and add to vegetables. Pour all into large casserole dish and bake at 350° until bubbly. Top with biscuit dough. Return to oven and bake until biscuits are done.

CHICKEN BROTH BAKE   Pat Parker

4 boneless, skinless chicken
  breasts
1 cup Italian bread crumbs

6 slices Muenster cheese
Sautéed mushrooms, if desired
1 can low salt chicken broth

Layer in large casserole dish 3 chicken breasts, ½ cup bread crumbs, 3 slices cheese, and sautéed mushrooms. Pour ½ can broth over and repeat layers. Bake covered at 350° for 45-60 minutes. Serves 6.

CHICKEN CASSEROLE   Ruth Yoder

4-6 boneless chicken breasts
Salt and pepper to taste
1 package Ritz crackers, crumbled
2 cans cream of chicken soup

1 cup chicken broth
2 tablespoons poppy seed
1 stick butter, melted
1 cup sour cream

Boil chicken, place in baking dish, and sprinkle salt and pepper on chicken. Mix cream of chicken soup, sour cream, and chicken broth and pour over chicken. Sprinkle poppy seed over that. Put cracker crumbs on top, and pour 1 stick melted butter over crackers. Bake at 350° for 30 minutes. Makes 4-6 servings.

CHICKEN CASSEROLE

Celesta Miller

2 cups celery, cut up
2 tablespoons onion
2 cups water
½ cup butter
⅛ teaspoon black pepper
½ teaspoon ginger
1¼ teaspoons poultry seasoning
1¼ teaspoons thyme

2½ teaspoons salt
1 can cream of mushroom soup
7 eggs, beaten
2-3 cups milk
4 quarts toasted bread, cubed
1 pint carrots, cut up or chopped
6 cups cooked, diced chicken

Bring celery, carrots, and onion to boiling point with 2 cups water. Add butter and let melt. Add seasonings and mushroom soup. Beat eggs, and then add to 2 cups milk. Add this to celery and onion mixture. Pour over bread crumbs and chicken in large bowl. Stir just until mixed. If it seems a bit dry, add more milk. Put in a large roaster and bake 1½-2 hours at 300°-325°. Yields 5-6 quarts.

Note: May be frozen to use as needed.

SAUCY CHICKEN CASSEROLE

Merlyn Mullett

1 (10¾ ounce) can cream of
  chicken soup, undiluted
1 (10¾ ounce) can cream of
  mushroom soup, undiluted
2 cups sour cream
¾ cup chicken broth
½ medium onion, chopped
1 cup sliced fresh mushrooms

½ teaspoon garlic powder
½ teaspoon salt
½ teaspoon poultry seasoning
¼ teaspoon ground black pepper
6 boneless chicken breast halves
Cooked noodles or rice
Chopped parsley

In a 13x9x2-inch baking dish, combine soups, sour cream, broth, onion, mushrooms, and seasonings. Arrange chicken on top of sauce. Bake uncovered at 350° for 1 hour or until chicken is tender. Serve chicken over noodles or rice. Garnish with parsley. Serves 6.

CHICKEN CHEDDAR BAKE

Judy Mullet

1 bunch fresh broccoli
5 medium potatoes
1 chicken, cooked and deboned
1 can cream of celery soup

½ cup mayonnaise
1 can Cheddar cheese soup
2½ cups buttered bread crumbs

Parboil broccoli for 3 minutes; slice potatoes and parboil 3 minutes. Butter 9x13-inch baking dish and place potatoes in dish. Next add broccoli and then chicken pieces. Mix soup and mayonnaise together and pour over chicken. Sprinkle top with buttered bread crumbs. Bake at 350° for 25-30 minutes.

DELICIOUS CHICKEN CASSEROLE   Mrs. Roger Helmuth, Sr.

SAUCE:

1 stick butter
½ cup flour
4 cups chicken broth
Salt and pepper to taste
1 pound cheese

1 can cream of mushroom soup
½ cup green pepper, diced
1 package wide noodles, cooked
1 (4 pound) chicken, cooked,
 deboned, and chopped

TOPPING:

1 stick margarine, melted   ¼ pound plus 5 crackers, crushed

Melt butter and add flour gradually. Add the broth and cook until thickened.
Melt cheese in gravy. Mix with rest of ingredients. Put mixture in a 2-quart
casserole dish.

Topping: Melt 1 stick margarine with crackers. Mix together and put on top
of casserole. Bake at 350° for 40-45 minutes. Makes 8-10 servings.

CHICKEN CREOLE   Cece Allen

3 pounds chicken pieces
1 medium onion, sliced
1 medium green pepper,
 cut in strips
½ cup diced celery
1½ teaspoons salt

1 teaspoon thyme
½ teaspoon paprika
2 tablespoons chopped parsley
1 (1 pound) can tomatoes
1 (4 ounce) can sliced mushrooms

Combine all ingredients and cook on high 4-5 hours in crock pot. Serve
over rice.

CHICKEN NORMANDY   Barbara Ann Yoder

1 box Stove Top dressing
2½ cups cooked, deboned chicken
2 eggs
½ cup melted butter
1 cup hot water

½ cup mayonnaise
1½ cups milk
1 teaspoon salt
Mushroom soup
Cheese

Spread Stove Top dressing in bottom of a 9x13-inch pan. Put chicken on
dressing. Beat eggs and mix next 5 ingredients. Spread mushroom soup
over that. Bake 40 minutes at 325°. Spread cheese over top and bake
another 15 minutes. Serves 12.

Not what we gain, but what we give,
Measures the worth of the life we live.

CHICKEN CHOW MEIN

Mrs. Robert Paul Yoder

4 tablespoons vegetable oil
2 cups thin onion strips
2½ cups diced celery
1 teaspoon salt
2 teaspoons sugar
1½ cups clear chicken broth

1 can bean sprouts (optional)
2 tablespoons (or more) cornstarch
3 tablespoons soy sauce
2 cups diced, cooked chicken
Chow mean noodles
Cooked rice

Heat oil in a 6-quart cooking kettle. Add onions and celery; sprinkle with salt and sugar. Add chicken broth; cover and simmer 10 minutes. Drain bean sprouts (save liquid). Mix cornstarch and soy sauce with bean sprout liquid. Add to the rest and cook and stir until thickened. Add bean sprouts and chicken; reheat. Serve with chow mein noodles and rice. Serves 4-6.

This can be made with any meat.

CHICKEN & RICE

Tina Nussbaum

1 can cream of celery soup
1 can cream of chicken soup
1 can water
1 cup rice

Salt and pepper
1 chicken, cut up
Paprika

Mix soups, water, and rice in casserole dish. Salt and pepper the chicken and lay on top. (You can use leg quarters also). Sprinkle with paprika and bake at 350° for 1¼ hours. Makes 4-6 servings.

CHICKEN AND RICE

Mrs. Freeman Schlabach

1 small chopped onion
1 cup chopped celery
4 tablespoons butter
2 cups cooked rice
2 cups chopped chicken

¼ cup chopped pimiento (optional)
1 cup chicken broth
1 can cream of mushroom soup
½ teaspoon salt
Dash of pepper

TOPPING: (OPTIONAL)
Bread crumbs

¼ cup shredded Cheddar cheese

Sauté onions and celery in butter. Set aside. Cook rice. Mix all ingredients together and pour into greased 9x13-inch casserole. Bake in 350° oven for 30-35 minutes or until bubbly and golden brown. Serves 8.

A topping of bread crumbs and ¼ cup shredded Cheddar cheese may be added before baking, if desired.

Foreign
Foods

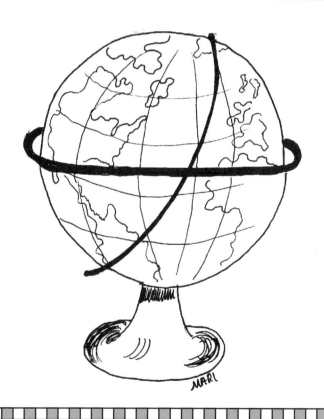

BURRITO CASSEROLE

Wanda Steiner, Faith Miller

2 pounds hamburger
2 small cans refried beans
1 package taco seasoning
10 soft tortillas
1½ cans mushroom soup

2 cups sour cream
Cheddar cheese, grated
Lettuce, grated
Tomatoes, diced
Additional sour cream to dab on
    top when served

Mix first 3 ingredients and fill tortillas. Mix mushroom soup and sour cream. Spread a little on the bottom of a 13x9-inch cake pan. Place burritos in pan and add the rest of the soup mixture on top. Bake 1 hour at 325°. Put Cheddar cheese on top and put back in oven until melted. Serve with lettuce, diced tomatoes, and sour cream. Delicious!

CHICKEN BURRITO

Lela Brenneman

Flour tortillas

HOT MIX:
1 tablespoon butter
2 medium onions, chopped
Garlic bulb (may use garlic salt)
5 tablespoons flour
1 cup chicken broth

1 cup milk
2 (4 ounce) cans chopped green
    chilies
¼ teaspoon salt
¼ teaspoon cumin

FILLING:
2-2½ cups cooked chicken
1 small can mushrooms
1 cup shredded white cheese

1 cup Cheddar cheese
Sour cream
Salsa

Hot mix: Melt butter and fry chopped onions and garlic. Blend in flour, then stir in broth, milk, chilies, salt, and cumin. Cook to boil. Simmer 5 minutes.

Grease 13x9-inch dish. Spread a little hot mix on each tortilla down center. Add chicken, mushrooms, and cheese. Wrap up and place in dish seam side down. Pour remaining sauce over that. Sprinkle with cheese. Bake uncovered at 350 for 20-30 minutes. Serve with sour cream and salsa. Serves 6-8.

SANTA FE ENCHILADAS

Regina Overholt

1½ pounds ground beef or pork
12 ounces tomato paste
1 cup water
½ cup chopped onion
Salt, if desired
1 package taco seasoning mix

8 ounces Cheese Whiz
4 ounces chopped green chilies,
   drained
12 flour tortillas
Shredded Cheddar cheese

Brown meat and drain. Add tomato paste, water, onion, salt, and season-ing. Cook until onion is tender. Add Cheese Whiz and green chilies. Lightly grease 9x13-inch pan. Spoon 2 tablespoons meat on each tortilla and roll up tightly. Top with remaining meat mixture and shredded Cheddar cheese. Bake at 350° until heated thoroughly. Serves 10-12.

TURKEY ENCHILADAS

Cynthia Helmuth

10 (6-inch) flour tortillas

SAUCE:
1 (16 ounce) can tomatoes, cut up
1 (15 ounce) can tomato sauce
1 cup finely chopped green pepper
½ cup sliced green onions

¼ cup snipped parsley or cilantro
1 teaspoon chili powder
½ teaspoon crushed red pepper
¼ teaspoon ground cumin

2 cups chopped cooked turkey
1 (3 ounce) package cream
   cheese, softened
1 cup (4 ounces) shredded sharp
   Cheddar cheese

Shredded lettuce and chopped
   tomatoes, if desired
Sour cream, if desired

Wrap the stack of tortillas tightly in foil. Heat in a 350° oven for 10 minutes.

Combine tomatoes, tomato sauce, green pepper, green onions, parsley or cilantro, chili powder, red pepper, and cumin in saucepan and bring to a boil. Reduce heat and simmer, uncovered, for 5 minutes. In mixing bowl, combine half the sauce, the turkey, the cream cheese, and half the shredded cheese. Spoon about ¼ cup of the turkey mixture onto each tortilla; roll tortilla. Place tortillas, seam side down, in lightly greased 9x13-inch baking pan. Bake, covered, at 350° for 20 minutes. Pour remaining sauce over tortillas; sprinkle with remaining cheese. Bake, uncovered, 8-10 minutes more. Serve with shredded lettuce and chopped tomatoes, and sour cream if desired. Serves 5.

Options: Substitute 1 quart of your favorite salsa for the sauce. Substitute browned ground beef for the turkey.

GRILLED FAJITAS

Silla Yoder

1 beef flank steak
1 envelope onion soup mix
¼ cup vegetable oil
¼ cup water
2 garlic cloves, minced
1 teaspoon ground cumin
½ teaspoon dried oregano

¼ teaspoon pepper
1 medium onion, thinly sliced
¼ cup Dale's seasoning
Green pepper, sliced
1 tablespoon cooking oil
8 (7-inch) flour tortillas

Place flank steak in glass dish. Pour the next 9 ingredients and Dale's seasoning over the meat. Cover and refrigerate overnight. Drain and discard marinade. Grill meat over *hot* coals until it reaches desired doneness, about 4 minutes per side for medium, 5 minutes per side for medium-well. Meanwhile in skillet, sauté onions and peppers in oil for 3-4 minutes or until crisp-tender. Slice meat in thin strips and place on tortillas. Top with vegetables. Roll up and serve immediately. Makes 4 servings.

SKILLET STEAK FAJITAS

Regina Overholt

½ cup A-1 steak sauce
½ cup medium or hot salsa
1 pound beef flank or bottom round
  roast, thinly sliced
1 medium onion, thinly sliced

1 medium green bell pepper, cut
  into strips
1 tablespoon margarine
8 (6½-inch) flour tortillas

Blend steak sauce and salsa. Place steak in glass dish; coat with ¼ cup salsa mixture. Cover and chill 1 hour, stirring occasionally.

In a large skillet, over medium heat, cook onion and pepper in margarine for 3 minutes or until tender. Remove and set aside. In same skillet, cook and stir steak for 5 minutes or until done. Add remaining salsa mixture, onion, and pepper; cook until heated through. Serve with tortillas and your favorite fajita toppings. Makes 4 servings.

MEXICAN CASSEROLE

Naomi Yoder

1 pound ground beef
½ cup chopped onion
2 (8 ounce) cans tomato sauce
¾ tablespoon chili powder

1 teaspoon salt
1 dozen flour tortillas, cut in half
2 cups shredded sharp cheese

Sauté ground beef and onion; drain fat. Stir in the tomato sauce, chili powder, and salt. In 1½-quart casserole dish, place alternate layers of meat sauce, tortillas, and cheese, ending with cheese. Bake at 325° for 45 minutes. Makes 10 servings.

MEXICAN CASSEROLE

Debbie Graber

1½ pounds hamburger, fried with
  salt and pepper
3 cups cooked rice
1 (15 ounce) can chili beans

1 (4 ounce) can diced green chilies
1 envelope taco seasoning
1 (16 ounce) can tomato sauce

TOPPING:
1 cup grated cheese
Crushed tortilla chips

Salsa and sour cream as
  condiments

Mix cooked hamburger, rice, beans, green chilies, taco seasoning, and tomato sauce together. Pour into casserole dish. Top with cheese and crushed tortilla chips. Bake at 325° for 45 minutes or until bubbly. Serve with salsa and sour cream.

MEXICAN HOTDISH

Mrs. David Wengerd

FLOUR TORTILLAS (MAKES 6):
1 cup flour
½ teaspoon salt
½ teaspoon baking powder

½ tablespoon lard or shortening
½ cup lukewarm water (scant)

FILLING MIXTURE:
1 pound ground beef
1 can chicken soup
1 can tomato soup
1 can cream of mushroom soup

1-2 tablespoons chili powder
1 pound grated cheese
1 onion, chopped
1 green pepper, chopped

Mix tortilla ingredients until it forms a ball. Divide into 6 balls. Roll each ball out on slightly floured surface. Roll until slightly transparent. Bake at 400°-450° on preheated pan for 1 minute on each side.

Brown beef; add onion and pepper; add soups and chili powder. Lightly grease 9x13-inch pan. Place 3 tortillas in the bottom. Put in half the soup mixture. Sprinkle with half the cheese. Place 3 tortillas on top. Add remaining soup, then cheese on top.

MEXICAN PIZZA

Silla K. Yoder

2 (8 ounce) cans refrigerated
  crescent rolls
1 (8 ounce) package cream cheese
1 cup sour cream
1 pound ground beef
1 package taco seasoning mix

1 (2¼ ounce) can sliced ripe olives,
  drained
1 medium chopped tomato
¾ cup shredded Cheddar cheese
¾ cup shredded mozzarella cheese
1 cup shredded lettuce

Flatten roll dough into an approximately 9x13-inch baking pan, lightly buttered to prevent sticking. Make sure dough is blended together so there are no cracks in crust. Bake at 375° for 8-10 minutes or until golden brown. Allow to cool.

Use medium size bowl and mix cream cheese and sour cream with a wire whisk. Spread evenly over crust. Chill 30 minutes.

Fry hamburger (crumbled) to brown and drain. Mix in taco seasoning, adding water according to directions on package. Simmer for 5 minutes, stirring. Spread over previous layer. Top with lettuce, tomatoes, olives, and cheeses. Cut and serve, or refrigerate.

MEXICAN TURKEY ROLL-UPS

Silla K. Yoder

2½ cups cubed cooked turkey
1½ cups (12 ounces) sour cream,
  divided
3 teaspoons taco seasoning,
  divided
1 (10¾ ounce) can condensed
  cream of mushroom soup,
  undiluted, divided

1½ cups shredded Cheddar
  cheese, divided
1 small onion, chopped
½ cup salsa
¼ cup sliced ripe olives
10 (7-inch) flour tortillas
Shredded lettuce
Chopped tomatoes
Additional salsa (optional)

In bowl, combine turkey, ½ cup sour cream, 1½ teaspoons taco seasoning, half of the soup, 1 cup of cheese, onion, salsa, and olives. Place ⅓ cup filling on each tortilla. Roll up and place seam side down in a greased 13x9x2-inch baking dish. Combine remaining sour cream, taco seasoning, and soup. Pour over tortillas. Cover and bake at 350° for 30 minutes or until heated through. Sprinkle with remaining cheese. Serve with shredded lettuce and chopped tomatoes. Top with additional salsa, if desired. Makes 5 servings.

MUCHO MEXICAN LASAGNA
Silla K. Yoder

1-1½ pounds ground beef, browned and drained well
1 package taco seasoning mix
½ teaspoon pepper
1 (16 ounce) jar homestyle mild salsa with garden peppers or distinction of your preference
1 package taco or fajita size flour tortillas
2 cups lowfat small curd cottage cheese

1 (8 ounce) package (2 cups) shredded Mexican cheese blend with Cheddar and Monterey Jack cheese with jalapeño peppers, divided (you can use 1 cup shredded Monterey Jack cheese with jalapeño peppers and 1 cup shredded Cheddar cheese)
1 egg
2 cups shredded lettuce
½ cup diced tomatoes
½ cup diced purple onion
½ cup sliced black olives

Combine browned and drained ground beef with taco seasoning mix, pepper, and salsa. Heat through. Set aside.

Cover the bottom and sides of a 9x13x2-inch baking dish with tortillas. Pour half of meat mixture over tortillas.

Combine cottage cheese, 1 cup of Mexican cheese blend, and egg. Pour half over meat mixture. Top with tortillas followed by remaining meat mixture then by cheese mixture.

Bake at 350° for 30 minutes. Remove from oven and sprinkle with remaining 1 cup Mexican cheese blend. Allow to melt slightly.

Sprinkle lettuce, tomatoes, onions, and olives diagonally across top of casserole. Serve while still warm.

Serve with sour cream, salsa, and guacamole on the side as desired.

SUPER NACHO
Irene Yoder, Melody Helmuth

1 pound hamburger
1 small onion, chopped
1 teaspoon salt
2 (16 ounce) cans refried beans
1 package taco seasoning

2 cups grated Monterey Jack cheese
1 (4 ounce) can chopped green chilies
1 cup grated Cheddar cheese
¾ cup hot taco sauce

Brown hamburger with onion and salt. Put in baking dish. Mix beans, seasonings, and Monterey Jack cheese, and spread on top of hamburger. Next add chilies and Cheddar cheese and spread taco sauce on top of everything. Bake in a 9x13-inch baking dish at 400° for 20-25 minutes. Serve with taco chips, shredded lettuce, tomatoes, sour cream, etc.

TACO PIZZA

Ramona Overholt

STEP 1 (CRUST):

2 tablespoons yeast
2 cups warm water, divided
4½ cups flour
1 tablespoon salt

1 tablespoon sugar
¼ cup oil
1 jar pizza sauce to spread over
  crust

STEP 2:

2 pounds ground beef
¼ cup onion
Pepperoni
Mozzarella cheese

Lettuce
Tomatoes
Cheddar cheese

Mix yeast and 1 cup warm water; let set 15 minutes. Add rest of ingredients and add 1 more cup warm water. Let rise 45 minutes. Punch down and spread on 2 greased pizza pans. Spread pizza sauce over crust.

Fry ground beef with onion. Drain; sprinkle on pizza. Add pepperoni and bake at 400° for 12-15 minutes. Sprinkle mozzarella cheese on top and bake again until completely done. Just before serving, garnish with chopped lettuce, tomatoes, and Cheddar cheese. Serve with sour cream and Thousand Island dressing!

TACO RICE

Barbara Ann Yoder, Melody Kauffman

1 pound hamburger
1 small onion, chopped
1 (16 ounce) can whole tomatoes,
  chopped up
1 cup rice
½ package taco seasoning (about
  1½ tablespoons)

Shredded cheese
Lettuce (or 1 cup each of sour
  cream and mayonnaise)
1 cup Bisquick baking mix
Enough water or milk to make a
  thin batter

Brown hamburger and onion. Drain tomatoes. Add enough water to the juice to make 2½ cups. Add tomatoes, juice, rice, and seasoning to hamburger. Mix and simmer 25 minutes, stirring occasionally. When ready to serve, top with shredded lettuce and cheese, OR mix equal parts sour cream and mayonnaise (about 1 cup each) and top with shredded cheese. Mix enough water or milk with Bisquick to make a thin batter. Pour over all and bake in a 9x13-inch pan at 350° until brown.

Trial is the school of trust!

EASY TACO SKILLET MEAL
Irene Yoder

1 pound ground beef
1 pint tomato juice
¾ cup water
1 package taco seasoning
Salsa or picante sauce
2 tablespoons brown sugar

1 cup rice
1 cup shredded Cheddar cheese
Shredded lettuce
Chopped onion
Sour cream

Brown ground beef in large skillet with lid. Add tomato juice, water, brown sugar, seasoning, and rice. Simmer 20 minutes or until rice is tender, stirring several times. Top with cheese and let it melt. Serve with lettuce, onions, sour cream, and salsa.

TACO SEASONING MIX
Alta Kauffman

¼ cup instant minced onion
3 tablespoons chili powder
2 tablespoons cumin
2 tablespoons salt

1 tablespoon crushed red pepper
  flakes
1 tablespoon minced garlic
1 tablespoon cornstarch
2 teaspoons oregano

Mix all ingredients and use as desired.

A BELZIAN SUPPER
Deborah Kauffman

FRY JACKS:
4 cups flour
4 teaspoons baking powder
1 teaspoon salt

2 tablespoons shortening
Enough water to make a soft
  dough

REFRIED BEANS:
4 cups dried kidney beans
1 onion, diced
1 bud garlic

Salt and pepper to taste
1 tablespoon shortening

Fry Jacks: Mix dry ingredients and shortening and add enough water to make dough soft and pliable. Knead dough; roll out thin (like a pie crust). Cut into squares and deep fry in hot oil until brown. Serve with refried beans.

Refried Beans: Cook beans until soft. Add onions, garlic, salt, and pepper; simmer approximately ½ hour. Mash beans with a potato masher; add shortening and continue to simmer until beans are thick.

POLISH KIELBASA STIR FRY

Elsie King Horst

1 pound Polish kielbasa
1 cup chopped onion
1 cup each of chopped mushrooms,
  broccoli, carrots, and green
  pepper, OR 1 package of frozen
  stir fry vegetables

Cooked rice
Cheese (preferably Velveeta)

Cut kielbasa into ½-inch pieces and fry on medium-high in 10-inch skillet with onion. When onion is transparent, add remaining vegetables. Stir frequently until vegetables are heated through and still crunchy. Can be served over rice, or rice and cheese can be mixed with meat and vegetables. Serves 8.

RUSSIAN BORSCHT

Mary Zook

4 tablespoons butter
4 cups carrots, shredded
1 large onion, chopped
2 cups celery, chopped
4 cups potatoes, diced
Water to cover
2 quarts tomatoes, chunk or juice
3 quarts beef broth (or broth made
  with bouillon)

2-3 cups leftover roast beef or
  canned chunk meat, optional
2 (15 ounce) cans red beets,
  rinsed and shredded
8 cups cabbage, coarsely
  shredded
Salt and pepper to taste
Dill to taste
Sour cream, optional

Combine butter, carrots, onion, celery, and potatoes; add just enough water to cover. Simmer just until tender. Add tomatoes, broth, meat, and red beets. Bring to boil. Add cabbage; simmer covered for 10 minutes. Season with salt, pepper, and dill. Serve with sour cream and fresh warm bread. Serves 10-12.

Pies

APPLE PIE

Emma Mae Yoder

4-5 apples
1 cup sugar
1 teaspoon apple pie spice

¼ teaspoon cinnamon
2 heaping tablespoons flour
Butter

Slice apples fairly thin. Mix sugar, spices, and flour together. Mix with sliced apples. Put in unbaked pie shell. Dot with butter. Cover with top crust. Spread a little cream and sprinkle some sugar on top crust. Bake at 325° for approximately 1 hour. Serves 6-8.

APPLE PIE FILLING

Irene Yoder

½ cup sugar
1 cup water
¼ teaspoon salt
½ teaspoon lemon juice
¼ cup Clear Jell
½ cup water

½ cup Karo syrup
1 teaspoon cinnamon
1 teaspoon butter
Allspice and nutmeg, optional
2-3 cups apples, sliced

Boil sugar and water. Add salt, lemon juice, and Clear Jell dissolved in ½ cup water. Cook until thickened, then add remaining ingredients. This is enough filling for 1 pie. Bake at 325° for 1 hour.

APPLE CREAM PIE NO. 1

Ruth Yoder

3 cups sliced apples

½ teaspoon cinnamon

CREAM FILLING:
⅔ cup sugar
2 eggs
2 tablespoons soft butter
⅛ teaspoon salt

2½ teaspoons vanilla
1 (3 ounce) package softened
   cream cheese

STREUSEL CRUMBS:
⅓ cup brown sugar
¼ cup flour

2 tablespoons butter
¼ cup chopped nuts

Put apples in pie shell and sprinkle with cinnamon.

For cream filling, cream the sugar, eggs, and butter for 2 minutes. Add salt, vanilla, and cream cheese; spoon over apples.

Streusel Crumbs: Mix sugar, flour, and butter to form coarse crumbs; add nuts. Top pie with crumbs. Bake at 375° for 45 minutes. Lower to 350° until pie is golden brown. Makes 6-8 servings.

APPLE CREAM PIE NO. 2

Ruth Yoder

CRUST:
1 stick margarine, softened
3 cups vanilla wafer crumbs

1 teaspoon cinnamon
¼ cup sugar

FILLING:
1 (14 ounce) can sweetened
  condensed milk
¾ cup sour cream

1 (3 ounce) package cream cheese
¼ cup lemon juice

APPLE TOPPING:
3 cups apples, peeled and sliced
1 tablespoon margarine
2 tablespoons water
½ cup sugar
2 teaspoons cinnamon
1 cup water

Reserved crumbs from crust
  mixture
½ cup chopped nuts
1 teaspoon cinnamon
1 tablespoon sugar

Crust: Stir mixture until well mixed. Press into 2 (8-inch) pie pans, reserving ½ cup of this mixture for topping.

Filling: Stir together first 3 ingredients, then add lemon juice. Mix well. Spread evenly over crumb crusts.

Apple Topping: Cook apples, margarine, and water just until tender. Remove from burner. Mix together ½ cup sugar, 2 teaspoons cinnamon, 1 cup water, and 3 tablespoons cornstarch. Add sugar, cinnamon, and water mix to apple mixture and cook until thickened. Cool. Pour over cream filling. Sprinkle with reserved crumbs, nuts, 1 teaspoon cinnamon, and 1 tablespoon sugar. Bake at 350° for 20-25 minutes or until set. Cool. Makes 2 (8-inch) pies.

FRENCH APPLE PIE

Jill Nussbaum

¾ cup sugar
1 teaspoon cinnamon

6 or 7 cups sliced apples
1½ tablespoons butter

TOPPING:
½ cup butter
½ cup brown sugar

1 cup flour

Mix sugar and cinnamon, then mix lightly through apples. Pour into pie shell. Dot with butter.

Mix ingredients for crumb topping and sprinkle on apples. Bake at 375° for 50-60 minutes.

CANDY APPLE PIE

Ruth Yoder

6 cups thinly sliced peeled baking apples
2 tablespoons lime juice
¾ cup sugar
¼ cup all-purpose flour

½ teaspoon ground cinnamon or nutmeg
¼ teaspoon salt
Pastry for (9-inch) double crust pie
2 tablespoons butter or margarine

TOPPING:
¼ cup butter or margarine
½ cup packed brown sugar

2 tablespoons heavy cream
½ cup chopped pecans

In a large bowl, toss apples with lime juice. Combine dry ingredients; add to the apples and toss lightly. Place bottom pastry in a 9-inch pie pan and fill with apple mixture. Dot with butter. Cover with top crust. Flute edges high; cut steam vents in top crust. Bake at 400° for 40-45 minutes, or until golden brown and apples are tender.

For Topping: Melt butter or margarine in small saucepan. Stir in brown sugar and cream; bring to boil, stirring constantly. Remove from heat and stir in pecans. Pour over top crust. Return to oven 3-4 minutes or until bubbly. Serve warm. Makes 8 servings.

Don't reject anyone whom God has accepted.

SOUR CREAM APPLE PIE

Carol Petersheim

2 tablespoons flour
¼ teaspoon salt
1 cup sugar
1 egg

1 cup sour cream
1 teaspoon vanilla
2 cups chopped apples

CRUMBS:
⅓ cup brown sugar
⅓ cup flour

1 teaspoon cinnamon
¼ cup butter

Stir together flour, salt, and sugar and set aside. Next stir together egg, sour cream, and vanilla. Add sour cream mixture to first mixture, then add chopped apples. Pour into pie crust. Bake for 15 minutes at 400° then turn back to 350° for 30 minutes.

While pie is baking, mix crumb ingredients together. Put crumbs on top of filling and return to oven until crumbs are browned. This recipe is one of Mrs. Simon Yoder's. She used it for her daughter's wedding then later it was used for her granddaughter's wedding.

SOUR-CREME APPLE PIE

Mrs. Gerald Lambright,
Martha Yoder, Carol Petersheim

3 tablespoons flour
1/8 teaspoon salt
3/4 cup sugar
1/4 teaspoon nutmeg

1 egg
1 1/2 cups dairy sour cream
1 teaspoon vanilla
2 cups diced apples

TOPPING:
1/3 cup brown sugar
1/3 cup flour

1 teaspoon cinnamon
1/4 cup butter or margarine

Sift together dry ingredients. Add egg, sour cream, and vanilla. Beat to smooth, thin batter. Stir in apples. Pour into a 9-inch, pastry-lined pie pan.

Mix topping ingredients and sprinkle over pie, then bake at 350° until golden brown. Makes 8 servings.

FRESH BLUEBERRY PIE

Mrs. Noah Yoder

1 (9-inch) baked pie shell
4 cups fresh (or frozen)
  blueberries, divided
1 cup sugar

3 tablespoons cornstarch
1/4 teaspoon salt
1/4 cup water
1 tablespoon butter or margarine

Line cooled pie shell with 2 cups blueberries. To make sauce, cook remaining berries with sugar, cornstarch, salt, and water over medium heat until thickened. Remove from heat; add butter and cool. Pour over berries in pie shell. Chill until serving time. If desired, serve with whipped cream. Other fruit can be used.

CLASSIC BANANA CREAM PIE

Silla K. Yoder

3 tablespoons cornstarch
1 2/3 cups water
1 (14 ounce) can Eagle brand
  sweetened condensed milk
3 egg yolks, beaten
2 tablespoons butter

1 teaspoon vanilla
3 medium bananas
Lemon juice concentrate
1 (9-inch) pie crust, baked and
  cooled
Whipped cream

In heavy saucepan, dissolve cornstarch in water. Stir in sweetened condensed milk and egg yolks. Cook and stir until thickened and bubbly. Remove from heat and add butter and vanilla. Cool slightly. Slice 2 bananas; dip in lemon juice and drain. Arrange on bottom of prepared crust. Pour filling over bananas. Cover and chill 4 hours or until set. Spread top with whipped cream. Slice remaining banana and dip in lemon juice and drain; garnish pie with bananas and whipped cream.

BOB ANDY PIE

Barbara Kauffman

⅓ cup butter or margarine
1 cup sugar
1½ tablespoons flour

2 eggs, separated
1 tablespoon cinnamon
1 tablespoon allspice
1½ cups milk

Cream butter or margarine, sugar, flour, and egg yolks. Add spices and milk. Beat 2 egg whites and mix with other ingredients until smooth. Pour into unbaked 9-inch pie shell. Bake at 350° for 40-60 minutes. Makes 6 servings.

BUTTERMILK CHESS PIE

Mrs. Sol Yoder, Sr., Ruth Yoder

½ cup butter
1½ cups sugar
2 tablespoons flour
Pinch of salt

4 eggs
1 teaspoon vanilla
⅔ cup buttermilk

Mix all together and pour into unbaked pie shell. Bake at 350° for 45-50 minutes, or until top is golden. Makes 1 pie.

Mrs. Sol Yoder, Sr., adds ⅓ chopped walnuts on top of pie.

A man is rich according to what he is, not according to what he has.

BUTTERSCOTCH PIE

Mary Joyce Miller

¼ cup water
½ cup brown sugar
1 tablespoon butter
⅛ teaspoon baking soda
Dash salt
1 cup sugar

½ cup flour
1 tablespoon cornstarch
1 egg yolk
1¼ cups water
1½ cups milk
1 teaspoon vanilla

MERINGUE:
4 egg whites
1 teaspoon cornstarch

¼ cup sugar
1 tablespoon corn syrup

Combine in saucepan water, brown sugar, flour, and cornstarch. Add egg yolk, 1¼ cups water, and milk. Bring to boil and cook 2 minutes. Remove from heat and add vanilla. Pour into baked 9-inch pie shell.

Beat egg whites until stiff peaks form. Add cornstarch, sugar, and corn syrup and beat until very stiff. Spread to edges of crust. Bake until meringue is golden brown. Makes 6-8 servings.

FLUFFY BUTTERSCOTCH PIE

Mrs. Gerald Lambright

1 (8 ounce) package cream
   cheese, softened
1 (6 ounce) package butterscotch
   morsels, melted

1 cup powdered sugar
½ cup milk
2 cups cream (whipped, enough to
   make 1 quart)

Whip cream cheese until soft and fluffy. Beat in melted morsels and sugar. Slowly add milk, blending thoroughly into mixture. Fold in whipped cream. Pour into 2 (9-inch) graham cracker pie shells. Freeze until firm and serve. Makes 12 servings.

Variations: May substitute 1 package chocolate chips instead of butterscotch morsels or ½ cup crunchy peanut butter.

PINEAPPLE CHESS PIE

2 eggs
1 cup sugar
½ cup brown sugar
1 tablespoon cornmeal
1 tablespoon flour

¼ cup milk
½ teaspoon vinegar
1 teaspoon vanilla
¼ cup butter
3 tablespoons crushed pineapple

Beat all ingredients together for 5 minutes. Pour into a 9-inch unbaked pie shell. Bake at 325° for 45 minutes. Serves 6.

SOUTHERN CHESS PIE

Donna Stephens

½ cup butter
1½ cups sugar
4 eggs
2 tablespoons cream

2 tablespoons cornmeal
2 tablespoons lemon juice
2 teaspoons vanilla

Combine and cream butter, sugar, and eggs. Beat 5 minutes on high speed, blending in remaining ingredients. Bake 1 hour at 325°.

PERFECT CUSTARD PIE

Drusilla Beiler

4 eggs
½ cup sugar
¼ teaspoon salt

½ teaspoon nutmeg
1 teaspoon vanilla
2 cups scalded milk

Put first 5 ingredients in blender and blend well. Slowly add scalded milk. Pour into unbaked pie crust. Bake at 400° for 10 minutes. Reduce heat to 325° and bake until set, about 15-20 minutes.

CHOCOLATE PIE

Melody Helmuth

2½ cups milk, divided
⅓ cup sugar
1½ tablespoons cocoa
2 rounded tablespoons cornstarch

1 tablespoon flour
¼ teaspoon salt
1 egg

Bring 2 cups milk, sugar, and cocoa to a boil. Blend ½ cup milk with remaining ingredients. Add to hot milk and bring to a boil, stirring constantly. Remove from heat. Cool, then pour into baked 9-inch pie shell. Top with whipped topping.

CHOCOLATE FUDGE PIE

Mrs. Gerald Lambright

1½ cups sugar (or less)
3 tablespoons cocoa
¼ cup melted margarine

2 eggs, beaten
½ cup evaporated milk or cream

Mix sugar and cocoa. Add margarine. Do not beat. Add eggs and stir in milk or cream. Bake at 400° for 10 minutes, then reduce heat to 350° and bake for 20-25 more minutes. Makes 1 small pie.

CHOCOLATE MERINGUE PIE

Jill Nussbaum

CHOCOLATE PUDDING FOR FILLING:
¼ teaspoon salt
2 tablespoons flour
2 tablespoons cocoa

1 cup sugar
3 egg yolks
2 cups milk

MERINGUE:
3 egg whites
Dash of salt

3 tablespoons sugar

Mix salt, flour, cocoa, and sugar. Beat egg yolks into milk. Add yolk and milk mixture gradually to dry ingredients. In heavy saucepan, cook on low heat, stirring constantly until thickened. Remove from heat. Let cool while mixing meringue.

Meringue: Beat egg whites and salt at high speed, adding sugar gradually.

Pour chocolate pudding into pie shell. Top with meringue. Bake at 350° for 15 minutes or until golden brown. Sprinkle sugar on meringue before baking. Peak meringue with spoon.

A family favorite—a *must* at family and church gatherings for 50 years. My mom's recipe.

MOM'S DELICIOUS CHOCOLATE PIE   Mrs. Robert Paul Yoder

4⅔ cups milk, divided
½ teaspoon salt
2 cups sugar
5 tablespoons flour
2 tablespoons cornstarch or Clear
  Jell

2½ tablespoons cocoa
4 eggs
2 teaspoons vanilla
1⅓ tablespoons butter

Heat 4 cups milk to boil in 6-quart kettle. In mixing bowl, mix sugar, salt, flour, cornstarch or Clear Jell, and cocoa. Beat eggs, then add eggs and ⅔ cup milk to the dry mixture. Mix well, then add to the boiling milk. Stir constantly until it boils. Take off heat, then add vanilla and butter. Cool. Pour into 2 (9-inch) baked pie crusts. Top with whipped cream.

Afflictions may test me,
They cannot destroy;
One glimpse of Thy love
Turns them all into joy. — Willett

FRIED PIES   Alta Kauffman

CRUST:
3 cups flour
1 teaspoon baking powder
1 teaspoon salt

½ cup shortening
¾ cup cold water

FILLING:
Your favorite pie filling

Oil for frying

GLAZE:
2 cups powdered sugar
1 teaspoon vanilla

2-3 tablespoons water

Combine flour, baking powder, and salt; cut in shortening with pastry blender until mixture resembles coarse meal. Sprinkle cold water 1 tablespoon at a time evenly over surface; stir with a fork until dry ingredients are moistened. Add more water if necessary.

Divide pastry in half; roll each portion to ⅛-inch thickness on wax paper. Cut into 5-inch circles. Put a spoonful of pie filling on each circle. Moisten edges with water, then fold in half, making sure edges are even. Press edges of filled pastry with a fork dipped in flour. Pour oil to depth of ½ inch in a Dutch oven. Fry pies in hot oil (375°) until golden brown on both sides, turning once. Drain well on paper towels.

Glaze: Combine powdered sugar, vanilla, and water. Drizzle over warm pies. Yield: 1 dozen.

COCONUT PIE IN ITS OWN CRUST

Mrs. Roger Helmuth, Sr.,
Ruth Yoder

4 eggs
1½ cups sugar
½ cup flour
¼ cup margarine

2 cups milk
1½ cups coconut
1 teaspoon vanilla
1 pinch salt

Put together in order given. Pour into greased 10-inch pie pan. Bake at 350° for 30 minutes or until golden brown, with center still soft. It sets more after baked. Makes 1 pie.

JAPANESE FRUIT PIE

Mrs. Freeman Schlabach

2 eggs
1 cup sugar
1 tablespoon vinegar
1 stick margarine, melted
Dash of salt

1 tablespoon flour
1 teaspoon vanilla
½ cup raisins
1 cup coconut
½ cup chopped nuts

Beat eggs and add the next 6 ingredients. Beat until smooth. Stir in raisins, coconut, and nuts. Pour into unbaked 9-inch pie shell and bake at 350° for 30 minutes or until set. Makes 1 pie.

CREAM CHEESE PINEAPPLE PIE

Mrs. Sol Yoder, Sr.

PINEAPPLE LAYER:
⅓ cup sugar
1 tablespoon cornstarch

1 (8 ounce) can crushed pineapple
  with juice

CREAM CHEESE LAYER:
1 (8 ounce) package cream cheese,
  softened to room temperature
½ cup sugar
2 eggs

1 teaspoon salt
½ teaspoon vanilla
1 (9-inch) unbaked pie shell
¼ cup chopped pecans

Combine sugar, cornstarch, and pineapple plus juice in a small saucepan. Cook over medium heat, stirring constantly until mixture is thick and clear. Cool. Set aside.

Blend cream cheese, sugar, and salt in bowl. Add eggs, one at a time, beating after each addition. Blend in milk and vanilla. Spread cooled pineapple mixture over bottom of pie shell. Pour cream cheese mixture over pineapple layer. Sprinkle with pecans. Bake for 10 minutes at 400°. Reduce heat to 325° and bake for 50 minutes. Cool.

CREAM CHEESE PIE
Ruth Yoder

½ cup butter
1½ cups graham crackers, crushed
¾ pound cream cheese
2 eggs
2½ tablespoons milk

½ cup sugar, divided
4 teaspoons vanilla, divided
2 teaspoons lemon juice
1 teaspoon grated lemon rind
1 cup sour cream

Melt butter and mix with crackers. Line a pie tin with cracker mixture, pressing down very firmly. Set aside. Place cream cheese, eggs, milk, ¼ cup sugar, 3 teaspoons vanilla, lemon juice, and lemon rind in an electric blender and mix for 1 minute at medium speed. Pour mixture into pie shell and bake at 375° for 20-25 minutes. Cool. Combine sour cream with remaining sugar and vanilla. Mix well and pour over cooled cheese pie. Bake for 7 minutes in 475° oven. Cool before serving.

LEMON CLOUD PIE
Elsie King Horst

FILLING:
¾ cup sugar
3 tablespoons cornstarch
1 cup water
1 teaspoon lemon peel

¼ cup lemon juice
2 beaten egg yolks
1 (3 ounce) package cream cheese

MERINGUE:
2 egg whites
¼ cup sugar

1 (9-inch) baked pie shell

In saucepan, combine sugar, cornstarch, water, peel, lemon juice, and slightly beaten egg yolks. Beat with rotary beater until well blended. Cook until thick, stirring constantly. Remove from heat and add cream cheese; stir until well blended. Cool while preparing meringue.

In small bowl, beat egg whites at high speed until foamy. Gradually add sugar, beating until meringue stands in stiff, glossy peaks. Stir into lemon mixture, spoon into crust. Chill at least 2 hours. (This pie does not soak the crust.) Serves 6-8.

Variations: Omit lemon juice and peel. Use 3 tablespoons cocoa and 1¼ cups water for Chocolate Cloud Pie.

Note: I cook my filling in the microwave, which cuts down on time spent stirring. It comes out perfect every time.

COOL LIME PIE
Edna Schrock

1 (8 ounce) package cream cheese
1 (14 ounce) can condensed milk
⅓ cup lime juice
1 drop of green food coloring,
  optional

2½ cups whipped topping
1 (9-inch) deep dish baked pie
  shell
Cool Whip whipped topping and
  lime slices for garnish

Cream the cream cheese until real smooth. Add condensed milk, lime juice, and food coloring and continue beating until creamy. Fold in whipped topping. Pour in a 9-inch baked pie shell. Makes 6-8 servings.

MY MOTHER'S MOCK MINCE PIE
Mrs. Freeman Schlabach

2 eggs
3 cups sugar
2 cups water
1 cup raisins
½ scant cup vinegar
1¼ cups bread crumbs

1 teaspoon cinnamon
1 teaspoon cloves
1 teaspoon nutmeg
½ scant cup butter
Cream and sugar for sprinkling on
  top crust

Beat eggs and add all the rest of the ingredients. Pour into unbaked 10-inch pie shell and put a top crust on. Brush top crust with cream and sprinkle with sugar. Bake at 350° until set.

COLORADO PEACH PIE
Rhoda Hilty

1 (9-inch) pie crust
4 cups sliced fresh peaches
1 cup sugar
2 tablespoons flour

¼ teaspoon salt
1 egg
1 cup sour cream
½ teaspoon vanilla

TOPPING:
⅓ cup brown sugar
⅓ cup flour

¼ cup butter
1 teaspoon cinnamon

Place peaches in pie crust. Beat the next 6 ingredients and pour over peaches. Make crumbs with the brown sugar, flour, butter, and cinnamon and sprinkle over top. Bake at 400° for 15 minutes then 350° for 20 minutes. Serves 6-8.

This is also good with plums.

OATMEAL PIE
Esther Mast

½ cup white sugar
½ cup butter, melted
3 eggs, beaten thoroughly
  one at a time

1 cup waffle syrup
3 tablespoons water
1 cup quick rolled oats

Mix sugar and butter, then eggs one at a time. Mix in syrup and water. Mix in rolled oats. Put in 1 (9-inch) unbaked pie crust. Bake at 375° for 30 minutes, or until set. Makes 6-8 servings.

PECAN PIE
Melody Helmuth

4 eggs
1½ cups Karo syrup
1 teaspoon vanilla
4 tablespoons butter, melted

¼ cup brown sugar
⅛ teaspoon salt
1 cup pecans

Mix all ingredients except pecans. Spread pecans over unbaked 9-inch pie shell and pour filling over top. Bake at 400° for 15 minutes, then at 350° for 30 minutes. Makes 6-8 servings.

CHEESECAKE PECAN PIE
Drusilla Beiler, Elva Miller

1 (8 ounce) package cream
  cheese, softened
1 large egg
⅓ cup sugar
¼ teaspoon salt
1 teaspoon vanilla

1 (9-inch) deep dish pastry pie shell
1¼ cups chopped pecans
3 large eggs, beaten
1 cup light corn syrup
¼ cup sugar
1 teaspoon vanilla

Combine first 5 ingredients; beat at low speed until smooth. Pour into pastry shell; sprinkle with pecans. Combine 3 eggs and remaining ingredients, mixing well. Spoon over pecan layer. Bake at 350° for 35 minutes or until set.

KENTUCKY PECAN PIE
Carolyn Eash, Irene Yoder

3 whole eggs, slightly beaten
1 cup white corn syrup
½ cup brown sugar

⅓ cup melted butter
1 teaspoon vanilla
1 cup pecans

Beat eggs lightly; add other ingredients except pecans and mix. Add pecans last. Pour into unbaked 9-inch pie shell. Bake at 350° for 50 minutes. Serve with ice cream and enjoy!

PECAN PIE

Debbie Graber

3 eggs
1 cup pancake syrup
½ cup brown sugar
⅓ cup margarine, melted

1 cup chopped pecans
Dash salt
1 teaspoon vanilla
1 unbaked pie shell

Combine all ingredients and pour into pie shell. Bake at 350°-375° until center is set.

The mother's heart is the child's schoolroom. — H. W. Beecher

FAVORITE PECAN PIE

Ellen D. Miller

3 eggs
⅞ cup brown sugar
½ cup light Karo syrup
1 teaspoon vanilla
⅛ teaspoon salt
6 tablespoons margarine, melted

1 tablespoon flour
½ cup water
¼ teaspoon nutmeg
1 cup pecans
1 tablespoon flour

Mix all ingredients (except pecans and 1 of the tablespoons of flour) lightly just until blended. Mix 1 cup pecans with 1 tablespoon flour. Fold in last. Pour in pan. Bake at 400° for 15 minutes, then at 325° for 15 more minutes, or until done. Makes 1 pie.

MARIE'S PECAN PIE

Mrs. Freeman Schlabach

½ teaspoon salt
1 cup sugar
2 tablespoons flour
2 tablespoons milk
1 teaspoon vanilla flavoring

1 teaspoon maple flavoring
2 eggs
½ cup corn or pancake syrup
½ cup melted margarine
½ cup pecans

Mix salt, sugar, and flour; add milk and flavorings. Add eggs; beat well. Add syrup and margarine and beat well. Stir in pecans. Pour into unbaked 9-inch pie shell. Bake at 350° for 30 minutes or until set. Serves 6-8.

Serve with ice cream and coffee.

PEANUT BUTTER PIE #1

Ruth Yoder, Regina Overholt

4 ounces cream cheese
1 cup confectioners sugar
½ cup crunchy peanut butter

1 cup heavy cream, whipped, or 9
  ounces non-dairy whipped topping
Chocolate syrup or cookie crumbs
  for garnish

CHOCOLATE-FLAVORED PIE CRUST:
1¼ cups chocolate cookie crumbs
  (20 cookies)

¼ cup butter, melted
1 teaspoon vanilla

Soften cream cheese in large bowl. Beat in confectioners sugar and peanut butter. Fold in whipped cream or whipped topping. Pour into pie crust; chill. Garnish with chocolate syrup or cookie crumbs.

Crust: Combine crust ingredients and press into a 9-inch pie pan. Bake at 375° for 10 minutes. Serves 6.

Regina uses 1 cup creamy peanut butter.

PEANUT BUTTER PIE

Mrs. Jonathan Yoder

2 cups milk, divided
½ cup sugar
½ teaspoon salt
4 tablespoons cornstarch
2 eggs, separated

1 tablespoon butter
1 teaspoon vanilla
Pastry for 1 (9-inch) pie crust
Whipped topping

PEANUT BUTTER CRUMBS:
½ cup peanut butter

¾ cup powdered sugar

Scald 1½ cups of the milk. Combine sugar, salt, and cornstarch. Add remaining ½ cup milk. Pour paste into hot milk and cook until thickened. Beat egg yolks. Pour small amount of hot mixture over yolks before adding them to milk. Cook 2 minutes longer. Remove from heat and add butter and vanilla. When cold, take a baked 9-inch pie shell and put a layer of peanut butter crumbs, then pudding and peanut butter crumbs. Top with whipped topping. Makes 1 pie.

Peanut Butter Crumbs: Mix together the peanut butter and powdered sugar until crumbly.

Good character, like good soup, is usually homemade.

FROZEN PEANUT BUTTER PIE
Emma Mae Yoder

¾ cup powdered sugar
1 (3 ounce) package cream cheese
½ cup peanut butter
2 tablespoons milk

1 (8 ounce) container whipped
 topping
1 baked pie shell
¼ cup chopped peanuts

Cream together powdered sugar and cream cheese. Add peanut butter and milk; mix well. Fold in whipped topping. Put in pie shell. Top with chopped peanuts. Freeze until firm. Serves 6.

DOUBLE LAYER PUMPKIN PIE
Ruth Yoder

4 ounces cream cheese, softened
1 tablespoon milk or half-and-half
1 tablespoon sugar
1½ cups whipped topping
1 (6 ounce) graham cracker pie
 crust
1 cup milk or half-and-half

2 (4-serving size) packages Jello
 instant vanilla pudding and pie
 filling
1 (16 ounce) can pumpkin
1 teaspoon ground cinnamon
½ teaspoon ground ginger
¼ teaspoon ground cloves

Mix cream cheese, milk or half-and-half, and sugar in large bowl with wire whisk until smooth. Gently stir in whipped topping. Spread on bottom of crust. Pour 1 cup milk or half-and-half into bowl. Add pudding mix. Beat with wire whisk until blended, 1-2 minutes. Stir in pumpkin and spices with wire whisk. Mix well. Spread over cream cheese layer. Refrigerate at least 3 hours. Garnish with whipped topping.

PUMPKIN PIE
Mrs. Roger Helmuth, Sr.

1 (8 ounce) package cream cheese
1 tablespoon milk
1 tablespoon sugar
1½ cups Cool Whip whipped
 topping
1 cup milk

2 packages instant vanilla pudding
1 (16 ounce) can pumpkin
1 teaspoon cinnamon
½ teaspoon ginger
¼ teaspoon cloves

Mix cream cheese, milk, and sugar until smooth. Stir in whipped topping and spread mixture on bottom of 2 baked pie crusts. Mix together milk and pudding, then stir in pumpkin, cinnamon, ginger, and cloves. Spread over cream cheese layer. Refrigerate 3 hours. Top with whipped topping. May be garnished with nuts. Makes 2 pies.

PUMPKIN PIE
Jo Ann Inhulsen

1½ cups cooked pumpkin
1 cup sugar
1½ cups milk, scalded
3 eggs, separated
½ teaspoon salt

1 tablespoon cornstarch
¼ teaspoon ginger
¼ teaspoon cloves
1 teaspoon cinnamon or 1½
    teaspoons pumpkin pie spice

Blend all ingredients except egg whites. Stir in last. Pour into a large unbaked pie shell. Bake at 425° for 10 minutes, then at 325°-300° until set. Makes 1 large pie.

PUMPKIN PIE FOR 3 PIES
Mrs. Henry Overholt, Sr., Celesta Miller

¾ cup white sugar
1⅔ cups brown sugar
5 eggs, separated
1½ cups pureed pumpkin
1 cup cream

4 cups milk
3 tablespoons flour
2 teaspoons cinnamon
1 teaspoon nutmeg
Pinch of salt

Mix sugars, egg yolks, pumpkin, flour, salt, cream, and spices. Fold in 1 cup milk; add rest of milk gradually. Add to pumpkin mixture with wire whisk. Mix well. Beat egg whites until stiff and fold into mixture last. Bake at 400° for 10 minutes then at 350° for 20-30 additional minutes. Makes 3 pies.

Celesta uses ⅓ teaspoon cloves and 1 tablespoon vanilla.

True love is one thing of which we can neither receive, nor give, too much.

FROSTY PUMPKIN PIE
Sharon Miller

1 pint vanilla ice cream
1 teaspoon cinnamon
½ teaspoon cloves
1 (9-inch) graham cracker crust
1 cup canned or cooked pumpkin
1 cup sugar

1 teaspoon pumpkin pie spice
½ teaspoon ground ginger
½ teaspoon salt
½ cup chopped walnuts
1 cup chilled whipping cream

Soften ice cream slightly and quickly stir in cinnamon and cloves. Spread in pie shell. Freeze until ice cream is solid. Mix pumpkin, sugar, pie spice, ginger, salt, and walnuts. Beat whipping cream until stiff. Stir into pumpkin mixture. Pour over ice cream in crust. Freeze several hours. Remove from freezer 10-15 minutes before serving. Makes 8 servings.

FROZEN PUMPKIN PIE

Mrs. Shirley Yoder

CRUST:
2 cups graham crackers
½ cup melted margarine

½ cup sugar
Cinnamon for sprinkling on crust

FILLING:
1 cup pumpkin
½ cup brown sugar
½ teaspoon cinnamon

¼ teaspoon nutmeg
½ gallon ice cream

Press graham cracker crust in 9x13-inch pan. Sprinkle with cinnamon. Bake at 350° for 10 minutes; cool. Mix rest of ingredients; pour into crust. Freeze. Cut in squares and serve.

SWEET POTATO PIE WITH NUT TOPPING

Ruth Yoder

2 cups cooked, pureed Georgia
  sweet potatoes
1 egg, slightly beaten
¼ cup milk
1 teaspoon vanilla

⅛ teaspoon salt
¾ cup sugar
¼ cup butter, melted
¼ teaspoon nutmeg

CARAMEL NUT TOPPING:
1 cup chopped pecans
¼ cup butter, melted

¼ cup light brown sugar

Mix first 6 ingredients together until mixture is smooth. Pour into unbaked cream cheese crust and bake for 35 minutes in 350° oven. Remove from oven and top with Caramel Nut Topping and bake for an additional 15 minutes.

Caramel Nut Topping: Combine all topping ingredients and mix well. Distribute evenly over sweet potato pie.

Never a soldier in fierce conflict
Could a higher honor bring,
Than the shut-in who's performing
Secret service for the King.

BEST EVER SWEET POTATO PIE   Ruth Yoder

1 cup whole milk, scalded
1 cup Carnation milk
1 cup cooked and mashed sweet
  potatoes
¾ cup white sugar
¾ cup brown sugar

3 tablespoons flour
½ teaspoon nutmeg
½ teaspoon cinnamon
½ teaspoon salt
3 eggs, separated

Scald whole milk. Mix Carnation milk, scalded milk, sweet potatoes, sugars, flour, spices and salt. Add egg yolks. Whip egg whites until stiff and fold in last. Pour into two 9-inch unbaked pie crusts. Bake at 400° for 10 minutes then at 350° for 45 minutes.

Variation: For crumb topping, mix 1 cup flour, 1 cup brown sugar, 1 cup oatmeal, and 1 stick softened butter. Add to top of pie before baking.

RAISIN CREAM PIE   Rhoda Coblentz

¾ cup raisins
3 cups water
1 cup brown sugar
6 heaping tablespoons flour
⅓ teaspoon salt

2 egg yolks
1¼ teaspoons vanilla
¼ teaspoon maple flavoring
1 tablespoon butter

Cook or simmer raisins in 2 cups of the water and add ½ cup of the brown sugar for 30 minutes. Combine remaining sugar, flour, salt, and beaten egg yolks with remaining 1 cup of water to make a smooth paste. Add this mixture to simmering raisins, and stir well until boiling. Remove from heat and add flavorings and butter. Pour cool filling into baked 9- or 10-inch pie crust and top with whipped cream. This makes a nice full pie.

RAISIN CREAM PIE   Mrs. Roger Helmuth, Sr.

2¼ cups milk
¾ cup brown sugar
4 level tablespoons cornstarch
2 eggs, beaten

1 tablespoon butter
1 teaspoon vanilla
1 cup raisins

Mix all together (except raisins) until thickened.

Cook raisins in a little water until soft. Drain. Add to pudding. Put in baked 9- or 10-inch pie crust, and top with whipped cream or Cool Whip whipped topping.

RAISIN MERINGUE BUTTERSCOTCH PIE   Ruth Yoder

RAISIN CRUNCH CRUST:
¾ cup raisins, finely chopped
⅓ cup pecans, finely chopped
½ cup butter, softened

¼ cup light brown sugar, packed
1 cup flour

BUTTERSCOTCH FILLING:
1 cup light brown sugar
6 tablespoons cornstarch
½ teaspoon salt
1½ cups milk
3 egg yolks, beaten

2 tablespoons butter
2 teaspoons vanilla
1 cup chopped raisins
1 cup sour cream

MERINGUE:
3 egg whites
¼ teaspoon cream of tartar

⅛ teaspoon salt
6 tablespoons sugar

Crust: Blend all ingredients together and press into a 9-inch pan. Prick with fork and bake at 375° for 8-10 minutes. Do not overbake.

Filling: In saucepan, blend brown sugar with cornstarch and salt. Stir in milk, stirring constantly over moderate heat until mixture thickens. Lower heat and cook until *very* thick, about 15 minutes, stirring constantly. Remove from heat, stir in beaten egg yolks, butter, vanilla, and raisins. Cover and cool until lukewarm. Stir in sour cream and pour into baked raisin crust. Top with meringue.

Meringue: Beat egg whites until foamy. Add cream of tartar and salt. Gradually beat in sugar, 2 tablespoons at a time, until sugar is completely dissolved. Bake meringue-topped pie at 400° for 8-10 minutes. Makes 8 servings.

TANGY RHUBARB PIE   Esther L. Miller

4 cups diced rhubarb
1½ tablespoons cherry or
   raspberry Jello
1 egg

1 tablespoon flour
1¼ cups sugar
½ teaspoon vanilla

TOPPING:
¾ cup flour
½ cup brown sugar

⅓ cup margarine

Mix rhubarb with Jello. Beat together the next 4 ingredients. Mix with rhubarb mixture. Pour in unbaked 9-inch pie shell. Mix topping and sprinkle over pie, if desired. Bake at 350° for 10 minutes and 300° for 25 minutes or until done.

FRENCH RHUBARB PIE

Barbara Kanagy

1 egg, beaten
1 cup sugar
1 tablespoon flour
1 tablespoon cream

2 tablespoons butter
1 teaspoon vanilla
2 cups diced rhubarb

CRUMBS:
½ cup brown sugar
¾ cup flour

¼ cup butter

Mix together egg, sugar, flour, cream, butter, and vanilla. Fold in diced rhubarb. Pour into 9-inch pie shell.

Crumbs: Mix together brown sugar, flour, and butter and spread on top of pie. Bake at 400° for 10 minutes; reduce heat to 350° until done. Serves 6.

RHUBARB CREME PIE

Mrs. James Mast

2 tablespoons butter
1 cup diced rhubarb
1 cup sugar
½ cup water
¼ cup sugar

1 egg
⅛ teaspoon salt
¼ cup cream
2 tablespoons cornstarch

TOPPING:
1 cup whipping cream, whipped

Nutmeg, if desired

1 (9-inch) pie shell, baked

Cook first 4 ingredients together until rhubarb is tender. Mix other filling ingredients together, add to cooking mixture, and bring to a boil again.

When cold, pour into pie shell. Top with whipped cream and sprinkle with nutmeg. Makes 6 servings.

SHOO FLY PIE

Drusilla Beiler

1 cup flour
⅔ cup brown sugar
2 tablespoons margarine
½ cup dark corn syrup
½ cup molasses

1 egg
¼ teaspoon salt
½ teaspoon baking soda
1 cup hot water
1 (9-inch) unbaked pie crust

Mix together until crumbly the flour, sugar, and margarine. Keep out ½ cup for topping. Blend rest of ingredients together, then into crumb mixture. Pour into crust and sprinkle reserved crumbs on top. Bake at 350° for 50 minutes.

WET BOTTOM SHOO-FLY PIE
Naomi Yoder

1 cup flour
⅔ cup brown sugar
1 tablespoon butter
⅔ cup hot water

1 cup dark molasses (I use light
   Karo syrup)
1 teaspoon baking soda
1 beaten egg
1 (8- or 9-inch) unbaked pie shell

Mix the first 3 ingredients into crumbs. Set aside ½ of this mixture. Combine hot water and molasses or Karo syrup, add baking soda and egg, and beat well. (I use a blender). Fold half of the crumbs into this mixture, but do not beat. Pour into pie shell and sprinkle remaining crumbs over top. Bake at 400° for 15 minutes, then reduce heat to 325° and bake for 20-30 minutes more. Delicious served warm with vanilla ice cream. Makes 1 pie.

AMISH SHOO-FLY PIE
Ruth Yoder

CRUMB MIXTURE:
2 cups flour
¾ cup brown sugar
⅓ cup lard, shortening, or butter

½ teaspoon nutmeg, optional
1 teaspoon cinnamon, optional

SYRUP MIXTURE:
1 cup molasses
2 eggs
1 cup hot water

1 teaspoon baking soda dissolved
   in hot water

Crumb Mixture: Mix ingredients together thoroughly in a bowl until crumbs are formed.

Syrup Mixture: In a separate bowl, mix syrup ingredients thoroughly. Pour half of the syrup mixture into unbaked pie crust-lined 8-inch pie plate, then add half of crumb mixture; repeat with the other pie plate. Bake at 400° for 10 minutes, then reduce heat to 350° and continue baking 50 minutes more. Cool before eating. Yield: 2 (8-inch) pies.

FRESH STRAWBERRY YOGURT PIE
Jo Ann Inhulsen

1 cup yogurt cheese
1 large container Cool Whip
½-¾ cup powdered sugar (to taste)
1 teaspoon vanilla

2 tablespoons instant starch
   (if filling seems runny)
Strawberries or other fresh fruit
   in season
2 (9-inch) baked pie shells

Beat yogurt cheese and Cool Whip until fluffy. Add powdered sugar and vanilla. Beat until light and fluffy. If using instant starch, add last and beat. Pie seems to hold up better if you use the starch. Spoon into pie shells and top with fresh fruit. Garnish with powdered sugar and serve.

You can also use store-bought plain yogurt if you're not into making your own!

STRAWBERRY PIE

Emma Mae Yoder

1 pint water
1 cup sugar
¼ cup strawberry Jello
¼ cup Clear Jell

¼ teaspoon lemon juice
Pinch of salt
¾ quart strawberries
Whipped cream

Bring ¾ pint water and sugar to boiling. Add Jello. Use remaining water to mix Clear Jell. Add to above mixture. Boil on low heat approximately 3 minutes. Add lemon juice and salt. Cool. Add strawberries. Put in baked pie shell and top with whipped cream.

CREAM CHEESE CRUST

Ruth Yoder

1 (3 ounce) package cream
  cheese, softened

¼ cup butter, softened
1 cup all-purpose flour

Combine cream cheese and butter. Blend well, then stir in flour. Shape dough. Place ball between 2 sheets of waxed paper. Roll out into a circle to fit deep dish pie plate. Remove 1 sheet of waxed paper and flute the edge of crust into pie plate.

CRISCO PIE CRUMBS

Debbie Graber

1 (5 pound) bag unbleached flour
1 (3 pound) can Crisco, minus 1
  cup

1 tablespoon salt
1 tablespoon baking powder
½ cup sugar

In a large mixing bowl, combine all ingredients. Blend with a pastry blender or fork until mixture resembles fine crumbs.

To use, take 1¼ cups crumbs and 3 tablespoons water, and roll out on floured wax paper. (Put a few drops of water under the wax paper to keep it from sliding!) I love this recipe; it's so handy!

PERFECT PIE CRUST

Mary Joyce Miller

6 cups flour
1 tablespoon sugar
1½ teaspoons salt
1½ teaspoons baking powder

2 cups shortening
1 egg, beaten
Cold water
2 tablespoons vinegar

Combine flour, sugar, salt, and baking powder. Cut in shortening. Put egg in measuring cup and water to measure 1 cup. Add vinegar. Pour into flour mixture all at once. Blend in just until dough holds together. Makes enough for 4 double pie crusts.

PIE CRUST
Jill Nussbaum

1¾ cups flour
1 teaspoon salt

½ cup Crisco oil
3 tablespoons cold water

Mix lightly with fork. Roll out between wax paper which has been sprinkled with flour. Makes a light, flaky crust. Makes 1 pie with top or 2 shells.

NEVER FAIL PIE CRUST
Ruth Yoder

3 cups flour
½ teaspoon salt
1 teaspoon sugar
⅛ teaspoon baking powder

1 cup shortening
1 egg
¼ teaspoon vinegar
5 tablespoons water or milk

In a large mixing bowl, combine the flour, salt, sugar, and baking powder. Add shortening and blend with a pastry blender and fork until mixture resembles fine crumbs. In small bowl, beat the egg and add vinegar and water. Pour over flour and mix with fork until dough forms. Roll out crusts for pie. Bake at 350° for 10-15 minutes. Makes 3 crusts.

A pie crust will be more easily made if all ingredients are cool.

SHAKE AND BAKE PIE CRUST
Drusilla Beiler

1 egg
1 tablespoon vinegar
Water
5 cups flour

2 cups Crisco shortening
1 teaspoon salt
⅓ cup brown sugar
1 teaspoon baking powder

Take a cup measure and put in the egg, vinegar, and fill with water. In a large Tupperware bowl, mix together all dry ingredients with shortening until crumbly. Then add liquids and put lid on Tupperware and shake for 30 seconds. Makes 10-12 pie crusts.

STIR AND ROLL PASTRY
Roxanna Linneber

2 cups sifted flour
1 teaspoon salt

¾ cup oil
¼ cup milk

Mix together flour and salt. Add oil and milk in small measuring cup. *Don't stir.* Pour liquids all at once in dry ingredients mixture. Form into ball. Roll out on wax paper on dampened counter with wax paper over dough.

This is really good flaky pie crust. I always get compliments.

Salads
&
Salad
Dressings

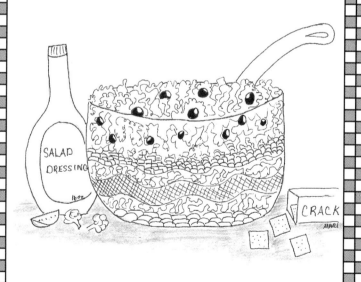

BROCCOLI SALAD

Donna Stephens, Melody Kauffman

1 large bunch fresh broccoli
8-10 slices bacon
1 cup mayonnaise
⅓ cup sugar

2-3 tablespoons vinegar
1 medium onion, chopped
½ cup raisins

Cut broccoli into bite-size pieces. Cut bacon in bits and fry. Mix mayonnaise, sugar, and vinegar. Pour dressing over broccoli, bacon, raisins, and onion and let stand 1 hour or more before serving. Makes 8-10 servings.

Donna adds ½ cup chopped pecans to her salad.

BROCCOLI & CAULIFLOWER SALAD

Mrs. Shirley Yoder

1 pound bacon
1 bunch each: broccoli and
   cauliflower

2 cups fresh mushrooms
½ cup slivered almonds
½-¾ cup shredded Cheddar cheese

DRESSING:
2 cups mayonnaise
2 tablespoons vinegar
¼ cup sugar

1 envelope Good Seasons Italian
   dressing mix

Fry bacon to a crisp and break in pieces. Cut up broccoli and cauliflower and slice mushrooms. Add slivered almonds and cheese.

Blend dressing, but do not mix in with vegetables until ready to serve.

BROCCOLI-CHEDDAR SALAD

Susan K. Yoder

3 cups broccoli florets
6 slices bacon, fried crisp, drained,
   and crumbled
½ cup shredded Cheddar cheese

1 cup mayonnaise
2 tablespoons vinegar
¼ cup sugar

Mix florets, bacon, and cheese. Combine mayonnaise, vinegar, and sugar and mix well. Pour over salad and toss. Cover and refrigerate until ready to serve. Makes 6 servings.

CARROT RAISIN SALAD

Ruth Yoder

⅔ cup California seedless raisins
2 cups grated carrots
1 cup, or more if desired, canned
   pineapple tidbits

⅓ cup mayonnaise
1 tablespoon lemon juice
¼ teaspoon salt

Combine raisins, carrots, and drained pineapple. Blend in mayonnaise, lemon juice, and salt. Chill thoroughly. Serve on crisp salad greens.

CARROT SALAD

Barbara Kanagy

2 pounds carrots, peeled and
  sliced
¾ cup vinegar
¼-½ cup oil
1¼ cups sugar

⅛ teaspoon pepper
1 green pepper, sliced
1 medium onion
1 tablespoon dry mustard, if
  desired

Cook carrots until soft. Mix all ingredients together and let set overnight. Keeps long in refrigerator.

CHINESE CHICKEN SALAD

Ruth Yoder

½ pound chopped chicken breast,
  cooked or baked
1 head lettuce, shredded
½ cup green onions

¼ cup sliced almonds
1 tablespoon sesame seed
½ package wonton skins, cut in
  strips and deep-fat fried

DRESSING:
2 tablespoons sugar
1 teaspoon salt
1 teaspoon Accent

½ teaspoon pepper
3 tablespoons vinegar
¼ cup oil

Toss together chicken, lettuce, green onions, almonds, and sesame seeds. Add crushed skins after dressing has been added.

For dressing, mix all ingredients together and add to salad.

Kindness is like snow:
It will make beautiful anything it covers.

CINDY'S PASTA SALAD

Merlyn Mullet

DRESSING:
1 large bottle zesty Italian dressing

SALAD:
1 (1 pound) box pasta, cooked
1 small jar pimientos
10-12 ounces pepperoni, chunked
1 pound provolone cheese, chunked

1 small can black olives, optional
Fresh mushrooms, sliced
1 bunch broccoli, cut up in small
  pieces

Pour Italian dressing over all. Let set several hours in refrigerator before serving.

COLE SLAW

Kathy Schrock

1 large head cabbage, diced
½ cup chopped onion
1 teaspoon celery seed
1 cup celery, chopped

1 green pepper, chopped
½ cup vinegar
2 cups sugar
2 teaspoons salt

Mix all together. This will keep its flavor indefinitely in the fridge, or it can also be frozen for later use.

DEVILED EGGS

Tina Nussbaum

8 hard-boiled eggs
Dash of salt
¼ teaspoon mustard

1½ tablespoons mayonnaise
4 teaspoons sugar

Cut hard-boiled eggs in half. Remove yolks and mash. Add rest of ingredients and refill the egg whites. Sprinkle with paprika and/or parsley flakes.

One's life will soon be past.
Only what's done for Christ will last.

STUFFED EGGS

Jonas and Kathy Schrock

1 dozen eggs
1 tablespoon flour or Clear Jell
½ cup sugar
1 teaspoon salt
1 cup cold water

1 egg
1 teaspoon mustard
2 tablespoons vinegar
3 tablespoons butter

Place eggs in boiling water. Bring to a boil and boil for 10 minutes. Cool in cold water. Peel them and split them lengthwise. Place on a serving dish. Remove the yolks and mash with a fork until free of lumps. Place other ingredients in blender and blend until smooth. Cook until thickened; cool. Mix cooled, cooked ingredients with yolks until smooth. Fill the eggs with it and garnish with parsley and paprika or as desired.

278

HAYSTACK
Judith Yoder, Silla Kay Yoder

Corn chips or white crackers, crushed
Rice, cooked in salt water
Lettuce, chopped
Tomatoes, chopped

Hamburger, fried and seasoned
Kidney beans
Grated cheese
Cheese sauce (see recipe below)
Chopped onions, optional

CHEESE SAUCE:
2 tablespoons butter
2 cups milk
2 tablespoons flour

1 teaspoon salt (or less)
⅛ teaspoon pepper
1 cup grated cheese

Put food on plate in order given until your stack is made. Fried potatoes may be used instead of rice.

Cheese Sauce: Brown butter in heavy saucepan. Add next 4 ingredients and cook until thickened. Add grated cheese and stir until melted. Sauce yields 2½ cups.

HOT CHICKEN SALAD
Laura K. Yoder

2 cups cooked and boned chicken
2 cups thinly sliced celery
1 cup toasted bread cubes or seasoned croutons
1 cup mayonnaise
½ cup chopped or slivered almonds

2 tablespoons lemon juice
½ teaspoon salt
½ cup shredded Cheddar cheese
1 cup toasted bread cubes
1 can French's French fried onions, optional

Heat oven to 350°. Mix all ingredients except cheese and 1 cup bread cubes. Pile lightly into ungreased 1½-quart baking dish. Sprinkle with cheese and remaining cup of bread cubes. Bake 20-30 minutes at 350° or microwave for 6 minutes. Serves 6.

LINGUINE SALAD
Sonia Hoffman

½ cup cucumber
½ cup celery
½ cup carrot
½ cup radish
½ cup broccoli
½ cup cauliflower
½ cup tomato

½ cup black olive
½ cup green pepper
1 (12 ounce) bottle Italian dressing
¼ cup Salad Supreme (spice section)
1 (1 pound) box linguine

Dice, slice, and chop vegetables. Cook about ½ of the box of linguine, breaking noodles into thirds. Drain. Add vegetables, Salad Supreme, and Italian dressing. Cover and refrigerate overnight or at least 6 hours.

LAYER SALAD

Roxanna Linnebar

1 head lettuce, chopped
1¼ cups diced onion
1 cup diced celery

½ cup diced green pepper
½ cup grated carrots
1 (20 ounce) bag frozen peas

DRESSING:
1 package Hidden Valley Ranch
  dressing mix

Buttermilk

TOPPING:
8 ounces sharp Cheddar cheese,
  grated

1 package fried bacon, crumbled

Put lettuce in bottom of cake oblong or large Tupperware bowl. Prepare all other ingredients in separate bowls or put in Ziplock bags. Mix Hidden Valley Ranch dressing with buttermilk. Refrigerate all ingredients overnight. Next day, layer ingredients over lettuce. Pour dressing over it. Crumble bacon over top. Sprinkle over all with grated cheese.

7 LAYER SALAD

Ruth Yoder

1 head lettuce, chopped
1 cup finely diced celery
4 cooked eggs, shredded
1 cup frozen peas

½ cup green pepper, chopped
½ cup sweet onion, chopped
1 package bacon, fried and
  crumbled

DRESSING:
2 cups mayonnaise

2 tablespoons sugar

TOPPING:
Hickory smoke salt

6 ounces shredded Cheddar cheese

Place ingredients in Pyrex dish in order given. Mix mayonnaise and sugar (for good taste add a little pickle juice!). Spread over salad. Sprinkle generously with hickory smoke salt then top with Cheddar cheese.

Note: This can be prepared the night before, covered securely with plastic wrap and refrigerated.

Nothing is all wrong.
Even a clock that has stopped running is right twice a day!

MACARONI SALAD

Mrs. Shirley Yoder

1 pound elbow macaroni
4 hard-boiled eggs
1 pound bacon, fried and crumbled

½-¾ cup shredded Cheddar cheese
4 tablespoons cucumber relish
Tomato wedges for garnish

DRESSING:
2½ cups mayonnaise
1 cup sugar
¼ cup mustard

2 teaspoons vinegar
¾ cup milk

Cook macaroni as directed on package; drain. Add rest of ingredients. Blend dressing well and mix into salad. Add tomato wedges on top for garnish. Makes 10-12 servings.

MACARONI SALAD

Alta Kauffman

1 pound macaroni shells
1 onion, diced
1 green pepper, diced
2 grated carrots
6 hard-boiled eggs, diced

2 cup mayonnaise
¼ cup vinegar
2 tablespoons mustard
1 can sweetened condensed milk
3 whole pickles, chopped

Cook macaroni in water until tender. Rinse in cold water; drain well. Mix with all other ingredients. Better if made in advance.

MACARONI SALAD

Roxanna Linneber

1 (4 ounce) can sliced mushrooms
1 (10 ounce) package frozen peas
2 (8 ounce) packages Oscar Meyer
  smoked ham lunch meat

1 (12 ounce) bag garden spiral
  noodles, cooked
4 tomatoes, chopped
1 green pepper, diced

DRESSING:
1 package Hidden Valley Ranch
  salad dressing

Buttermilk

Bring mushrooms and juice to a boil in saucepan. Add peas. Cover and simmer 3 minutes. Uncover and add ham. Cook until dry. Mix with cooked noodles, tomatoes, and green pepper.

Make Hidden Valley Ranch buttermilk dressing as directed on package. Stir into salad.

ORANGE-ALMOND SALAD

Barbara Kauffman

DRESSING:
1/4 cup vegetable oil
2 tablespoons sugar
2 tablespoons vinegar

1/2 teaspoon salt (optional)
A few drops hot sauce

SALAD:
6 cups romaine lettuce
5 cups iceberg lettuce
1 1/2 cups fresh orange sections, or
  mandarin oranges, drained

1/4 cup slivered almonds, toasted
2 green onions, sliced
1/4 cup cooked, crumbled bacon

Mix dressing and refrigerate unless ready to serve salad immediately.

Mix salad. Just before you are ready to serve it, pour dressing over it and mix well. Makes 4-6 servings.

ORIENTAL CABBAGE SALAD

Irene Yoder

DRESSING:
1/2 cup oil
2 tablespoons vinegar
1 teaspoon Accent
1/2 teaspoon pepper

1 or 2 seasoning packets
2 tablespoons sugar
1 teaspoon salt

SALAD:
1/2 head cabbage
2 tablespoons chopped green
  onions
1 chopped green pepper
2 packages Ramen noodles (beef
  or chicken)

1/2 cup sunflower seeds
1 (2 1/2-ounce) package slivered
  almonds
Red pepper for garnish

Mix dressing. Add cabbage, onions, and peppers. Let set several hours. Before serving, add noodles (uncooked), sunflower seeds, and almonds. Garnish with red pepper.

PEA SALAD

Ann Mast

1 can peas
2 hard-boiled eggs
1/2 cup salad dressing

1/2 teaspoon mustard
Salt to taste
Sugar to taste

Mix and serve.

ORIENTAL COLE SLAW

Donna Stephens

SLAW:

2 pounds cole slaw mix
1 bunch green onions, cut up
1 cup toasted, sliced almonds

1 cup sunflower seeds
2 packages Ramen noodles,
crushed (any flavor)

DRESSING:

½ cup oil
¼ cup sugar

¼ cup vinegar
Ramen seasoning packet

Mix first 4 ingredients together. At serving time, crush Ramen noodles over salad and toss with dressing. (This slaw is not good left over.)

POTATO SALAD

Betty Yoder, Mrs. Roger Helmuth, Sr.,
Mrs. David Wengerd, Barbara Kanagy, Rhoda Hilty

12 cups cooked, shredded
potatoes
1½ cups celery, diced

½ of a medium onion, chopped
finely
1 dozen eggs, boiled and chopped

SAUCE:

3 cups Miracle Whip salad
dressing (or Kroger brand)
4 teaspoons salt

6 tablespoons mustard
2 cups sugar
½ cup milk

Combine potatoes, eggs, celery, and onion. Mix together dressing ingredients and pour over potato mixture. If you make this exactly like the recipe, you'll get compliments every time. Makes 18-20 servings.

Barbara puts 1 tablespoon mustard and ¼ cup vinegar in her potato salad.

24 HOUR POTATO SALAD

Melody Helmuth

6 cups cooked, shredded potatoes
6 hard-boiled eggs, diced
¾ cup diced celery

1-2 tablespoons finely chopped
onions

DRESSING:

1½ cups Miracle Whip salad
dressing
¼ cup mustard
1¼ teaspoons salt

1 teaspoon celery salt
¼ cup milk
2 tablespoons vinegar
1 cup sugar

Combine potatoes, eggs, celery, and onions. Mix together dressing ingredients and pour over potato mixture. Mix lightly. Can be made up to 24 hours ahead of time. Makes 12 servings.

TACO SALAD

Heidi Kauffman

1 (8 ounce) container sour cream
1 package taco seasoning
1 (8 ounce) package cream cheese
1 small onion, chopped

½ head lettuce, shredded
1 (8 ounce) package shredded
  cheese
1 tomato, diced

Combine sour cream, taco seasoning, and cream cheese and spread on bottom of 9x13-inch pan. Chop onion and sprinkle over mixture. Put lettuce, cheese, and diced tomato on top.

TACO SALAD

Martha Kauffman

1 large can crescent rolls
1 pound ground beef
1 package taco seasoning
1 (8 or 12 ounce) can refried beans
1 (8 or 12 ounce) can salsa

1 (8 or 12 ounce) container sour
  cream
1 (8 or 12 ounce) package
  Monterey Jack cheese
Chips of choice
Lettuce and tomatoes to taste

Roll out crescent rolls into a 9x12-inch pan and bake at 350° for 10 minutes. Brown beef and mix with taco seasoning. Follow taco directions. Layer all of the above ingredients and sprinkle with chips. Bake at 350° for about 20 minutes. Add lettuce and tomatoes after baking.

THREE BEAN SALAD

Deborah Kauffman

DRESSING:
1 cup sugar
½ cup salad oil

¾ cup vinegar
Salt, to taste

BEAN SALAD:
1 can green beans
1 can yellow beans
1 can kidney beans

1 stalk celery, sliced thin
1 green pepper, chopped
1 medium onion, sliced thin

Combine sugar, oil, vinegar, and salt. Beat well or run in blender for a few seconds. Pour over salad ingredients and stir gently. Stir several times the first day. Make at least 24 hours before serving.

No life is hopeless unless Christ is ruled out.

MARINATED TOMATOES

Faith Miller

3 large fresh tomatoes, sliced
⅓ cup olive oil
¼ cup red wine vinegar
¼ teaspoon pepper, optional
½ teaspoon salt
½ garlic clove, minced

2 tablespoons chopped onion
1 tablespoon chopped fresh
   parsley or 1 teaspoon dried
   parsley
1 tablespoon chopped fresh basil
   or 1 teaspoon dried basil

Arrange tomatoes in a large shallow dish. Combine remaining ingredients in a jar; cover tightly and shake well. Pour over tomato slices. Cover and refrigerate for several hours. Serves 8.

VEGETABLE PIZZA

Viola Miller

2 packages crescent rolls
2 (8 ounce) packages cream
   cheese
¾ cup salad dressing

1 package Hidden Valley Ranch
   dressing mix
Cauliflower, broccoli, green pepper
   (optional), and carrots
Grated cheese

Bake the crescent rolls 10-12 minutes at 325°. Combine the next 3 ingredients and spread over rolls. Arrange vegetables over dressing mix and top with shredded cheese. Serves 12.

VEGETABLE PIZZA

Dorothy Schlabach, Melody Kauffman

¼ cup margarine
2 tablespoons sugar
¼ cup boiling water
1 package yeast
¼ cup very warm water
1 small egg, beaten
1½ cups flour
1 teaspoon salt

1 pint sour cream, or 2 (8 ounce)
   packages cream cheese
1 cup salad dressing
1 package ranch dressing mix
Raw vegetables (broccoli,
   cauliflower, onion, carrot, tomato,
   cucumber, sweet pepper, etc.)
Shredded cheese

Combine margarine, sugar, and boiling water; stir until dissolved. Cool to lukewarm. Dissolve yeast in very warm water; add egg, flour, and salt. Add to first mixture and mix with very greasy fingers. Spread in pizza pan. Bake at 325° until golden brown.

Combine sour cream or cream cheese, salad dressing, and ranch dressing mix; mix well. Spread over cool crust. Use your choice of finely chopped or sliced vegetables and arrange over dressing mix. Top with shredded cheese. Makes 6-8 servings.

Dorothy uses crescent rolls for crust.

YOGURT SALAD
Pat Parker

1 head lettuce
1 cup peanuts
2-3 navel oranges, cut up

2 bananas, cut up
1 (8 ounce) container fruit yogurt
   (raspberry works nicely)

Cut up lettuce. Add peanuts, oranges, bananas, and yogurt. Blend well. Serve immediately. Makes 6 servings.

ANGEL HASH SALAD
Martha Yoder

1 (No. 2) can crushed pineapple
1 (No. 2) can fruit cocktail
2 tablespoons cornstarch
¼ cup sugar

2 egg yolks, beaten
1 cup whipped topping
¼ cup chopped nuts
2 cups miniature marshmallows

Drain fruit and reserve juice. In a saucepan, combine cornstarch and sugar; mix well. Add 1 cup of reserved juice and egg yolks. Blend well and cook over medium heat until thickened, stirring constantly. Cool thoroughly. Fold in whipped topping, nuts, marshmallows, and drained pineapple and fruit cocktail. Cover and chill overnight. Serves 10.

CHERRY FLUFF SALAD
Ruth Yoder

1 can cherry pie filling
1 can Eagle brand milk
1 small can crushed pineapple,
  drained

⅓ cup lemon juice
1 cup chopped pecans
1 large container Cool Whip
  whipped topping

Mix together and refrigerate or freeze.

COTTAGE CHEESE SALAD
Betty Yoder

2 cups whipped topping
1 (3 ounce) box Jello, any flavor

1 cup cottage cheese
1 cup well-drained pineapple

Stir first 2 ingredients until well blended, then add cottage cheese and pineapple. Pears can be used instead of pineapple.

COTTAGE CHEESE SALAD

Rachel Swarey,
Mrs. Freeman Schlabach,
Mrs. Gerald Lambright

1 pound marshmallows
½ cup milk
1 (8 ounce) package cream cheese
1 pint cottage cheese

Pinch of salt
1 cup cream, whipped
1 can crushed pineapple
Nuts, optional

Melt marshmallows and milk in double boiler or saucepan. Stir in cream cheese, cottage cheese, and a pinch of salt. Chill. Beat the cream and add to mixture. Add the pineapple. Add nuts, if desired. This is delicious!

CRANBERRY SALAD

Celesta Miller

1 large box orange Jello
2 large boxes raspberry Jello
6 cups boiling water
6 cups cold water
2 cups apples

2 oranges
Orange peel from the 2 oranges
2 cups cranberries
Sugar to taste
3 cups crushed pineapple and juice

Add boiling water to Jello to dissolve. Add cold water and let cool until it congeals. Grind or put through blender the apples, oranges, cranberries, and orange peel. Add sugar to taste, and add to Jello with pineapple. Makes 1 gallon.

CRANBERRY SALAD

Barbara Hershberger

1 quart raw cranberries
1 quart white sugar
⅔ cup water

2 small boxes raspberry Jello
3-4 apples, diced

Cook cranberries and sugar in water in covered dish until cranberries pop open. Uncover and boil 8 more minutes. Add Jello and apples. Put into serving dish and chill until firm.

CRANBERRY SALAD

Mrs. Merle Overholt

3 packages strawberry Jello
3 cups boiling water
3 cups ice cubes
1 can crushed pineapple, drained

2 large apples, diced
1 can whole berry cranberry sauce
½ cup chopped nuts

Dissolve Jello in boiling water and add ice cubes. Stir until partially set and remove any ice. Add fruits and nuts. Refrigerate until firm.

CRANBERRY PINEAPPLE SALAD
Denise Smith

1 (6 ounce) package raspberry
  Jello
1¾ cups boiling water
1 can cranberry sauce
1 (8 ounce) can crushed
  pineapple, undrained

½ cup orange juice
1 tablespoon lemon juice
½ cup chopped walnuts
2 cups whipped cream

In a bowl, dissolve Jello in boiling water. Stir in cranberry sauce, pineapple, orange juice, and lemon juice. Chill until partially set. Stir in nuts and whipped cream. Pour into an 11x7x2-inch dish, chill until firm, and cut into squares. Serve each on a lettuce leaf and top with a dollop of mayonnaise. Serves 12.

FROZEN CRANBERRY SALAD
Alta Kauffman

1 (12-15 ounce) package
  cranberries
2 cups sugar
1 large can crushed pineapple,
  well drained

1 pint whipping cream, whipped
10 large marshmallows, cut up, or
  equivalent in small
  marshmallows

Put cranberries in blender; add sugar and blend until fine. Let stand for 2 hours. Mix all ingredients and put into pan and freeze. Remove from freezer 30 minutes before serving to soften a little. Delicious! Try it even if you don't like cranberries!

GRANDMA'S CRANBERRY SALAD
Faith Miller

3 apples, cored
1 orange, peeled (save ½ of the
  orange's peeling)
2 cups cranberries

1 cup sugar
1 box red Jello, made according to
  package directions

Grind or chop apples, orange, and cranberries, and also the half of the orange's peeling. Mix together with sugar and Jello (already made with 1 cup boiling water and 1 cup cold water). Let set and jell. This has been passed on from my mom and grandmother. A favorite!

Great works are performed not by strength but by perseverance!

CREAM CHEESE JELLO
Barbara Hershberger

2 large packages lime, raspberry, or orange Jello
4½ cups boiling water

1 (8 ounce) package cream cheese
1 cup Sprite
2 cups whipped cream

Dissolve Jello in water and blend in cream cheese. Let cool. Add Sprite and whipped cream and mix thoroughly. Let jell.

When God sends man to a lion's den, He goes there with him.

CREAM CHEESE SALAD
Miriam Yoder

1 (6 ounce) package lemon Jello
3 cups boiling water
1 (8 ounce) package cream cheese
1 cup marshmallows

1 cup crushed pineapple
2 tablespoons mayonnaise
½ cup grated cheese
3 cups Cool Whip whipped topping

Mix Jello with water. Add cream cheese and marshmallows. Let cool until slightly jelled. Then add remaining ingredients and chill until ready to serve. Makes 10-12 servings.

FINGER JELLO
Judith Yoder

5 tablespoons gelatin
2 cups cold water
1½ cups water

12 ounces Jello
½ cup sugar

Soak gelatin in 2 cups cold water. Heat 1½ cups water, Jello, and sugar until boiling. Remove from heat and add the gelatin/water mixture. Pour into cake pans and chill until firm. Cut into squares and serve.

FESTIVE FRUIT SALAD
Ruth Yoder

1 (20 ounce) can pineapple chunks
½ cup sugar
3 tablespoons all-purpose flour
1 egg, lightly beaten
2 (11 ounce) cans mandarin oranges, drained

1 (20 ounce) can pears, drained and chopped
3 kiwi fruit, peeled and sliced
2 large unpeeled apples, chopped
1 cup pecan halves

Drain pineapple, reserving juice. Set pineapple aside. Pour juice into a small saucepan and add sugar and flour. Bring to a boil quickly. Stir in egg and cook until thickened. Remove from heat. Cool. Refrigerate. In a large bowl, combine fruits and pecans. Pour dressing over and blend well. Cover and chill for an hour. Makes 12-16 servings.

GELATIN FRUIT SALAD

Ellen D. Miller

2 cups boiling water, divided
1 (3 ounce) package lemon Jello
2 cups ice cubes, divided
1 (3 ounce) package orange Jello

1 (20 ounce) can crushed
  pineapple, liquid drained and
  reserved
2 cups miniature marshmallows
3 large bananas, sliced

COOKED DRESSING:
1 cup reserved pineapple juice
⅓ cup sugar
1 egg, beaten
2 tablespoons cornstarch

1 teaspoon vanilla
1 cup whipped topping
½ cup finely shredded Cheddar
  cheese for sprinkling on top

In mixing bowl, combine 1 cup water and lemon Jello. Add 1 cup ice cubes, stirring until melted. Add pineapple. Pour in 13x9x2-inch pan. Refrigerate until set. Repeat with orange gelatin, remaining water, and ice. Stir in marshmallows. Pour over lemon layer. Combine all dressing ingredients except whipped topping and cook until thickened. Cool and refrigerate. When ready to serve, arrange bananas on top of Jello. Combine dressing with whipped topping and spread over bananas. Sprinkle with cheese. Makes 12-16 servings.

JELLO SALAD

Martha Kauffman

3 regular size boxes Jello
3 cups hot water
1 cup cold water

4 or 5 bananas
1 can pineapple tidbits or chunks

TOPPING:
½ cup pineapple juice
1 cup sugar
2 tablespoons flour

1 (8 ounce) package Philadelphia
  cream cheese
2 packages of Dream Whip mix

Combine the Jello with the hot and cold water. Save ½ cup pineapple juice for topping. Add all the pineapple, the rest of the juice, and the bananas. Let this chill and set.

Topping: Combine reserved pineapple juice, sugar, and flour and bring them to a boil. Add cream cheese to the mixture and turn the heat on low and melt the cream cheese in the mixture. Let this cool. After it cools, add Dream Whip mix packets to the mixture and spread on top of Jello.

HOLIDAY MOLD

Viola Miller, Ruth Yoder

2 cups ginger ale, divided
1 small package orange Jello
½ teaspoon vanilla
Pinch of salt
1 teaspoon lemon juice

1 can mandarin oranges
2 bananas, sliced
½ cup cream, whipped
Coconut and orange slices to
    garnish

Heat 1 cup ginger ale to dissolve Jello. Add vanilla, salt, lemon juice, and remaining ginger ale. Let thicken. Add orange slices, bananas, and whipped cream. Pour into mold. Decorate with coconut and orange slices. Makes 10 servings.

LIME FOAM SALAD

Judi Wagher

1 small package lime Jello
1½ cups boiling water
1 (8 ounce) package cream cheese,
    cut in pieces and softened

1 (8 ounce) container Cool Whip
    whipped topping

Combine Jello and water. Cool slightly. Add cream cheese and Cool Whip. Beat in blender or food processor at high speed until well blended. Pour into 4-cup mold and refrigerate until firm. Makes 6-8 servings.

LIME JELLO SALAD

Esther Mast

2 (6 ounce) packages lime Jello
3 cups boiling water
¾ cup sugar

5 cups cold water
1 cup shredded cabbage
1 cup chopped celery

Combine Jello and sugar in boiling water and stir until dissolved. Stir in cold water. Let cool off until it starts to set, then add cabbage and celery. Pour into a mold and refrigerate until firm.

PEACH BAVARIAN

Deborah Kauffman

1 (16 ounce) can sliced peaches
2 (3 ounce) packages peach or
    apricot flavored gelatin
½ cup sugar

2 cups boiling water
1 teaspoon almond extract
1 (8 ounce) container frozen
    whipped topping, thawed

Drain peaches, reserving ⅔ cup juice. Chop peaches into small pieces; set aside. In a bowl, dissolve gelatin and sugar in boiling water. Stir in reserved syrup. Chill until slightly thickened. Stir extract into whipped topping; gently fold into gelatin mixture. Fold in peaches. Pour into an oiled 6-cup mold. Chill overnight. Unmold. Makes 8-10 servings.

LITE JELLO SALAD

Verda Overholt, Barbara Kauffman, Ruth Yoder

2 small boxes sugar free cherry Jello
2 cups boiling water
1 can lite cherry pie filling

1 (20 ounce) can crushed pineapple in natural juice
1 cup chopped nuts

Mix and dissolve Jello in boiling water. Cool, and when Jello is syrupy, add pie filling, pineapple, and nuts. Spray Jello mold with Pam, and pour Jello into mold. Makes 10-12 servings.

Serve with cottage cheese. This is pretty in the round Tupperware mold, serving the cottage cheese in the center. Also good to use grape Jello and blueberry pie filling.

PEACH PARTY SALAD

Sharon Miller

2 small packages orange Jello
2 cups boiling water

2 cups fresh or frozen peaches

SAUCE:
½ cup white sugar
3 tablespoons flour
1 egg
1 tablespoon butter

1 (20 ounce) can crushed pineapple
1 cup miniature marshmallows
1 cup shredded Cheddar cheese
1 cup whipped cream

Dissolve Jello in boiling water. Drain pineapple; add enough water to peach juice to make 1½ cups liquid. Add ¾ cup juice to Jello. Chill until syrupy. Spread peaches over bottom of pan. Add Jello and chill until firm.

Combine sugar, flour, egg, and remaining juice. Cook over low heat, stirring until thick and smooth. Stir in butter. Let mixture cool, then chill. Fold pineapple, marshmallows, shredded cheese and whipped cream into sauce mixture. Spread over Jello. Chill several hours or overnight. Makes 12 servings.

RED-HOT APPLESAUCE JELLO

Tina Nussbaum

2 cups hot water
½ cup red hots candies

1 (3 ounce) box lemon Jello
1 cup applesauce

Put water and red hots in a saucepan and bring to a boil. Stir until red hots are dissolved. Add Jello and stir. Pour into serving dish. Let cool and then stir in applesauce. Place in refrigerator until Jello is firm. Makes 4 servings.

The Lord gets His best soldiers out of the highlands of affliction.

STRAWBERRY PRETZEL SALAD

Martha Kauffman,
Rose Yoder, Candy (Miller) Knepp

1ST LAYER:
1½ sticks butter

2 cups crushed pretzels

2ND LAYER:
1 (8 ounce) package cream cheese
1 cup sugar

1 (8 ounce) container Cool Whip
whipped topping

3RD LAYER:
2 cups boiling water
1 (6 ounce) package strawberry
Jello

2 (10 ounce) packages frozen or
fresh sliced strawberries (fresh is
much better)

First Layer: Mix butter and pretzels and bake in a 9x13-inch pan for 10 minutes at 375°-400°.

Second Layer: Mix together the cream cheese, sugar, and Cool Whip whipped topping. Spread over cooled crust and refrigerate for 30 minutes.

Third Layer: Dissolve Jello in boiling water and add sliced strawberries. Pour over cream cheese layer and refrigerate.

Candy says it doesn't sound good together but is delicious.

COLONIAL HOUSE ITALIAN DRESSING

Elsie Yoder

1½ cups Puritan oil
¼ of a small onion
½ cup red wine vinegar
1 section of a clove of garlic
½ teaspoon salt
1 teaspoon oregano

¼ cup sugar
1 teaspoon pizza seasoning
½ teaspoon celery salt
1 teaspoon parsley flakes
1 teaspoon Parmesan cheese
Dash of pepper

Put in blender and mix together for a few minutes. Makes 1 pint.

FRENCH ISLAND DRESSING

Doris Eash

3 cups mayonnaise
1 cup sugar
¼ cup vinegar
½ cup ketchup
½ cup oil
2 teaspoons mustard

1 teaspoon paprika, optional
1 teaspoon Worcestershire sauce
½ teaspoon salt
1 tablespoon chili powder
1 slice (½-inch thick) onion

Put all ingredients in blender and blend.

293

FRENCH DRESSING

Drusilla Beiler, Ruth Yoder

2 cups mayonnaise
1½ cups sugar
¼ cup vinegar
½ cup ketchup
2 teaspoons mustard

2 teaspoons paprika
½ teaspoon salt
4 teaspoons water
½ cup cooking oil

Put all ingredients in mixer and blend.

Drusilla Beiler adds ½ teaspoon Worcestershire sauce and ½ teaspoon garlic salt.

ITALIAN DRESSING

Esther L. Miller

1 cup mayonnaise
½ small onion
2 tablespoons vinegar
1 tablespoon sugar

¾ teaspoon Italian seasoning
¼ teaspoon salt
¼ teaspoon garlic salt
⅛ teaspoon pepper

Blend ingredients together and let stand a few hours before serving. Yield: 1½ cups.

MEXICAN SALAD DRESSING

Mrs. Gerald Lambright,
Barbara Kauffman

1 medium onion
⅓ cup vinegar
⅔ cup salad oil
2 tablespoons mustard
3 tablespoons mayonnaise or
  salad dressing

¾ cup sugar
1 teaspoon celery seed
1 teaspoon salt
½ teaspoon black pepper

Put in blender or food processor and liquefy. Delicious on tossed salad or taco salad.

My family eats more salad if I serve it with this dressing. Makes about 1½-2 cups.

If God numbers our hairs, will He not also number our tears?

Soups
&
Sandwiches

ASPARAGUS SOUP
Sonia Hoffman

¼ cup unsalted butter
1 onion, finely chopped
1 celery stalk, finely chopped
4 cups chicken stock
3 pounds asparagus, trimmed and
  cut into 1-inch pieces

2 baking potatoes, peeled and cut
  into 1-inch cubes
2 tablespoons fresh basil, chopped
2 cups heavy cream
Salt and white pepper

In a large saucepan, melt the butter over medium heat. Add onion and celery and sauté until translucent, 2-3 minutes. Add the stock, asparagus stalks and about ⅔ of the tips, potatoes, and basil. Bring to a boil, reduce heat, and cover and gently simmer until vegetables are tender (about 20 minutes). In small batches, puree the soup in a blender; strain and return to pan. Stir in cream; season with salt and white pepper. In small saucepan, cook reserved tips 3-4 minutes. Drain. Serve soup and garnish with cooked tips. Serves 6-8.

BROCCOLI CHEESE SOUP
Linda Zook

3 tablespoons margarine
6 cups water
6 chicken bouillon cubes
8 ounces thin noodles
1 teaspoon salt

2 (10 ounce) packages frozen
  chopped broccoli, or 1 medium
  bunch fresh broccoli
6 cups milk
1 pound Velveeta cheese
Pepper to taste

Melt margarine in saucepan; add water and bouillon cubes. Heat to boiling and stir until cubes are dissolved. Add noodles and salt; cook 3 minutes. Stir in broccoli (which has been cooked). Cook 4 minutes. Reduce heat; add milk and cheese. Add pepper to taste. Makes 4 quarts.

CANADIAN CHEESE SOUP
Jill Nussbaum

2 medium carrots, cut in 1-inch
  pieces
2 stalks celery, cut in 1-inch pieces
1 small-medium onion, quartered
2 cups water

2 bouillon cubes (chicken or beef,
  or 1 each)
2 cups milk
¼ cup flour
2½ cups shredded Cheddar cheese

Put carrots, celery, onions, bouillon cubes, and water in blender. Process until vegetables are finely chopped. Pour into saucepan; cover and cook until vegetables are tender. Put milk and flour in blender. Process until smooth. Stir in vegetable mixture. Stir in cheese.

For variety, add broccoli, basil, and a few slices of Velveeta. Be creative. Delicious.

CHEESE CHOWDER SOUP

Ruth Yoder

1 cup celery
1 small onion
1 stick butter
4 cups chicken broth
2 cups diced potatoes
1 cup sliced carrots

2 cups milk
2 teaspoons salt
2-3 cups deboned chicken
1 cup Velveeta cheese
1 cup Cheddar cheese

THICKENING:
1 cup milk

5 tablespoons flour

Cook celery and onions in butter. Add chicken broth and rest of vegetables. Cook until tender. Add milk and salt.

Mix flour and milk together and add to soup to thicken.

Stir in chicken and cheese; cook just until heated through. Do not boil.

MISSOURI CHEDDAR CHOWDER SOUP

Mrs. Jonathan Yoder

2 cups chopped potatoes
1 cup each of carrots and celery
  (celery is optional)
1/4 cup chopped onion
1/4 cup flour
1 1/2 teaspoons salt

1/4 teaspoon pepper (or more)
1/4 cup butter
2 cups milk
2 cups shredded sharp Cheddar
  cheese
1 cup chopped cooked ham

Combine vegetables with water to cover in saucepan; simmer for 10 minutes. Blend flour, salt, pepper, and butter in saucepan and cook until bubbly, stirring constantly. Stir in milk and cook until thick. Cook 1 minute and remove from heat. Stir in cheese until melted. Add to undrained vegetables with ham. Cook just until heated through. Do not boil. Makes 4 servings.

A really happy man is the one
who can enjoy the scenery when he has to take a detour.

QUICK GOLDEN STEW

Marialice Yoder

4 carrots, cut into 1-inch pieces
1 1/2 cups peeled and diced potatoes
2 medium onions, cut into chunks
Water to cover

1 (10 ounce) package frozen peas
2 cups cubed ham
1 can cream of celery soup
1 (8 ounce) jar cheese spread

In a large saucepan, combine carrots, potatoes, onions, and just enough water to cover. Cook, covered, until vegetables are tender, about 10 minutes. Add peas and ham; continue to cook 5 more minutes. Drain water. Stir in soup and cheese. Heat through. Makes 4-6 servings.

HAM CHEDDAR CHOWDER SOUP   Carolyn Eash, Drusilla Beiler

2 cups water
2 cups diced potatoes
½ cup diced celery
½ cup diced carrots

¼ cup minced onions
1 teaspoon salt
¼ teaspoon pepper

SAUCE FOR CHEDDAR CHOWDER:
¼ cup butter, melted
¼ cup all-purpose flour
2 cups milk

2 cups Cheddar cheese, grated
1 cup finely cut ham

Bring all chowder ingredients to boil, then reduce heat to simmer until vegetables are tender. Add Cheddar Chowder Sauce.

Sauce: Blend together ingredients and cook over medium heat, stirring often until smooth textured. (Do not bring to boil.) Makes 8-10 servings.

CHICKEN RICE SOUP   Mrs. Noah Yoder

1 chicken (less can be used)
2 quarts water
½ cup chopped celery
1 onion, chopped

Parsley (optional)
1 cup rice
Salt and pepper to taste

Cut up chicken into pieces. Place in cooking pan to cook; add water, celery, onion, and parsley. Cook slowly until chicken is tender. (I prefer to have chicken simmer awhile before adding vegetables.)

Rice can be cooked separately in salt water. Drain and add to chicken just before serving. Is also delicious omitting the rice and adding carrots and potatoes. Serves 6.

CHICKEN OR CLAM CHOWDER   Mrs. Freeman Schlabach

2 cups potatoes
1 cup carrots
1 cup celery
2 cups broth or water
2 cups chicken or clams
1 medium onion

1 cup milk
2 tablespoons flour
Salt and pepper to taste
4 tablespoons butter
½ pound Velveeta cheese

Cook potatoes, carrots, and celery in the broth or water until soft. Add chicken or clams and onion. Make a paste from the milk and flour, and add to soup while it is simmering. Add butter and cheese last. Makes 8 servings.

CHUNKY SOUP

Paul and Ruth Yoder

2½ gallons water
¾ cup beef base
2 large cans beef broth
1 stick butter
4 quarts tomato juice
1¾ cups sugar
¼ cup salt (or less)
4 quarts carrots

2 quarts beans
3 quarts peas
4 quarts potatoes
2 cups flour
8 pounds hamburger
2 large onions, chopped
Salt and pepper

Heat together until boiling 2½ gallons water, beef base, beef broth, butter, tomato juice, sugar, and ¼ cup salt. Cut vegetables into small cubes. Cook separately in salted water, then add to mixture. (Canned veggies may be used.) Add enough water to flour to make a smooth paste to thicken soup. Fry hamburger in some butter with chopped onions, salt, and pepper. Mix hamburger and drippings with soup. (6 quarts beef chunks may be used instead of hamburger.) Makes about 30 quarts. Pressure cook it for 30 minutes at 10 pounds pressure.

CLAM SPINACH BISQUE

Drusilla Beiler

1 stick of butter
1 onion, pureed
2 cloves garlic, minced
1 (10 ounce) can chopped clams
⅓ cup flour
2 cups half-and-half

2 cups heavy cream
1 tablespoon chicken base
Salt and pepper
1 can cream of chicken soup,
   diluted with milk
1 small box of frozen spinach

Melt half of butter in a large pot. Add onion and garlic. Then add clams and sauté. Make paste of ½ stick butter and flour, then add onion and clam mixture. Add rest of ingredients. Simmer until spinach is tender. Do not boil. Season to taste with salt and pepper. Delicious. Serves 8-10.

CHILI

Cissy Allen

⅓ cup chopped onion
⅓ cup chopped celery
¼ cup chopped green pepper
1 clove garlic
2 tablespoons butter
1 pound ground beef

2 cans spicy chili beans
1 can tomato sauce
1 teaspoon pepper
1 teaspoon salt
1 teaspoon chili powder

In large skillet, sauté vegetables in butter until tender. In separate pan, sauté meat until brown and crumbly. Drain well. Add to vegetables. Add remaining ingredients. Cover and simmer for 45 minutes to an hour.

CHILI

Jo Ann Inhulsen

1 pound hamburger
1 large onion, chopped
2 cloves garlic, crushed
1 can whole tomatoes
2 medium stalks celery, sliced
2-3 tablespoons chili powder
2 teaspoons salt

1 teaspoon sugar
1 teaspoon Worcestershire sauce
½ teaspoon red pepper sauce,
   optional
1 (15 ounce) can kidney beans
Corn chips
Sour cream

Cook and stir hamburger, onion, and garlic. Add rest of ingredients except beans. Bring to boil and simmer 1 hour. Add beans and continue simmering 15 minutes. Serve with corn chips and sour cream.

CHILI SOUP

Marialice Yoder

1 pound beef
1 medium onion
1 (1 quart) jar tomatoes, chunked
1 (1 quart) jar thick tomato juice
2 teaspoons chili powder
   (or 1 package)

1 teaspoon salt
½ teaspoon cumin, optional
¼ teaspoon black pepper
2 tablespoons brown sugar
1 (16 ounce) can kidney beans
Shredded sharp Cheddar cheese

In saucepan, brown beef and onion. Drain fat. Stir in all remaining ingredients except cheese. Cover and simmer 20 minutes. Top each serving with cheese. Makes 6 servings.

DADDY'S FAVORITE CHILI

Ellen Schlabach

1½ pounds hamburger
2 (15½ ounce) cans kidney beans
2 (6 ounce) cans tomato paste
1 quart whole tomatoes

2 cups water
2 packages mild chili seasoning,
   or to taste
½ scant cup onions

While hamburger is browning, chop beans coarsely and add to browned hamburger. Put hamburger/bean mixture in a large soup pot. Next add tomato paste and stir until smooth. Add rest of ingredients and stir well. Simmer for 20 minutes.

Put leftover chili in tortillas and serve with sour cream and/or cheese and chips. Serves 8.

WHITE CHILI

Jo Ann Inhulsen

3 cans white great Northern beans
3 cans cream of mushroom soup
3-4 cups cooked chicken
1 can green chilies, chopped
1 small onion, chopped and sautéed

2 cups milk
1 (8 ounce) package Monterey
 Jack cheese, shredded
Sour cream and picante sauce for
 garnish

Puree one can beans in blender. Add all ingredients except cheese, and heat thoroughly. Stir constantly. When hot, add cheese and stir until melted. Garnish with sour cream and picante sauce. Serve with chips.

CREAMY ONION SOUP

Ruth Yoder

½ cup celery, finely diced
⅔ cup green onion, including some
 of the tops, sliced thin
¼ cup butter
¼ cup flour
4 cups milk

1 cup chicken broth
½ cup sharp cheese, shredded
1½ teaspoons salt
⅛ teaspoon pepper
¼ teaspoon MSG

Sauté onion and celery in butter until tender. Blend in flour. Gradually stir in milk and broth. Stir in rest of ingredients until well blended.

FRENCH ONION SOUP

Cissy Allen

3 onions, sliced in rings
3 tablespoons butter
Salt and pepper to taste
1 tablespoon flour
5 cups beef bouillon

Pepperidge Farm seasoned
 croutons
Parmesan cheese
Swiss cheese (about 6 ounces)

Sauté onions in butter until golden. Add salt, pepper, and flour. Cook 5 minutes. Add bouillon and simmer 30 minutes. Place soup in 4 bowls. Sprinkle croutons on top, then sprinkle Parmesan cheese on top, and then a slice of Swiss cheese on top of that. Pour in broiler until cheese melts.

Prayer contains the soul's needed nutrition:
Do you have a balanced diet?

POTATO SOUP

Martha Yoder

¼ cup butter
2 cups onion, finely chopped
4 medium potatoes, peeled and
  cubed

½ cup celery, chopped
4 cups chicken stock
Salt and pepper to taste
1½ cups whole milk

Melt butter in saucepan and add onions. Cook until tender and transparent. Add potatoes, celery, broth, and seasoning. Simmer until vegetables are tender. Add milk just before serving and heat through well. Do not boil. Serves 6.

ROMANIAN SOUP*

Mary Zook

4 cups potatoes, diced
1 cup carrots, diced
2 tablespoons chopped onion
Water to cover
1-2 chicken bouillon cubes
1 quart milk

1 cup corn
2 cans cream of chicken soup
Velveeta to taste
1 cup frozen peas, thawed
Salt and pepper

Cover potatoes, carrots, and onion with water. Add bouillon cubes. Cook until vegetables are soft. Add milk, corn, and soup and heat slowly, stirring often. After soup is heated, add several slices Velveeta, or to taste. Just before serving, add peas. Season with salt and pepper. Makes 4-6 servings.

*Christian Aid Ministries served this soup when we packaged Christmas bundles for the poor people in Romania. Thus it was given the name "Romanian Soup". It's one of our favorites.

SPICY POTATO SOUP

Rachel Swarey

1 pound hamburger
1 onion
4 cups cubed potatoes
24 ounces tomato juice
4 cups water

2 tablespoons salt
1½ tablespoons pepper
1 or 2 big carrots
Celery, if desired

Fry hamburger and add onion. When onions are tender, add rest of ingredients. Simmer for 1 hour or until vegetables are soft. Makes 16 servings.

TACO SOUP

Ann Mast

3 pounds hamburger
Salt
Pepper
1 medium onion, chopped
6 tablespoons flour
2 packages taco seasoning

2 cans refried beans
3 quarts tomato juice
¾ cup brown sugar
Taco chips
Shredded cheese
Sour cream

Brown hamburger and season with salt, pepper, and onion. Add flour, taco seasoning, beans, tomato juice, and brown sugar. Simmer ½ hour over low heat. Serve with taco chips, shredded cheese, and sour cream.

HEARTY TOMATO SOUP

Ruth Yoder

1 medium onion, finely chopped
2 tablespoons butter
1 (3 ounce) package cream cheese
2 cans condensed tomato soup
1 soup can milk

½ teaspoon paprika
½ teaspoon sweet basil leaves
⅛ teaspoon garlic powder
Sieved egg yolk for garnish,
 if desired

In medium saucepan, cook and stir onion in butter until onion is tender. Stir in cream cheese. Gradually stir in soup and milk; beat with rotary beater until smooth. Add seasonings. Heat, stirring frequently, but do not boil. If desired, garnish each serving with sieved egg yolk. Makes 4 servings.

TURKEY CHOWDER

Barbara Kanagy

1 cup finely chopped green onion
1 cup finely chopped carrots
1 cup finely chopped celery
¼ cup butter
¼ cup flour
2 cups turkey broth or bouillon
2 cups half-and-half

¼ teaspoon salt
⅛ teaspoon white pepper
Dash red pepper
2 cups cooked and diced turkey
1½ cups shredded sharp Cheddar
 cheese

Sauté onions, carrots, and celery in butter until soft but not brown. Blend in flour. Stir in gradually the broth, then the half-and-half, salt, white and red pepper, and turkey. Add cheese last. Serve as soon as cheese melts. Serves 6.

CAMP STEW

Mrs. Henry Overholt, Sr., Ruth Yoder, Mrs. Robert Paul Yoder (Amanda)

3 pounds hamburger
2 pounds sausage
2 fryers or 1 large hen
3 pounds onions
5 pounds potatoes

1 cup regular and 1 cup hot
  barbecue sauce
2 cups ketchup
8 cups corn
Salt and pepper to taste

Fry hamburger and sausage. Cook chicken meat and debone. Peel and dice potatoes and onions; cook in a 12- to 16-quart kettle with 1 quart broth until tender. Add meat, barbecue sauce, and ketchup. Bring to a good boil, add corn, and serve. Makes approximately 10 quarts.

You may can or freeze. Delicious. Tastes a lot like "Brunswick Stew".

VEGETABLE SOUP

Sara Jean Yoder

2 quarts (about 12 large) peeled
  and chopped potatoes
1½ quarts (about 6 medium)
  peeled and cubed tomatoes
1 quart shelled lima beans
1 quart corn

1 quart sliced carrots (more or less)
2 cups sliced celery
2 cups chopped onion
1½ quarts water
1½ teaspoons salt, or according to
  taste

Combine vegetables and water in a large kettle and cook until soft.

The soup can be varied by adding 1 quart beef broth and meat according to taste, plus ½ cup barley, 1 cup cabbage, and ¼ cup green pepper. Season accordingly.

BRUNSWICK STEW

Susan K. Yoder

2½-3 pounds chicken, cut up
6 cups water
1 teaspoon salt
2 pounds boneless pork shoulder
  roast
3½ pounds boneless chuck roast
4 pounds potatoes, peeled and cut
  into ¾-inch cubes
3 medium onions, chopped
2 (17 ounce) cans whole kernel corn

2 (14½ ounce) cans tomatoes,
  sliced
1 (14 ounce) bottle ketchup
1 can tomato soup
½ cup vinegar
¼ cup Worcestershire sauce
1 teaspoon hot pepper sauce
¾ teaspoon salt
¼ teaspoon pepper

Cook chicken in water. Remove chicken from bones, reserving broth. Remove fat from broth. Meanwhile, roast pork in a 325° oven for 2 hours, or

(Continued on next page)

until thermometer inserted in the thickest part registers 170°. Cool. Shred meat. Roast beef until tender. Cool and shred meat. (You should have 10-12 cups chicken, pork, and beef, total.) In a 10-quart kettle, combine broth, potatoes, and onions. Bring to a boil, reduce heat, and cook for 10 minutes. Stir in corn, undrained tomatoes, ketchup, soup, vinegar, Worcestershire sauce, hot pepper sauce, salt, and pepper. Return to boiling. Reduce heat; simmer uncovered for about 30 minutes. Stir in meat and cook until heated through. Makes 16-18 servings.

BEEFY BUNWICHES   Irene Yoder

3 pounds hamburger
1 cup chopped onion
Seasonings as desired (see
  directions for examples)
1 tablespoon salt

¾ teaspoon pepper
¾ cup oatmeal
3 pounds cabbage
3 cups shredded cheese

DOUGH:
4 cups milk
1 cup sugar
4 eggs
2 tablespoons salt
2 cups mashed potatoes

1 cup shortening
4 tablespoons yeast (dissolved in 1
  cup water)
16 cups flour (or more, as needed)

Fry hamburger and onion until brown. Season as desired. Chili powder, oregano, and sweet basil are good. Add salt and pepper. Drain. Mix in oatmeal, cabbage, and cheese.

Prepare dough (a regular bread recipe can be used). Roll and cut into 5x7-inch pieces. Place about ½ cup of hamburger mixture in center of dough. Pinch shut. Bake at 350° until golden brown. Makes 30 bunwiches.

ITALIAN SUB SANDWICH   Elsie Yoder

Sub rolls
Salad dressing
Salami, sliced
Sliced ham

Swiss cheese, sliced
Sliced tomatoes
Italian dressing
Lettuce

Cut each sub roll in half and cover each half with salad dressing. On one half layer salami and ham, about 1-2 slices each. Top with cheese and broil until cheese is melted. Top with tomato slices and dribble with Italian dressing. Add lettuce and top with other bun half.

CHEESY SALSA CHICKEN SANDWICHES
Ramona Overholt

½ cup salsa
4 boneless and skinless chicken
  breast halves
4 slices cheese (preferably
  Velveeta)

4 Kaiser rolls, split
Mayonnaise
Lettuce
Tomato slices

Pour salsa over chicken; cover. Refrigerate 1 hour or overnight to marinate. Drain.

Grill or broil chicken 5-7 minutes on each side or until cooked through. Top with slices of cheese. Grill or broil until cheese is melted. Spread rolls with mayonnaise and fill with lettuce, tomato, and chicken. Makes 4 sandwiches.

We are always in the wrong key when we sing our own praises.

HAM SPREAD FOR SANDWICHES
Elsie Yoder

½ pound margarine, softened
3 tablespoons prepared mustard
3 tablespoons poppy seed
1 teaspoon onion powder
1 tablespoon Worcestershire
  sauce

½ cup mayonnaise
1 pound ham, sliced thin
½ pound Swiss or American
  cheese
3 dozen Pepperidge Farm rolls
  or small homemade dinner rolls

Mix first 6 ingredients together and spread on each side of rolls. Fill with ham and cheese. Cover with foil and bake for 20 minutes. You can also use 30 hamburger buns and make them open face and put under broiler for a few minutes.

HOT HAM-N-CHEESE BUNS
Silla K. Yoder

½ pound ham
½ pound sharp cheese
⅓ cup sliced onions
2 hard-cooked eggs, sliced

½ cup sliced peppers
3 tablespoons salad dressing
½ cup chili sauce

Cut the ham and cheese into ¼-inch cubes. Combine them with the onions, eggs, peppers, and salad dressing blended with chili sauce. Mix it well and spread the mixture in 10 split wiener buns. Wrap each one in foil and twist the ends. Bake at 400° for 10 minutes or until the buns are hot.

JUICY HAMBURGERS

Silla Yoder

1½ pounds ground beef
¾ cup quick oatmeal
¼ cup chopped onion
1 teaspoon sugar
¼ teaspoon black pepper

1 teaspoon salt
½ teaspoon hickory smoke salt
½ cup tomato juice
Few drops liquid smoke

Mix all ingredients well and shape into patties. Fry on both sides until done. Great served with honey mustard and pepper relish. Makes 6-8 servings.

SLOPPY JOE PIZZA

Marialice Yoder

1 pound ground beef
¾ cup frozen corn, defrosted
¾ cup prepared barbecue sauce
½ cup sliced green onions
1 teaspoon salt

1 large (12-inch) Italian bread shell
  or prepared pizza crust
1½ cups shredded Colby/Jack
  cheese

Heat oven to 425°. In large nonstick skillet, brown ground beef over medium heat for 8-10 minutes or until no longer pink. Pour off fat. Stir corn, barbecue sauce, green onions, and salt into beef; heat through.

Place bread shell on baking sheet or pizza pan. Spoon beef mixture over top; sprinkle with cheese. Bake at 425° for 12-15 minutes until cheese melts. Cut into 8 wedges. Makes 4 servings.

Happy, quiet, well-behaved children in only 30 minutes.

PIMIENTO CHEESE SPREAD

Mrs. Freeman Schlabach

1 pound Velveeta cheese
1 stick butter
1 cup Miracle Whip salad dressing

1 (4 ounce) jar drained pimientos
2 tablespoons sugar
1 tablespoon vinegar

Combine all ingredients and let stand until room temperature. Blend well and refrigerate, covered.

PIZZABURGERS SANDWICHES

Ruth Yoder, Miriam Yoder

1 pound hamburger
1 can pizza sauce
1 can cream of mushroom soup

1 teaspoon oregano
1 teaspoon garlic salt
Mozzarella cheese

Brown and drain hamburger. Add pizza sauce, soup, oregano, and garlic salt. Heat until ingredients are heated through. Spoon onto hamburger buns and top with cheese. Broil just until cheese melts. Serve hot.

PITA BREAD OR POCKET BREAD   Ruth Yoder

1 tablespoon dry yeast
1½ cups warm water
1 teaspoon sugar
1 tablespoon vegetable oil
1 tablespoon sugar

1 teaspoon salt
1½ teaspoons ground cumin seeds
1½ cups whole wheat flour
2 cups flour

Stir together yeast, warm water, and 1 teaspoon sugar until dissolved. Add, beating thoroughly, the rest of ingredients in the order given.

Place in greased bowl and grease top. Cover and let rise until double, about 1 hour; punch down dough. Cut into 6 parts. Shape each into a ball; cover and let rise until double, about 30 minutes. Sprinkle 2 large baking sheets with cornmeal. Roll each ball into a 7-inch circle and place on baking sheet. Cover and let rise 30 minutes more. Bake at 450° for 12 minutes until lightly browned and puffed. Cut each in half and fill with a variety of fillings. (See following filling recipe). Makes 12 servings.

PITA BREAD FILLING   Ruth Yoder

1 pound hamburger
1 small onion, chopped
1 package taco seasoning
¾ cup Thousand Island or Italian
  salad dressing

7 cups shredded lettuce
2 tomatoes, chopped
1 cucumber, chopped
1 cup grated cheese

Sauté hamburger, onion, and taco seasoning in skillet and drain. Mix dressing over lettuce, tomatoes, cucumbers, and cheese. Fill pockets and enjoy.

Also good to have a cold filling. Add ham and omit hamburger mixture.

QUICK PIZZA   Melody Kauffman

Bread
Pizza sauce
Garlic salt

Pepperoni or bologna, optional
Cheese

Toast the bread, then spread 1-2 tablespoons pizza sauce on each slice. Sprinkle with garlic salt. Add several small slices of pepperoni or bologna, if desired, and top with a slice of American or Velveeta cheese. Place on broiling pan and broil until cheese is bubbly, 2-3 minutes.

SANDWICH FILLING

Lela Brenneman

1½ pounds ground ham
1 pound ground beef, browned
5 pieces toast, crumbled fine

1 can mushroom soup
1 pint milk
2 onions, finely chopped

Combine ingredients and place in a long baking dish. Bake in a 350° oven for 1 hour, stirring often. Serve on warm buns. Makes about 24-26 sandwiches.

SCRUMP-DELICIOUS BURGERS

Silla K. Yoder

1½ pounds ground beef
3 tablespoons finely chopped
  onion
½ teaspoon garlic salt
½ teaspoon pepper
1 cup (4 ounces) shredded
  Cheddar cheese

⅓ cup canned sliced mushrooms
6 bacon strips, cooked and
  crumbled
¼ cup mayonnaise
6 hamburger buns, split
Lettuce leaves and tomato slices,
  optional

In medium bowl, combine beef, onion, garlic salt, and pepper. Mix well. Shape into 6 patties ¾-inch thick.

In a small bowl, combine the cheese, mushrooms, bacon, and mayonnaise. Refrigerate.

Grill burgers over medium hot coals for 10-12 minutes, turning over once during the last 3 minutes. Spoon ¼ cup cheese mixture onto each burger. Serve on buns with tomatoes and lettuce, if desired. Makes 6.

SLOPPY JOSEPHINES

Silla Yoder

2 pounds hamburger
3 teaspoons minced onion
Dash hickory smoke salt
Dash pepper and salt
Dash of red pepper

½ teaspoon Louisiana hot sauce
½ cup sour cream
Pimiento cheese
Mayonnaise
Sesame seed hamburger buns

Fry hamburger with minced onion. Add seasonings and sour cream; simmer 5 minutes. Put meat mixture on bottom half of hamburger bun, then put a thin layer of pimiento cheese over that. Broil until cheese is oozy. Put mayonnaise-smeared top half of hamburger bun on top of hamburger mixture. Serve immediately.

SOUTH CAROLINA SANDWICHES

Mrs. Henry Overholt, Sr.

3 pounds hamburger
1 (8 ounce) package cream cheese

1 can cream of mushroom soup
1 cup cheese

Fry hamburger. Add rest of ingredients and heat well. Put on bread or hamburger buns.

People take our example far more seriously than they take our advice.

TOASTED CHEESE SANDWICHES

Silla Yoder

8 slices bread
Mayonnaise

16 small slices cheese
Butter

Smear bread in the inside with mayonnaise. Layer 2 slices cheese on a slice of bread. Cover with the other slice of bread. Smear outside of sandwich with butter and toast in skillet until dark brown or until cheese is completely melted.

For variation, add chopped ham, Spam, or any meat. *Delicious* served with soup.

TUNA BURGERS

Linda Kauffman, Jill Nussbaum

1 can cream of mushroom soup
1 (7 ounce) can tuna, drained
¼ cup chopped onion and/or
  ¼ cup green pepper, chopped

Hamburgers buns
Butter

Mix cream of mushroom soup, tuna, and onions and/or peppers. Spread evenly on hamburger buns. Brush top of buns with butter, and place on cookie sheet. Bake at 350° for 7-10 minutes. Makes 6-8 servings.

EGG SALAD SANDWICH

Mrs. Henry Overholt, Sr.

1 dozen hard-boiled eggs
1 small onion, chopped
1 teaspoon salt
Season-All or other spices
1 cup mayonnaise

1 tablespoon sugar
Dash of pepper
Chopped celery or celery seed
  (optional)

Mash hard-boiled eggs with potato masher and add other ingredients. It is delicious on buttered bread still warm. Makes 6 servings.

Vegetables

ASPARAGUS CASSEROLE

4 cups crushed saltine cracker
crumbs
1 or 2 cans asparagus
4-6 slices Velveeta cheese

½ cup butter
1½ cups milk or the amount to fill
casserole ⅔ full
Dash of salt and pepper

Alternate layers of crackers, asparagus, cheese, and butter, then add milk.
Season with salt and pepper. Bake in a 9x13-inch casserole dish for 35-40
minutes at 350°. Top with crumbs and cheese, if desired.

ASPARAGUS EGG MEDLEY   Alta Kauffman

2 (15 ounce) cans asparagus
spears, or 1½ pounds fresh
asparagus, cooked
¼ cup butter
¼ cup flour
½ teaspoon salt

2 cups liquid (asparagus liquid plus
milk)
1 cup cheese
6 hard-boiled eggs, sliced
½ cup corn flakes

Drain asparagus, reserving liquid; set aside. Melt butter; blend in flour and
salt. Cook, stirring until mixture is smooth and bubbly. Stir in liquid; heat to
boiling, stirring constantly, until thickened. Remove from heat and add
cheese, stirring until melted. In a 2-quart casserole dish, alternate layers of
asparagus, egg slices, and cheese sauce. Sprinkle corn flakes on top and
bake at 350° for 15-20 minutes or until hot and bubbly. Serves 6.

BLUSHING SNOWBALLS   Lena Schrock

6 medium apples
1½ cups hot water
1½ cups sugar
18 marshmallows

1 teaspoon lemon juice
1½ cups cinnamon candies
1 cup flaked coconut

Peel apples and core, being careful to leave them whole. Put the water,
sugar, marshmallows, lemon juice, and candies into a larger pan, and stir
over *low heat* until well blended. Cook apples in this syrup until tender, not
mushy. Drain and cool apples, then gently roll them in coconut. Real tasty
with chicken or turkey meals.

BAKED BEANS
Tina Nussbaum

1 (15 ounce) can pork and beans
⅓ cup ketchup

½ cup brown sugar
½ cup onion, diced

Spray small casserole pan with Pam. Mix ingredients and bake at 350° for 1 hour or 250° for 2 hours. *Easy and good.* Serves 4.

BARBECUED BEANS
Mrs. Freeman Schlabach

1 (40 ounce) can pork and beans
1 small onion, diced
¼ cup diced pepper, optional

1-1½ cups barbecue sauce
1-2 cups barbecued pork

Mix together all ingredients and bake slowly in a 4-quart pot at 275°-300° for several hours. Makes 8 servings.

BBQ GREEN BEANS
Ruth Yoder

10 slices bacon, diced
1 large onion, chopped
4 cups green beans, cooked
¾ teaspoon salt

½ cup brown sugar
¾ cup ketchup
3 teaspoons Worcestershire sauce

Fry bacon and onion together until onion is tender and bacon is fried. Combine all ingredients and bake or cook slowly for 1 hour.

Do good things everywhere you go.
After awhile, the good you do will return to help you.

BROCCOLI CASSEROLE
Linda Zook

2 small boxes frozen broccoli
4 strips bacon, fried
8 ounces Velveeta cheese

¼ cup milk
⅔ stack Ritz crackers, crushed
½ cup butter or margarine, melted

Cook broccoli until tender. Place in casserole. Crumble bacon over broccoli. Melt cheese with milk and pour over broccoli. Top with Ritz cracker crumbs. Pour melted butter or margarine over top. Bake at 350° for 30 minutes. Serves 4.

BROCCOLI CASSEROLE

Cissy Allen

1 can cream of mushroom soup
2 eggs
½ teaspoon salt
¼ cup mayonnaise
Onion juice

2 packages chopped frozen
broccoli
½ cup grated Cheddar cheese
Cracker crumbs

Mix mushroom soup, beaten eggs, salt, mayonnaise, and onion juice. Cook broccoli and stir into mixture. Put into greased casserole dish. Cover with cheese and cracker crumbs. Bake at 350° for 30 minutes.

BROCCOLI CASSEROLE

Ruth Yoder

2 (10 ounce) packages frozen
broccoli or fresh broccoli
2 eggs, beaten
1 onion, chopped
1 cup chopped celery
2 cans cream of mushroom soup,
or 2 cans cream of celery soup

1 cup mayonnaise
1 cup sharp Cheddar cheese,
cubed
1 package herbed stuffing mix
½ cup butter, melted

Cook broccoli until tender. Combine eggs, onion, celery, soup, and mayonnaise. Place layer of broccoli in a 3-quart casserole dish. Add layer of cheese, then a layer of stuffing mix. Pour a small amount of sauce over top. Repeat layers until all of ingredients are used. Top with a layer of stuffing mix. Sprinkle melted butter on top of stuffing mix. Bake at 350° for 30 minutes. Serves 8-10.

BROCCOLI CORN SCALLOP

Barbara Kanagy

2 tablespoons onions
2 tablespoons butter, divided
1 tablespoon flour
1¼ cups milk
8 ounces cheese

12 ounces whole kernel corn
½ cup cracker crumbs
2 (10 ounce) packages frozen
broccoli spears, cooked and
drained

Sauté onion in 1 tablespoon butter. Blend in flour; add milk and cook. Keep stirring until thickened. Add cheese and stir until melted. Stir in corn and ¼ of cracker crumbs. Arrange broccoli in long (9x13-inch) baking dish. Pour sauce over broccoli. Sprinkle remaining crumbs and butter over casserole. Bake at 350° for 30 minutes. Makes 8 servings.

BROCCOLI-RICE CASSEROLE

Barbara Hershberger,
Sonia Hoffman, Barbara Ann Yoder

1 stalk celery, chopped
1 onion, chopped
½ stick butter
1 box frozen broccoli, cooked
1 can cream of chicken soup

1 small jar Cheese Whiz
Tabasco sauce and pepper to
taste
1 cup raw rice, cooked

Sauté celery and onion in butter. Add cooked broccoli, soup, sautéed onion and celery, Cheese Whiz, Tabasco sauce, and pepper to cooked rice. Bake in greased casserole at 350° until bubbly, about 45 minutes. Better fixed the day before.

Barbara Ann adds cream of mushroom soup to hers instead of cream of chicken. Makes 8-10 servings.

CABBAGE CASSEROLE

Jill Nussbaum

1 medium head cabbage
2 cups seasoned white sauce
Salt to taste

Crackers, crushed
Butter
Grated Cheddar cheese, optional

WHITE SAUCE:
4 tablespoons butter
4 tablespoons flour

½ teaspoon salt
2 cups milk

Cut cabbage medium fine. Cook until tender. Drain. Prepare white sauce. Put ½ cabbage in greased 8x8x2-inch casserole dish. Sprinkle with salt and crushed crackers and dot with butter. Add rest of cabbage.

Pour white sauce over top. Sprinkle with salt and cracker crumbs and dot with butter. Bake at 350° for 30 minutes. For extra flavor, add grated Cheddar cheese and let melt.

To make sauce: Melt butter over low heat in saucepan. Blend in flour and salt, stirring until smooth and bubbly. Remove from heat and stir in milk. Bring to boil, stirring constantly. Boil 1 minute.

Sanctified afflictions are spiritual promotions.

315

CABBAGE WITH CHEESE

Mrs. Noah Yoder, Ruth Yoder

3 cups shredded cabbage
1 teaspoon salt
½ cup boiling water

¼ cup light cream
½ cup grated cheese

Cook cabbage in boiling salted water until tender, about 6-9 minutes. Drain. Add cream and cheese. Place over low heat; stir until cheese melts and coats cabbage. Makes 4 servings.

Is also good using less cream and cheese.

Ruth adds 1 (8 ounce) can French fried onion rings during the last 5 minutes of baking.

SWEET-AND-SOUR RED CABBAGE

Elsie Brenneman

2 tablespoons bacon drippings
   or cooking oil
¼ cup packed brown sugar
3 tablespoons vinegar
1 cup water

¼ teaspoon salt
Dash of pepper
4 cups shredded red cabbage
2 apples, peeled and sliced

In large skillet, combine drippings or oil, brown sugar, vinegar, water, salt, and pepper. Cook for 2-3 minutes or until hot, stirring occasionally. Add cabbage; cover and cook for 10 minutes over medium-low heat, stirring occasionally. Add apples; cook, uncovered, for about 10 minutes more or until tender, stirring occasionally. Makes 6-8 servings.

CARROT CASSEROLE

Rhoda Yoder

12 carrots, cooked and sliced
½ pound Cheddar cheese, sliced
1 stick butter
¼ cup flour
2 cups milk
2 tablespoons dried onion

1 teaspoon salt
½ teaspoon mustard
¼ teaspoon celery salt
⅛ teaspoon pepper
Bread crumbs for topping

Alternate layers of carrots and cheese slices in casserole dish. Melt butter; stir in flour, milk, and spices, stirring until thickened. Pour sauce over carrots and cheese. Top with fine bread crumbs and bake at 350° for 25 minutes. Makes 8-10 servings.

CANDIED CARROTS
Ruth Yoder

1 pound carrots
3 tablespoons butter

¼ cup brown sugar

Slice carrots; cook in small amount of salted water until tender. Drain. Melt butter and add brown sugar; stir until mixture bubbles. Add carrots and simmer gently until carrots are coated. Place into serving dish. Makes 5-6 servings.

Variation: Add ¼ cup orange juice or 1 cup pineapple.

CARROTS-N-CHEESE
Silla Yoder

2 pounds carrots
1 stick butter

½ pound Velveeta cheese
Toasted bread crumbs

Cook carrots and place in casserole dish. Melt butter and cheese. Pour over carrots. Make toasted bread crumbs in skillet with butter; put crumbs on top of casserole. Bake at 350° for 30 minutes. Makes 8-10 servings.

CORN CASSEROLE
Mrs. Merle Overholt

3 eggs, well beaten
¼ cup flour
2 tablespoons sugar
2 cups (½ pound) shredded sharp
    processed cheese

2 cans (4 cups) whole kernel corn,
    drained
10 slices bacon, cooked and
    crumbled

Combine eggs, flour, and sugar. Beat well. Add shredded cheese and corn. Stir in about ¾ of the bacon. Turn mixture into an ungreased 10x6x1½-inch baking dish and sprinkle remaining bacon over top. Bake at 350° for 30 minutes, or until knife inserted in center comes out clean. Makes 8 servings.

DELICIOUS CORN DISH
Judi Wagher

1 can cream style corn
1 can whole kernel corn and liquid
1 cup dry spaghetti, broken in
    small pieces

1 cup cubed Velveeta cheese
1 stick butter, melted
2 tablespoons chopped onion

Mix together above ingredients and place in greased 2-quart casserole dish. Cover and bake at 350° for ½ hour. Uncover and bake for an additional ½ hour. Makes 6-8 servings.

CORN BAKE
Laura K. Yoder

2 eggs, beaten
1 (12 ounce) can evaporated milk
1 quart corn, drained
2 tablespoons minced onion
2 tablespoons diced pimiento,
  optional

1 cup shredded Monterey Jack
  cheese or Cheddar cheese
1 teaspoon salt
½ stick butter, browned
½ cup shredded cheese
1 cup bread crumbs

Beat eggs. Add milk and beat again. Add corn, onion, pimiento (if using), 1 cup cheese, and salt; brown and add butter. Pour into a 2-quart casserole dish and sprinkle ½ cup cheese on top. Cover and cook in microwave on high for 8 minutes; turn dish and cook another 5 minutes. Sprinkle with crumb topping and heat 2 more minutes. Remove cover and brown 5 minutes. Makes 12 servings.

BAKED EGGPLANT WITH HAM
Barbara Kanagy

Juice of 1 lemon
1 cup water
1 large eggplant
¼ cup minced onion
1 cup cooked ham, diced

2 tablespoons butter or margarine
1 egg, beaten
¼ cup shredded cheese
½ cup buttered bread crumbs

Combine lemon juice with water. Peel eggplant. Dip in lemon water; dice and dip again. Rinse in cold water. Parboil diced eggplant about 10 minutes.

Sauté onion and ham in butter or margarine; add eggplant and egg. Mix well. Put mixture in greased 1-quart casserole. Combine cheese and crumbs and sprinkle over top. Bake at 350° for 40 minutes. Makes 4 servings.

FETTUCCINE SPEEDY
Pat Parker

8 ounces fettuccine noodles
¼ cup garlic spread
¼ cup butter

½ cup light cream
½ cup Parmesan cheese
2 tablespoons parsley

Cook noodles. Melt garlic and butter slowly in microwave or on stove top. Add rest of ingredients and toss. Cover with grated cheese, if desired. Makes 4-6 servings.

GREEN BEAN CASSEROLE

Barbara Hershberger

3 cups French-style green beans, cooked and drained
1 can cream of mushroom soup
1 small can French-fried onion rings
Dash of salt and pepper
Garlic salt
Minced onion
Milk
Buttered bread crumbs and grated cheese for topping

Combine all ingredients except milk and topping ingredients in a greased baking dish. Add enough milk to bring to surface. Cover with foil and bake at 325° for 40 minutes, stirring once during baking. Remove tin foil after baking and sprinkle with buttered bread crumbs and grated cheese. Makes 6 servings.

GREEN BEAN DISH

Rose Yoder

4 large potatoes, cubed
1 pound hot dogs or 1 pound browned hamburger
1 quart green beans

SAUCE:
2 cups milk
½ pound cheese
½ cup flour
2 teaspoons salt

Put potatoes, meat, and beans in a 2-quart casserole dish. In a saucepan, heat milk enough to melt cheese. Add flour and salt. Pour over potatoes, meat and beans. Bake at 300° for 2 hours. Serves 10-12.

HARVARD BEETS

Ruth Yoder

2 cans beets, sliced or diced
⅜ cup sugar
3 tablespoons cornstarch
¾ teaspoon salt
⅜ cup vinegar or lemon juice
¾ cup beet juice
1½ tablespoons butter

Drain juice from beets and save liquids in a 2-quart saucepan. Combine sugar, cornstarch, and salt. Add vinegar or lemon juice and beet juice. Mix thoroughly and cook until juice is thickened. Add beets and heat thoroughly. Just before serving, add butter. Makes 6 servings.

HOMINY CASSEROLE

Roxanna L. Linneber

1 large can yellow hominy
1 large can white hominy
1 small can chopped green chilies
4 tablespoons butter
16 ounces sour cream

1½ cups shredded Monterey Jack
cheese
Dash of salt and pepper
1 teaspoon chili powder, optional

Butter a 2½-quart casserole dish. Combine all ingredients and bake for 45 minutes at 350°.

Do what you can, where you are, with what you have.

BAKED HOMINY AND CHEESE

Elsie Brenneman

1 egg
2 (15½ ounce) cans white or
yellow hominy, rinsed and
drained
12 ounces processed American
cheese, cubed
¾ cup milk

½ small onion, finely chopped
3 bacon strips, cooked and
crumbled
1 tablespoon butter or margarine,
melted
¼ teaspoon pepper
Chopped fresh parsley, optional

In a large bowl, beat egg. Add hominy, cheese, milk, onion, bacon, butter or margarine, and pepper; mix well. Spoon into a greased 11x7x2-inch baking dish. Bake uncovered at 350° for 45 minutes or until bubbly and top begins to brown. Let stand a few minutes before serving. Garnish with parsley, if desired. Makes 8 servings.

LIMA BEAN CASSEROLE

Sara Jean Yoder

2 packages frozen or fresh lima
beans
2½ cups milk
4 tablespoons butter
3 tablespoons flour

½ pound Swiss cheese (or other)
3 tablespoons onion, chopped
1 can mushrooms (or mushroom
soup)
½ cup toasted crumbs

Cook lima beans. Drain. Make cream sauce of milk, butter, and flour. Add cheese and onion. Combine all ingredients except crumbs and put in casserole. Top with crumbs. Heat at 350° until hot.

MUSHROOM CASSEROLE
Elva Miller

6 slices white bread, buttered
½ cup chopped onions
½ cup chopped celery
½ cup chopped green pepper
1 stick butter

1 pound sliced *fresh* mushrooms
2 eggs
1 cup milk
1 can cream of mushroom soup
½ cup mayonnaise

Butter bread and cut into cubes. Sauté onion, celery, and green pepper in butter. Add mushrooms and heat. Layer bread cubes and mushroom mixture in a 9x13-inch pan. Mix eggs, milk, mushroom soup, and mayonnaise. Pour on top and bake at 325° for 1 hour.

MACARONI AND CHEESE
Mrs. Freeman Schlabach,
Jill Nussbaum

3 tablespoons butter
2½ cups uncooked macaroni
1 teaspoon salt

¼ teaspoon pepper
½ pound Velveeta cheese
1 quart cold milk

Melt butter and pour over macaroni. Stir well and add salt and pepper. Cut cheese in pieces and add. Also add milk. Pour into greased casserole dish. Bake 1½ hours at 325°. Don't cover and don't stir. Comes out golden and creamy.

MACARONI & CHEESE
Ruth Yoder

1 cup dry macaroni
1 cup cottage cheese
1 cup dairy sour cream

1 cup Velveeta cheese, cut up
1 cup sharp Cheddar cheese, grated
2 eggs, beaten

Cook macaroni according to package directions; drain. Combine cottage cheese, sour cream, Velveeta, Cheddar cheese, and eggs in buttered 2½-quart casserole. Add cooked macaroni; fold in thoroughly. Bake at 350° for 45 minutes. Yields 6-8 servings. This is very good.

ONIONS IN CHEESE SAUCE
Alta Kauffman

6 large onions
½ cup grated cheese
2 cups white sauce or mushroom
  soup

2 tablespoons butter
1 cup cracker crumbs

Cut onions in half and boil until tender, but not falling apart. Drain and place in greased dish. Mix cheese into white sauce and pour over onions. Melt butter in skillet and add cracker crumbs. Stir until coated. Sprinkle over onions. Bake 20 minutes at 350°.

ONION CASSEROLE

Jill Nussbaum

8 medium onions
1 cup butter
30 crackers, crushed
2 small cans mushroom soup

4 eggs, beaten
1-1½ cups milk
Grated cheese

Cut onions in ¼-inch rings. Sauté in butter until clear. Keep enough crackers back to garnish top. Put remaining crackers in bottom of greased casserole dish. Mix onions, soup, eggs, milk, and cheese. Pour on top of crackers. Top with crackers and more cheese. Bake at 350° for 20 minutes. Especially good with Vidalia onions.

Holiness is not the way to Christ;
Christ is the way to holiness.

CHEESE POTATO PUFF

Silla K. Yoder

12 medium potatoes, peeled
  (about 5 pounds)
1 teaspoon salt, divided
¾ cup butter

2 cups (8 ounces) shredded
  Cheddar cheese
1 cup milk
2 eggs, beaten
Fresh or dried chives, optional

Place potatoes in large kettle and cover with water. Add ½ teaspoon salt and cook until tender. Drain. Mash potatoes until smooth. In a saucepan, cook and stir butter, cheese, milk, and remaining salt until smooth. Stir into potatoes. Fold in eggs. Pour into greased 3-quart baking dish. Bake uncovered at 350° for 40 minutes or until puffy and golden brown. Sprinkle with chives, if desired. Serves 8-10.

DELICIOUS GRILLED POTATOES

Lydia Knox

8 large potatoes
8 teaspoons dried minced onion
8 teaspoons butter

Salt
Pepper
8 squares foil

Peel potatoes and cut into strips. Place one serving potatoes onto foil; sprinkle 1 teaspoon onion on each. Dot with butter. Salt and pepper to taste. Seal edges well. Place on grill until tender, approximately 30 minutes. Makes 8 servings.

FAVORITE BAKED POTATOES
Elsie King Horst

8 medium potatoes
1 cup half-and-half
½ cup butter

Salt and pepper
1 onion
Paprika

Cook potatoes with skins on. Cool. Peel and shred into a 9x13-inch pan. Heat half-and-half, butter, salt, and pepper. Grate onion into milk mixture and pour into potatoes. Sprinkle with paprika and bake at 350° for 45 minutes. Makes 8-10 servings.

Variation: Add 1 can cream of mushroom soup and grated cheese for scalloped potatoes.

Note: May be prepared ahead and kept in refrigerator until ready to bake.

CHEESE SAUCE FOR BAKED POTATOES
Tina Nussbaum

1½ tablespoons butter
1 tablespoon flour
½ teaspoon salt

¼ teaspoon pepper
1 cup milk
1 cup grated cheese

Melt butter over low heat. Add flour, salt, and pepper. Stir constantly until well blended. Gradually add milk, stirring constantly. Cook until thick and smooth. Add grated cheese. Serves 4.

Optional: Add diced mushrooms, green peppers, and onions.

CHILI FOR BAKED POTATOES
Linda Zook

2 pounds hamburger
1 (16 ounce) can chili hot beans
1 tablespoon taco seasoning
1 cup salsa
4 cups tomato juice

1 cup water
1 tablespoon brown sugar
1 teaspoon salt
1 teaspoon cumin

Brown hamburger and drain. Add remaining ingredients and simmer for 1-1½ hours. Delicious on baked potatoes.

SOUR CREAM DRESSING
FOR BAKED POTATOES
Ruth Yoder

1 cup mayonnaise
1 cup sour cream
1 tablespoon parsley flakes

1¼ teaspoons dill weed
1 teaspoon seasoned salt
½ teaspoon or more onion powder

Blend together thoroughly. Makes 2 cups.

POTATO TOPPING
Lela Brenneman

1 pound hamburger
⅓ cup peppers
¼ cup onion
1 tablespoon butter
2 tablespoons flour
1 cup milk

¼ pound Cheddar cheese
¼ pound American cheese
⅛ teaspoon red pepper
Pinch of dry mustard
Pinch of hot pepper sauce
Salt and pepper to taste

Fry hamburger with peppers and onion. Stir in butter and sifted flour. Blend with fat. Add milk slowly, stirring to mix in. Cook until thick; add cheese and seasoning. Season to taste with salt and pepper. Makes 3 cups.

GOLDEN PARMESAN POTATOES
Alta Kauffman

6 large potatoes
¼ cup flour
¼ cup Parmesan cheese
¾ teaspoon salt

⅛ teaspoon pepper
⅓ cup butter
Chopped parsley

Pare potatoes and cut into quarters. Combine flour, cheese, salt, and pepper in a bag. Moisten potatoes with water; put in bag and shake to coat well with cheese mixture. Melt butter in 9x13-inch pan. Place potatoes in pan and bake 1 hour at 375°, turning once during baking. When golden brown, sprinkle with parsley.

Note: You may use Cheddar cheese powder instead of Parmesan cheese if you desire.

OVEN-FRIED POTATOES
Lela Brenneman, Merlyn Mullet

4 large baking potatoes, unpeeled
¼ cup vegetable oil
1-2 tablespoons Parmesan cheese
½ teaspoon salt

¼ teaspoon garlic powder
¼ teaspoon paprika
⅛ teaspoon pepper

Wash unpeeled potatoes and cut lengthwise into 4 wedges. Place skin side down in a 13x9x2-inch baking dish or pan.

Combine remaining ingredients and brush over potatoes. Bake in a 375° oven for 1 hour, brushing with oil/cheese mixture at 15 minute intervals. Turn potatoes over for last 15 minutes. These are wonderful with any roasted meat or fine as a snack. Makes 4 servings.

MASHED POTATO TIPS

Ruth Yoder

Instead of using cold milk when whipping mashed potatoes, use some of the salt water in which the potatoes were cooked, plus a generous amount of dry milk and butter. Potatoes will not cool down as quickly and they're *fluffy.*

Turn care into prayer and God will turn midnight into music.

MASHED POTATO CASSEROLE

Mrs. John Nissley

3 pounds mashed potatoes
1 (8 ounce) package cream
  cheese, room temperature
¼ cup butter
½ cup sour cream

2 eggs, beaten
½ cup milk
¼ cup onion, chopped fine
1 teaspoon salt
Pepper to taste

Mix potatoes, cream cheese, and butter; add sour cream. Mix eggs with milk, then add to potato mixture. Add onions, salt, and pepper. Pour into a buttered casserole and refrigerate overnight. Bake at 350° for 45 minutes.

POTATO BAKE

Lena Schrock, Barbara Ann Yoder,
Rhoda Coblentz, Martha Kauffman

2 pounds potatoes, cooked and
  shredded
½ cup melted butter
1 teaspoon salt
¼ teaspoon pepper

½ cup chopped onion
1 can cream of chicken soup
1 pint sour cream
2 cups grated cheese, Velveeta or
  Cheddar

TOPPING:
2 cups crushed corn flakes

¼ cup melted butter

Mix together. Put in a 4-quart casserole dish and top with crushed corn flakes mixed with melted butter. Bake at 350° for 1 hour. Serves 8.

WHITE SAUCE MIX

Ruth Yoder

1 cup flour
4 cups dry powdered milk

4 teaspoons salt
1 cup butter

Mix white sauce mixture well! For thin sauce, use ⅓ cup milk and ⅓ cup mix. For medium sauce, use ½ cup mix and 1 cup milk. For thick sauce use 1 cup mix and 1 cup milk.

Bring to a boil. For cheese sauce, add cheese after it boils...preferably Velveeta. If you prefer some spice, add Tabasco pepper sauce.

RANCH POTATO CASSEROLE
Elva Miller

6-8 medium potatoes
½ cup sour cream
½ cup prepared ranch dressing

¼ cup cooked, crumbled bacon
2 tablespoons parsley
1 cup shredded Cheddar cheese

TOPPING:
½ cup shredded cheese
2 cups slightly crushed corn flakes

¼ cup melted butter

Cook potatoes until tender; quarter and set aside. Combine sour cream, dressing, bacon, parsley, and 1 cup cheese. Place potatoes in a greased 9x13-inch baking dish. Pour sour cream mixture over potatoes and toss gently. Top with cheese. Combine corn flakes and melted butter and sprinkle over casserole. Bake at 350° for 40-45 minutes.

STUFFED BAKED POTATO
Ruth Yoder

3 pounds hamburger
1 cup chopped green peppers
½ cup chopped onions
½ cup pimiento or red pepper,
  chopped
¼ cup butter
⅜ cup flour
¼ cup dry mustard

3 cups milk
¾ pound Cheddar cheese
¾ pound American cheese
½ teaspoon hot pepper sauce
Salt to taste
Seasoning salt, optional
Chili powder, optional

Fry hamburger, peppers, onions, and pimiento or red pepper. Stir in butter and then flour and dry mustard. Add milk slowly, stirring constantly. Cook until thickened, then add cheese and seasonings. Serve on baked potato. Delicious!!

SWEET POTATO CASSEROLE
Mrs. Jonas Schrock

5 medium sweet potatoes
1 teaspoon salt
1 cup brown sugar
3 tablespoons flour
2 tablespoons butter

8 large marshmallows or 1 cup
  miniature marshmallows
½ cup chopped nuts
1 cup thin cream

Cook potatoes until tender; drain and cool. Cut in half lengthwise and arrange in a greased 9x13-inch shallow baking dish. Mix salt, sugar, and flour and pour over potatoes. Dot with butter, marshmallows, and nuts. Pour cream over all. Bake at 350° for 45-50 minutes.

SWEET POTATO SOUFFLÉ

Donna Stephens

7-8 sweet potatoes
1½ cups sugar
¾ cup flour
¾ cup canned milk

3 eggs
2 teaspoons vanilla
2 sticks butter or margarine,
   melted

Peel, slice, and boil potatoes until soft. Drain and cool potatoes. Mash and add sugar, flour, milk, and eggs. Add vanilla and melted butter or margarine. Bake in a 9x13-inch dish at 350° for 25-30 minutes. Top with marshmallows and brown. Serves 8-10.

RICE AND MUSHROOMS

Ruth Yoder

2 small onions, chopped
¼ cup bell peppers
1 stick butter
1 pound rice (2 cups)

1 small can mushrooms
1 can beef consommé
2 soup cans water
1 cube beef bouillon

Fry onions and pepper in butter. Mix all ingredients together and put in a 3-quart baking pan. Bake at 350° for 1 hour and 15 minutes. Makes 15 servings.

BUTTERNUT SQUASH BAKE

Silla K. Yoder

⅓ cup butter or margarine,
   softened
¾ cup sugar
2 eggs

1 (5 ounce) can evaporated milk
1 teaspoon vanilla extract
2 cups mashed, cooked butternut
   squash

TOPPING:
½ cup Rice Krispies cereal
¼ cup packed brown sugar

¼ cup chopped pecans
2 tablespoons butter or margarine

In a mixing bowl, combine butter and sugar. Beat in eggs, milk, and vanilla. Stir in squash (mixture will be thin). Pour into a greased 11x7x2-inch baking pan. Bake uncovered at 350° for 45 minutes or until almost set.

Combine topping ingredients and sprinkle over casserole. Return to oven for 5-10 minutes or until bubbly. Makes 6-8 servings.

SQUASH CASSEROLE

Marialice Yoder

2 cups sliced yellow squash,
   cooked and drained
2 cups crumbled cornbread
1 can cream of chicken soup
1 small onion, chopped

½ cup melted butter
3 eggs, beaten
Sage to taste (approximately
   ½ teaspoon)

Mix and bake at 350° in 8-inch baking pan.

*Satan trembles when he sees
the weakest Christian on his knees.*

SQUASH CASSEROLE

Mrs. Paula Yoder

4 cups squash
1 cup milk
1 stick melted margarine
2 eggs
1 cup cracker crumbs

½ teaspoon salt
¼ teaspoon pepper
1 tablespoon sugar
1 small onion
1 cup grated cheese

Shred squash and mix together with rest of ingredients. Bake at 350° for
30-40 minutes.

SUMMER SQUASH BAKE

Rhoda Coblentz

½ cup water to cover bottom of
   baking dish
Yellow summer squash
Onions
Salt

Pepper or basil
Butter
Sliced cheese to put on top,
   optional

Slice raw yellow squash thinly (using also some zucchini if desired, to
make it colorful), into desired size (4-quart recommended) baking dish to
about ¼ full. Now slice onions to cover the squash. Then sprinkle with salt
and pepper or basil. Repeat this 2 or 3 times. Dot top with butter, then
cover and bake 1 hour at 350°. Upon removing from oven, sliced cheese
may be put on top. Serves 7 people.

This will shrink.

SPINACH CHEESE BAKE
Laura K. Yoder

1 (10 ounce) package frozen
  chopped spinach
2 teaspoons flour
2 eggs, beaten
1 (3 ounce) package cream
  cheese, cubed

¾ cup American cheese, cubed
¼ cup butter, melted
1½ teaspoons minced onion
½ teaspoon salt

TOPPING:
½ cup fine bread crumbs
½ stick butter

⅓ cup Parmesan cheese

In 1½-quart covered casserole dish, cook spinach on high setting of microwave for 6 minutes, stirring once halfway through. Stir in flour, then eggs, cheeses, butter, onion, and salt. Mix well. Cook on high for 9-11 minutes stirring twice. Remove from oven.

Measure bread crumbs into glass 1-cup measure and slice or grate ½ stick butter over crumbs. Heat on high until butter is melted, about 1 minute. Stir until crumbs are well coated. Sprinkle over spinach mixture and top with Parmesan cheese. Brown as desired. Makes 4 servings.

TASTY TOMATO BAKE
Barbara Kanagy

2 strips bacon
2 cups soft bread crumbs
¼ cup chopped green pepper
¼ cup chopped onion
6 medium tomatoes
1 tablespoon sugar

2 tablespoons flour
1 teaspoon salt
⅛ teaspoon pepper
Dash of sage
⅓ cup grated or shredded sharp
  processed cheese

Fry bacon. Remove strips and drain. Leave about 3 tablespoons fat in skillet. Add bread crumbs; toss. Add green pepper and onions; sauté lightly. Peel tomatoes; cut into cubes and add to bread mixture.

Combine sugar, flour, salt, pepper, and sage. Sprinkle over tomatoes; toss lightly. Spoon mixture into greased 1½-quart casserole. Crumble bacon over top, then cheese. Bake at 350° for 20-30 minutes. Serves 4.

Be not forgetful to entertain strangers
for thereby some have entertained angels unawares.

329

TOMATO OKRA GOULASH
Ruth Hershberger

1 quart whole canned tomatoes
1 cup chopped onions
1½ cups sliced okra
1½ pounds browned hamburger

1 teaspoon salt
⅓ teaspoon garlic powder
⅛ teaspoon red pepper
Chopped peppers, optional

Brown and drain hamburger. Add all ingredients together in a 2-quart saucepan. Simmer gently for 45 minutes, stirring occasionally. Serve over cooked brown rice. Chopped peppers are very good added while cooking. Serves 4-6.

VEGETABLE CASSEROLE
Mary (Mrs. Paul) Miller

1 (1 pound) bag California blend
    vegetables, frozen
8 ounces cubed Velveeta

1 stick margarine
½ small box Ritz crackers, crushed

Cook vegetables in a saucepan until almost done. Drain. Put in a 2-quart baking dish. Sprinkle with cubed cheese. Mix together melted margarine and crushed crackers. Put on top. Bake at 350° for 15 minutes or until bubbly. Makes 6 servings.

YAM BALLS
Ruth Yoder

3 cups cooked yams
¼ cup butter
¾ cup brown sugar
2 tablespoons milk

¼ teaspoon salt
⅛ teaspoon grated lemon rind
8 marshmallows
½ cup crushed corn flakes

Mash yams and add butter, sugar, milk, salt, and lemon rind. Scoop up ¼ cup of the mixture. Center with a marshmallow. Cover with more yam and shape into balls. Roll balls into crushed corn flakes. Place in buttered baking dish and bake at 350° for about 20 minutes.

Miscellaneous

BEEF JERKY

Celesta Miller

Beef, sliced
½ cup soy sauce
½ cup liquid smoke
Salt

Pepper
Garlic salt, optional
Lemon pepper

Soak about 30 thin strips of meat ¼-inch thick overnight in soy sauce mixed with liquid smoke in refrigerator. Place the meat on a baking sheet and sprinkle with salt, pepper, garlic salt (if desired), and lemon pepper to taste on both sides, separating strips so they don't touch each other. Place the baking sheet in the oven which has been preheated to no more than 150°. The oven door may be left open a crack to speed the drying. Dry for 8-10 hours overnight.

Note: When finished, the jerky should be dry and leathery, not brittle. Store in paper bag.

INDIAN BEEF JERKY

Alta Kauffman

2 pounds lean meat, no fat,
   cut into ½-inch strips
2 cups water
1 teaspoon garlic powder
1 teaspoon onion powder

1 teaspoon meat tenderizer
1 teaspoon salt
1 teaspoon black pepper
1 teaspoon baking soda

Mix all ingredients and marinate 48 hours. Put in food dehydrator 12 hours. Very good!

*If you cannot be content with what you have received,
be thankful for what you have escaped.*

CASSEROLE SAUCE MIX

Sara Jean Yoder

2 cups dry powdered milk
¾ cup cornstarch
¼ cup Instant chicken or beef
   bouillon granules

2 tablespoons dried onion flakes
1 teaspoon dried basil, optional
1 teaspoon thyme, optional
½ teaspoon pepper

Mix well. Store in airtight container.

To substitute for one can condensed soup, combine ⅓ cup dry mix with 1¼ cups water in saucepan. Cook and stir until thickened.

PEANUT BUTTER SPREAD
Ruth Yoder

1 cup boiling water
2 cups brown sugar
2 tablespoons light Karo syrup

1 teaspoon maple flavoring
2 cups marshmallow creme
3 cups peanut butter

Remove boiling water (with sugar, Karo syrup, and maple flavoring added). Blend in marshmallow creme and peanut butter. Stir until smooth.

*Why try to buy or "steal" salvation
when you can have it as a gift? — Romans 6:23*

CHOCOLATE SYRUP
Celesta Miller

3 tablespoons cocoa
½ cup sugar
Dash of salt

¼ cup plus 2 tablespoons water
2 tablespoons butter
1 teaspoon vanilla

Mix cocoa, sugar, and salt. Add water. Cook several minutes and add butter and vanilla.

DUMPLINGS
Jo Ann Inhulsen

3 tablespoons shortening
1½ cups flour
2 teaspoons baking powder

¾ teaspoon salt
¾ cup milk

Cut shortening into flour, baking powder, and salt until mixture resembles fine crumbs. Stir in milk. Drop dough by spoonfuls onto hot boiling meat or vegetable stew. (Do not overcrowd dumplings). Cook uncovered 10 minutes. Cover and cook 10 minutes longer. Best if eaten right away.

Herb or cheese dumplings are a nice touch. Use fresh herbs, such as parsley or sage.

When you run your life, you ruin it because the "I" has been added.

LO-FAT CULTURED BUTTERMILK
Rhoda Coblentz

1 gallon skim milk   2 cups buttermilk (store bought)

Heat milk to lukewarm. Remove from heat and stir buttermilk. Cover and let set in fairly warm spot or away from draft until thick. Then using mixer or wire whip, beat until nice and smooth. Pour into jars and refrigerate. Makes 4½ quarts.

This may be used as starter as it stays good for a long time. This same procedure may be used to make cultured sour cream, but omit the whipping and just refrigerate when thick.

BRINE TO CURE MEAT
Kathy Schrock

8-10 cups water   1 tablespoon liquid smoke
1 cup Tender Quick   ½ teaspoon salt water
1 handful brown sugar

Stir this together until dissolved. Add raw meat and let it soak for 3 days in a cool place. Then put meat in a roaster and bake at 325° for several hours until tender. This can be used for pork, turkey, or chicken, etc. It tastes just like ham. The brine can be stored in the fridge and reused up to 6 weeks.

MEAT BRINE
Mrs. Roger Helmuth, Sr.

1½ cups sugar cure   1 cup Tender Quick
1 teaspoon spice which comes in   2 tablespoons liquid smoke
   with sugar cure   1½ gallons water

For whole turkey or large roast, make deep slashes through middle of the meat. Soak meat 24 hours, or it can be soaked up to 48 hours. Bake. Tastes like ham, and it also takes care of the wild taste in deer roast.

SMOKED TURKEY BRINE
Elsie Brenneman

Turkey   7 cups water
1 cup Tender Quick   2 tablespoons liquid smoke

To make turkey taste smoked, make a brine of 1 cup Tender Quick and 7 cups water. Make enough to cover turkey. Drain after 3 days and brush 2 tablespoons liquid smoke over turkey. Wrap in foil and bake at 200° overnight. Do not put salt on it.

YOGURT

Jo Ann Inhulsen

1 gallon milk
Dairy thermometer
Wire whisk

1½ cups yogurt culture (plain unflavored yogurt)

Bring milk, thermometer, and wire whisk to a full boil and boil for 1 minute. Place in cold water to cool down to 120°-110°. Remove from water and add yogurt culture and stir with wire whisk, which was kept in boiling milk. Pour boiling water over inside of lid to sterilize it. Place lid on cultured milk and let set for 1 hour. Put in refrigerator until set. Take out 1½ cups of yogurt for culture for your next batch of yogurt.

It is very important to keep everything you use sterile or you will not have success with this recipe.

PLAIN YOGURT

Rhoda Coblentz

1 gallon skim milk
4 tablespoons plain gelatin, softened in ¾ cup cold water

2 cups plain yogurt
1 cup powdered milk

Heat milk to 180° or until milk steams but *not* boiling. Remove from heat and add gelatin which has been dissolved in cold water. Stir well. Cool to 120°.

Put 2 cups plain yogurt in blender pitcher and add powdered milk and some of the cooled milk. This mixture should be 112° or a bit warmer than lukewarm. Pour into bowl and set into barely warm oven, that has been heated but turned off again. Usually takes 1½ hours to set. If it goes much longer, turn oven on for about 1 minute or just enough to heat air in the oven again.

For flavored yogurt, you may beat in any flavor Jello you with as soon as it is set. Makes 1 gallon.

SWEET-N-SOUR SAUCE

Alta Kauffman

½ cup mayonnaise
½ cup brown sugar

½ cup honey
½ cup mustard

Mix and serve. Delicious with chicken nuggets.

SALT SUBSTITUTE

Mrs. Noah Yoder

1 teaspoon chili powder
2 teaspoons powdered oregano
2 teaspoons black pepper
3 tablespoons paprika
1 tablespoon garlic powder
(not garlic *salt*)

2 tablespoons dry mustard
6 tablespoons onion powder
(not onion *salt*)
3 tablespoons poultry seasoning

Put all ingredients into a jar, seal tightly with the lid, and shake well.

COUGH SYRUP

Barbara Kanagy

1 pint honey
4 ounces glycerine

Juice of 2 lemons

Mix and use as desired. May be given to children as often as needed for cough.

Man says "Do,"
but God says, "It's done!" All now is "Finished."
Believe on the Soul.

CRUMBLY SOAP

Esther L. Miller

10 cups water
9 cups melted fat (not hot)
½ cup ammonia

½ cup borax
½ cup sugar
1 can lye

Mix water, melted fat, ammonia, borax, and sugar in a plastic pail in the order given. Sprinkle in lye. Stir and let set 5-10 minutes. Then stir again. Stir frequently the first hour and a half. Thereafter, every hour throughout the day. If there is liquid left at the end of the day, stir several times next morning.

Let set in pail several days, then cover soap or put in airtight container to prevent drying out. The mixture may look separated at first, but will absorb and be nice and crumbly by stirring. Makes approximately 2 gallons.

To use, put hot water in washing machine. Start agitator and add 1 cup soap and let agitate several minutes before adding clothes.

HOMEMADE PAM
Ruth Hershberger, Silla Yoder

1½ cups white shortening
1½ cups flour

1½ cups vegetable oil

Beat shortening and flour together until very smooth. Beat in oil until blended. Place in container and store in refrigerator. Use pastry brush to spread in baking pans. (Bread pans, cake pans, muffin tins, etc.) Economical, and will save you from needing to use waxed paper in your muffin tins or cake pans.

Dare to discipline!
We may not salvage some members of the present generation,
but perhaps we can preserve the next.

NOSE DROPS
Barbara Hershberger

¼ teaspoon salt

4 ounces water

Combine salt and water. Four drops every 4 hours. Not harmful to babies. Recommended by doctors.

WINDOW CLEANER
Barbara Hershberger

1 pint alcohol
1 teaspoon liquid dishwashing soap

½ cup sudsy ammonia

Put all ingredients in a gallon jug and fill with water.

PLAY DOUGH
Barbara Hershberger, Ruth Hershberger

2 cups flour
1 cup salt
4 teaspoons cream of tartar

2 cups water
4 tablespoons oil
2 teaspoons food coloring

Combine flour, salt, and cream of tartar in a saucepan. Stir in water, oil, and food coloring.

Cook over medium heat, stirring constantly, until a ball forms. Remove from heat and knead until smooth. Store in covered container. Will keep for months.

Oh, I'm the queen of my little kitchen
What a wonderful privilege is mine,
As I reign in my little queen-dom
giving my pots and pans all a shine.

You see, I've been given a calling
So great, how it blesses my heart!
The business of feeding my family,
Tis a wonderful culinary art.

The planning of meals and preparing
Is a challenge that calls for great skill,
how to balance the proteins and veggies
good dietary rules to fulfill.

On the top of the list is to please hubby,
and consider his favorite food,
while using the resources I'm given
coming up with a menu that's good.

So I chop and stir with great fervor
As I blend and I mix and I baste,
Adding herbs and seasonings important
So each dish will be pleasing to taste.

It's nice not to be rushed in my cooking
When there's plenty of time to prepare,
But a simple meal, too, can be special
When it's served with kind loving care.

My heart is so filled with God's blessings
as I consider the gift of each day,
for the heart of the home is the mother
setting the tone with the words that I say.

May my home and my heart reach to others
with hospitality warmed by your love,
So that others may come to know Jesus
By these gifts you've sent from above.

—Ruth Hershberger

INDEX

340

343

J

JELLIES, JAMS, AND PRESERVES

M

MISCELLANEOUS

MUSHROOMS

O

OKRA

ONIONS

ORANGES

P

PASTA

PASTRY

PEACHES

PICKLES

PIES

349

Montezuma Amish Mennonite Cookbook II

Melvin & Ruth Yoder
Rt. #2, Box 182 • Montezuma, GA 31063
Phone 912-472-8921

Please send_____ copy(ies) of the *Montezuma Amish Mennonite Cookbook II*

@ $17.95 each _____

Georgia residents add applicable sales tax _____

Postage and handling @ $ 3.00 each _____

Name _____

Address _____

City_____ State_____ Zip_____

Make checks payable to Montezuma Amish Mennonite Cookbook II.

Montezuma Amish Mennonite Cookbook II

Melvin & Ruth Yoder
Rt. #2, Box 182 • Montezuma, GA 31063
Phone 912-472-8921

Please send_____ copy(ies) of the *Montezuma Amish Mennonite Cookbook II*

@ $17.95 each _____

Georgia residents add applicable sales tax _____

Postage and handling @ $ 3.00 each _____

Name _____

Address _____

City_____ State_____ Zip_____

Make checks payable to Montezuma Amish Mennonite Cookbook II.

Montezuma Amish Mennonite Cookbook II

Melvin & Ruth Yoder
Rt. #2, Box 182 • Montezuma, GA 31063
Phone 912-472-8921

Please send_____ copy(ies) of the *Montezuma Amish Mennonite Cookbook II*

@ $17.95 each _____

Georgia residents add applicable sales tax _____

Postage and handling @ $ 3.00 each _____

Name _____

Address _____

City_____ State_____ Zip_____

Make checks payable to Montezuma Amish Mennonite Cookbook II.